The Scarecrow Author Bibliographies

ALLEN GINSBERG:

An Annotated Bibliography, 1969-1977

by

MICHELLE P. KRAUS

The Scarecrow Author Bibliographies, No. 46

THE SCARECROW PRESS, INC.
METUCHEN, N.J., & LONDON
1980

FLORIDA GULF COAST
UNIVERSITY LIBRARY

Library of Congress Cataloging in Publication Data

Kraus, Michelle P   1953-
    Allen Ginsberg : an annotated bibliography,
1969-1977.

    (The Scarecrow author bibliographies ; no. 46)
    Includes indexes.
    1. Ginsberg, Allen, 1926-   --Bibliography.
Z8342.5.K7 [PS3513.I74]   016.811'54   79-27132
ISBN 0-8108-1284-3

Copyright © 1980 by Michelle P. Kraus

Manufactured in the United States of America

To Mom, Dad, Grandma Fanny and brother Andrew,
who all in their own ways influenced
the development of this work.

ACKNOWLEDGMENTS

I would like to take this opportunity to acknowledge the efforts of all the people who helped make this bibliography possible: the library staff of the Harlan Hatcher Graduate Library of the University of Michigan; the library staff of the Paterson Free Public Library (in particular Mr. Leo Fictelberg, Director); the library staff of the Allen Ginsberg Papers, Rare Book and Manuscript Library; Columbia University (in particular, Mary Bowling, reference librarian and bibliographer); my translators who all donated their time--Dr. David Burrows, Barbara Delaney, Laura Pickett, Celeste Nastri, Vera Tolar, Hedicko Weyman, Giovani Blumer, Miguel Pagliere; other research aides--Beth Greenberg and Ann Rea; Bill Kortum of the WBAI staff; Bob Rosenthal, Neil Hackman, and Michael Scholnick, who all worked on compiling the Ginsberg master list of audio-tapes; Gordon Ball for his invaluable assistance; The Education Film Library Association (43 West 61 Street, New York, N.Y. 10023, 212-246-4533) for the list of films they compiled; The National Institute of Arts and Letters for supplying information from their files; Bell and Howell Micro Photo Division (Wooster, Ohio 44691) for making available their underground newspaper collection; Elsa Dorfman and Fred McDarrah for each compiling a list of her/ his work on Ginsberg; Mary Beach for all the information on Ginsberg work appearing in French; Bert Britton, owner of Books & Co. (939 Madison Avenue, New York, N.Y. 10021), for allowing me to rummage through his shelves of alternative publications; Kenneth Bondor for his donated photographic work; Sally Bondor for her encouragement; Judy Ann Caracio, my proofreader; Pat Gross for her typing expertise; and finally Denise Mercedes, Penny, Peter and Julius Orlovsky, Ted Berrigan and everyone else who colored my frequent visits to Ginsberg's home. Thanks also to my attorney and friend Frederick Testa. Too numerous to list are all the individuals and groups who responded to my requests for information.

In particular, special thanks are extended to my friend and consultant, Lynn Miller of the Douglass College Library, Rutgers University; Sharon Hogan of the Harlan Hatcher Graduate Library of the University of Michigan; my research assistants and friends, Mark Nolden and Louis Cohen; my translator and former teacher, Dr. David Burrows of Douglass College, Rutgers University; my mentor, Dr. Warren Susman of Rutgers College, Rutgers University; Bob Rosenthal, Ginsberg's secretary, 1977-1978, without whom this project would have been much more difficult; Steven Taylor, Ginsberg's summer secretary (1978); the poet himself, Allen Ginsberg; and my family, without whom this project could not have become a reality.

TABLE OF CONTENTS

SECONDARY WORKS

vii

CONTEMPLATION ON BIBLIOGRAPHY

If you want to know the Devil, find out his system, Blake advised. This extensive (1969-77) bibliography covers not only the traditional literary publications of a Poet but also cinema shadows, vocal tones tape-recorded, interviews transcribed and printed in whole or part, television apparitions, newspaper images especially underground, niteclub blues, even secret CIA or FBI reports, media documents and fragments of a public self, a sort of work of art, or Happening, named Allen Ginsberg.

I did not exactly plan this large persona though it was within literary bounds set by Walt Whitman and other sympathetic precursors. My original ideal was actually spare and brilliant: to publish nothing but purest gemwork like Rimbaud, with no dross left over prosaic vulnerable quotidian un-eternal tendentious to bore the eager youthful reader seeking Visionary Diamond. Rimbaud-Whitman, mad Sanity, was my ideal.

Kerouac's teaching of the sacramental quality of spontaneous utterance, later interpreted as a practice of Bodhisattvic open-ness, led me to this plethora of letters in all dimensions. An early impulse to treat scholars, newsmen, agents, reporters, interviewers and inquirers as sentient beings equal in Buddha-nature to fellow poets turned me on to answer questions as frankly as possible. All situations from Queen Elizabeth Hall, London, to Rocky Flats' Rockwell Corporation Plutonium Plant railroad tracks, to the classrooms of the Jack Kerouac School of Disembodied Poetics at Naropa Institute thus become Dharma-Gates. "Dharma-gates are endless, I vow to enter all."

Diabolic egoism? Unthinkable to presume in advance that this path might lead to a Hell of media Selfhood replicated vulgar, obnoxious Ginsberghoods troublemaking throughout America with spiteful lecherous loudmouth hypocritic trips, projecting cowardly errors of spirit, chemistry, and aesthetic form o'er the world, in Ossianic yawps.

The avid reader who has this bibliographic list of every traceable image and utterance I made for a decade, now has materials to find me out, lay my skeleton system on the table, and examine it for symmetry or misshapen-ness, public beauty or queer form.

The presumption was of prophecy, part Blakean inspiration, part ordinary mind from Whitman---that is to say, the poet who speaks from his frank heart in public speaks for all Hearts. "Who touches this book touches a man. " ... "One touch of nature makes the whole world kin. " ... "What oft was thought but ne'er so well expressed. "

Another presumption that runs thru these letters is the Grand Conspiracy of Governments, that the State is a lie as Kenneth Rexroth said. Thus this bibliography includes many poems and interviews touching on corruption of the U. S. Narcotics Bureaucracy, CIA involvement with Indochinese opium trafficking, Surveillance-State Censorship, war psychosis, alterations of National consciousness involving grass and LSD, physical assassination and character assassination of heroes by police agencies. I thought I was being overheard by public and secret police mind all along, taking part in mental fight for America's "soul. " A secret war: most citizens were careless or indifferent to details of massive brainwash perpetrated on themselves by their armies, industries, police agencies and public media interconnected by alcohol, nicotine and money to the powers that be. So all "statements" listed here make an attempt to break thru to public consciousness with some detail of Personal life at variance from the Establishment cover story. I was conscious that my gossip would go into the inner ear of media Government bureaucracies, somewhere to be recorded, have its effects, alter an official brain cell here or there, waken a provincial genius in Iowa, liberate a professor at midnite in Wichita, trouble the head of the CIA some sleepless dawn wondering should he learn to medi-

tate or not, flash in a rock star brainpan rousing mortal consciousness, comfort an anonymous old lady in the Bronx with repetition of her grief sympathetic powerful unobstructed compassionate,
seduce a youth to meditative blues in New Jersey.

Certain errors of judgement emerge by hindsight: advocacy
of LSD legalization would now be accompanied by prescription for
meditation practice to qualify its use. I would extend my self-hood
less widely in sympathy with "movement" contemporaries whose subconscious belief in confrontation, conflict or violence encouraged
public confusion and enabled police agents to infiltrate and provoke
further violence and greater confusion. We were finding "new reasons for spitefulness," Kerouac complained. Experience with Buddhist sitting practice since 1971 has left me more open to such criticism. We need greater space, it is vanity not to include our errors
in the universe. My practice of mantra chanting and Hindu theistic
public ceremony now seems relatively naive to me, that is to say
inexperienced and unlearned, inefficient for its time, leading to spiritual delusion of Godhood rather than breakthru of common awareness. On the other hand that's too narrow a judgement, too humor-
less, of total "Hippie" effect, in the American War scene. I wish I knew
then (1969) what I know now: how to sit silent following the breath
---traditional nontheistic mindfulness.

From a literary point of view, I hope this book will help myself and others keep chronologic inventory of fugitive essays, interviews, letters, poems and aesthetic deeds, which otherwise have
been lost in masses of "faded yellowed press clippings," university
archives, manila envelopes and home-made filing cabinets full of
electric paper. My intention was to leave a record, in some Akashic
Heaven if not on contemporary earth; I'm glad it's brought down to
earth by Michelle Kraus. In fact, she started underground, realizing that the fugitive speech imagery of Underground Press was closer
to literary history beauty than the more truncated and style-censored
"above ground" newspaper interview prose. I did have in mind that
everything said, written or aesthetically imaged would be accounted
in later decades by scholars who might uncover behind the police-

state commercial version of Beat Poetics another version composed
by poets alone, single handed, or with company of friends, working
for a sangha in new Consciousness beyond the reach of public illu-
sion---a version of late XX century America as a gnostic story,
full of humor and public double entendre such as the expansion of
poetic consciousness to vivify the police and their Capitalist-Com-
munist wars, and the confident adventure of visionary seekers to
encompass ordinary mind: self and its fabulous trips into politics, nonself discovering eternal geography, newspaper-headlined
Egolessness, strophic Ego confession, cosmic war conspiracies,
empty loves and deaths, city meditations, country crazy wisdom
studies that occupied body, speech and mind of this poet for a decade.

Allen Ginsberg
Bedrock Mortar Hermitage
September 13, 1978

ALLEN GINSBERG: AUTOBIOGRAPHIC PRECIS

Grammar High School Paterson New Jersey, B. A. Columbia College 1948; associations with Jack Kerouac, Wm. S. Burroughs, Herbert H. Huncke & Neal Cassady begun 1945 NYC and next decade after with Gregory Corso, Peter Orlovsky companion 1954 & poets Michael McClure, Philip Lamantia, Gary Snyder & Philip Whalen in San Francisco became known 1955 on as "Beat Generation" and/or "San Francisco Renaissance" literary phases; acquaintance with William Carlos Williams 1948 & study of his relative-footed American speech prosody led to Empty Mirror early poems with W. C. W. preface, as later Williams introduced Howl.

Illuminative audition of William Blake's voice simultaneous with Eternity-vision 1948 and underground bust-culture Apocalypse-realization conduced to 8-month stay NY State Psychiatric Institute & later preoccupation with Gnostic-mystic poetics and politics, residence in India & Viet-Nam Japan visit 1962-3, mantra chanting beginning with Hare Krishna Mahamantra and Buddhist Prajnaparamita (Highest Perfect Wisdom) Sutra same years, & experiment with poetic effects of psychedelic drugs beginning 1952 and continuing with Dr. Timothy Leary through Cambridge experiments 1961: certain texts Howl part II (1955) and Wales Visitation (1967) were written during effects of Peyote & LSD respectively.

Travel began early 1950's half year Mayan Mexico, several voyages years Tangiers-Europe late 50's on, earlier merchant marine sea trips to Africa & Arctic, half year Chile Bolivia & Peru Amazon 1960, half year Cuba Russia Poland Czechoslovakia culminating May Day 1965 election as King of May (Kral Majales) by 100, 000 Prague citizens.

Literary Awards: obscenity trial with Howl text declared legal by court S. F. 1957, Guggenheim Fellowship 1963-4, National

Institute of Arts and Letters Grant for poetry 1969. Contributing Editor: Black Mountain Review #7 edited by Robert Creely; Advisory Guru: The Marijuana Review; writing published variously in Yugen, Floating Bear Mimeo, Kulcher, Big Table, City Lights Journal, "C", Evergreen Review, Fuck You/A Magazine of the Arts, Atlantic Monthly, Life, New Yorker, Look, New York Times, Izvestia, Rolling Stone, Underground Press Syndicate, etc.

Participated in college poetry readings & NY Literary scene '58-'61 with Leroi Jones & Frank O'Hara; Poet's Pull My Daisy, Robert Frank film 1959; early Trips Festivals with Ken Kesey Neal Cassady & Merry Pranksters mid-'60's; Vancouver '63 & Berkeley '65 Poetry Conventions with Olson, Duncan, Creely, Snyder, Dorn & other poet friends; Albert Hall Poetry Incarnation, readings with Vosnesensky in London, and anti-Vietnam War early Flower Power marches in Berkeley 1965.

Attended mantra-chanting at first Human Be-in San Francisco 1967; conferred at Dialectics of Liberation in London & gave poetry readings with poet father Louis Ginsberg there and in NY; testified U.S. Senate hearings for legalization of psychedelics; arrested with Dr. Benjamin Spock blocking Whitehall Draft Board steps war protest NY same year. Teargassed chanting AUM at Lincoln Park Yippie Life-Festival Chicago 1968 Presidential convention, then accompanied Jean Genet & William Burroughs on front line Peace "Conspiracy" march led by Dave Dellinger.

Mantric poetics and passing acquaintance with poet-singers Ezra Pound, Bob Dylan, Ed Sanders, & Mick Jagger led to music study for tunes to Wm. Blake's Songs of Innocence & of Experience: this homage to visionary poet-guru William Blake, occasioned by visit West Coast to touch a satin bag of body-ashes the late much-loved Neal Cassady, was composed one week on return from police-state shock in Chicago, & recorded summer 1969. Chanted OM to Judge and Jury December 1969 Anti-War-Conspiracy trial Chicago; thereafter interrupted by Miami Police on reading poetry exorcising police bureaucracy Prague & Pentagon, rapid Federal Court Mandatory Injunction declared texts Constitutionally protected from police censorship. Pallbore funerals late Kerouac & Olson, last few '60's winters spent outside cities learning music milking cows & goats.

A. G. , February, 1970

CHRONOLOGIC ADDENDA

1971--Began daily hour subvocal-mantra heart meditation, Swami Muktananda teacher; brief journey Bengal Jessore Road Calcutta to E. Pakistan refugee camps & revisit Benares. Jamming at home & recording studios w/Dylan & Happy Traum learned Blues forms. Kaddish play mounted N. Y. Chelsea Theater. Researched & publicized CIA subsidization Indochinese opium traffic; assembled 16 phono albums Collected Poems Vocalized 1946-71 from decades' tape archives. Completed second album Blake Songs.

1972--Began study Kagu lineage Tibetan style Buddhist meditation, Chögyam Trungpa, Rinpoche teacher; took Refuge and Boddhisattva vows; extended poetic praxis to public improvisation on blues chords with politic Dharma themes. Adelaide and Central Australia meeting with Aboriginal song-men, Darwin Land travel with Russian poet Andrei Vosnesensky. Jailed with hundreds of peace protestors, Miami Presidential Convention; essays in defense of Tim Leary, Abbie Hoffman, John Lennon etc. from Federal Narcotics Bureau entrapment, as member of P. E. N. Freedom to Read Committee.

1973--Poetry International London & Rotterdam; meetings with Basil Bunting & Hugh MacDiarmid, tour Scotland/Inner Hebrides. Taught poetics Naropa Seminary; all Autumn retreat Buddhist study including month's 10 hour daily sitting practice.

1974--Inducted member American Academy & Institute of Arts and Letters. National Book Award for Fall of America; apprenticed rough carpentry wooden cottage neighboring Gary Snyder Sierra land; with Anne Waldman founded Jack Kerouac School of Disembodied Poetics, Naropa Institute now 1111 Pearl Street, Boulder, Colorado 80302; co-director teaching subsequent summers.

1975--Poetics school solidified; poet-percussionist on Bob Dylan's Rolling Thunder Review tour, filmed improvised blues at

Kerouac's grave; First Blues with lead sheet music notation published.

1976--Reading Academie der Kunste, Berlin with Wm. Burroughs; First Blues recordings produced by John Hammond Sr.;
several months fall seminary retreat with Chögyam Trungpa.

1977--Read thru Blake's entire Works, wrote "Contest of
Bards," narrated TVTV film Kaddish, presented poetry/music
Nightclub Troubadour L.A. under Buddhist auspice, thereafter N.
Y. Other End & Boston Passim folk clubs. Journals: Early '50's
Early '60's, Grove Press, N.Y., ed. Gordon Ball. Read with
Robert Lowell St. Mark's, N.Y. Taught Blake's Urizen Naropa
Institute spring, summer discoursed on "Literary History Beat
Generation 1940's." Attended U. of Cal Santa Cruz L.S.D. Con-
ference, visited Kuai.

POETRY BOOKS

Howl and Other Poems. City Lights Books, SF, 1956.
Kaddish and Other Poems. City Lights Books, SF, 1961.
Empty Mirror, Early Poems. Totem/Corinth, NY, 1961.
Reality Sandwiches. City Lights Books, SF, 1963.
Ankor Wat. Fulcrum Press, London, 1968.
Airplane Dreams. Anansi/City Lights Books, SF, 1968.
Planet News. City Lights Books, SF, 1968.
The Gates of Wrath, Rhymed Poems 1948-51. Four Seasons, Bo-
       linas, 1972.
The Fall of America, Poems of These States. City Lights Books,
       SF, 1973.
Iron Horse. Coach House Press, Toronto / City Lights Books, SF,
       1974.
First Blues. Full Court Press, NY, 1975.
Mind Breaths: Poems 1972-77. City Lights Books, SF, 1978.
Poems All Over The Place--Mostly Seventies. Cherry Valley
       Editions, NY, 1978.

PROSE BOOKS

The Yage Letters. (w/Wm. S. Burroughs), City Lights, SF, 1963.
Indian Journals. David Hazelwood/City Lights, SF, 1970.
Improvised Poetics. Anonym Books, Buffalo, 1971. Distr. by City
       Lights, SF.
Gay Sunshine Interview. Grey Fox Press, Bolinas, 1974.
Allen Verbatim: Lectures on Poetry etc. McGraw-Hill, 1974.
The Visions of the Great Rememberer. Mulch Press, Amherst,
       Mass., 1974.

Chicago Trial Testimony. City Lights Trashcan of History Series,
#1, SF, 1975.
To Eberhart from Ginsberg. Penmaen Press, Lincoln, Mass., 1976.
Journals: Early Fifties Early Sixties. Grove Press, NY, 1977.
As Ever: Collected Correspondence Allen Ginsberg & Neal Cassady,
Creative Arts, Berkeley, 1977.

ANTHOLOGIES, INTERVIEWS, ESSAYS, BIBLIOGRAPHIES, PHOTO
CAHIERS

The New American Poetry 1945-1960. D. Allen, Ed., Grove Press,
NY, 1960.
A Casebook of the Beat. T. Parkinson, ed., Thomas Y. Crowell,
NY, 1961.
The Marihuana Papers. D. Solomon, ed., Bobbs-Merrill, NY, 1966.
The Experience of Literature. L. Trilling, ed., Holt, Rinehart,
NY, 1967.
Paris Review Interviews. (w/Tom Clark), 3rd Series, Viking, NY,
1967.
The Poem in Its Skin. Paul Carrol, ed., Big Table/Follet, Chicago,
1968.
Modern American Poetry. New & revised edition, L. Untermeyer,
ed., Harcourt Brace & World, NY, 1969.
Playboy. (interview with Paul Carrol) Chicago, April 1969.
Norton Anthology of Poetry. WW Norton Co., NY, 1970.
Scenes Along the Road. A. Charters, ed., Gotham Book Mart, NY,
1970.
Allen Ginsberg Bibliography 1943-67. G. Dowden, ed., City Lights,
SF, 1971.
Poetics of the New American Poetry. Allen & Tallman, eds.,
Grove, NY, 1973.
The Beat Book. A. & G. Knight, eds., California, Pa., 1974.
Loka: Journal of Naropa Institute. Anchor/Doubleday, NY, Vol 1-
1975, Vol 2-1976.
Understanding Poetry. Brooks & Warren, eds., Holt Rinehart Win-
ston, NY, 1976.
The New Oxford Book of American Verse. Oxford, NY, 1976.
The New Naked Poetry. Berg & Mexey, eds., Bobbs-Merrill, NY,
1976.

PHONOGRAPH RECORDS

Howl and Other Poems. Fantasy-Galaxy Records #7013, Berkeley,
1959.
Kaddish. Atlantic Verbum Series 4001, NY, 1966. (o. p.)
Wm. Blake's Songs of Innocence & of Experience tuned by A. G.
MGM Records, NY, 1970 FTS 3083 (o. p.)
Blake Album II. Fantasy-Galaxy Records, to be released?
First Blues: Songs. John Hammond Sr., Prod., NY, to be re-
leased?

FOREWORD

For a quarter of a century Allen Ginsberg has been haunting
the American consciousness. Acknowledged almost from the first
of his many publications as a major poetic voice (called even "the
Walt Whitman of our time"), he has read his works at all of the
important (and at many of the less important) American colleges
and universities and in halls all over the world. Holder of a Guggenheim Fellowship and a National Book Award, he has also been
a motion picture actor and a recording artist (as well as a composer
of sorts). But at no time has his prominence been limited to his
work in the arts. Famous as the "wild shaman" of the Beat Generation, he used the public fascination with him and the movement to
urge new attitudes toward drugs and various forms of sexuality. A
Jewish poet from New Jersey, he has reported visions, taken LSD,
chanted mantras, practiced Yoga and meditated. Yet through all of
this he has insisted on talking in a specifically American idiom, always recalling his own deep relationship to an American poetic and
intellectual tradition: Melville, Whitman, William Carlos Williams.
He has been a merchant seaman, a dishwasher, a market research
analyst. He has been a resident of a madhouse and a sojourner in
India. A financial success (complete with business manager), he
has maintained the simplest of life-styles. He was one of the more
important anti-war activists. Life magazine interviewed him; a
Senate committee listened to him; local governments jailed him;
foreign countries expelled him. No other poet in our history has
been so fully newsworthy; no other has achieved quite the same
celebrity status, even in this age of celebrities.

While it is easy to see the reasons for the public fascination,
Ginsberg's life and work present a special challenge to the historian
of culture in our time. Clearly a central figure, Allen Ginsberg

has spoken to his generation and for it--at least a significant part of it. Yet somehow he is more than a voice and even more than a personality, more than the sum total of his work and deeds, his words and actions. His biography tells us everything--and yet nothing; his poetry will always strike us as important (and perhaps will even continue to move generations to come) but somehow may never be able to stand alone in greatness apart from his time and his place. And yet Ginsberg will remain as one of the crucial keys to the second quarter of twentieth-century American culture; future cultural historians who fail to understand him will somehow never understand that period and its meaning.

For Allen Ginsberg is part of American mythology, a mythic presence of archetypal significance. In a profound sense it is possible to suggest that the mythic type prefigured his actual public appearance. By what may seem remarkable coincidence, in the Winter Number of Partisan Review in 1943, Columbia Professor Lionel Trilling published a short story, "Of This Time, of That Place." It dealt with the complex relationship between a college teacher of literature and two of his students, one a normal and routine young man of limited talent and imagination who manages to "achieve" and "beat" the system, the other quite literally insane but brilliant and often profound in the wild confusions of his own involved rhetoric. The author's affection is plainly directed to the second student. Ginsberg himself did not enter Columbia until the fall of 1943. Yet Diana Trilling recalls this story in her essay "The Other Night at Columbia: A Report," based on a 1956 performance by Ginsberg at his Alma Mater. In that essay, Mrs. Trilling remembers Ginsberg as an undergraduate, most particularly as a student of her husband. She remembers him as a "case"--"a gifted case, a guilt-provoking and nuisance case, but, above all, a case." The fact that Trilling had recently published his story seemed to have made things more difficult. People would call and ask whether in fact the "crazy" student was not really sane.

Had not Trilling in his brilliant story given us the archetype of the poet, of the man of letters for our time? And had not Ginsberg come along and given life to the archetype? In his narrative, Trilling invents a paper from his mad student on the theme "Who I am and why I came to Dwight College."

> Materialism, by which is meant the philosophic concept and not the moral idea, provides no aegis against the question which lies beyond the tangible (metaphysics). Existence without alloy is the question presented. Environment and heredity relegated aside, rags and old clothes of practical life discarded, the name and the instrumentality of livelihood do not, as the prophets of the dismal science insist on in this connection, give solution to the interrogation which not from the professor merely but veritably from the cosmos is given. I think, therefore I am (cogito etc.) but who am I? Tertan I am, but what is Tertan? Of this time, of that place, of some parentage, what does it matter?

Surely the rhetoric is not Ginsberg's, but just as surely many of the ideas and much of the stance of Tertan, the "crazy" student who yearns to be a poet-philosopher are emblematic of what Ginsberg as a poet-leader of his generation is to be. Buried deep in Tertan's rhetoric is much that is basic to the vision of the so-called New Left and most particularly its poetic voice.

The mythic Ginsberg continues, then, to haunt the student of our recent cultural past. It has a significance that transcends the particular facts and achievements of the living Allen Ginsberg. Indeed, from perhaps the Trilling story up through the 1977 brilliant dramatization of the Beat Generation in Martin Duberman's Visions of Kerouac (in which Ginsberg appears lightly disguised as Irwin Goldbook), the mythic Ginsberg has been a part of our national fiction as well as part of other aspects of our national life. In the long range of our cultural history the mythic Ginsberg may prove even more significant than the real poet and newsmaker himself.

The appearance, then, of this major bibliographical study is not only welcome but essential. We need to understand more urgently than ever before all aspects of this most special figure in our cultural life. No bibliography, of course, can do more than point the way through the literature in our search for truth and meaning. But such a work is an indispensable beginning in our search for the real Allen Ginsberg, and the archetype as well, that helped shape a period in our development as a culture.

Warren I. Susman
Rutgers University

INTRODUCTION

Allen Ginsberg--poet, prophet, voice of the nation--has fascinated me for many years. He is a barometer of social change, the poet of our decade, the spokesman of a generation, the center of thought for a particular segment of our society. He mirrors overall social turmoil and later change. As a researcher of contemporary American culture and history, I am impressed by the breadth of his development, his expansiveness, over the last years. He is the supreme manipulator of the media, yet the prime subject of manipulation. He is an enigma, a symbol, a hero and guru. Often paralleled to Walt Whitman, he sings the song of America.

I have spent two years completing this annotated bibliography of work by this man (as of 1968) and that which has been written about him from 1969 through 1977. Through this endeavor, I seek to bring under bibliographic control previously inaccessible information which rebels against more traditional forms of classification. Interdisciplinary or underground research has yet to be incorporated entirely into a research library classification system such as that of the Library of Congress. As a result, such information is often not available to the general public. Ginsberg falls within the realm of both; not only is his work interdisciplinary (spanning such areas as poetics, literature, culture, history and Eastern thought), but also it is underground, originating from alternative sources, outside the mainstream of publishing. Despite the efforts of editors of standard indexes, these sources are generally omitted because of the often ephemeral nature of their existence and their deliberate inaccessibility. A game plan or strategy by which to complete such research is illustrated through the types of information gathered here.

This bibliography is the product of both a traditional and nontraditional search procedure. The traditional search took me to the more standard library research tools, including Besterman, Bibliographic Index, Bulletin of Bibliography, Essay and General Literature, The American Humanities Index, Popular Periodicals Index, Comprehensive Index to Little Magazines, Articles in Twentieth Century Literature, Alternative Press Index, American Literary Scholarship, MLA Bibliography and Abstracts, Humanities Index, Social Science Index, Readers' Guide to Periodical Literature, The Year's Work in English Studies, Abstracts of English Studies, Publishers Weekly, Forthcoming Books, Books in Print, Paperback Books in Print, Cumulative Book Index, Dissertation Abstracts

International, Comprehensive Dissertations Index, Chicorel Series, The National Union Catalogues, Book Review Index, Book Review Digest, major newspaper indexes including the New York Times, and film and audio-visual indexes. However, it is the nontraditional search which took me on the never-ending journey. Since material on Ginsberg is often omitted from the above-listed indexes for a variety of reasons, the researcher must first play with the existing subject headings and reap the information which is there, but not visible because of the limitations of any arbitrary classification system. Then, having gleaned what does exist, the researcher must look beyond the given to the other sources which publish Ginsberg material. The first stop was an underground newspaper collection (covering 1963-1975) available on microfilm from Bell and Howell. It is the only collection of its kind and a storehouse of information which again is difficult to enter because of the lack of subject indexing. The collection (included here in Appendix C-1) is arranged alphabetically by the title of the underground publication and then chronologically. The researcher must scan page after page of information to discover subject contents of this collection. Despite the tedious nature of the task at hand, the character of this decade was revealed from a particular perspective. The social temper of our culture passed before my eyes, as I read of current events and movement issues of this time. Beyond this collection there were other special collections/catalogs to be discovered and investigated. Most crucial of these was the collection housed with the poet himself, Allen Ginsberg. This collection will eventually join the existing deposit at the Allen Ginsberg Papers, Rare Book and Manuscript Library, Columbia University. After reviewing my preliminary manuscript, the poet opened his personal papers to me thus inviting me aboard the journey through the land of Allen's "F.Y.P.C." ("Faded Yellowed Press Clippings," a designation intrinsic to the Ginsberg papers). "F.Y.P.C." serves as a general heading for newspaper articles, press releases, notes, magazine articles, and ephemera within the Ginsberg papers. Long, short, big and small cartons filled with overstuffed folders were placed before me, and somehow made their way back to my parents' house.

As my visits to Ginsberg's Lower East Side apartment became more frequent, my initially bourgeois sensibilities altered. The poverty of the streets confronted me on all sides. The two dominant ethnic groups, the older, Yiddish-speaking population and the more recently arrived Spanish-speaking population, exist in tension. A heightened awareness was necessary for survival in this area, which is also a mecca for young poets from the St. Mark's Church Poetry Project. Rumor has it that besides several funeral parlors and a church coupled with a school, an auto theft ring operates on his street. The outer door of his tenement building was always locked and the procedure for opening the door well rehearsed. A dirty sock was kept for someone throwing the key to the person waiting below the window. Allen lives with Peter Orlovsky and Denise Mercedes (a "punk rocker"). Despite the seeming normality of having two roommates, a different situation really did exist. At no time have I ever seen only three people in the small

The Ginsberg Collection and "Faded Yellowed Press Clippings"

apartment. There was a constant throng of young poets and "punk rock" people coming or going, as Allen's secretary, Bob Rosenthal, attempted to deal with the continuously ringing telephone and the apartment activities.

I am grateful to all my unemployed friends who came with me and aided my research endeavors; before long I had my own set of keys and was welcome to come and go at my own discretion and at any hour. I and my team of researchers earnestly continued through the spring digesting the wall of books, papers, magazines and ephemera in Allen's place. One underground source led to another. One item revealed a clue for several others within the alternative publishing community. There were connections throughout the entire publishing network. The information I found here sent me out into the alternative press community seeking answers to clues discovered in this manner.

The information included in this bibliography, then, is specific to its subject. It includes selections from gay periodicals, underground newspapers and alternative publications that often exist in mimeographed forms only. None of the other available bibliographies of Ginsberg's work extends beyond the late 1960's; each is limited in its own way. As a result, I have chosen to begin my study where the most comprehensive work stopped. This work is that edited by George Dowden and Laurence McGilvery, Bibliography of Works by Allen Ginsberg, October, 1943 to July 1, 1967, published by City Lights (San Francisco) in 1971. Although the work officially ends in 1967, it has some listings into the latter part of the 1960's. The chronology adopted by McGilvery includes citations which are listed alphabetically by the title of the journal involved. Unless the reader is familiar with the literature, it is a difficult tool to use.

The other Ginsberg bibliographies available include an article by Morris Dickstein, "Allen Ginsberg and the 60's" which appeared in Commentary (49, January 1970, pp. 64-70). The article includes a bibliography which extends into the middle 60's with minimal although accurate listings. In Richard Kostelanetz's collection of articles and bibliographic essays that include Allen Ginsberg, Master Minds; Portraits of Contemporary American Artists and Intellectuals (Macmillan Co., 1967, 1969), the citations available extend only into 1968. The Thomas Merrill volume on Ginsberg (Allen Ginsberg, part of the Twayne United States Authors Series) couples a "selected bibliography" with a series of analytical essays. It is primary and secondary in its scope, but not extensive in its listings which are both evaluative and descriptive. Two French bibliographies are available: one by Christine Tysh, Allen Ginsberg, étude de Christine Tysh: choix de poèmes, bibliographie, illustrations (Paris: Seghers, 1974/Poètes d'aujourd'hui 221), available in French or English, which has minimal listings; the other is located within Jacqueline Starer's Les Ecrivains beats et le voyage, published in 1977 by Didier in Paris (in French only). Since this bibliography covers all the major writers of the Beat Movement, its individual treatment of Ginsberg is limited. Nonetheless, it is an excellent research tool for the period and genre.

The years covered by this annotated bibliography are 1969 through 1977. Primary works from 1968 are included, as well as some material from 1978, particularly that which was prepared within the time frame of this compilation, but published later. The primary book section includes works from 1968 (which predate the framework of this compilation) because although they were officially published in 1968, they did not appear commercially until 1969. As a result, the book reviews of these works are also included in the secondary section. It includes other bibliographies, primary books, poems, pamphlets, essays/statements, interviews, excerpts of interviews, records, photographs, films, television and radio programs, tapes, audio-visual productions; secondary books, reviews, articles (in newspapers and periodicals), works in translation and other categories specific to the material analyzed. All items are annotated, except those unavailable for examination.

I have decided to list all entries in the SECONDARY WORKS section (except Part V-G, Photographs) alphabetically by author's last name (with anonymous material interfiled by title). This system also is used in the PRIMARY WORKS section for Parts III, IV, and VI-C (see Table of Contents), with the remaining parts filed alphabetically by title. A particular concern of the poet and the bibliographer is the chronological development of his work over the years, as well as the geographical patterns that developed. Thus, a chronological list of his primary books, letters, essays/statements and interviews is included in the back of the book as Appendix D.

Many unusual pieces of Ginsberg writing border on classification as ephemera because of the ambiguity of their later publication. Also note that a statement/essay will often appear in a variety of forms in different underground publications. The major clearinghouses of underground literature (Underground Press Syndicate and Liberation News Service) share articles and often remain deliberately vague about publication details. Indicating the original source of information is difficult, if not impossible. Bibliographically, this presents a research dilemma which is intrinsic to the material discussed. I have attempted to deal with the situation as simply as possible by indicating the chronological origin of the material. Usually the main entry is the first underground newspaper to carry the information and is the origin of the statement/essay. Then it is sent on and shared by the other members of that particular underground press service, so the entry will list these as reprints. For further information on the membership of the individual services, see the underground newspaper address file in Appendix C-2. It is arranged alphabetically by the title of the publication and has a key for explanation of the abbreviations used.

There are inconsistencies noticeable in the film, television and radio programs, audio-visual and photography sections because of the search problems encountered. Each of these sections is selec-

tive because no comprehensive indexes are available. A prime source for this information was the "F. Y. P. C. " file. Despite all efforts to be comprehensive, the bibliographer admits the short-comings in these areas. The photography section is different be-cause it usually notes photographs which are printed alone without accompanying text. The two major photographers of Ginsberg are noted. One is Elsa Dorfman. A complete list of her work on Allen Ginsberg will be made available through her gallery, the Witkin (41 East 57th Street, New York, N. Y. , 212-355-1461). A list of the work of the other, Fred McDarrah of the Village Voice, is included in this section. His work is for sale. Do not contact him for re-search purposes.

Appendix B expands the tape section by including a list of tapes prepared by the staff of Allen Ginsberg. It includes tapes from the 1960's to the present that are or will be on deposit at the Allen Ginsberg Papers, Rare Book and Manuscript Library, Colum-bia University, or in Ginsberg's private collection in his home. Al-though some of this material predates the time frame of this com-pilation, it is included in full because it has never before appeared in print. (Permission from the poet is necessary to use any ma-terial on deposit at Columbia.) A separate list of tapes owned by Pacifica Broadcasting was also made available through WBAI in New York City. These programs are cross-listed with the Ginsberg master list whenever possible; the remainder are listed separately (within the radio broadcast section of the main portion of the bib-liography). A list of special non-print holdings of the Paterson Free Public Library (250 Broadway, Paterson, N. J. 07501; 201-881-3770) is also included in the tape section for the reader's use.

The individual foreign language subsections throughout this work are uneven because the information available was inconsistent. Some languages were more accessible to Ginsberg scholarship than others. To compensate somewhat for the inconsistencies, Appendix C-3, 4 lists the names and addresses of the major translators and pub-lishing houses in each language (whenever possible) for further ref-erence, as well as including foreign language periodicals which have been referred to in the bibliography.

Appendix A contains a list of the general material available at the Allen Ginsberg Papers, Rare Book and Manuscript Library, Columbia University. A decision was made not to compile informa-tion from these earlier deposits into this bibliography because, to date, they are unindexed and uncategorized beyond general listings. Until more work is completed on these deposits it is impossible for anyone to locate material. Information from the Ginsberg Collection of personal papers (from his home) which is included here was de-posited in 1978 at Columbia University. Special permission (in writ-ing) from the poet is necessary for permission to see these papers.

Opposite: The author working with Ginsberg at home. Photo cour-tesy of Kenneth Bondor.

This bibliography unifies a particular set of experiences and information for me. It is the end product of many years of research together with personal growth and experience. It includes ideas which have shaped my development as a scholar in this field, as well as the thoughts of my mentor, Warren Susman, in his introduction. It symbolizes a chapter of my life, along with a segment of our culture. It presents a game plan for finding the hidden treasures of a crucial segment of our literature and culture as revealed through the works by and about Allen Ginsberg. It facilitates research in a crucial chapter of American culture and history. With humor I recall the opening words of Ginsberg's introduction to a William Burroughs bibliography, * "Who has time to read such big bibliographies?..." Everyone, I hope; scholars, researchers and anyone interested in Allen Ginsberg and contemporary American culture and history. What mortal has enough hours in his life to be so prolific, and to generate so much thinking? Allen Ginsberg.

---

*Joe Maynard and Barry Miles (comps.). William S. Burroughs, A Bibliography, 1953-1973/"Unlocking Inspector Lee's Word Hoard." Intro. by Allen Ginsberg. Charlottesville, Va.: University Press of Virginia, 1978.

Allen Ginsberg

PRIMARY WORKS

I. BOOKS

[Primary books from 1968 have been included because
although they were officially published in 1968, they
did not appear commercially until 1969. Also reprints
of earlier works are cited with the original publication
date in parentheses.]

A. ENGLISH LANGUAGE

1 Airplane Dreams: Compositions from Journals. San Francisco:
House of Anansi, City Lights Books, 1968; USA Edition 1969.
[Originally published in Canada by the Vietnam war-refugee
House of Anansi, Toronto 1968, these "Airplane Dreams" are
now reprinted in the Mother Country by City Lights, San
Francisco, California 94133, in conjunction with the original
publisher.]
      Notes (by Ginsberg and the editor): "These are compositions
from journals kept decades 1948-1968, a few solid fragments typed
up published out of context, not exactly poems, nor not poems:
journal notations put together conveniently, a mental turn-on printed
across the border by long hair youthful exiles disunited from these
states by the war of sighs and spears. "

2 Allen Verbatim: Lectures on Poetry, Politics, Consciousness.
Ed. by Gordon Ball. New York: McGraw-Hill, 1974.
      A delight to read. It includes some bibliographic refer-
ences in the notes at the end of each chapter. According to Gordon
Ball, "these chapters are a selection from transcriptions of approxi-
mately twenty hours of informal lectures and conversations. In
terms of portraying Allen and the range and depth of his multiple
interests and attentions, they are by no means comprehensive ...
nor are they entirely 'verbatim' as much was edited (deleted or re-
phrased or restructured) to reduce repetition and fat normal in conversation but awkward in reading (although spoken language has been
retained as much as possible). "

3 Ankor Wat. London: Fulcrum Press, 1968; with photographs
by Alexandria Lawrence.
      First 100 copies signed & numbered by Ginsberg contain
biography on inside of cover. The Ginsberg collection has number 15
and is signed.

1

4 Bixby Canyon Ocean Path Word Breeze. New York: Gotham
      Book Mart, 1972.
                One long poem with pictures (May 28, 1971). The front
and back piece are by Jack Kerouac. Ginsberg laments: "O
Kerouac / thy broken / car behold... ".

4a Careless Love, Two Rhymes. Wisconsin: The Red Ozier
      Press, 1978. (Chapbook, limited edition).

5 Empty Mirror: Early Poems, with introduction by William Carlos
      Williams. New York: Totem/Corinth Books, 1970, second
      printing; original ed., 1961.
                Notes on p. 63: This new edition of Empty Mirror was
designed by Joan Wilentz and printed by the Profile Press of N.Y.C.
The poems were set in Garamond type; Baskerville was used for
the front matter and Caslon 540 Italics was used for display.

6 The Fall of America; Poems of These States, 1965-1971. San
      Francisco: City Lights Books, 1972.

7 First Blues: Rags, Ballads, and Harmonium Songs, 1971-1974.
      New York: Full Court Press, 1975.
                "Dedication: To Ministrel Guruji Bob Dylan" According
to Ginsberg, ... "I've left most first drafts and improvisions fixed in
their original wordings, useful to myself and others to see how raw
mind actually sings. " June 30, 1975.

8 The Gates of Wrath: Rhymed Poems, 1948-1952. California:
      Grey Fox Press, 1972. Distributed by Book People, 2940
      Seventh St. : Berkeley, California 94710.
                "Hindsight, " after thoughts (p. 56): "The Gate of Wrath
manuscript was carried to London by lady friend early fifties: it
disappeared, and I had no complete copy till 1968 when old typescript was returned through Bob Dylan--it passed into his hands
years earlier. By sweet coincidence, I returned to this rhymed
mode with Dylan's encouragement as fitted for musical song. Tuned
to lyric guitar, composing on harmonium, chant or improving on
rhythmic chords in electric studio, I began 'perfecting' use of this
mode two decades after W. C. W. 's wise objection, dear reader, in
same weeks signatur'd below. " (Allen Ginsberg, December 8, 1971)

9 Gay Sunshine Interview. Introduction by Allen Young. San
      Francisco: Grey Fox Press, 1974.
                See INTERVIEWS for further information.

10 Howl and Other Poems. San Francisco: Grabhorn and Hoyem,
      1971, (1956).
                This is a special edition of Howl from 1956 "with recent
minute revisions by the author and one addition of a related poetic
fragment. The names, written in 1957, published in the Paris Review for Spring 1966 and here first collected with the poem. The
title page bears the signature of the poet. The drawing for the
cover is by Robert LaVigne. This edition, limited to 275 copies,

was printed on handmade paper from Goudy Modern type in the Summer of 1971 by Robert Grabhorn & Andrew Hoyem of San Francisco. "

11   Howl and Other Poems.   Introduction by William Carlos Williams.   San Francisco: City Lights Books, May 1971.   24th printing; Jan. 1973, 25th printing (orig. ed. , 1956).

12   Improvised Poetics.   Edited with an introduction by Mark Robison.   San Francisco: Anonym Press (P. O. Box 313 Occidental, Calif. 95465), 1972.
        "Printed in a limited edition of two thousand copies, one hundred of which are signed and numbered by the author. "   According to the editor, Mark Robison, "the following is a discussion of modern poetry between Allen Ginsberg, Michael Aldrich, Edward Kissam and Nancy Bleeker at Ginsberg's farm in Cherry Valley, New York on November 26, 1968. "   See "Selected Bibliography" of Ginsberg's work.

13   Indian Journals, March 1962-May 1963:   Notebooks, Diary, Blank Pages, Writings.   San Francisco: Dave Haselwood Books, 1970; second printing, June 1971.
        The Ginsberg collection edition is a work copy of the June 1971 printing with corrections.

14   Iron Horse.   Toronto, Canada: The Coach House Press, 1972.   Printed in an edition of 1, 000 copies, Jan. 1973.   48 pp.

15   Iron Horse.   San Francisco: City Lights Books, 1974.
        A long poem.

16   Journals: Early Fifties, Early Sixties.   Edited by Gordon Ball.   New York: Grove Press, Inc. , 1977.

17   Kaddish and Other Poems.   San Francisco: City Lights Press, 1961; ninth printing, February 1969; thirteenth printing, Sept. 1972; fourteenth printing, March 1974.

18   Mind Breaths: Poems 1972-1977.   San Francisco: City Lights Books, 1978: Pocket Book Series No. 35.
        The Ginsberg collection copy is dated "received December 11, 1977" and signed by Ginsberg with corrections written into the work copy.   One correction worth noting encompasses an addition to the copyright page written in below the Library of Congress information: "Diligent readers will find 22 additional poems, rhymed, many with music notation, published as First Blues: Rags, Ballads and Harmonium Songs, 1971-1974, New York: Full Court Press, 1975, to correlate with Mind Breaths, supplementing the volume. "

19   The Moments Return.   A poem by Allen Ginsberg with three drawings by Robert LaVigne, San Francisco: Grabhorn-Hoyem, 1970.   20 pp.
        One of 200 copies.

20 Open Head. Victoria, Australia: Sun Books Pty. Ltd., 1972.
    This consists of two books, back to back, Open Head by Allen
    Ginsberg on one side, Open Eye by Lawrence Ferlinghetti on
    the other. Black and white photographic portraits of each
    poet on their respective covers. The Ginsberg collection copy
    includes Ginsberg's correction written into his work copy.
    The following poems are included in Open Head: "Elegy For
    Neal" pp. 1-3; "On Neal's Ashes" p. 4; "Rain-Wet Asphalt
    Heat, Garbage Curbed Cans Overflowing" pp. 4-5; "Memory
    Gardens" pp. 5-8; "Friday The Thirteenth" pp. 8-11; "Memory
    Milarepa" p. 12; "September On Jessore Road" pp. 12-17.

21 Planet News, 1961-1967. San Francisco: City Lights Books;
    second printing February 1970; later printing May 1974 (orig.
    ed., 1968). The Pocket Poets Series Number 23.

21a Poems All Over The Place: Mostly Seventies. Allen Ginsberg.
    Cherry Valley, N.Y.: Cherry Valley Editions, 1978.

22 To Eberhart from Ginsberg. Lincoln, Mass.: Penmaen Press,
    1976, with illustrations by Jerome Kaplan. The first edition
    was printed in limited number in March, 1976.
        "An Historic Document from the Beat era published now for
the first time. Allen Ginsberg's remarkable 1956 letter to Richard
Eberhart and Eberhart's 'West Coast rhythms' with comments by both
poets." Ginsberg clarifies his intent in writing Howl and offers a
fresh interpretation of his words.

23 T.V. Baby Poems. San Francisco: Beach Books, Texts & Docu-
    ments, 1968, n. 2 (Distributed by City Lights Books; London:
    Cape Goliard Press, Ltd., Sept., 1967; New York: Grossman
    Publishers Inc., 1968 in association with Cape Goliard Press,
    Ltd., London.

24 The Visions of the Great Rememberer. Amherst, Mass.: Mulch
    Press, 1974.
        "With letters by Neal Cassady; Drawings by Basil King."
Part One is a prose journal. Part Two is "intrapersonal relations"
notes for the story. From the jacket cover, "(This) is a Memoir of
Jack Kerouac and Neal Cassady taking off from the text of Kerouac's
recently published Visions of Cody."

25 The Yage Letters. William Burroughs and Allen Ginsberg. San
    Francisco: City Lights Books, sixth printing, 1971 (orig. ed.,
    1963).
        The Ginsberg collection copy is signed and dated, "Naropa
1977" as well as inscribed: "For Allen Ginsberg all the best from
the bujos and the brew. William Burroughs"

B. TRANSLATIONS

Dutch

26 Proef m'N tong in je oor. [Selected Poems]. Amsterdam: Uit-
geverij De Berige Bij, 1973. (Van Miereveldstraat, 1, Amsterdam). Een keuze uit de dichtbundels Howl, Kaddish en
Reality Sandwiches alsmede enkele andere tekstin. Vertaald
uit het Amerikaans door Simon Vinkenoog.

French

27 Howl and other poems. Paris: Christian Bourgois Editeur,
1977; (Bilingual). Traduit de l'américain par Jean-Jacques
Lebel et Robert Cordier.
    This edition of Howl is complete as compared to the origi-
nal 1956 American work. However, it adds "Psalm III" and "Green
Automobile," both of which were omitted in the Christian Bourgois
editions of Reality Sandwiches in 1967 and then in 1972. This edition concludes (on pp. 90-93) with "Notes Ecrites Lorsqu 'Howl'
Finit Par Etre Grave Sur Disque" ["Notes written on finally recording
'Howl'"] which is reprinted from Fantasy, Spoken Word Series, 7006,
copyright 1959 by Fantasy Records, Inc. (not properly cited in this ed.).

28 Journaux Indiens. Paris: Christian Bourgois Editeur, 1977. Traduit de l'americain (par François et) Philippe Mikriammos.
    Peculiarly Jacques François is listed on the inside jacket
cover but not on the title page. The following explanation is given:
"Cette édition française est dédiée a la mémoire de Jacques François
qui avait entrepris avant sa disparition une permière traduction. " C.
B. ("This French edition is dedicated to the memory of Jacques
François who before his disappearance had undertaken a first translation of this text. ") The notes on pp. 246-267 describe the people,
terminology, places, Hindu/Indian words from text. This is a complete version of Indian Journals (as compared with the original English edition in 1970) with the addition of the above-mentioned notes.
"These notes came out of collaboration between Allen Ginsberg and
Fernanda Pivano for the Italian edition of Indian Journals. A certain number of them were reviewed, completed or entirely added
for the present edition by Gérard-Georges Lemaire, Philippe Mikriammos and Philippe Payelle. "

29 Kaddish. Paris: Christian Bourgois Editeur, 1976. Text corrected for Bourgois Edition by Author, 1976, traduit de l'américain par Mary Beach, adapté par Claude Pélieu. (Bilingual).
    This translation contains "Notes" from pp. 213 to 216 of
proper names, places, terms, etc. , that all appear in the 1967
edition on pp. 140-144.

30 Kaddish et Sandwiches de Réalité. Poems choisis et traduits
par Mary Beach et Claude Pélieu avec la collaboration de l'auteur,
Paris, Union Générale d'Editions, Collection (10-18), 1972.
(Bilingual.)

31 Les Lettres du Yage, traduit de l'américain par Claude Pélieu et Mary Beach. Paris: Éditions de l'Herne, 1970.

32 Planet News. Poemes traduits de l'américain par Mary Beach et Claude Pélieu. Note introduction de Claude Pélieu. Notes concernant Planet News compilées par Claude Pélieu, Mary Beach avec l'assistance d'Allen Ginsberg (notes assemblees NYC, Cherry Valley, 1970). Paris: Christian Bourgois Éditeur, 1971. (Bilingual.)
"Notes and Notules" only in French from pp. 329 to 344 include all sorts of items which need further clarification. Introduction by Claude Pélieu, "La télévision était un bébé rampant vers la chambre de la mort." This is a stream of consciousness critique of individual poems which ends with a poem by Claude dealing with images of Ginsberg.

33 Reality Sandwiches. Paris: Christian Bourgois Éditeur, 1972, pour la traduction française/traduit de l'américain par Mary Beach et Claude Pélieu. (Bilingual.)
Included are "Notes sur 'Reality Sandwiches'" (pp. 171-75).
The order of the "Notes" reflects the text of the poems. They indicate formal names, terms, places, etc. This is not a complete edition (as compared to the original English 1963 edition). The following poems are omitted: "The Green Automobile," "Over Kansas," "Malest Cornifici Tuo Catullo," "Blessed be the muses," "Psalm III," "Tears," "Ready to Roll," "Wrote This Last Night," "Squeal," "American Change," "Funny Death," and "Battleship Newsreel."
There is a title change in "Back from Europe" to "Back on Times Square, Dreaming of Times Square." One addition is the back cover note by Claude Pélieu written in Gun Hill in 1972, which builds upon Ginsberg's "afterthought" in a stream of consciousness poetic discussion of the work.

German

34 Das Geheul und Andere Gedichte. (Howl and Other Poems.) Einfürhrung von William Carlos Williams (Introduction.) Nachwort von Walter Höllerer (Afterword). München, Germany: Ausgabe Limes Verlag, 1970. Ins Deutsche übertragen von Wolfgang Fleischmann und Rudolf Wittkopf/Funfte auf 2000 limitierte Auflage 1970.
This German edition of Howl does not include "Earlier Poems: 'An Asphodel,' 'Song,' 'In Back of the Real,'" but does add "At Apollinaire's Grave" from Kaddish. In addition there is an afterword "Zu Allen Ginsbergs Gedichten" ("To All of Allen Ginsberg's Poems") by Walter Höllerer (pp. 85-86) which comments upon "Howl" the rebel of tradition. He indicates the European impulse to imitate this rebellion and praises Ginsberg for his gifts for "his voice is a snake-like twisting or the language."

35 Indisches Tagebuch. München, Germany: Carl Hanser Verlag, 1972. Übersetzt von Carl Weissner (translated by Carl Weissner). Printed in Germany.

This is the complete version of the original Indian Journals, copyrighted in 1970 by the poet.

36 Iron Horse. Göttingen, Germany: expanded media editions #10, Oktober 1973. Übersetzung 1973 by Carl Weissner (Translator). Cover Design by Bobby Geldner.
Beautifully completed version of Iron Horse in German with the skillful inclusion of photographs by Norman Mustill, Gerard Belart, Fred W. McDarrah, Richard Avedon, Claude Pélieu.

37 Planet News. Gedichte (Auswahl) [Selections]. München, Germany: Carl Hanser Verlag, 1969, 1970. Aus dem Amerikanischen von Heiner Bastian.
The German edition excludes the following poems: "This form of Life needs Sex," "Sunset S.S. Azemour," "Seabattle of Salamis took place off Perama," "Stotras to Kali Destroyer of Illusions," "Why is God Love, Jack," "Morning," "I am a Victim of Telephone," "Today," "Big Beat," "Cafe in Warsaw," "Drowse Murmurs," "Who Be Kind To," "Studying the Signs," "Portland Coliseum," "Carmel Valley," "A Vision in Hollywood," "Chances 'R'," "To The Body," "Holy Ghost on the Nod over the Body of Bliss," "Wales Visitation."

38 Der Untergang Amerikas [The Fall of America]. München, Germany: Carl Hanser Verlag, 1975. Aus dem Amerikanischen von Carl Weissner.
Selections from The Fall of America with notes, including: "Dedication to Walt Whitman," "Beginning of a Poem of These States," "These States into Los Angeles," "Hiway Poesy L.A. to Wichita," "Kansas City to St. Louis," "A Vow," "Done, Finished with the Biggest Cock," "An Open Window on Chicago," "Returning North of Vortex," "Crossing Nation," "Violence," "Over Denver Again," "To Poe: Over the Planet, Air Albany-Baltimore," "Northwest Passage," "In a Moonlit Hermit's Cabin," "Rain-wet asphalt heat, garbage curbed can," "Death on All Fronts," "Friday the Thirteenth," "D.C. Mobilization," "Ecologue," "Guru Om," "Have You Seen This Movie?" and "After Words."

Italian

39 Diario Indiano [Indian Journals]. Rome, Italy: Arcana Editrice, 1973. Introdizione, tradizione et note di Fernanda Pivano.
Text all in Italian with original photographs and drawings. From pp. lxi-lxiv "Mantra: Da Chaitanya" a short article by Ginsberg appears (original source: Fresh Planet, n.1., v.1, 1967--underground newspaper). "Nota All Edizione Italiana del Diario Indiano" on page 1 was prepared by the poet for this edition. This text mentions the passage of time since the origin of these journals and updates the reader about Ginsberg's activities regarding his personal meditation, teachers and mantras.

40 Jukebox All' Idrogeno/"Il Messaggio E: Allargate L'area Della Conscienza" [Hydrogen Jukebox]. Italy: Arnoldo Monadori, 1974, Text bilingual; indice Italian.

In this anthology of selections from Ginsberg's work the following is included from Howl: "Howl," "A Supermarket in California," "Transcription of Organ Music," "Sunflower sutra," "America," "In the Baggage Room at Greyhound," "An Asphodel," "Song," "Wild Orphan," "In Back of the Real." The included selections from Kaddish are complete (as compared to the original English edition). "The Change: Kyoto-Tokyo Express" is included from Planet News, as are three prose statements: Notes on Howl from Fantasy Records, "Poetry, violence, trembling lambs (NYC: August 1959)," and the comment on the second edition of Kaddish from its back cover, 1961 (San Francisco, August 28, 1963). The introduction has been prepared by Fernanda Pivano.

41 Mantra del Re di Maggio [Mantra of the King of May]. Italy: Arnoldo Mondadori, 1973, 1976. (Bilingual)
This anthology of Ginsberg work includes as an introduction a conversation between Fernanda Pivano and Ginsberg. From Reality Sandwiches: "The Green Automobile," "On Burroughs' Work," "Over Kansas," "Malest Cornifici Tuo Catullo," "Dream Record: June 8, 1955," "Blessed be the Muses," "Fragment 1956," "A Strange New Cottage in Berkeley," "Scribble," "Psalm III," "Tears," "Ready to Roll," "Wrote this Last Night," "American Change," "Back on Times Square, Dreaming of Times Square," "My Sad Self," "Funny Death," "Battleship Newsreel," "I Beg You Come Back & be Cheerful." Included from Planet News: "Who Will Take Over the Universe?," "Television was a Baby Crawling Toward that Deathchamber," "This Form of Life needs Sex," "Sunset 'S.S. Azemour'," "Describe: The Rain on Dasaswamedh," "Death News," "Patna-Benares Express," "Why is God Love, Jack?" "Wales Visitation," "Pentagon Exorcism." Includes an autobiography and interview with Ginsberg by Thomas Clark.

42 Testimonianza a Chicago [Chicago Trial Text]. Torino, Italy: Gulio Einaudi, editore, 1972, 2nd printing. Translation by Fernanda Pivano.
On pp. ix-xxvi, "Il processo di Chicago" by F. Pivano; pp. 3-98, "Testimonianza per il processo di Chicago 1969" (Italian only); pp. 101-113, "Ginsberg la chiamo: Solitudine Publica" ("Ginsberg spelled it out: Public Solitude").

Japanese

43 Uchū no Iki. (Literal translation, "Breath of the Universe.") Tokyo: Shobun-sha, 1977. [Allen Verbatim: Lectures on Poetry, Politics, Consciousness.] Japanese.

44 Selected Poems of Allen Ginsberg. Tokyo: Shichosya, 1975, 2nd edition. Translator Yu Suwa. (Orig. ed., 1969).
This collection includes from Howl and Other Poems: "Howl," "Footnote to Howl," "A Supermarket in California," "Transcription of Organ Music"; from Empty Mirror: "Fragment," "The Shrouded Stranger," "The Trembling Veil," "After Dead Souls," "Gregory Corso's Story," "Metaphysics," "The Night-Apple," "Sun-

set," "Marijuana Notation," "Paterson"; from Reality Sandwiches: "Sakyamuni Coming Out from the Mountain," "Ready to Roll," "A Strange New Cottage in Berkeley"; from Kaddish and Other Poems: "To Lindsay," "To Aunt Rose," "The Lion for Real," "At Apollinaire's Grave," "Death to Van Gogh's Ear," and parts from "Kaddish."

Portuguese

45 Cadernas de poesia/ Uivo (e outros poems) [Howl and Other Poems]. Lisbon, Portugal: publicações dom quixote, 1973. Selections and translation by José Palla e Carmo.
The following selections from Howl and Other Poems are included: "Howl," "Notes... on Howl," "Song," "In Back of the Real"; from Reality Sandwiches: "On Burroughs Work," "Psalm 3," "My Sad Self"; from Kaddish: "Poem Rocket," "At Apollinaire's Grave," "Death to Van Gogh's Ear"; from Planet News: "First Party at Ken Kesey's with Hell's Angels," "Uptown," "Pentagon Exorcism"; from The Fall of America: "War Profit Litany," "Imaginary Universes," "Death on all Fronts," "D.C. Mobilization."

Spanish

46 Cartas del Yage [Yage Letters], with William Burroughs. Buenos Aires, Argentina: Ediciones Signos, March 1971, 1st edition. Traducción de M. Lasserre.
This is identical to the English edition.

City Lights List

[The following list of books by Allen Ginsberg in foreign language editions was made available through the efforts of City Lights Publishing House. The dates of publication were unavailable due to a theft in 1977 which destroyed many of their records. The reader is advised to contact City Lights for further information (1562 Grant Avenue, San Francisco, California 94133/(415)362-3112), the foreign publishing house directly or the main translator in that particular language. The addresses for the publishers and translators can be found in the Appendix.]

47 Selected Poems. Rhodos, Niels Brocks Gard, Strandgade 36, 1401 Kobenhagan K DENMARK.

48 The Yage Letters (with Wm. S. Burroughs). Stig Vendelkaers DENMARK (op).

49 Selected Poems. Arvi A. Karisto, Osakeyhtio, Hameenlinna, FINLAND.

50 Prose Selections (Chicago Trial Testimony & Encounters with Ezra Pound, etc.). Editions du Seuil, 27 rue Jacob, 75005 Paris FRANCE.

51 The Fall of America. Librairie Ernest Flammarion, 26 rue Ra-
cine, Paris 6, FRANCE.

52 Selected Poems. Editions Seghers, 6 Place St-Suplice, 3 Blvd de
Latour-Maubourg, Paris, FRANCE 75005.

53 The Yage Letters. Limes Verlag, Spielgelgasse 9, Wiesbaden
WEST GERMANY.

54 Selections from Planet News & Fall of America. Heyne Verlag.
(No country cited.)

55 Howl & Other Poems, Kaddish. Akmon Publishers, 3 Mavromihali
St., Athens, GREECE (forthcoming).

56 Selected Poems. Europa Könyukiado, Budapest V, Vorosmarty
Ter 1 HUNGARY.

57 Selected Poems. Reshafim, c/o Bar-David, P. O. Box 1104,
Tel-Aviv ISRAEL (forthcoming).

58 Selected Poems. Publicações Dom Quixote, rua Luciano Cor-
derio 110, Lisbon, PORTUGAL.

59 Planet News, Reality Sandwiches. Mondadori Editore, 20122 Milano, Via Bianca di Savoia, ITALY.

60 Kaddish. Shicho Sha Ltd., 3-15 Ichigaya Sadoharacho, Shinjuku-
Ku Tokyo JAPAN.

61 The Yage Letters. Producciones Editoriales, Avda. Jose Antonio
810, Barcelona 13 SPAIN.

62 Chicago Trial Testimony, Editorial Fontamara, SA, Apad. de Cor-
reos 678 Barcelona SPAIN.

63 The Fall of America. Visor Libros, Calle de Roble 22, Madrid
20 SPAIN (forthcoming).

64 Howl & Other Poems. Visor Libros, Isaac Peral 18, Madrid 14
SPAIN. (forthcoming).

65 Wichita Vortex Sutra. Tusquets Editor, Calle Rosellon 285, Barcelona 9 SPAIN.

66 Selected Poems. FIBs Lyrikklubb, Sveaveagen 68, Stockholm
SWEDEN.

II. POEMS/PROSE IN PERIODICALS
AND BOOKS

A. SELECTED POEMS AND PROSE

67 "After Thoughts," Sebastian Quill, 2 (Spring 1971): unpaged.

68 "After Wales Visitacione," La Huerta Magazine, (1973):
    unpaged.

69 "America," Laomedon Review, 1:1 (Dec./Jan. 1975): 4-6.

70 "Anti War Games," Ramparts (published by Noah's Ark, Inc.,
    Berkeley, Cal.) 9:10 (May 1971): 40-42.

71 "The Argument: Last words spoken by the bard to the boy on a
    train between Washington and N.Y.," from "Contest of Bards,
    III, Epilogue." Roof IV, 1:4 (1977): 15.

72 "Auto Poesy: On the Lam from Bloomington," fervent valley 1
    (Spring 1972).

73 "Ballad of Tommy the Traveler," The Herald, XCII: 15 (Febru-
    ary 8, 1971): 3.

74 "Bayonne Tuscarora," from These States. American Poetry
    Review, 1:1 (November/December, 1972).

75 "Big Beat," ERA, VI:4 (June 1974): 2.

76 "Bixby Canyon Ocean Path Word Breeze," Berkeley Barb, 13: 14:
    322 (October 15-21, 1971): 13. (with drawing titled "Allen
    Discovering America.")

77 "By Air Albany-Baltimore," Look, 33 (November 4, 1969): 34;
    Skidmore 1970 (Yearbook) pp. 130-131, with photographs
    pp. 127-129, and a reprint of a postcard from the poet to
    Barbara D'Andrea of Skidmore College.

78 "Cabin in the Rockies," Loka 2, A Journal from Naropa Institute,
    New York: Doubleday, 1976, p. 156.

79 "Chicago to Salt Lake by Air," Northwest Passage, 9 (August 19,
    1969): 18-19; The Spectator, IX: 6 (October 21, 1969): 11-
    12. (with photo of Ginsberg.)

80 "Christmas Blues," Unmuzzled Ox, 1:4 (Autumn 1972): unpaged.
(with photograph of Ginsberg, no credit.)

81 "C'mon Jack...," Gay Sunshine, 29/30 (Summer/Fall, 1976):
unpaged, p. 36. (1 line poem).

82 "Come Back Christmas," Columbia Today, 2:3 (December 1976):
21.

83 "Contest of Bards," Roof IV, December 1977, n.p.

84 "Continuation Long Poem 'These States' Northwest Passage,"
Earth Read-Out, #022: 0611170 (undated): 3-5.

85 "Crossing Nation," door, 4:18 (March 22-April 12, 1973): 14.

86 "D.C. Mobilization," The Washington Post (April 30, 1974): B1.

87 "Dateless Dream Song," Bombay Gin, 4 (Summer-Fall, 1977):
unpaged.

88 "Death on All Fronts," door, 4:18 (March 22-April 12, 1973):14.

89 "Describe: the rain on Dasaswamedh," Focus, The Sunday Camera's Magazine (July 17, 1977): 24.

90 "Don't Grow Old," Berkeley Barb, 8:577 (September 3-9, 1976);
River Styx 2 (Winter 1977): unpaged; A Shout in the Street,
A Journal of literary and visual art, 1:1 (undated): (unpaged)
49.

91 "A Dream (related to W. C. Williams)," Gay Sunshine, 29/30
(Summer/Fall 1976): unpaged, p. 36.

92 "Easter Sunday," Focus, The Sunday Camera's Magazine (July 17,
1977): 24; The National Observer (June 9, 1973): n.p.

93 "Ecologue," American Review, 16 (February, 1973): 124.

94 "Ego Confession," Chicago Review, 27:1 (Summer 1975): 36-
37.

95 "Elegy Che Guevara," Berkeley Tribe, 5:25:105 (July 30, 1971-
August 6, 1971): 13.

96 "Elegy for Neal Cassady," Paris Review, 14:53 (Winter 1972):
76-9.

97 "Energy Vampire," Kuksu, Journal of Backcountry Writing (July
1974): 55-56.

97a Esthetics Contemporary, Kostelanetz, Richard (ed.). Buffalo,

N. Y. : Prometheus Books, 1977.
See under POEMS/PROSE IN SELECTED ANTHOLOGIES.

98   "Everybody Sing," Berkeley Barb, 17:21 (May 25-31, 1973):
18; Gay News 28, 26 July-8 August 1973?, p. 8.
"Rhythm similar to 'How you gonna keep 'em down on the
farm after they've seen paree.'"

99   "Exemplary Buddhist Shocker." Bastard Angel, 2 (Spring 1974):
13.

100   "Flying Elegy," Colorado-North Review XIV: 1 (Fall 1977):
26; Skyway Peninsula 1 [1977]: p. 1 (cover), with cover
graphic by Steve Brooks.

101   "For Henry Herman, M.D. from friend in time of mental war
and distress." The Marijuana Review 1:5 (July 4, 1969):
unpaged.

102   "Friday the Thirteenth," Klipsun 1970 (1970): 140-142; Rolling
Stone, 60 (June 11, 1970): 28-29.

103   "G. S. Reading Poesy at Princeton," Antioch Review, 30 (Fall/
Winter 1970-1971): 334-5.

104   "Galilee Shore," Focus, The Sunday Camera's Magazine (July 17,
1977): 25.

105   "Gospel Noble Truths," Stupa, Naropa Institute Student Magazine, v. 3, n. 9, n.p. (inside back cover).

106   "Grant Park/Thursday August 29, 1968," Seed, 6:6 (January 20,
1971): 34.

107   "Hadda Be Playing on the Jukebox," Sevendays, Preview Editions: 7 (April 19, 1976): 14.

108   "Have You Seen This Movie?" AFS (Alternative Feature Service):
13 (September 10, 1971): 1-2; Georgia Straight, 5:13 (October 26, 1971): 13. Space City 3:16 (Undated): 9. The Staff
(September 24, 1971).

109   "Hearing 'Lenore' Read Aloud at 203 Amity Street," Focus,
The Sunday Camera's Magazine (July 17, 1977): 24; A Hundred Posters 23 (November 1977).

110   "Heroic Ecstasy," Rolling Stone, 204, January 15, 1976,
p. 39.
See "Rolling Thunder Stones" below.

111   "Hospital Window," The Painted Bride Quarterly 3:3 (Fall 1976):
9-10. Photograph of Ginsberg on page 11.

112 "House of the Rising Sun," Berkeley Barb 17:19: 404 (May 11-17, 1973): 13. Photograph of Ginsberg by Sam Silver; Gay News (July 26-August 8, 1973?): 8; Georgia Straight 7:294 (May 24-31, 1973): 12-13.

113 "Hum Bom!" Nola Express, 91 (October 7, 1971): 32.

114 "Hymmnn," International Education, A Bi-Annual Journal 1:2 (Spring 1972): 36.

115 "I Lay Love on My Knee," Gay Sunshine 33/34, Summer/Fall 1977 (Special Double Issue), n. p. (back cover).

116 "Jaweh and Allah Battle," Holy Beggars Gazette, A Journal of Chassidic Judaism (Special Double Issue), (Winter-Spring 1975): 26-27; WIN, 10:11 (March 28, 1974): 12.

117 "July 4, 1969," Fruit Cup 0:IV (1969): unpaged, [p. 3].

118 "King of May, " Good Times, 11:17 (April 30, 1969): 2.

119 "Kral Majales," Chinook, 1:5 (September 18, 1969): 6; Georgia Straight 3:48 (March 7-13, 1969); It 57 (May 23-June 5, 1969: 28; Los Angeles Free Press, 6:238 (February 7-13, 1969); Photographs of Allen Ginsberg.

120 "Lion Roars Sun Set Over Rockies' East Slope," Loka, A Journal from Naropa Institute, New York: Doubleday, 1975, p. 72.
   "This spontaneous linked verse poem was spoken into a tape recorder by Chögyam Trungpa and Allen Ginsberg.... August 1, 1974."

121 "Local Noise" (with Anne Waldman), Rolling Stone, 204, January 15, 1976, p. 39. See "Rolling Thunder Stones" below.

122 "Mabillon Noctambules," Big Sky 10 (1976): unpaged, [p. 130].

123 "Manhattan Thirties Flash," New York Quarterly, 2 (Spring 1970): 15.

124 "May King's Prophecy," Strike Newspaper, Yale University (May 2, 1970): unpaged [p. 3].

125 "Memory Gardens," Evergreen Review, 14:80 (July 1970): 27, with illustration.

126 "Message II," Era 1:4 (June 1974): 2.

127 "Midnight Streets," Midwest Quarterly 15:1 (August 1973): 53.

} "Morning," Daily Planet 1:VIII (January 24, 1970): 5, 7, with cartoon of Ginsberg in sneakers.

129 "Mr. Sharpe the carpenter from Susanville," Kuksu, Journal
     of Backcountry Writing 4 "Work" (1975): 54.

130 "Mugging," New York Times Magazine, 1 (January 5, 1975):
     7; The Poetry Project Newsletter 20 (December 1974): un-
     paged, [pp. 7-8].

131 "My own voice rose to Heaven in elation," Rolling Stone, 204,
     January 15, 1976, p. 39. See "Rolling Thunder Stones" be-
     low.

132 "N.Y. Youth Call Annunciation," ("A come all-ye"). Scottish
     International (September 1973): unpaged, [pp. 20-21] (song
     without score).

133 "New York Blues." ("A walking blues"). Scottish International
     (September 1973): unpaged centerfold, [pp. 20-21] (song).

134 "The Night Apple," Distant Drummer, 65 (December 25-Janu-
     ary 1, 1970): 3-4.

135 "Night Gleam," Gay Sunshine, 22 (March 1974): 24; Transat-
     lantic Review 52 (Autumn 1975): 17.

135a Oh How Glad Will You Dance With Me, Ed. by Lia Levi.
     Barcelona, Spain: Artes Gráficas Oriente Plaza Riusi Tau-
     let, II, n.d. (oversized color photographic compilation,
     12"x 11" horizontal).
          This is an alternative publication published in Spain but
     written in English. It includes a "trip programmer" in the form of
     two computer "punched cards" which serve as the table of contents
     for the work of Dylan and Ginsberg included. Of Ginsberg's poetry,
     "Sunflower Sutra," "Laughing Gas," "Mescaline," "Lysergic Acid,"
     "The Change," "Witchita Vortex Sutra" are all included.
          "A series of verbal and visual images makes up this
     work. Its purpose is to achieve a communion, a unity between the
     two media. That's the basic idea, the proposal. But through the
     formalized lay out breathes a deeper and more complex goal: a re-
     creation of the words and images that have shaped and moved a
     whole generation of young people and artists everywhere.
          "Lia Levi belongs to that generation and, through her art,
     she gives us her own version, her own experience and hung-ups [sic].
     Her book should be viewed as a trip she makes with her images
     through Bob Dylan's and Allen Ginsberg's words."

136 "On Burroughs' Work," The Literary Tabloid 1:2 (April 1975):
     27 (in review of Allen Verbatim by John E. Schoen).

137 "On Jessore Road," New York Times, (December 17, 1971): 41.

138 "One Day," Unmuzzled Ox 13:76 (undated): 101.

139 "An Open Window on Chicago," Paris Review, 54 (Summer
     1972): 27.

140 "Pentagon Exorcism," Ann Arbor Sun 3:1 (January 6, 1975):
12.

141 "The Planet is Finished," door, 4:18 (March 22-April 12, 1973):
14.

142 "Please Master," Berkeley Barb, 17:16:401 (April 10-26, 1973):
17; The Eulenspiegel Society Pro-Me-Thee-Us (Sexual Minorities Report) (?1973): 32-33; Gay Sunshine 16 (January-
February 1973): 9; Georgia Straight, 7:281 (February 22-
March 1, 1973): 12-13.

143 "A Poem," (untitled) Kumanitu, 1 (Spring 1974): 54. (from
Teton Village 1973 series).

144 "A Poem for You," Williamette Bridge, 3:32 (August 7, 1970):
15.

145 "Poem on Meditation," Rolling Stone, (May 23, 1974).

146 "Police State Blues," Harbinger (October 1970-December 1970):
10-11 (centerfold), with collage by Joseph LaDenta; Helix,
11:14 (April 2, 1970): 13; Toothpick, Libson & The Orcas
Islands, The Wiater/Scott Issue 2:1-2:3 (Fall 1972): 1-3.
(one hand written version, followed by a typed version).

147 "Pralim IV," Los Angeles Free Press, 07:06 (2/6/70): 30.

148 "Punk Rock You're My Big Crybaby," Juice 2 (1978): unpaged.

149 "Put Down Yr Cigarette Bag," Sixpack 6 (Winter 1973/74): 25-
27.

150 "Returning North at Vortex," Partisan Review, 37:2 (1970): 180-
3.

151 "Returning to the Country for a Brief Visit," Chicago, October
1973, European Edition, n.1, n.p.; New Departures, 7/8 and
10/11, n.d., p. 69; The Beat Diary, by Arthur and Kit
Knight (ed.), Pennsylvania: n.p., 1977, [p. 79].

152 "Rolling Thunder Stones," Rolling Stone, 204, January 15,
1976, p. 39. Nine poems from the Rolling Thunder Revue
Troupe newsletter: I. no title, October 31, 1975; II. no
title, November 1, 1975; III. "Rolling Thunder Sunrise Ceremony."
November 5, 1975. ("Verses improvised with Australian Aborigine
song-sticks at request of medicine-man Rolling Thunder"); IV. "Heroic Ecstasy," November 8, 1975; V. "Snowy Blues," November 10,
1975; VI. "My own voice rose to Heaven in elation," November 12,
1975; VII. "Local Noise" (with Anne Waldman), November 15, 1975;
VIII. "To the Six Nations at Tuscarora Reservation," ("Adaption of
traditional Zen thanks-offering for food.") November 18, 1975; IX.
no title. December 4, 1975. All with photograph of Allen Ginsberg

and Bob Dylan "Dylan and Ginsberg at Kerouac's grave, Lowell, Massachusetts."

153   "Rolling Thunder Sunrise Ceremony," Rolling Stone, 204, January 15, 1976, p. 39. See "Rolling Thunder Stones" above.

154   "September on Jessore Road," Berkeley Barb (October 1-7, 1971; The East Village Other 6:44-45 (December 23, 1971): 11-13; Westport Trucker, 2:20 (44) (1972?): 4 with two illustrations by Allen Ginsberg.

155 "Sickness Blues," After-Image 1 (December 1977): 22; Sitting Frog (1976): unpaged, [p. 53].

156   "Snowy Blues," Rolling Stone, 204, January 15, 1976, p. 39. See "Rolling Thunder Stones" above.

156a   "Some Different Considerations in the Mindful Arrangement of Open Verse Forms on the Page," City Lights Journal, ed. by Mendes Monsanto. San Francisco: City Lights Books, 1978, no. 4, p. 137.

157   "Songs of Experience--A Divine Image," Logos, 3:1 (March 1970): n. p.

158   "Spring Anti-War Games," Quicksilver Times, III: V (March 17-30, 1971): 8.

159   "Stool Pigeon Blues," Bombay Gin 4 (Summer-Fall 1977): unpaged.

160   "A Strange New Cottage in Berkeley," Folio, (May 1977): 1. (A publication of KPFA-FM 94, Berkeley, California.)

161   "Sunflower Sutra," Laomeden Review 1:1 (December/January 1975): 4-6.

162   "Sweet Boy, Gimme Yr Ass," Gay Sunshine. 26/27 (Winter 1975/76): unpaged, [p. 36].

163   "T.S. Eliot Entered My Dreams," City Lights Journal, Mendes Monsanto (ed.). San Francisco: City Lights Books, 1978, no. 4, pp. 61-65.
      This prose piece was prepared in Casper, Wyoming on April 13, 1977. It concerns itself with the musings of Ginsberg as he addresses a question to Eliot of his dream: "And yourself ... what did you think of the domination of poetics by the C.I.A.?"

164   "Tear Gas Rag," Scottish International (September 1973): 23.

165   "Thoughts on a Breath," Southwest Review 60:1 (Winter 1975): 37-40.

166 "Thoughts Sitting Breathing," Chicago, 1 European Edition
(October 1973): unpaged; Georgia Straight 7:296 (June 7-14,
1975): 12-13 (with photograph).

167 "Thus Crosslegged on Round Pillow Sat in Teton Space," Rolling
Stone, 161 (May 1974): 46+.

168 "To Dulles Airport," Bombay Gin (undated) (unpaged): [6-10].

169 "To Mike," Bastard Angel 2 (Spring 1974): 13.

170 "To the Six Nations at Tuscarora Reservation," Rolling Stone,
204, January 15, 1976, p. 39. ("Adaption of traditional Zen
thanks-offering for food.") See "Rolling Thunder Stones"
above.

171 "Troust Street Blues," Berkeley Barb 17:19:404 (May 11-17,
1973): 13; Gay News 28 (July 26-August 8, 1973?): 8;
Georgia Straight 7:294 (May 24-31, 1973): 12-13; Westport
Trucker 2:21(45) (February 2-March 1972): 5.

172 "2 AM Dirty Jersey Blues," Fervent Valley 4 (Summer 1974):
unpaged [p. 33]. ("First stanza has chord notations for 12
bar blues. Caesuras are spaced.")

173 "Ungaretti in Heaven," Books Abroad, 44 (Autumn 1970): 615.

174 "Uptown," The Tufts Observer. II:10 (May 25, 1977): 7.

175 "V," Focus, The Sunday Camera's Magazine (July 17, 1977):
24.

176 "VI," Focus, The Sunday Camera's Magazine (July 17, 1977):
24.

177 "Violence," Sub 70 3:1'6 (undated): unpaged.

178 "A Vow," Ann Arbor Sun 2:10 (May 17-31, 1974): 15; Georgia
Straight 8:353 (July 18-25, 1974): 20.

179 "Walking into King Sooper After Two Weeks Retreat," (September 16, 1975), Loka 2, A Journal from Naropa Institute,
New York: Doubleday, (1976).

180 "A War Profit Litany (To Ezra Pound)," Focus, The Sunday
Camera's Magazine (July 17, 1977): 24.

181 "What Would You Do If You Lost It?" Berkeley Barb 17:19:404
May 11-17, 1973): 13; Chicago 1, European Edition (October 1973): unpaged; Georgia Straight 7:294 (May 24-31,
1973): 12-13.

182 "The Wisconsin Alliance Blues," Wisconsin Patriot 2:4 (May
1972): 7.

183 "Xmas Gift," Bastard Angel 2 (Spring 1974): 13.

184 "You Might Get in Trouble," Waves 6:1 (Autumn 1977): 21.

B. SELECTED EXCERPTS FROM POEMS

184a Excerpt from "America," in The United States, A World Power, by Litwak, et al., New Jersey: Prentice-Hall, Inc., 1976.

185 Excerpt from Ankor Wat. Liberation News Service (January 1, 1969): 120 (Massachusetts Edition).
      Note (Miles, International Times): "In 1965 after the Albert Hall poetry reading the presence of so many poets and poetic feeling in London inspired us to publish a magazine of their work. I asked Allen Ginsberg for a title for the magazine and one evening we ran through his journals and selected a piece written in Cambodia. Thus the Long Hair magazine came out including Allen's long poem Ankor Wat of which this is a part."

186 Excerpt from "Bixby Canyon Ocean Path Word Breeze," Footnotes, Magazine of Lehman College, n.d., p. 7.

187 "From the Car Crash Poem," Seventies, III:1 (Spring 1972): 83.

187a Excerpt from "The Change," in America in Our Time: From World War II to Nixon--What Happened and Why, by Godfrey Hodgson. New York: Doubleday and Co., Inc., 1976, p. 324.

188 Excerpt from "Done, Finished with the Biggest Cock," Ethos, n.d., v. 8, n. 2, pp. 15-17.

189 Excerpt from "Elegy for Neal Cassady," Footnotes, Magazine of Lehman College, n.d., p. 9.

190 Excerpt from The Fall of America. The Standford Observer. (May 1976): 3.

191 Excerpt from "The Green Automobile," Mouth of the Dragon 3 (undated): 104.

192 Excerpts from "Howl," Win VI: 15 (Sept. 1970):18-19. (With photograph of Allen Ginsberg.); Contemporary Music and Music Cultures, by Bruno Nettl, et al., Englewood Cliffs, N.J.: Prentice-Hall, Inc., 1975; A Study of Future Worlds, by Richard A. Falk, New York: The Free Press, 1975; On Taking God Out of the Dictionary, by William Hamilton, New York: McGraw-Hill, 1974, pp. 414-15; The Free and the Unfree, A New History of the U.S., by Peter N. Carroll and David W. Noble, New York: Penguin Press, 1977, p. 17 and Chpt. 16; Bombs, Beards and Barricades, 150 Years of Youth in Revolt, by Anthony Esler, New York: Stein and

Day, 1971; America in Our Time, From World War II to Nixon, by Godfrey Hodgson, New York: Doubleday, 1976, p. 322; Leisure and Popular Culture in Transition, by Thomas M. Rando, St. Louis, Mo.: C. V. Mosby Co., 1975; Literature, Obscenity and Law, by Felice Flanery Lewis, Carbondale, Ill.: Southern Illinois University Press, 1976.

193 Excerpts from Iron Horse. Bastard Angel 1, (Spring 1972) pp. 4-6; The Journal, (August 7, 1973): n. p.: Kliatt (Paperback Book Guide), September 1974, n. p.

193a Excerpts from Kaddish, " in Kegan, Robert (ed.), The Sweeter Welcome, Voices for a Vision of Affirmation: Bellow, Malamud and Martin Buber, Needham Heights, Mass.: Wexword Press, 1977 (paperback edition); orig. ed. 1976), p. 16; The Free and the Unfree, A New History of the U.S., by Peter N. Carroll and David W. Noble, New York: Penguin Books, 1977, pp. 22 and 29.

194 "Unpublished Fragment: 'The Names,'" Folio 15: 1 (Fall-Winter 1977-78): 50.

194a Excerpts from Planet News, in The Free and the Unfree, A New History of the U.S., by Peter N. Carroll and David W. Noble, New York: Penguin Press, 1977, p. 61.

195 Excerpts from "September on Jessore Road," Footnotes, Magazine of Lehman College, n.d., p. 10; The Grand Rapids Press, "Wonderland"/The Sun Press Magazine. (July 29, 1973): 4.

196 "From These States: 'Sonora Desert-Edge,'" New American Review, 11, (1971): 11.

197 "Excerpts from 'Sunflower Sutra,'" The Journal, (August 7, 1973): n. p.; Soundings: An Interdisciplinary Journal, 59:2 (1976): 204-225; also in On Taking God Out of the Dictionary, by William Hamilton, New York: McGraw-Hill, 1974.

198 "From These States: 'A Vow,'" New American Review, 11 (1971): 9.

199 "Excerpt from 'Wichita Vortex Sutra,'" Ethos, n.d., v. 8, n. 2, pp. 15-17.

C. SELECTED EXCERPTS FROM PROSE

200 "Allen Verbatim," Paideuma, Fall 1974, v. 3, n. 2, p. 253.
        Excerpts from Allen Verbatim: chapter 4, "Poetic Breath and Pounds Usura" and chapter 5, "The Death of Ezra Pound."

201 "Crossing Nation," (Journals, June 19, 1968). The East Village Other. 24 March 1970, v. 5, n. 16, p. 10, with photograph by Kelvin Brodie.

202 " 'The Dream of Tibet' from New York Journals, August 1960" and "Dream: Mycenae--September 2?-1961 from the Mediterranean section of Allen Ginsberg's early journals 1952-62..." Attaboy! (1976), pp. 68-74.

"The Dream of Tibet" was reprinted in William Burroughs' The Retreat Diaries (New York: The City Moon, 1976, Broadcast No. 3), a limited edition of 2,000 copies; that and "Dream: Mycenae..." were later published in Ginsberg's Journals, edited by Gordon Ball (New York: Grove Press, Inc., 1977).

203 "Hearing: Called One Day," (April 1961). Unmuzzled Ox, 1976, v. IV, n. 1, pp. 100-104.

"This is from Early Journals, which Gordon Ball is editing for publication by Grove Press."

204 "From Indian Journals," (December 13, 1962). Focus, The Sunday Camera's Magazine, 17 July 1977, p. 25.

205 "Journals: Early Fifties Early Sixties, by Allen Ginsberg/ Two days in the life of one of the major 'beat' poets of the fifties and sixties, from his new book, a diary-in-poetry form...," Christopher Street, May 1977, v. 1, n. 11, pp. 18-23.

Two excerpts from Journals are included: "Politics on Opium" and "Subliminal," with a full page photograph courtesy of Grove Press.

206 "From the Journals," (Ezra Pound, 1968). Roof: an anthology of poetry from the Naropa Institute, Boulder, Colorado, n.d., n.p.

Roof is a magazine published quarterly by Segue Press. As a result it is not listed separately in the Anthology section.

206a From the Journals. Prose excerpts in The Beat Diary, by Arthur and Kit Knight (eds.). Pennsylvania: n. p., 1977, pp. 31-34 and 162-66.

D. POEM TRANSLATIONS

Czech

207 "Básĕn Raketa" ["Poem Rocket"], Svĕtová Literatura 1969. Prague, Czechoslovakia: n.p., 5-6, pp. 145-146. Translation by Jan Zábrana.

208 "Kvílení" ["Howl"], Sešity pro literaturu a diskusi. Duben 30 (1969): 9-13. Translation by Jan Zabrana.

209 "Kyselina lysergová" ["Lysergic Acid"], Světová Literatura 1969. Prague, Czechoslovakia: n. p., 5-6, pp. 147-149. Translation by Jan Zábrana.

210 "Transkripce varhanní hudby" ["Transcription of Organ Music"], Světová Literatura 1969. Prague, Czechoslovakia: (n. p.) 5-6: pp. 140-142. Translation by Jan Zábrana.

211 "Ve skladišti zavazadel Greyhoundu" ["In the baggage room at Greyhound"], Světová Literatura 1969. Prague, Czechoslovakia: n. p., 5-6, pp. 143-144. Translation by Jan Zábrana.

Danish

212 "I Am a Victim of Telephone," Drive-In Digte/Non-Stop Neon-Nat Lys-Auis (Dan Turèll). Denmark: Borgen, 1976, n. p.

213 "Ignu," Drive-In Digte/Non-Stop Neon-Nat Lys-Aus (Dan Turèll). Denmark: Borgen, 1976, n. p.

214 "My Sad Self," Drive-In Digte/Non-Stop Neon-Nat Lys-Auis (Dan Turèll). Denmark: Borgen, 1976, n. p.

French

215 "A Vendre" ["For Sale"], Les Temps Modernes, 32 (Aout-Septembre 1976): 444-447. Translated by Jean-Jacques Lebel.

216 "America," ellipse, (Québec: Faculté des Arts, Université de Sherbrooke), 8/9 (1971): 104-109. Translation by Jean Basile. English and French.

217 "At Apollinaire's Grave," ellipse (Québec: Faculté des Arts, Université de Sherbrooke), 8/9 (1971): 114-123. Translation by Joseph Bonenfant. English and French.

218 "Aubord de la Galilee" ["Galilee Shore"], Planète Plus. Avril-Mai 1971, n. p.

219 "A Crazy Spiritual," entretiens, beat generation, 1975, p. 73. (English).

220 "Howl," Actuel, 10-11 (juillet-août, 1971): 16-19, with illustration of wrecked civilization by E. Thomas with superimposed photograph of Ginsberg, "dessin de Magaudoux." Translation by Jean-Jacques Lebel; ellipse (Québec: Faculté des Arts, Université de Sherbrooke), 8/9 (1971): 80-100. Translation by Jean-Jacques Lebel. French and English; La Poesie de la Beat Generation. Translation by Jean-Jacques Lebel.

221 Hurlement [Howl and Other Poems]. French Canadian transla-

tion of this work by Jacques-Serge Neven, c/o Les Ateliers Globus Enr., 4489 Rue Garnier, Montréal, 177. n.p., n.d. Publication of this manuscript form translation has not been verified. The translation itself includes: "Amerique" ["America"]; "Hurlement I, II, III" ["Howl I, II, III"]; "Pour Faire Suite a Hurlement" ["Footnote to Howl"]; "Un Supermarche En Californie" ["A Supermarket in California"]; "Transcription De Musique D'Orgue" ["Transcription of Organ Music"].

222   "Quotation from 'Kaddish,'" entretiens, beat generation, 1975, p. 74. (English).

223   "Kral Majales," Planète Plus, Avril-May 1971, n.p.

224   "On Jessore Road," Antholgie Planète and Opus International. Translation by Mary Beach and Claude Pélieu; entretiens, beat generation, 1975, pp. 236-245. Bilingual-translation by Mary Beach and Claude Pélieu.

225   "Sunflower Sutra," ellipse (Québec: Faculté des Arts, Université de Sherbrooke), 8/9 (1971): 110-114. Translation by Monique Grandmangin. English and French.

226   "A Supermarket in California," ellipse, (Québec: Faculté des Arts, Université de Sherbrooke), 8/9 (1971): 101-103. Translation by Roch Carrier. French and English.

227   "To Aunt Rose," entretiens, beat generation. 1975, pp. 74-75. (English).

German

228   "Ego-Beichte," ["Ego-Confessions"], Akzente (Zeitschrift für Literatur). [Accents (Journal for Literature)], 23:6 (December 1976): 551-555.

229   "Es Musste Auch Nochaus Der Jukebox Drohnen," ["It Hadda Be Playing on the Jukebox."] Deutsch Heft, literatur zeitschrift, [German Notebook, literary news], 8:6 (Juni 1977): 1-5.

230   "Das Geheul" ["Howl"], Exempla, Eine Tübinger Literaturzeitschrift Texte Aus Nordamerika, [Example, Texts from North America], 3:1 (1977): 5-16. Translation by Jörg Ross.

231   "Liebesgedicht nach einem Thema von Whitman" ["Love Poem on Theme by Whitman"], Podium, 11 (1974): 131. Austrian journal; translation by Doris Müchringer.

232   "The Moment's Return," PERI, Loseblattsammlung zeitgenössischer Kunst und Dichtung. [PERI, Collection of pages of current art and poetry]. Mainz, Germany: Robert Kaufman, Verlag Edition, 1969.

This appears to be a small 12-page catalogue for Robert Kaufman published by him in Mainz. He is a concrete poet. Ginsberg's "The Moment's Return" is included on the first two unnumbered pages in English as an introduction to the following concrete poetry.

233 "Returning to the Country for a Brief Visit," Ottersberger Abreiss (April 21-27th, 1974). Herausgeber: Mananaum, Zeitschrift für die Künste; Druck: Schülerdruckerei manufaktur, Ottersberg. Translation by Michael Kurtz.
German lithograph calendar (1 page per week) which includes poetry in German, English, Russian and Chinese; and prints in various colors. The poetry always appears in the original language and is translated on the other side into German.

234 "Die Schlacht von Jahweh und Allah," ["Jaweh and Allah Battle"], Exempla, Eine Tübinger Literaturzeitschrift Texte Aus Nordamerika, [Example, Texts from North America], 3:1 (1977): n.p. Translation by Jörg Ross. (Bilingual).

Italian

235 "Hadda Be Playing on the Jukebox," Expresso, 1976, n. 15, p. 55. Translation by Giola Zannino Anglolillo.

236 "No More Yelling," Agenda, 8:2 (Spring, 1970): 36. Translation by Giuseppi Ungaretti. (Italian).

237 "Rain-Wet Asphalt Heat, Garbage Curbed Cans Overflowing," ["Colre di asfalto lucido sulla strada bidoni straboccanti di rifiuti"], Fuori! (fronte unitario omossessual rivoluzionario italiano/mensile di liberazione sessuale), 1972, lug. ago, n. 2, p. 4, with photo by Fernanda Pivano (Red Rock, Denver, Colorado, May '72) of Allen Ginsberg.

238 "Song and Sunflower Sutra," Italy: Verona, F. Riva, 1969, nomero 62. Translation by Fernanda Pivano. (Bilingual)
Two poems, in English and Italian translation respectively. Special edition: "concilium typographicum," manila (high quality rag) with frayed edges, bound in orange, red and gold with beige flowers, with separate matching book box.

Norwegian

239 "Fantasiverdver," ["Imaginary Universes"], Vinduet, 1974, 28 yr., n. 3, p. 23.

240 "Inskripsioner Pa Veggen, Tolyte Bas Herretoalettet, Syracuse Flypass" ["Graffiti 12th Cubicle Men's Room Syracuse"], Vinduet, 1974, 28 yr., n. 3, p. 23.

241 "Kontinentet Pa Tvers," ["Crossing Nation"] Vinduet, 1974, 28 yr., n. 3, p. 23.

242 "Over Neals Aske" ["On Neal's Ashes"] <u>Vinduet</u>, 1974, 28 yr.,
     n. 3, p. 23.

Polish

243 "Ameryka, " ["America"], <u>Tematy</u>, (1969), n. 29 & 30, pp. 159-
     162. Translation by Jerzy Niemojowski.
     Polish literary magazine published outside of Poland in
New York and London; in the Polish language.

244 "Ignu, " <u>Tematy</u>, (1969), n. 29 & 30, pp. 162-166. Translation
     by Jerzy Niemojowski.
     Polish literary magazine published outside of Poland in
New York and London; in the Polish language.

245 "Nocne Jablko" (Poem), <u>nowywyraz, miesiecznik literacki
     m todysch</u>. Lipiec-sierpien, 1975, n. 7-8, p. 58. Transla-
     tion by P. K. Boczkowski.
     Polish literary magazine from Warsaw.

Rumanian

246 "Un Magazin cu autoservire in California" ["A Supermarket in
     California"], <u>secolu/20</u>, Summer 1976, n. 185, n. 6,
     1976, p. 41. (Union of Rumanian Writing-Publisher).

Russian

247 "Jessore Road, " 15 <u>Literature Gazeta</u> (Moscow), (December 9,
     1971), n. p.

Spanish

248 "Yahve y Ala Combaten" ["Jaweh and Allah Battle"], <u>El
     Nacional</u>, 15 de Febrero de 1976, n. p. (Caracas, Vene-
     zuela). Translation by Antonia Arráiz Parra.

III.   POEMS/PROSE IN SELECTED ANTHOLOGIES

[The reader is directed to the Chicorel Index Series.
(New York: Chicorel Library, 1970) for further references regarding anthology listings of individual poems
in print and on disc which have not been included because the lists are too extensive.   See volumes 4 (Chicorel Index to Poetry in Collections, in Print, on Discs
and Tapes, and Cassettes), 5A-B (Chicorel Index to
Poetry in Collections: Poetry in Print) and 6A (Chicorel
Index to Poetry in Retrospect) for the individual listings.
They have not been incorporated in this bibliography because Chicorel does not supply the publication dates for
such (or complete citations, i.e. editor, publisher, place
and date).   It has been impossible in terms of this work
to indicate whether they were published after or before
1969.   Other Chicorel Indexes to refer to for information gathered throughout this work are Volume 7 (Chicorel Index to the Spoken Arts in Discs, Tapes and Cassettes) and Volume 20 (Chicorel Index to Poetry and
Poet: Literature).]

A.   ENGLISH LANGUAGE

249   Allen, Donald M. (ed.).   The New American Poetry 1945-
        1960.   New York: Grove Press, Inc., 1960.   (London:
        Evergreen Books Ltd.).
              Allen Ginsberg is cited among the third group of poets
in the collection, "The Beat Generation."   The other four groups
are "The Black Mountain Poets," "The San Francisco Renaissance,"
"The New York School," and "the younger poets."   Includes "Howl
[parts I and II]," pp. 182-190; "Kaddish [parts I, II, IV, V]," pp.
194-201; "Malest Cornifici Tuo Catullo," p. 179; "Message," p. 194;
"Sather Gate Illumination," pp. 190-94; "The Shrouded Stranger,"
pp. 178-79; "Sunflower Sutra," pp. 179-81; "A Supermarket in California," p. 181.

250   Allen, Donald and Tallman, Warren (eds.).   The Poetics of the
        New American Poetry.   New York: Grove Press, Inc., first
        edition, 1973.
              In the preface by Warren Tallman, Ginsberg is compared to
Walt Whitman: "Thus it isn't surprising to discover one of Walt's
more direct inheritors, Allen Ginsberg--who also shines--speaking
for all concerned when he 'woke up alive and excited' and decided
poetry should be that way too!" (pp. 318-350)   It includes the fol-

lowing Ginsberg essays: "Notes for Howl and Other Poems" (Independence Day, 1959); "Introduction to Gasoline" (Amsterdam, Holland Oct. 57); "When the Mode of the Music Changes the Walls of the City Shake" (1961); "Poetry, Violence, and The Trembling Lambs" (1959); "Prose Contribution to Cuban Revolution" (Oct. 16, 1961/ Athens, Greece); "How Kaddish Happened" (March 20, 1966); "Some Metamorphoses of Personal Prosody" (Sept. 10, 1966); "On Improvised Poetics" (Independence Day 1973).

251   Allison, Alexander W., et al. (eds.).   The Norton Anthology of Poetry.   New York: W. W. Norton & Co., Inc., 1975, revised edition.
      This is a college text which provides a chronological survey of major poetry from anonymous lyrics of the thirteenth and fourteenth centuries through literature of the twentieth century.   Includes "To Aunt Rose," p. 600.

252   Barnet, Sylvan; Berman, Morton; and Burto, William (eds.). An Introduction to Literature, Fiction, Poetry, Drama. Boston: Little, Brown and Company, 1973.   5th edition. Includes "A Supermarket in California," p. 491.

253   Bender, Todd, et al. (eds.).   Modernism in Literature.   New York: Holt, Rinehart and Winston, 1977. Includes "Sunflower Sutra," p. 349.

254   Berg, Stephen and Mezey, Robert (eds.).   The New Naked Poetry, Recent American Poetry in Open Forms.   Indianapolis: The Bobbs-Merrill Co., Inc., 1976.
      Includes "Bayonne Turnpike to Tuscarora," pp. 69-73; "Friday the Thirteenth," pp. 77-79; "Memory Gardens," pp. 74-76; "This form of life needs sex," pp. 61-63; "Thus Crosslegged on Round Pillow Sat in Teton Space," pp. 80-83; "Wales Visitation," pp. 66-68; "Who Be Kind To," pp. 63-65.

255   Bradley, Sculley, et al. (eds.).   The American Tradition in Literature.   New York: Grosset & Dunlap, 1974, volume 2, 4th edition.
      Includes "Howl," p. 1722; "A Supermarket in California," p. 1722; plus biographical and bibliographical information on Ginsberg.

256   Brady, Frank and Price, Martin (eds.).   Poetry Past and Present.   New York: Harcourt Brace Jovanovich, Inc., 1974.
      This is a softcover textbook. Includes "America," p. 440.

257   Brooks, C. and Warren, Robert Penn (eds.).   Understanding Poetry.   New York: Holt, Rinehart and Winston, 1976, fourth edition.
      The excerpt from Howl on p. 162 is utilized in "Questions" which discusses rhythms of poetry.   "My Sad Self"

is included in the chapter. "Representative Poems of Our Time" (p. 415) and "A Supermarket in California" in the chapter "Tone; Against the Establishment" (p. 159).

258   Cahill, Susan and Cooper, Michele F. (eds.). The Urban Reader. New Jersey: Prentice-Hall, 1971. Includes "By Air, Albany-Baltimore."

259   Carruth, Hayden (ed.). The Voice That Is Great Within Us: American Poetry of the 20th Century. New York: Bantam Books, Inc., 1970.
         This anthology celebrates the last "sixty years of American poetry.... Yet whatever else an anthologist may be, he is a worker in time, a kind of historian. His aim is the present, but his material is the past and the further back he looks the deeper he sees. Hence as his anthology moves from early to late his criteria of selection progressively changes from narrow to broad, from deep to shallow...." Includes "Death to Van Gogh's Ear!" pp. 576-80; "Message," pp. 574-75; "Poem Rocket," pp. 572-74; "To Aunt Rose," pp. 575-76.

260   Checchia, Anna (ed.), con la collaborazione di Pirani, Renata Coen. This Century, This World-Problems & Events Seen By British & American Writers. Bologna: Nicola Zanichelli Editore, S. P. A. (All in English except the introduction which is in Italian).
         This reader includes a section of "The Beat Generation" which refers to Ginsberg: "When he wrote America he was a young man, at the beginning of his career, full of resentment against a civilization which allowed no room for poetry and idealism, and strongly determined to create a new world by destroying the old order.... Ginsberg's attitude has not changed but the explosiveness has been taken out of him. His poetry has been anthologized and read by the most backward 'squares,' his unconventional metres have been widely imitated, 'pot' and homosexuality have been absorbed in the American social tissue. America has nevertheless failed to become angelic, failed to fulfill her promises, and Ginsberg, the rebel, has had to experience the final blow, the indignity of success." Includes "America," pp. 161-62. The anthology on p. 160 includes a biographical statement as well as a selected bibliography.

260a   Christ, Carol T. (ed.). The Finer Optic; The Aesthetics of Particularity in Victorian Poetry. New Haven, Conn.: Yale University Press, 1975.
         Includes excerpt from "Wales Visitation," pp. 22-23.

261   Dabaghian, Jane (ed.). Mirror of Man, Readings in Sociology and Literature. Boston: Little, Brown and Company, 1975.
         Sociology as seen through contemporary writers including Allen Ginsberg. Others include Mario Puzo, Anthony Burgess and Truman Capote. Contains "Kaddish," p. 400.

262 Davis, Joseph K.; Broughton, Panthea R.; and Wood, Michael
  (eds.). Literature. Illinois: Scott, Foresman and Company, 1977.
  Includes "A Supermarket in California," p. 568.

263 Deloach, Allen (ed.). A Decade and Then Some, Contemporary
  Literature--1976. New York: Intrepid Press, 1976. (c/o
  P. O. Box 1423, Buffalo, New York 14214).
  In the "Editor's note" (p. ix) Ginsberg is mentioned
as a steady contributor to this "anniversary issue ... this anthology" which is dedicated to the memories of Louis Ginsberg
and Walter Lowenfels and Charles Reznikoff. Includes "Broken
Bones," p. 121 and "Prayer Blues," p. 121.

264 deRoche, Joseph (ed.). The Heath Introduction to Poetry and
  a Brief History. Massachusetts: D. C. Heath and Company,
  1975.
  This is an anthology of works of poetry beginning with
anonymous works of the 8th century and continuing to the modern
work of the 20th century. Includes "In back of the real," p. 410
and "A Supermarket in California," p. 409.

265 Ellman, Richard (ed.). The New Oxford Book of American
  Verse. New York: Oxford University Press, 1976.
  This is an anthology of poetry which "begins with
Anne Bradstreet, who died in 1672, and ends in Imamu Amiri
Baraka (LeRoi Jones), born in 1934...." Ginsberg is mentioned
in the Editor's Introduction in his attempt to "out confess confession." Includes "Dream Record: June 8, 1955," p. 930;
"Hymmnn," p. 928; "On Burroughs' Work," p. 929; "Sunflower Sutra,"
p. 923; "A Supermarket in California," p. 922; "Wales Visitation,"
pp. 931-32; and an excerpt from "Kaddish," pp. 924-27.

266 Fagin, Larry (ed.). Adventures in Poetry. New York: The
  Poetry Project, St. Mark's Church In-the-Bowery, Spring
  1972, n. 9, (unpaginated).
  Available from editor, Larry Fagin, at 437 East 12th
Street, Apt. 18, New York, New York 10009. Includes "New
England in the Fall: Autumn Gold" (Auto Poetry to Hanover,
New Hampshire, October 17, 1966), pp. 39-46.

267 Ferlinghetti, Lawrence (ed.). City Lights Anthology. San
  Francisco: City Lights, 1974.
  This anthology "leads off with Allen Ginsberg's journal
notes of his 'Encounters with Ezra Pound,' skips through Huey
P. Newton, Ericka Huggins, and Herbert Marcuse, then touches
all the bases with Genet, Bukowski, McClure, Creeley, Kerouac,
Norse, DiPrima, Snyder, Brautigan, and more, and more, and
more."

268 Fleming, William (ed.). Arts & Ideas. New York: Holt,
  Rinehart and Winston, Inc., 1974.

Includes "Howl," pp. 399-400 and "A Supermarket in California," p. 411.

269 Grigson, Geoffrey (ed.). Unrespectable Verse. London: The Penguin Press, 1971.
Includes "America," pp. 259-62 and "A Supermarket in California," pp. 172-73.

270 Hamilton, Leo and Zeiger, Arthur (eds.). In the Modern Idiom, An Introduction To Literature. New York: Thomas Y. Crowell Company, Inc., 1973. (published simultaneously in Canada by Fitzhenry and Whiteside, Ltd. in Toronto). A biographical sketch until 1972 is included. Includes "Last Night in Calcutta," pp. 427-28; "Sunflower Sutra," pp. 428-30; "A Supermarket in California," pp. 430-31; "Who Be Kind To," pp. 424-27.

271 Hunter, J. Paul (ed.). The Norton Introduction to Literature, Poetry. New York: W. W. Norton & Co., 1973. Includes "Howl [part I]," p. 448 and "A Supermarket in California," p. 294.

272 Hurst, Michael E. Eliot (ed.). I Came to the City. Boston: Houghton Mifflin Co., 1975. This book is a collection of essays and comments on the urban scene. Includes "A Supermarket in California," p. 124, and "Uptown," p. 159.

273 In Person (part of series Variations [A Contemporary literature program]). New York: Harcourt Brace Jovanovich, Inc., 1975. Includes "Song."

274 Junkins, Donald (ed.). The Contemporary World Poets. New York: Harcourt Brace Jovanovich, Inc., 1976. "This is a book of contemporary poems ... international in scope." Biographical information is supplied on pp. 351-52 and an excerpt from "Wichita Vortex Sutra," pp. 352-59.

275 Katzman, Allen (comp.). Our Time; An Anthology of Interviews from the East Village Other. See Kohn, Jaakov, under INTERVIEWS section.

276 Kennedy, X. J. (ed.). An Introduction to Poetry. Boston: Little, Brown and Company, 1974, third edition. (A later edition was published in 1976.) This is a college edition which asks the reader to compare the Ginsberg poem, "In Back of the Real" (p. 404) to "Flower in the Crannied Wall" by Tennyson and "To See a World in a Grain of Sand" by Blake.

277 Knodt, Kenneth S. (ed.). Pursuing the American Dream. New Jersey: Prentice-Hall, Inc., 1976. This is a collection of political writings including poetry, fiction and essays. Includes "America" p. 265.

278 Esthetics Contemporary, Kostelanetz, Richard (ed.). Buffalo,
    N. Y. : Prometheus Books, 1977.
    "Esthetics Contemporary is an incomparable collection of
essays in general esthetic principles relevant to the avant-garde arts. . . .
Works by some of the most important practioners ... of 'the new art'
are included. . . . " (Allen Ginsberg, among others). [From Press
Release from Frederic A. Brussat/Cultural Information Service.]

279 Laughlin, J. , with Glassgold, Peter and Martin, Frederick R.
    (eds.). New Directions 36. New York: New Directions
    Publishing Co. , 1978.
    Includes "Don't Grow Old [six poems I-VI], " p. 4.

280 LaValley, Albert J. (ed.). The New Consciousness. Massa-
    chusetts: Winthrop Publishers Inc. , 1972.
    This is an anthology which contains essays about the "new
consciousness. " In the chapter highlighting Ginsberg the Morris
Dickstein article is included plus some of Ginsberg's poetry. The
cover has a facsimile of Ginsberg in the center.

281 Leyland, Winston. Orgasms of Light: The Gay Sunshine
    Anthology, Poetry, Short Fiction, Graphics. San Francisco:
    Gay Sunshine Press, 1977.
    "This volume contains the best of the poetry, short fic-
tion and graphic work that has appeared in the pages of Gay Sunshine
Journal during the years 1970-1977 under the editorship of Winston
Leyland. " Included is the work of Allen Ginsberg: "A Dream [re-
lated to W. C. Williams]," p. 85; "Night Gleam," p. 90; "Spring Anti-
war Games," p. 88; "Sweet Boy, Gimme Yr Ass, " p. 87; "Troust
Street Blues," pp. 89-90. Other than the poetry and prose cited elsewhere, on p. 86 a reproductoin of the cover of the Gay Sunshine Journal which featured the famous interview by Allen Young is included.
See the INTERVIEW section for an annotation of the Young work.

282 Lief, Leonard and Light, James F. (eds.). The Modern Age
    Literature. New York: Holt, Rinehart and Winston, 1976.
    This is a basic introductory text for English literature
which includes expository writing, fiction, drama and poetry in three
sections: 1) Influential Voices, 1848-1917; 2) The Long Armistice,
1918-1939; 3) Under the Volcano, 1939-1976. "The basic emphasis
of the text is historical, but an alternative table of contents has been
provided for instructors who prefer to emphasize theme. . . . " An index and "selective glossary of literary terms" is included. Ginsberg's poems are "America," pp. 706-7; "Sunflower Sutra," pp.
708-9; "A Supermarket in California," p. 705.

283 McMichael, George (ed.). Concise Anthology of American Lit-
    erature. New York: Macmillan Publishing Co. , Inc. , 1974.
    This is a college text which includes a chronological sur-
vey from the literature of colonial America through the literature of
the twentieth century. The preface to the poems includes biographical and bibliographical information. Included are "America," p.
1771; "Sunflower Sutra," pp. 1769-70; "A Supermarket in California,"
p. 1768.

284 Moore, Geoffrey (ed.). The Penguin Book of American Verse.
New York: Penguin Books. 1977.
Includes "America," pp. 528-30; "Death News," pp. 537-
38; "Death to Van Gogh's Ear!" pp. 533-36; "My Sad Self," pp. 531-
33; "A Supermarket in California," pp. 525-27; "Uptown," p. 538;
"A Vow," pp. 538-39; and an excerpt from "Howl," pp. 520-26.

285 Morgan, Pete (ed. and intro. by) C'mon Everybody, Poetry of
the Drama. London: Corgibooks Transworld Ltd. , 1971.
This is an anthology which "ranges from the lyrical po-
etry of Brian Patten to the concrete poetry of Ian Hamilton Finaly."
Includes "Big Beat," p. 40; "Liverpool Muse," p. 39; "Seabattle of
Salamis Took Place Off Perama," p. 41.

286 Muscatine, Charles and Griffith, Marlene (eds.). The Borzoi
College Reader. New York: Alfred A. Knopf, 1974. 2nd ed.
Includes "A Supermarket in California," p. 141.

287/8 Ollier, J. S. ; Mosher Jr. , H. ; and Rodgers, J. (eds).
American Literature, An Anthology, 1912-1972. Paris:
Classiques Hachette, 1973.
An anthology in English about American Literature for
the French university. On page 314 biographical and critical infor-
mation about Ginsberg is included as well as a "selected bibliography."
Includes "Howl," pp. 315-20.

289 Poulin Jr. , A. (ed.). Contemporary American Poetry. Boston: Houghton Mifflin Company, 1975, (orig. ed. 1971).
The biographic information on pp. 430-432 includes a list
of published "poetry" books, published "correspondence and interviews," published "bibliographies" and published "biographical and
critical studies." A biographical statement follows. This is an excellent undergraduate college text because of the wide variety of
poets included. The works by Ginsberg include "America," pp. 144-
45; "Flashback," pp. 150-51; "Footnote to Howl," p. 143; "Howl,"
pp. 135-42; "Love Poem on Theme by Whitman," p. 146; "On Neal's
Ashes," p. 150; "Psalm III," p. 147; "Wales Visitation," pp. 147-49.

290 Rice, Donald L. (comp.). The Agitator: A Collection of Diverse
Opinions From America's Not-So-Popular Press. Chicago:
American Library Association (A Schism Anthology), 1972.

291 Robinson, Cecil (ed.). Mexico and the Hispanic Southwest in
American Literature. Tucson: The University of Arizona
Press, 1977.
Excerpts of poems from Reality Sandwiches appear on
pages 26-27, 30, 35, 38, 211, 272-73, and 274 and are used out
of context to illustrate particular points.

292 Rothenberg, Jerome and Quasha, George (eds.). America a
Prophecy, A New Reading of American Poetry from Pre-
Columbian Times to the Present. New York: Random
House, 1973.

Includes "The End," p. 32; "Mescaline," pp. 140-43; "Psalm IV," p. 284; "Sunflower Sutra," pp. 383-84.

293 Roy, Emil and Roy, Sandra (eds.). <u>Literature 1</u>. New York: Macmillan, Inc., 1976.
This is an "introduction to literature" textbook whose contents are "arranged according to five elemental approaches to literature: structure, characters, point of view, symbol, and theme...." There are two tables of contents, one oriented to the above listed "approaches" and the second arranged alphabetically by the author's last name. Ginsberg is included under the "Point of View" section. Includes "America," pp. 366-68.

294 Ryan, Betsy (ed.). <u>Loving, Dying, Living: Faces of America</u>. New York: Scholastic Book Services, 1976.
Includes "A Supermarket in California."

295 Ryan, Betsy (ed.). <u>Search the Silence, Poems of Self-Discovery</u>. New York: Scholastic Book Services, 1974.
Includes "Song," pp. 77-79.

296 Shapcott, Thomas (ed.). <u>Contemporary American and Australian Poetry</u>. Queensland: University of Queensland Press, 1976.
A biographical blurb and selected bibliography is included on page 88, plus "Ecologue," pp. 88-98.

297 Simon, John O. (ed.). <u>City of Buds and Flowers, A Poet's Eye View of Berkeley</u>. Berkeley, California: Aldebaran Review, 1977, #25, p. 29. (2209 California, Berkeley, California 94703).
1500 copies printed May 1977 on Edna at Shameless Hussy Press, Oakland, by John Oliner Simon and Sarah Kennedy. Typesetting is by the East Coast Print Center. <u>City of Buds and Flowers</u> is issued as <u>Aldebaran Review</u>, No. 25. <u>Aldebaran Review</u> is a continuing series of books of poetry. The introductory note citing the source of the Ginsberg poem "A Strange New Cottage in Berkeley," p. 29, is incorrect.

298 Srinivas, Krishna. <u>Great American World Poets, An Assessment</u>. India: Poet Press India, 1976. (20-A, Venkatesan Street, Madras - 17 - India).
"Amazing gems of American Verse lie scattered in the following pages." Includes excerpts from over 1000 poets, arranged by "guest editors" to illustrate particular, often geographical, segments of what the editor assumes to be American culture. In section 13 on "American University Poets," arranged by guest editor, Dr. Orville C. Miller, a part of a Ginsberg poem is included without a source of origin.

299 Stein, Agnes (ed.). <u>The Uses of Poetry</u>. New York: Holt, Rinehart & Winston, Inc., 1975.

This is a classroom text which is arranged by topics. Key poems are analyzed in detail. Ginsberg's selections are not analyzed as such. Included are "The End," p. 385 and "In back of the real," p. 248.

300   Strand, Mark (ed.).   The Contemporary American Poets: American Poetry Since 1940.   New York: Meridian Books, 1969. (Published simultaneously in Canada by Nelson, Foster & Scott Ltd.)
       On page 367 a short biography and bibliography can be found.   Also includes "America," pp. 91-93, "Sunflower Sutra," pp. 94-95; "A Supermarket in California," pp. 90-91.

301   Trungpa, Chögyam (Rinpoche at Lama Fdn.).[No Title].   San Cristobal, New Mexico: Lama Fdn., 1974.
       Compilation of material from the visit of Chögyam Trungpa, Rinpoche, in the winter of 1973.   Includes "Prayer Blues," pp. 37-38 and "What Would You Do If You Lost It?" pp. 24-26.

302   Untermeyer, Louis (ed.).   50 Modern American & British Poets.   McKay, 1973.

303   Untermeyer, Louis (ed.).   Modern American Poetry.   New York: Harcourt Brace & World, 1969.   New and Revised Edition.

304   Van Doren Stern, Philip (ed.).   The Pocket Book of America. New York: Pocket Book/Simon & Schuster, 1975.   Expanded, revised, updated version of the original 1942 edition. Includes "A Vow," pp. 461-62.

305   Wakeman, John (ed.).   World Authors, 1950-1970.   Wilson, 1975.

306   Waldman, Anne (ed.).   The World Anthology, Poems from The St. Mark's Poetry Project.   New York: Bobbs-Merrill Co., Inc., 1969.
       "The World, a New York City literary magazine, began in the Fall of 1966 during a lull in the poetry magazine 'scene' on the Lower East Side.... This anthology is a selection of works from the first twelve issues of The World (extending from Fall 1966 through Spring 1968) of which there were never more than 500 copies at a time.   Rather than arrange the poets in alphabetical order or make a categorical arrangement of works from individual issues, once they were all selected, I decided to think of the book as one giant issue of The World...." from Anne Waldman's introduction.   Includes "A Methedrine Vision of Hollywood," pp. 52-54 and "Morning," pp. 51-52.

307   Waldman, Anne (ed.).   Another World, A Second Anthology of Works from The St. Mark's Poetry Project.   New York: Bobbs-Merrill Co., Inc., 1971.
       This anthology is dedicated to Jack Spicer, Frank O'Hara,

Jack Kerouac and Charles Olson. Includes a jacket cover statement by Ginsberg, and his "Rain-Wet Asphalt Heat, Garbage Curbed Cans Overflowing...," p. 230.

308 Young, Ian (ed.). The Male Muse, A Gay Anthology. Trumansberg, New York: Crossing Press, 1973.
According to the publisher this is a "collection of contemporary gay poetry edited by Ian Young. Features 35 poets including Allen Ginsberg, Robert Duncan, Tennessee Williams, Paul Goodman, John Wieners, Christopher Isherwood...."

B. TRANSLATIONS

Czech

309 Sešity pro literatura a diskusi. Duben 30 (1969), Ročník Ctvrtý.
Czechoslovak magazine which includes works by and about Allen Ginsberg.

310 Světová Literatura 1969. Prague, Czechoslovakia: n.p., 5-6.
Czechoslovak book which includes work by and about the poet Allen Ginsberg.

Greek

311 Mastoraki, Jennie. Συγχρονη Ποιηση Αλλεν Γκινψηερyκ.
Athens, Greece: "Boukoumanis" Publications, 1974.
This text includes selections from Howl, Kaddish and Other Poems, Reality Sandwiches, Planet News and The Fall of America.

Italian

312 Poesia degli Ultimi Americani [Poetry of the Last Americans].
Italy: Feltrinelli Milano, 1973. Bilingual. Translator Fernanda Pivano.
Ginsberg's work is included as follows: p. 94, "Aether"; p. 95, "Etere"; p. 120, "Love Poems on Theme by Whitman"; p. 121, "Poesia d'amore su un tema di Whitman"; p. 122, "To an Old Poet in Peru"; p. 123, "A un vecchio poeta del Peru"; p. 126, "Sather Gate Illumination"; p. 127, "L'illuminazione del Sather Gate." Biographical notes including Ginsberg are contained on pages 354-359.

Japanese

313 Di Prima, Diane (ed.). War Poems. Japan: Poets Press, Inc. (orig. ed. 1968), 1972. Japanese.
The collection includes two poems by Ginsberg: pp. 35-69, "Wichita Vortex Sutra" translated by Yuzuru Katagiri and pp. 70-71, "Pentagon Exorcism" translated by Yu Suwa.

Polish

314 Wizjonery I Buntownicy wiersze/wspótezesnych poetów w amery-
kańskich. Wybrala, przelozyla i opatrzyla Poslowiem
Teresa Truszkowska. Poland: Wydawnictwo Literackie
Krakow, n. d.
      This Polish anthology includes the following works by
Ginsberg: Z tomu Skowyt i nne poematy [Howl and Other Poems],
"Skowyt ["Howl"] II, III," pp. 97, 99; Przypisek do "Skowytu"
["Footnote to Howl"], p. 103; "Sutra o stoneczniku" ["Sunflower
Sutra"], p. 105; Transkrypcja na muzyke organowa [Transcription of
organ music] p. 109; "W przechowalini bagazu linii Greyhound" ["In
the Baggage Room at Greyhound"], p. 113; Z tomu "Kaddish"[Kaddish I
I, III], pp. 119, 127; "DoCiotki Rózy" ["To Aunt Rose"], 129; "Wier
sz-rakieta" ["Poem Rocket"], 133; Z tomu sandwicze rzechzywistóscy
[Reality Sandwiches], "Pisane ostatnieg nocy" ["Wrote This Last
Night"], p. 139; Z tomu Wieści z planety [Planet News], "Warszawska
Kawairnia ["Café in Warsaw"], p. 141.

Russian

315 Современная Американская Поэзия [Contemporary American
Poetry], 1973.
      Includes selected poems by Ginsberg on pp. 359-72.

Spanish

316 Barnatan, M. R. (ed.). Antologia de la 'Beat Generation'/
Selecciones de Poesia Universal. Barcelona, Spain: Plaza
& Janes, S. A. Editores, 1970. Bilingual.
      On pp. 70-71 there is a short biographical note on Gins-
berg. From pp. 72-87 there is a truncated version of "Howl [Part
I]". On pp. 88-93 "Song" is included. On pp. 94-123 a truncated
version of "Kaddish" is given. From pp. 124-5 there is "To Lindsay." Finally from pp. 126-7 "Message" is included.

317 La Escritura en libertad/Antologia de poesía experimental.
Selection, foreword and notes by Fernando Millan y Jesús
Garcia Sánchez. Madrid, Spain: Alianza Editorial, 1975,
pp. 40-42.
      This is an anthology of experimental poetry: futuristic,
concrete, etc. Every item is in the original language. The author's
name is not listed on the page by the poetry and can only be located
through the index. The Ginsberg work included is in this experimental mode on pages 40-42.

Ukrainian

318 To The Sources. Edited by Ivan Drach. Soviet Union: Dnipro
Publishers, 1972. Ukrainian.
      Includes "A Supermarket in California," pp. 263-65.

IV. INTERVIEWS

A. ENGLISH LANGUAGE

319 Aldrich, Michael R. "Exclusive--Ginsberg on Marijuana. "
  Part 1, Grass Roots Gazette, no. 3, July 1973?, pp. 1, 4-
  6, 14 with illustrations of Ginsberg.
  This is a conversation between Michael R. Aldrich, Research Director of AMORPHIA and Allen Ginsberg; Re: Marijuana
Law Reform. Taped May 25, 1973, San Francisco. In this conversation Ginsberg defines his role in marijuana reform. (Organi-
zationally this conversation is weak, plus there are gaps in the text
itself.) Ginsberg's actual involvement goes back to 1958. In re-
constructing his story he alludes to a talk with then "up-and-coming
political leader" Edward I. Koch, on the legalization of marijuana.

320 "Allen Ginsberg: Interview. " Unmuzzled Ox, 3:2, 1975, pp. 14-25.

321 "Allen Ginsberg ... Rennie Davis and the Underground Press. "
  Georgia Straight, 7:298, 21-28 June 1973, p. 11.
  This discussion between Ginsberg and the Georgia Straight
staff centers on the underground press coverage of the Miami Convention and the allegations of CIA involvement with both the Yippie
leaders and the Underground Press Syndicate itself. It seems that
Allen Ginsberg is criticizing Paul Krassner for his allegations about
Rennie Davis, and Tom Forcade for his reporting (UPS). "Everybody was accepting the UPS reporting inspired by Tom Forcade.
But Forcade also, in addition to attacking Abbie and Jerry in jail,
levelled his hand at David Dellinger, who was on a 30-day fast, and
said, 'We ruined Abbie and Jerry and we'll ruin you if you don't
watch out,' which I have a record of--a tape.... And that's the
failure of the whole underground--its own bad faith...."
  See Forcade, Tom. Open Letter. Georgia Straight, 26
July - 2 August 1973, v. 7, n. 303, p. 1. , under LETTERS TO GINS-
BERG in the Secondary Works section of this bibliography; also, "Dear
Readers of the Georgia Straight. " Georgia Straight, 20-27 September
1973, v. 7, n. : 311, p. 1, letter (by Allen Ginsberg) under LETTERS
AND CORRESPONDENCE in the Primary Works Section.

322 Ann Arbor Argus, Interview, 1:5, 14-28 April 1969, pp. 12-13,
  with photographs by Neil Montone.
  "Allen Ginsberg was also at the Buffalo LEMAR Conference, where he granted a series of Argus interviews, here pasted together in the semi-conscious way they happened with much help by
Jaakov Kohn of East Village Other. " These conversations take place
at the conference referred to above. (In the midst of conversation,

Ginsberg spots Leslie Fiedler and they go to talk with him.) In
this series of conversations Ginsberg talks about the power of the
media, his interaction with it, the system (the Pentagon), drugs,
William Burroughs and his own state of mind and body.
  As a closing note he talks about the "Pornography and
Censorship Conference at Notre Dame where he and Peter Orlovsky
were the keynote speakers." He notes they left before mace was
used to prevent the students from actually seeing Flaming Creatures.
In general he comments on government surveillance, people and
the current times.

323 Bageant, Joseph L. "Allen Ginsberg--Beat Saint." Rocky
    Mountain Musical Express, October 1977, pp. 14-15, with
    photographs by Jerry Aronson.
    Joseph Bageant, because of his desire to interview
Ginsberg, is invited to hear Ginsberg lecture at Naropa Institute in
Boulder. Bageant in this piece (which is as much a critique on culture as an interview of Ginsberg) attempts to measure the distance
that Ginsberg has traveled over the last twenty years. Ginsberg the
man is older and his poetry more mature. "No more sirens. Instead, a settling down to a quieter pursuit of Buddhism, poetry's
craft ... and young boys, the homely details of love, work and
burial.... Due to the American self-realization movement and a
score of others, freedom and individuality are flourishing. Things
are lightened up, thank God, since the days of the Beat Vision.
Apocalyptic Jewboys who once roamed Harlem's anonymous nights
now teach poetics at modern Buddhist universities. Allen, who was
along for the whole flipped-out saxophone ride, often says he's tired.
I don't doubt it. But if Jack Kerouac and Charlie Parker will par-
don my boundless optimism, I think America has gotten over her
20th Century blues."

324 Barg, Barbara. "Allen Ginsberg and William Burroughs."
    Out There, 7, n.d., p. 18.
    This is a one-page excerpt from an interview in which
both Allen Ginsberg and William Burroughs respond to Barbara
Barg's questions on fiction. Burroughs refers the questions to Ginsberg who explains the activities of "young, experimental writers....
It's taking those methods of juxtaposition, surrealism without a central section of metaphors and using it as a sort of baseball game...."

325 Belov, Miriam and Elliot Sobel. "Poet in Dharmaland/An In-
    terview with Allen Ginsberg." The New Sun, 1:4, March
    1977, pp. 12-15, 35, with photographs by Chana Benjamin
    (including cover photograph, "Exclusive Interview/Buddhist
    with a Beat: Allen Ginsberg.")
    The introduction to this interview is in spontaneous mind
thought--"Space/time capsule explodes. Images flash ..." --and
concludes--"against the sounds of the lower east side--horns honking
and voices yelling, telephone ringing--and Peter Orlovsky somewhere
in the apartment, we talk on a warm afternoon in New York City."
    The interview itself, centers on the "sublime" 1970's and
encompasses Ginsberg's thoughts on action for this decade. Many of

the issues discussed here are topical for Ginsberg. They include the combination of Buddhist meditation and poetry at Naropa Institute in Boulder, Colorado and the use of practical meditation, politics and egolessness.

From here the interviewer leads us to the "orgiastic 80's" in which the descriptive words must connotate "awareness." Allen, for a moment, returns to his thoughts on his father's gentle death of old age and illness, and then proceeds. His prophetic words are laden with anticipation for the future.

326 Billotte, Louise. "Ginsberg Reflects /' ... Famous Some /Day in Heaven.'" Berkeley Barb, 8:577, 3-9 September 1976, p. 11, with photograph (Simon & Schuster, credit) and poem, "Don't Grow Old."

Ginsberg is interviewed jointly by Louise Billotte of the Barb and a male interviewer from the College Press Service at the Varsity Townhouses at Naropa Institute. It is a thoughtful piece on his thoughts, particularly those on his father's death. There is some division in what the two interviewers want to discuss with the poet, but in the end there is continuity. "The talk goes from Allen's Buddhist present to his Beatnik past to the tour with Dylan." In the end, they discuss Kerouac, Naropa and the candidacy of Jerry Brown. Interestingly enough, Louise Billotte is "a fellow Buddhist and also a distant relative" which explains her desire to talk with Allen about his father's death. This interview provides some valuable insights into Allen Ginsberg, the "famous" poet who has played the game well, but continues to pay the price.

327 Bockris, Victor. "The Egolessness of Heroes /Conversations with Allen Ginsberg." National Screw, June 1977, pp. 6-10 with photographs by Gerard Malanga and excerpts on page 8 from First Blues by Ginsberg (Full Court Press, New York, 1976).

In this interview Ginsberg discusses the relationship of ego and certain heroes. Among those included are Patti Smith and her idolized "Rimbaud"; Jimmy Carter; Bob Dylan; Chögyam Trungpa; Rinpoche; John Lennon; Paul McCartney; Gary Gilmore; and William Burroughs. Each is set before you by Ginsberg in a visually creative article which weaves both horizontally and vertically, often splashed with photographs of those being discussed. In essence he sees Jimmy Carter as "a deistic or theistic-minded person, (who) might take his ego seriously enough to start an atomic war on some moral issue connected with divine principles." Nonetheless he voted for him in 1976. He sees Dylan as "--the kind of nobility you don't often see--the nobility of a great bard.... He's a great poet in the sense of great orator." Chögyam Trungpa is cited as a personal hero of Ginsberg's, for "he seems to have carried forward a practical, visible, programmatic practice of egolessness, and provided a path for other people to walk on."

Comments on Gary Gilmore: "See, the problem is he doesn't want to live and he doesn't want to die, so let him kill his ego if he's that sincere."

In closing Ginsberg, of course, includes his thoughts on

William Burroughs: "I think he played a major role in either cataly-
zing or expressing the change of consciousness that overcame the
United States in the last two decades, which resulted in disillusionment on the part of the general public with self-mystifying government." Last, in passing through these remarks, Ginsberg includes
references to work by Bob Dylan which should surface in the near
future in the form of a film, edited from all the film shot on The
Rolling Thunder tour.

328 Bockris-Wylie. "Allen Ginsberg Special/An Interview on
    Heroes/A Self-Portrait." Drummer, 282, February 12,
    1974, pp. 3-4, with photographs, including collage: "Heroes
    are boring and the acceptance of their boringness is some-
    thing that is significant & useful." Reprinted in Georgia
    Straight, May 2-9, 1974, pp. 12-13, "Ginsberg 'On Heroes,'"
    with drawing of Ginsberg among unidentifiable heroes, by
    Finart and a cover caricature by Craig; also in Berkeley
    Barb, May 17-23, 1974, pp. 12-13.
       "This is neither interview nor essay, but transcription of
conversation edited slightly, condensed, punctuated, contexted and
prose-timed by Bockris-Wylie, thus not precisely my text, though
'tis my words" [Allen Ginsberg, 11 February '74]. "We asked Allen
Ginsberg what he thought about the Star System and the effect of the
hero-leaders. He told us what he thought and portrayed a few major figures whose lines have crossed his" [Bockris-Wylie].

329 Bockris-Wylie. [no title]. Unmuzzled Ox, Interview, LV:1,
    1976, p. 140, with photograph by Craig Vander Lende.
       This appears to be an excerpt from a larger unidentified
interview by Bockris-Wylie. The complete excerpt is included below:
       "BW: How did you feel when you shaved off your beard?
       AG: I felt years ago.
       BW: Yeah, well it's an old question, but...
       AG: I didn't feel anything. I shave it every year."

330 Brandenburg, John. "Ginsberg Packs 'em In to Hear His Dark
    View of America." Oklahoma City Times, April 25, 1974,
    p. 10.
       This is an interview presented in correlation with Allen
Ginsberg's reading and informal sessions at the University of Oklahoma. It is laden with quotes from Ginsberg concerning the plight
of American civilization and his poetry.

331 Cargas, Harry J. "An Interview with Allen Ginsberg." Nim-
    rod, 19:1, Fall/Winter 1974, pp. 24-29, with illustration.
       Ginsberg and Cargas talk about poetry as the "rhythmic
articulation of feeling," and about Ginsberg, himself, who has "been
given the freedom of live language, dancing like fire on my tongue."
Allen Ginsberg discusses his writing patterns and habits. He pinpoints "the bardic practice of chanted, sometimes rhymed improvisation" which is often linked with "dancing." For according to him,
"the nearest hint of that is the behavior of Mick Jagger who sings
language that he composes and dances at the same time."

332 Carroll, Paul. "Playboy Interview." Playboy, XVI: 4, April
      1969, pp. 81-92, 236-244.
          "A candid conversation with the hippie-guru poet laureate
of the new left and the flower children." Carroll and Ginsberg
start talking about the Beats, and continue onto life in general, sex,
and the metaphysics of the world. Carroll speculates, "but for all
his earthly profanity, I sensed about him improbably enough, something of the holy man." (Ginsberg plays with the writing style of
the Playboy journalist in his responses.)

333 Castro, M. "Ezra Pound (1885-1972) 'A Noble Poet Nobly Ele-
      gized.'" Outlaw III 11, 17 November - 14 December 1972, pp.
      12-23, with photographs. See Allen Verbatim, pp. 179-87.
          "November 1st, the night of Alan Ginsberg's [sic] reading
at Webster College was also the night in which Ezra Pound passed
on. Ginsberg didn't learn of Pound's death until an hour and a half
after the reading around midnight, when he was gathered with a
smaller group of students interested in politics at Kirk House on the
Webster Campus. What follows is a transcription of Ginsberg's
verbal response as recorded by KDNA which was broadcasting the
Kirk House discussion live. Some editing has been done to avoid
repetition.... A discussion ensued about demon worship and the like,
and the importance of not clinging, when Harry Cargas (head of Webster College's English Department) entered" with the news. Ginsberg
responds, "Ahhhh for Ezra Pound.... He was the greatest poet of
the age.... Someone who opened up fresh new forms in America
after Walt Whitman.... As to Pound's Karma, you could say, Ahhh!"

334 Chowka, Peter Barry. "Poet at Mid Century." East West,
      February 1978, pp. 52-55 with photographs by Chowka.
          Although published in February of 1978, this interview
took place "in early December" (1977) in Boston after Ginsberg gave
"a four-night performance at a folk music club off Harvard Square....
Late one afternoon before he was to perform, he talked with me
about his present work and the directions his life is taking." So,
Allen and Peter takl informally about Allen's travels along the road
of life. They discuss his writing, his teaching at Naropa, his relationship to his teacher, Chögyam Trungpa, the generalized effect
of breath meditation on America and the personal effect on the poet.

335 Clark, Thomas. "The Art of Poetry VIII: Allen Ginsberg, An
      Interview." End of the Year, 1975, unpaged, pp. 22-23.
          This is an excerpt from the original Thomas Clark inter-
view in The Paris Review, 37, 1966. The full interview was later
published in Writers at Work, Paris Review Interviews. Ed. by
George Plimpton, with an Introduction by Alfred Kazin. New York:
Penguin Books, 1977 (orig. ed., The Viking Press, 1967).

336 Clarke, Gerald. "Checking in with Allen Ginsberg." Esquire,
      79:4 (April 1973): 92-95, 169, 170. Preview by College Press
      Service, March 14, 1973, p. 6. Subtitled, "Notes on Passing
      in life-in-progress."
          Clarke's article on Ginsberg is interspersed with quotes

from Ginsberg's poetry which serve as an introduction to each new thought topic. The article flows from social concerns to the reason for existence, to Ginsberg's lovers, and back to reality.

337 Colbert, Alison and Anita Box. "Conversations, A Talk with Allen Ginsberg. " Partisan Review, 38:3, 1971, pp. 289-309. Reprinted as "The West End excerpts of an interview with Allen Ginsberg by Alison Colbert and Anita Box," West End, 1:1, Winter 1971, pp. 32-43.
    "Also present were Miles, rock editor of International Times, a London underground paper, and Jim Anderson, a photographer." A lively conversation which begins with a discussion of Ginsberg's relationship to Blake and Song of Innocence, the conversation then progressed to the question on Ginsberg's mind of the "larger consciousness" necessary for revolutionaries. He stated "what I would propose is using actual meditation ... as a necessary ritual stabilizing influence in any kind of action. "

338 "A Conversation with Allen Ginsberg. " The Organ, 1:1, July 1970, pp. 4-9.

339 "Corso, Ginsberg, Orlovsky, April 1973, Salem State College, Kerouac Symposium, Salem Massachusetts," later published in Gone Soft, v. 1, n. 3, Spring 1974.
    This is a discussion between the audience and the poets in which the poets comically preach to the audience and themselves about the evils of smoking and drinking.

340 "Craft Interview with Allen Ginsberg. " New York Quarterly, 6, Spring 1971, pp. 12-40.
    "The sixth in a series of Craft interviews with outstanding poets on the general subject of style and parody and technique in writing. " Technical interview with Ginsberg, not a dialogue. The questions by the New York Quarterly seem rigid. This rigidity even seems to structure Ginsberg's replies until the end when he breaks free. This article includes photographs of Ginsberg which are more revealing than the words.
    This interview was later published in The Craft of Poetry: Interviews from the New York Quarterly. New York: Doubleday and Co. , 1974, pp. 53-78. Ed. by William Packard. Includes a "Selected Bibliography" until 1973 on p. 78 and a photo of Ginsberg.

341 Desruisseaux, Paul. "Are we ready for two Ginsbergs? /All in favor say Om!" Pacific Sun, 16-22 May 1974, pp. 12-14, with photograph "Louis Ginsberg and his famous son" by Julian Solmonson.
    This article serves as a review of the father and son poetry reading at San Francisco State and as an interview with both Louis and Allen Ginsberg. It blends the insights of the critic with the perspectives of the poets. "Last week at San Francisco, the thousand students crammed into McKenna Theater to hear the Ginsbergs witnessed a poetic balancing act that would require a lot of doing to undo. " Although the students came to hear Allen, "spiritual

godfather of the counter culture," there was a warm response to
Louis's work. Biographical information on both poets is included.
Allen responds to questions regarding the National Book Award. An
important fact is revealed in that it was "Captain William Handrahn
of the S. F. P. D. ... [who] ... ordered copies of the book (Howl)
taken from the shelves of City Lights in what became the first test
of California's obscenity law ... " (in 1957).

342 "Ecology and Progress/Ginsberg...," Octopus (Ottawa, Canada), 2:16, 11 December 1969, p. 4 with photograph.
This is an interview between Allen Ginsberg, the Octopus
staff and a group of people. Ginsberg finds little difference between
the idea of religious apocalypse and ecologial apocalypse. He even
succeeds in convincing his audience. "So in other words, the metaphors of apocalypse are all literally being articulated as a result of
our technological feedback thing." He highlights the work of Gary
Snyder and his book, Earth Household, in the name of ecology. He
discounts progress, "I am absolutely against progress. I don't want
to move ahead." The Octopus staff concluded, "How do you argue
against someone like that?"

343 End of the Year, Interview, 1975, unpaged, pp. 22-23.
In the Western Haiku Issue of this literary magazine there
is "Haiku conversation between Allen Ginsberg and Gary Snyder"
(June 16, 1974) in which Ginsberg discusses Kerouac and Snyder
(mostly Kerouac) as masters of America Haiku.

344 Faas, Ekbert (ed.) Towards a New American Poetics: Essays
& Interviews: Olson, Duncan, Snyder, Creeley, Bly, Ginsberg. Santa Barbara, California: Black Sparrow Press,
1978.
The "interview" (pp. 269-288) was conducted in 1974. It
is a carefully documented literary analysis of Ginsberg's work com-
mencing with "The Shrouded Stranger." The influence of "Cézanne,
Kerouac and Burroughs" on his work are discussed, as well as that
by William Carlos Williams and Walt Whitman. Ginsberg's contact
with Olson and indirect influence by Lawrence is noted. "I think I
am indebted to Lawrence more indirectly through Kerouac and Burroughs. ... " Some time is spent on Ginsberg's interactions with
Burroughs and in particular his "cutups." Although Ginsberg finds now
"that Burroughs' cutup things are very similar by hindsight now to
regular mindfulness meditations procedure" there was a break between the two for a short time. "Because for one thing he was
really going into something very radical in terms of introspection
of his consciousness and something which I didn't get myself into
until many years later. ... " Ginsberg's later development is then
discussed through his development of "mantra poetics" and his per-
sonification of "the national psyche." The pivotal point is "The
Change." In the end, Ginsberg discusses his writing style in relation to that of others. Ginsberg then introduces Faas to the
process of the actual "graphing of the movement of the mind." Faas
responds to Ginsberg's instructions about breathing and mind focus,
and the process is illuminated through the dialogue.

345 "First Thought Is Best Thought. " Scottish International, September 1973, pp. 18-23, with photographs (some by Ian Dryden, others uncredited) and poems/songs "New York Blues," "NY Youth Call Annunciation" and "Tear Gas Rag" listed elsewhere in the bibliography.

   "An earlier section of this interview in which Allen Ginsberg discusses Watergate, the reimposition of censorship, the middle classes and Scottish poetry appears in the August issue of The Glasgow Review.... Allen Ginsberg, the most influential poet of the twentieth century, recently visited Scotland, and, between visiting Samyè-Ling, the Tibetan Buddhist monastery near Dumfries, celebrating with Hugh Macdiarmid the latter's 81st birthday and touring the highlands, gave a press conference and four extraordinary readings.... " This interview takes place at a press conference at Glasgow's Arts Council Centre at which time he speaks about his most recent work. "The poems are about broken bones more than sex. " He also responds to a question about Kerouac titling "Howl.... I sent him the text and he sent me back a long letter about a lot of other matters. He also said 'I got your Howl today, and it was really beautiful and a nice poem' and he underlined it, sort of shrewdly. "

346 Foehr, Stephen and Richard Lutz. "American Mantra: An Interview with Allen Ginsberg. " The Straight Creek Journal, 1:15, May 18, 1972, pp. 1, 10, with drawing of profile on front page (p. 1).

   This is an interview with Allen Ginsberg after a major anti-war demonstration in Boulder. It encompasses his thoughts on political action. He sees the "futility" of violence and recommends active yet "silent" sessions. "If you could get a 1,000 people down saying 'Ah-h-h-h, Ah-h-h-h' for several hours in unison, it would create such a sound vibration in the center of the city that it might transfer a good deal of consciousness and particularly transform the aggression of the hard-hat truck driver who would otherwise be inclined to smash and attack. "

347 Fox, Herb. "Allen Ginsberg Interview/Cosmic Comments from Greying Guru. " Santa Barbara News & Review, VI: 19 (221), May 20, 1977, pp. 28-30 with two photographs by Vern Salzbrunn.

   "A fool draws a large circle in the sand and determined to find the circle's beginning, runs around and around it until exhaustion puts an end to the obvious, yet impossible quest. " This quote from the interviewer sets the tone of his opening remarks. Ginsberg responds to questions about his past and present, along with those about his image. In particular when questioned about his being " 'everywhere' at the right time" he responds: "You've got to remember some of the right time and right place is a comment on interpretation. Things are going on everywhere, always in every corner with every little ant and every little cockroach. So it's a question of poetry making the moment conscious ... finding words to searchlight the moment. So the impression made is I might have been everywhere, but it's probably [only] where I've been writing poems.

So they sound more romantic than they really were. " Ginsberg goes on to talk about his current practice of meditation, politics (the impending "revolution of consciousness") and society.

348 Fraser, David. "The Trees Are Our Allies. " Fifth Estate, 4:13 (91), 30 October - 12 November 1969, pp. 8-9, with photographs by Howie Epstein/LNS; (Recorded and transcribed). Reprinted in Chinook 2:7, 1970, p. 5; Extra, 2:3, 16 December 1969, p. 10; Good Times II: 4, 27 November, 1969, pp. 10-11; Los Angeles Free Press 7:5:289, 30 January 1970, pp. 33, 35, part 2; San Diego Door 2:8, 10 September 1970, p. 4; and Win VI:4, March 1970, pp. 20-21, 24. Also included in The Movement Toward a New America, Mitchell Goodman (comp.). Philadelphia: Pilgrim Press; New York: Alfred A. Knopf, 1970.
    "This interview with poet Allen Ginsberg took place at 10 A.M. October 15 driving from Detroit's inner city to Macomb College where he was reading at John Sinclair Defense Fund and a benefit for the Ann Arbor Argus." Ginsberg struggles with the vocabulary of the Movement espoused by the interviewer from the Fifth Estate. He resorts to the musings of William Burroughs who said, "Once a problem is posed, it becomes insoluble." Having confronted the language barrier, Ginsberg proposes ecological unity for the movement and quotes from Gary Snyder who pointed out "the exploited masses are not just blacks and hippies and the Chinese, the exploited masses are the trees and the fish in the sea, those are the exploited masses, the rest of the sentient beings of the planet." Ginsberg sees the Movement in global and ecological terms and criticizes the Movement in the Detroit area for its lack of this perspective. The real issue is that "there's a threat to the existence of the entire planet."

349 Freeman, Deborah. "Interview with Ginsberg." Green Revolution, Official Journal of the School of Living (SOL, v. 31) 12:3, February-March 1974, pp. 11-14, with photographs.
    Throughout this interview Ginsberg has as much trouble as I do with Freeman's style of questioning. Finally he responds by first categorizing her as "a hippy girl" and then "I, too, have a certain resentment ... each one of these questions came from a very specific category of thought, social category of thought ... There's a frame of reference: What's this frame of reference I'm being surrounded with? By the terminology, the point of view sounds like a teeny bopper magazine." Before this actual confrontation various topics regarding Ginsberg's life are discussed. Nonetheless, throughout there is a sense of tension between Ginsberg and the interviewer for he is "interpreting the question first and then answering it."
    Finally there are some closing words of wisdom from Ginsberg on "non-attachment ... if you see something horrible, don't cling to it ... and if you see something beautiful, don't cling to it either ..."
    Interestingly enough this interview was previewed in The Green Revolution (SOL, v. 30), 12:2, December-Jnauary 1973-1974: "Deborah Freeman to ask unusual questions and get unusual answers from Allen Ginsberg and Swami Satchidananda."

350 Geneson, Paul. "A Conversation with Allen Ginsberg." Chicago Review, 27:1, Summer 1975, pp. 27-35.
"This conversation is an edited version of a spontaneous
discussion which took place after class at the Naropa Institute in
Boulder, Colorado." The discussion deals with poetry as "a spoken
thing," academics, America, and the possibility of establishing a
"school of poetics" within Naropa Institute.

351 Gengle, Dean. "Interview: Allen Ginsberg." The Advocate,
228, November 16, 1977, pp. 25, 28, with cover illustration by Dennis Forbes.
Ginsberg talks about his most recent projects and thoughts
on his society in a lively interview. First on the list is his activities at the Kerouac School of Poetry at Naropa Institute in Boulder,
Colorado (site of the interview). He explains how the school came
into being. He then highlights the publication of his new book,
Journals, edited by Gordon Ball and the forthcoming record from
Columbia Records, First Blues. "What is interesting about this
record is that Columbia sat on it for about a year because it has a
lot of dirty words and gay songs on it. I did a book called First
Blues, which has a lot of old-time, funky gay rags and blues." Apparently there is some overlap between the two. This, however, is
the first album of his "own music." Last, Ginsberg is working on
"a new book of poems covering 1971 to '77 called Mind Breaths--
poems written more or less under Buddhist influence. A lot of very
interesting gay material in it, including a long poem called 'The
Contest of the Bards,' which I've subtitled, 'A Punk Epic.' It is, I
think, one of the first largescale, elegant, epic-style poems written
in America having a primarily gay theme, kind of daringly ordinary
treatment of an actual love scene between the two men, or the man
and the boy. So that's coming out from City Lights (publishers)."
In conclusion his recommendations for the community
include the development of "old-fashioned, classical Buddhist, nontheistic meditation practice, centered on the breath.... It would be
useful if everybody in America would take on themselves a little bit
of meditation practice as a basis from which to begin judging the
political emotions of the American scene. That would be a big help."

352 Giangreco, Dennis. "An Interview with Allen Ginsberg." Westport Trucker, 2:22 (46) ("Eighth-ninth"), 1972, pp. 8-9, with
photograph by U News and artwork by David Doyle. Continued 2:23 (47), 1972, pp. 8-9, with photograph imposed on illustration.
"The following interview was recorded for KBEA/KBEY
on Wednesday, February 9, and was aired in part on those stations....
present at the interview were Steve Bell and Steve Litman of KBEY,
Jim Vogt, Bill Dehart, and Kevin Powd of UMKC and Dennis Giangreco of the Trucker." Ginsberg opens the session chanting and
accompanying himself on the harmonium, "Aum, ha." He then talks
for a while about his thoughts on chanting and meditation. Indeed
he sees poetry as a "prophetic art."
Ginsberg is amazed at the mythmaking which surrounds
his image and offers general comments on the state of his life in

America. In fact he picks up his harmonium and improvises "a little tune. " At this point, he would like to continue with a discussion of the "CIA involvement with opium. "
In part two he takes the discussion to the CIA involvement with opium, to Vietnam and then links it all to the Junk problem on the streets. A general discussion of drugs follows and then Allen chants to the Indian yogi, "Ganja Shiva. " He mentions his work with Dylan soon to be released on Apple. Finally, gay liberation is tied "to the beginning of the Universe.... 'The end of the universe will be pure sound ... ' (Allen strikes a chord on the harmonium and chants) ... OM!"

353 "Ginsberg. " Intrepid, Self-Interview, 18/19, 1971, pp. 52-61.
Ginsberg conducts this "self-interview" in Cherry Valley on July 1, 1968, by asking the questions and answering them too. "Now ... I wanted to talk to myself. We all talk to ourselves all the time actually.... One is constantly interviewing oneself. Everybody's always interviewing themselves all the time. So if one first talks to oneself what kind of answers would come up--What kind of questions would come up?... " And through this format, Ginsberg articulates the most recent thoughts in his mind: consciousness, Vietnam and drugs.

354 "Ginsberg and Swami A. C. B. P. " Chinook, 2:16, 30 April 1970, pp. 6-7, Part II, with three photographs by Ted Benhari/Good Times. [Part I unavailable].
"The following is part II of a conversation between Allen Ginsberg and His Divine Grace A. C. Bhaktivedanta Swami Prabhupada which took place at the Radha Krishna Temple in Columbus, Ohio. Part I was published in last week's issue of Chinook. Both parts are reprinted from Back to Godhead by authorization of the Boulder Krishna Temple. " Allen Ginsberg and Prabhupada exchange words before their preparation for an appearance together at Ohio State University. Allen colors the conversation by questioning him. Their conversation spans the general metaphysical, theoretical and personal. Prabhupada reveals "I know that you are not ordinary man. " Allen responds with a confession of his earthly sins. A discussion follows about farming, and their later joint appearance. Allen and Peter Orlovsky then sing Blake's "To Tirzah," to which "Prabhupada listens with open-eyed amusement and delight. "
See also entry below.

355 "Ginsberg and Swami A. C. B. P. " Chinook, 2:17, 17 May 1970, pp. 6-7, continuation Part II [see entry above], with photograph of Allen Ginsberg by Shunneson.
The conversation opens where it left off with Blake. Ginsberg is offered "two flower garlands" and this chapter closes. The next day--May 12--Prabhupada and Allen Ginsberg discuss the poet's work. Prabhupada believes that "poetry comes out of deep love for something. " The work of Mirabai, ("a devotee") whose songs were poetry, is discussed. They continue with a discussion of the future of civilization and the world, and then turn to topics of devotion, religion and their personal experiences.

356   "Ginsberg--Arts 1." Georgia Straight, Interview, 3:49, 14-20
      March 1969, pp. 10-11 with two photographs.
      In part I, "What's Happening to Me," Ginsberg catches us
all up with his current state of being. "I just quit smoking." He
also works out his feelings regarding sex, identity and age. In
part II, "Chicago," he comments on his experiences at the Chicago
convention as a credentialed guest reporting for the Eye (a Hearst
magazine). He and a friend are forcibly removed as are others
(reminiscent of Prague). "So that was happening on the floor of
the convention and in the convention hall ... meaning in a sense
there was no legal nomination. Meaning therefore there was no legal
election. Meaning there is no legal government in America now."

357   "Ginsberg Interview." Good Times, 3:16, 17 April 1970, p. 11.

358   Golden, Daniel. "Allen Ginsberg/Politics of Emptiness." City
      on a Hill, 11:4, October 1977, pp. 3-7.
      This is an interview with Allen Ginsberg videotaped at a
colloquium on LSD at the University of California at Santa Cruz, in
which he comments on his most recent acid experience on his flight
to California yesterday, and highlights "punk rock ... a new expression of old message...." Beyond this videotaped message, Golden
follows Ginsberg around as he chats with Dr. Albert Hofmann, dis-
coverer of LSD regarding "U.S. Intelligence connections," a young
woman accompanied by a Time magazine reporter on her intended use
of acid, and others. After a heated LSD debate, Ginsberg leads a
meditation session.

359   Goodwin, Michael, Richard Hyatt and Ed Ward. "Q: How Does
      Allen Ginsberg Write Poetry?/A: By Polishing His Mind."
      City Magazine, 7:52, 13-26 November 1974, pp. 30-34,
      with photographs by Richard Hyatt.
      A City interview by Michael Goodwin, Richard Hyatt and
Ed Ward under the subject heading of "A City Special Reports:
Books." As a prelude to this interview the editors announce a free
joint reading of Allen Ginsberg, Gary Snyder and Philip Whalen on
November 22 at the De Young Museum, Golden Gate Park. Allen
Ginsberg shares his knowledge on his process of writing, polishing
his mind," which stems from a self-conscious awareness of the
thought process. He compares this to "a fish coming down the
stream. So when the fish comes down the stream of the whole phenomenon of consciousness, you just take out a hook and let it down.
It's a question of getting it while it's going by, doing it rapidly, in
the sense that it's a special event, like somebody jumping out a window...." He indicates the tool of meditation and its effect, the influence of Chögyam Trungpa, his teacher and how this relates to
"Kerouac's basic principle for his spontaneous writing,..." In further detail Ginsberg talks about the mechanics of his actual writing
and the "tinkering" which takes place. Pound's work and influence
are discussed. And in the end Ginsberg talks about his new work
Allen Verbatim and forthcoming First Blues, Rags and Songs. His
philosophy which pervades this discussion and others is "that the
interview and the media were ways of teaching. If you talk to people

as if there were future Buddhas, or present Buddhas, any bad Karma coming out of it will be their problem rather than yours...."

360 Gross, Amy (guest editor). "We Talk to ...." Mademoiselle, 69, August 1969, pp. 343-5, (telephone interview--Cherry Valley).
         The topic of discussion in this brief interview is social change and action. Ginsberg's remedy is one which urges individual growth. "People have to trust their own nature and heart, and if they deal with each other in a heartfelt way, they will be changing the nature of interpersonal relations, which determine larger social relations." In response to a query on his motivation for writing poetry, he explains, "I'm looking into the crystal ball of my own unconscious, to articulate the apprehensions, intuitions, fears I find in my own head...." This is obviously an interview meant for popular consumption because the questions and answers are short, sweet, superficial and tend to be within the realm of expectation. I wonder if the context of the remarks is always accurate because the interviewer never seems to cut below the surface of "the public imagery" of Ginsberg, although he says, "I find being the subject of public imagery an embarrassment, I'd rather have personal contact with people...."

361 Harris, James T. "Beard, Beer, Moon: An Interview with Allen Ginsberg." Alternative Feature Service 1:13, 10 September 1971, pp. 1-4, with photographs by Karma Patrol/ AFS. Reprinted in Chinook, 3:34, 16 Sept. 1971, p. 5, as "Allen Ginsberg on Leary"; In Good Times, 4:28, 17-30 Sept. 1971, pp. 14-15, with two photos, as "Just Call Me Allan [sic]"; in The Great Speckled Bird, 4:42, 18 Oct. 1971, pp. 10-11 with two photos (by Hank Lebo/Good Times and Benhari/Good Times), as "Ginsberg: Beard, Beer, Moon"; in Harry, 12, Oct. 1971, pp. 3, 15, with photos as "Ginsberg and the Drunken Guru or Drooling in Your Beard"; and in Space City, 3:16, 21-27 Sept. 1971, pp. 8-9, with two photos, as "Allen Ginsberg."
         "The interview took place August 21st in Allen's North Beach apartment. It's a small room with only a mattress, a cluttered desk and multitude of cardboard boxes filled with letters, tapes and manuscripts." Ginsberg, America's priest of high poetry discusses a meeting in a bar with Chögyam Trungpa who convinced him to cut off his beard. Then he discusses the habits police must acquire to survive in operating with dope dealers, and the "Mafia and CIA" influence on the drug market. He then focuses on Timothy Leary's "Shoot to Live" mantra when the interviewer tries to confront Ginsberg with Leary's advocation of violence.
         Finally they close on Ginsberg's reflections of the enormity of life's work. Ginsberg is presently working on a vocalized assemblage of his poetry 1946-1971. There "will be a complete set of notes in the recording, the meaning of each poem, the occasion it was written, the occasion it was read, and what it means in relation to other poems...."

362 Head, Robert. "Interview with Allen Ginsberg." Nola Express,
    67, 30 October-12 November 1970, pp. 4-5 with photographs
    by Murph Dowouis. Continued in 69, 27 November-10 De-
    cember 1970, pp. 10-11. Reprinted in Berkeley Barb, 11:
    19:274, 13-19 November 1970, pp. 10-11, with two photos,
    as "An Interview with Ginsberg"; in Chinook, 2:42, 12 No-
    vember 1970, pp. 6-7, with photos, as "An Interview with
    Allen Ginsberg"; and continued in Chinook, 2:45, 3 Decem-
    ber 1970, p. 7.
        Ginsberg prescribes "a minimum of one hour daily sitting,
    meditation, contemplation of one form of yoga or another with or
    without a teacher but at least one hour daily best in the morning
    around dawn" for political activists. "So if we're going to have a
    spiritual revolution we better have the means and tools and the wea-
    pons of a spiritual revolution.... The net effect of Leary's alliance
    with the Weathermen on me so to speak has been to move me fur-
    ther left into actual practice of research into inner space." All of
    this is in response to the recent activities of Tim Leary and the
    state of the Movement. He concludes on a more personal level when
    he comments upon personal space: "silence seems almost a more
    beautiful form of prayer than love-making."

363 "Interrogation of a Businessman by the Interior Police." Kali-
    flower, 3:17, 26 August 1977, 6 pages in length.
        "The following interview took place on July 26 and August
    19, 1971. It was transcribed by hand, typed, and on August 19
    and 23 the typescript was read and corrected by the speakers."
    "Star" interviews "Crescent" (who is Allen Ginsberg). At no time
    are either parties formally introduced; Star is representative of the
    communal alternative structure and an old friend of Allen Ginsberg.
    Much of their rap centers on Star's "Interrogation" of the poet con-
    cerning his mainstream activities. In his own defense, the poet
    mentions his farm community which cost $20,000 annually to main-
    tain. Yet Star attacks him because of his contributions to mass
    culture, his agile manipulation of the system and political abilities.
    In that context Ginsberg attacks the entire publishing system, par-
    ticularly in reference to poetry. In the end, he offers Gary Snyder's
    vision of returning "to tribal culture." Star takes issue with the
    patronage system of the New York male writers that he came into
    contact with when he spent time with Ginsberg in 1958. Ginsberg
    fends off all these attacks with an argument referring to his state
    of reality and barrage of activities.

364 "Interview with Allen Ginsberg." The Noiseless Spider, IV:1,
    Fall 1974, pp. 2-15. (English Club of University of New
    Haven).

365 Johnson, Bryan. "Allen Ginsberg: radical crusader on retreat
    (Being beatific beats being Beat)." The Globe and Mail, 4
    September 1976, p. 1 with superimposed drawing of Buddha
    on Ginsberg by Yenkins.
        Johnson interviews Allen Ginsberg as he teaches Yeats
    at Naropa Institute in Boulder, Colorado. As an introduction, he

describes Ginsberg as he teaches and provides background information on both the teacher and the school. The conversation centers for a long while on his involvement with Buddhism, past and present. Finally the interviewer gets to his Big Question. "Isn't it true," he asks, "that most people don't consider Ginsberg a real poet at all? Don't they generally think of him as just some guy who got a lot of publicity for using dirty words, who has now faded into total obscurity?" Ginsberg replies, "Well,... except that a lot of those poems with dirty words are being taught in schools--so I probably have more impact than ever.... I don't want to sound vain, but I'm more in demand at a higher price than I've ever been. I can get $1,500 a night to read at universities--that's why I can afford to work here all summer for nothing." The interview closes with Bryan Johnson's evaluation of Ginsberg's current musical endeavors, "musically, they sound awful to me." Some lyrics are included for the reader's reference.

366 Jones, Lauren, Barbara Weinberg and David Fenton. "Interview with Allen Ginsberg." Ann Arbor Sun, 2:10, 17-31 May 1974, pp. 14-15, 22, with cover caricature of Ginsberg, and photographs (4) by Barbara Weinberg and another by Francesca Carr/Gay Sunshine. Reprinted in Georgia Straight, 8:353, 18-25 July 1974, pp. 13, 20, as "Ginsberg Raps."

This interview is taken from a transcript of an afternoon spent with the poet, in which he talks about his recent experiences with meditation and correlates these experiences to his original interests. "The basis of my poetics always was a visionary thing beginning with a breakthrough in 1948...." He indicates Neal Cassady's, Kerouac's and Peter Orlovsky's influence here and talks about his trip to India (with Peter in 1962-63) and his visits to Gary Snyder in Zen monasteries in Kiete. Ginsberg moves on in response to a question about the spiritual and political state of the Movement, which leads him to comment upon the old Movement leaders. He proceeds to comment upon the CIA and its relationship to drug traffic (note the research he completed for Alfred McCoy, The Politics of Heroin in Southeast Asia), SLA and the Movement in general. He closes with his remarks concerning John Sinclair, White Panther leader. "The reason John actually got in trouble was that he was organizing in Detroit the first communal mixing of black and white artists in a large scale that was having international reverberations with black and white musicians and poets."

366a Katzman, Allen (comp.). Our Time: An Anthology of Interviews from the Village Other. See Kohn, Jaakov, under INTERVIEWS section.

367 Koch, Kenneth. "Allen Ginsberg Talks About Poetry." New York Times Book Review, 23 October 1977, section 7, pp. 9, 44-46, with photograph by Paul Barry Chowka.

This is a "long conversation" between the poets Allen Ginsberg and Kenneth Koch in which Allen talks about his "poetry." They discuss the influence of "experience, mental states, and breath" on the actual process of writing. Allen's twentieth-century poetic mentors are explored and his new Journals are highlighted. This is an analytically literary discussion between two poets who have known each other "for 25 years" and who at last have had their "first long conversation."

368 Kohn, Jaakov. "I Saw the Best Minds of My Generation ..."
     East Village Other, 4:15, 12 March 1969, pp. 6-7, 19,
     with photograph by Raeanne Rubinstein. Continued in 4:16,
     19 March 1969, pp. 4, 12. Part II, with photograph by
     Andrew Whittuck. Interview reprinted in Our Time: An
     Anthology of Interviews from the East Village Other, comp.
     by Allen Katzman. New York: Dial, 1972, pp. 115-27.
          Ginsberg and Kohn talk about Ginsberg's place in the
     Movement for Ginsberg has changed from "promoting meat joy" (free
     sexuality) to "cosmic consciousness" because "the body is not a suf-
     ficiently stable location for identity since the body can't feel good
     permanently." Burroughs' transition from a "good lay" and The
     Pornography and Censorship Conference at Notre Dame are both dis-
     cussed. Kohn and Ginsberg finish talking about drug dealing, drug
     traffic, the city (NYC) politics, anti-Semitism, the military industrial
     complex and his development in music.

369 Krown, Johnny. "Journey to the EAST." View from the Bot-
     tom, 1:3, 27 [i.e., 17] November 1969, p. 10.
          Krown reminisces, speculates and directly questions Allen
     Ginsberg. "How does it feel Allen? Kerouac is dead, Neal is dead.
     Burroughs is off in Tangier, silent?" Skillfully he weaves this fabric
     by first questioning, then selecting commentary by others i.e. re-
     porters, and then coming back to Ginsberg in the here and now.
     Ginsberg muses, "Comradeship gave us confidence.... We grew on
     each other and learned from each other and that's how it was. We
     helped each other along. We were lucky." Krown concludes, "I
     smiled as he finished, for I realized that we were the ones who were
     lucky. Who's to say where we might be if Kerouac and Cassady
     hadn't been around."

370 Lanser, Hinda. " Jew in the Loft," Six-Thirteen Magazine,
     February 1976, Premier Issue, pp. 52-67 ("Allen Gins-
     berg: Blowin' in the Breeze," pp. 64-67), with photographs
     and illustrations.
          Three interviews are included here. The third is with
     poet Allen Ginsberg. Although they "spoke with Ginsberg for six
     hours, ... a great deal of the interview has been edited out.... For
     now we are limiting ourselves to two major facets: Ginsberg the
     poet, because that is how he sees himself, and Ginsberg the Jew, be-
     cause that is how we see him...." Originally this information was
     gathered by Editor Hinda Langer, but later re-edited by another staff
     person. The actual editing of this interview takes place on an Am-
     trak from Grand Central Terminal, NYC to Buffalo, New York. The
     text is interspersed with the editor's train (travel) associations and
     thoughts. (The introduction and conclusion establish the train ride
     sequence.) The editor brings into focus an image of a painting of

a "giant silent buffalo" in the train station. In closing he thinks
"about the lonely, impotent buffalo back in the station, and Allen
Ginsberg's fears of the heart." The interview is judgmental and
arranged for the editor's convenience. Ginsberg in his notes refers
to this as a "castrated transcript." In essence, Ginsberg talks
about his fellow poets, Jack Kerouac, William Burroughs, and Neal
Cassady and their search for "Supreme Reality." He reveals his
family roots in secular Judaism and discusses his conception of the
Messiah.

371   Lemon, Denis and Stephen MacLean.   " 'Turn On, Tune In, and
        Drop Up' A Conversation with Allen Ginsberg." Gay News
        (London), 27, July 12-25, 1973, pp. 10-12, with two photo-
        graphs.
        This interview took place after the Press Conference at
the Poetry Festival International, June 28, 1973 (Fernanda Pivano
of "the Italian Gay Lib movement FUORI" was along). Denis Lemon
and Stephen MacLean talk with Ginsberg about the gay scene in America, Europe and London, the corruption of "capitalism," William
Burroughs, Mick Jagger and David Bowie. (Ginsberg's "Main reason
for coming was to go, re-establish contact with William Burroughs,
'cause I haven't seen him in a long time.'") "Allen will be giving
a poetry reading in aid of the National Youth Theatre at 8:00 pm on
Sunday, July 22" at the Shaw Theatre, London. In the end, they
discuss "running around the gay scene in London...."

372   Lester, Elenore. "Allen Ginsberg Remembers Mama." New
        York Times, II, 6, February 1972, p. 1, column 4, with
        photographs of Ginsberg.
        A warm and touching article about Elenore Lester's re-
sponse to the form of Kaddish and her later communications with
Ginsberg before going to review the play, "Kaddish," a theater video
work to open at the Chelsea Theater Center. "Ginsberg did the
adaptation, working it from a screen play by Robert Frank." Lester
and Ginsberg talk about "Kaddish," Naomi, and the world. It is a
refreshing, revealing dialogue between the two. Ginsberg's retrospective vision of his mother's illness and situation reveals careful
thought. "Ginsberg went on to say that his experience with his
mother had helped him in dealing with his own life and the people
with whom he was involved himself."

373   Levine, Sharon. "Puns, Poetry and, Sour Creme--Lunch with
        Allen and Louis Ginsberg." American Jewish Ledger, 31
        January 1976, pp. 7-8, with photograph of the two.
        The American Jewish Ledger interviews Louis Ginsberg
and family (Edith, stepmother and grandson/nephew Allen, Jr.) on a
visit to Allen's on the Lower East Side. After a tour of his living
quarters, the "entourage" goes to "Hamer's Dairy Restaurant" for
lunch. Reference is made to a joint reading, but no details are
given. Allen is himself. The Ledger tries to define him and his
family in terms of their concerns as a Jewish newspaper. "The
Ginsbergs are undoubtedly a family affair holding fast to old ties.
Allen Ginsberg, though somewhat apart from the Jewish community,

represents a sizable segment of its youth. Despite his break with traditional Yiddishkite, the questions he poses have been the age-old quest of the Jew. The poet's journey to India, in search of self and immortality, marks a definitive trend in modern Jewish culture. The recent outcry and estrangement of the young Jew is an indication, that Ginsberg's experience is one of a Hebrew and not of an outcast, as some would brand him." Allen Ginsberg's opening remarks adequately summarize his feelings, "I'm sick of Jewish newspapers, questioning me about religion..."

374 Leyland, Winston (ed.). Gay Sunshine Interviews. San Francisco: Gay Sunshine Press, 1978, volume one.
       This volume includes the Allen Young interview (q.v.) with Allen Ginsberg originally published in the Gay Sunshine (1974) from pp. 95-128 with photograph by Elsa Dorfman. Although the volume is published in 1978, it contains a crucial interview from 1974.

375 Litterine, Lynn. "Allen Ginsberg: Olde garde isn't so avant anymore." The Philadelphia Inquirer, 10 December 1977, pp. 7-8A with photograph.
       Lynn Litterine interviews Allen Ginsberg after an hour-long radio broadcast with Arlene Francis in which "he talks and sings about lots of things. He sandwiches meditation instructions, theories of poetics and songs about death in between the commercials for coats, banks and non-dairy creamers." With Litterine, they walk down the street from the studio further discussing his lifestyle, thoughts and current work. "You can alter the world by pointing out to people the basis of their own mind. That's why I still write. It's not doing me any good anymore. I would rather go live in a monastery or on a farm at this point." The photographer of the above-listed photograph caught Ginsberg in a rare moment because it reveals his age and vulnerability.

376 Loewinsohn, Ron. "The Breathing Center of Poetry and Politics: Allen Ginsberg Interview." The Daily Californian, 10 March 1972, n.p.

377 Logos, Interview, 3:1 March 1970, unpaged. Reprinted from Strobe Magazine, 1969.
       This interview with Allen Ginsberg offers "random samples of some of Allen's raps" at the Sheraton-Mount Royal Hotel (November 1, 1969) before a reading at McGill. Ginsberg's message is that "the only path that people can follow safely at this point is the path of tenderness towards themselves and other people and to nature." "Songs of Experience--A Divine Image" (a poem) is included.

378 Lovell, John. "Breath Is What Concerns Poet Ginsberg, He Explains." Press Herald, 27 April 1974, p. 26, with photograph.
       Lovell sets the tone of the reading with his comments on the audience and the cost of the appearance. He shares some of Ginsberg's thoughts with us on meditation, the National Book Award,

and "his next scheduled appearance in a couple of days at the Library of Congress. " At the Portland, Maine, reading Ginsberg and Bhagavan Das sat crosslegged, chanted and read on "a big Oriental rug. " Indeed, as the reviewer remarks, "Ginsberg seemed to have left his generation ... to sing Hindu chants in Portland to the hip children of the seventies. "

379 Lupoff, Dick. "Allen Ginsberg: Interview ..." Changes, n.d., pp. 1-2, with photograph by Lupoff.
    This San Francisco interview was conducted after the production of Kaddish opened in New York, but before Ginsberg left for a tour to Australia. Ginsberg reveals the history of his work on Kaddish that began after his work with Robert Frank, the film maker. "The starting point was an attempt to make the poem, which involves mental images, flashbacks, simultaneous and overlapping events, more linear for the screen. " These activities encompassed his first attempts to translate the work into a film in 1963. As for Ginsberg's activities, he recently completed recording with Dylan, an album Holy Soul Jellyroll. In closing, he comments upon his dedication to Kaddish, as a work of art. Lupoff concludes, "Ginsberg cites others with whom he's been associated: 'Burroughs wrote Naked Lunch for himself, Kerouac wrote On the Road for himself, I wrote Kaddish for myself. We had to write for ourselves. Then commercial success just came. '"

380 Maine Edition, August/1974, pp. 7-11 with photographs taken at Bates College Reading, 1/74, by Cort Roberts.
    "The following interview with poet, Allan Ginsberg [sic] was conducted after a reading at Bates College, in the home of John Tagliabue, January 29, 1974. The condition of the interview was of drunkenness, and humor. Recorded on a tape recorder, in a stairway from the apartment. The quality of the recording is extremely poor. The transcription involved some twenty-two hours of work. I have made every effort to transcribe the tape exactly. I am afraid though that there are errors. If anyone would like a copy of the recording, contact me and arrangements will be made. " Despite the misspelling of Ginsberg's first name and various other words, there is some substance to this conversation in which Ginsberg and his cohorts discuss his reading at Bates at which time he offered a collage of past and present poems (including "Howl"). The interviewers compare their personal reactions for "Howl" to Ginsberg's everchanging motivation for reading the work. Ginsberg used music at the reading. As a result his oral style and the influence of chanting on his work are discussed. Toward the end, the interview sinks to the level of drunken banter about sexual preferences and habits.

381 Maroney, Tom. "Where have you gone, Allen Ginsberg?" Acton Minute-Man, 15 December 1977, p. 5. Also reprinted in the following Boston area newspapers: Bedford Minute-Man, Billerica Minute-Man, Burlington Times-Union, Concord Journal, The Hansconian, Lexington Minute-Man.
    This is a short interview with Allen Ginsberg after a reading in the Boston area which the interviewer attended. Ginsberg

read "Kaddish." The interview itself is conducted at the home of
Elsa Dorfman (whom Maroney refers to as "a woman whom I had
seen at the reading") and on the way to a coffeehouse appearance.
Ginsberg responds to questions about his current activities and
thoughts. Nothing new is revealed in this dialogue.

382   Mottram, Eric.   New Departures, Interview, 7/8 and 10/11,
      n.d., pp. vi-vii.
      This is an excerpt from an interview with Ginsberg for
the BBC regarding the "Albert Hall Poetry Incarnation" which was
never broadcast.   There are also various references to Ginsberg
throughout this literary serial, plus some poetry.

383   Nolan, Frank.   "Allen Ginsberg: poet-musician, shaman and
      bard."   Polar Star, XXIX:24, 14 April 1972, p. 8 with two
      photographs.
      Ginsberg talks about himself, the discovery of Alaska,
politics, the war and his use of mantra and song in his new work.
"Actually, I've been thinking of myself as poet-musician...." Excerpts from his "improvised song 'Caribou Blues'" are included.
This interview was conducted during the poet's stay when he was
reading at the University of Alaska in Fairbanks.

383a Obst, Lynda Rosen (ed.).   The Sixties.   New York: Rolling
      Stone Press, Random House, 1977, designed by Robert
      Kingsbury.
      This compilation includes a 1965 interview with Allen
Ginsberg, "Coming to Terms with the Hell's Angels," from pages
160-163 (with photographs, p. 160 by Larry Keenan, Jr., p. 161
two by Jeffrey Blankfort, p. 162 by Baron Wolman and p. 163 by
Jim Marshall).   Essentially this interview describes Ginsberg's
confrontation with Hell's Angels which is resolved through chanting
and "Ken Kesey's statesmanship and his common sense."

383b Packard, William (ed.).   The Craft of Poetry: Interviews
      from the New York Quarterly   See "Craft Interview ..."
      under INTERVIEWS section.

384   Portugés, Paul.   "An Interview with Allen Ginsberg."   Boston
      University Journal, XXV:1, 1977, pp. 47-59.
      Ginsberg and Portugés chat for some time in July 1976
about the influence of Tibetan meditation and C. Trungpa (Ginsberg's
meditation teacher) upon Ginsberg's work and his person.   Ginsberg
began his serious meditation efforts in 1970-71.   "And that's the
reason for the Naropa Kerouac School of Disembodied Poetics; originally Trungpa asked me to take part in the school because he wanted
his meditators to be inspired to poetry because they can't teach unless they're poets--they can't communicate."

385   Prescott, Bill and Pierre Joris and Steve Kushner.   "A Talk
      with Allen Ginsberg."   Taped at Annandale-on-Hudson,
      New York (Bard College), December 3, 1969.   (According to
the National Union Catalogue for 1977 this was published "In a whole

issue of a magazine of prose published by and for members of the
community of Bard College'" [Bard Observer?].)
    Ginsberg and these men talk about the police bureaucracy
in the United States and elsewhere, images of Moloch, personal
habits, Chicago, the coming trial, politics, Lennon, John Sinclair,
the need to break away in order to write, the South, Mexico, Burroughs, Genet, junk, other drugs, the Mafia and the Pentagon, and
Ginsberg's reason for writing. Ginsberg indicates that he writes
out of a need to communicate. "It's a form of meditation. I have
to find out what I'm thinking. Literally, I find out what is on my
mind. Or I articulate it out front, where I can see it,... Also,
in social terms, the bardic function, set side by side, or inside,
the mass media, is a corrective, to mass hallucination. Because
the bardic thing is personal communication of actual data as far as
you really see it or feel it from unconscious sources, uncensored.
Whereas the mass media hallucination is a censored reality. So
poesy's a corrective to mechanical robot reduplication of castrated
and manipulated news.... So that's one reason I write. To say
what I could say when I was alive." In the end, this is a comprehensive interview between Ginsberg and these other men which indicates the social climate of the times. The items discussed are those
which are important to the Movement and culture. In all a valuable
social/cultural document is presented.

386 "Raps with Allen Ginsberg." All Hands Abandon Ship, 2:6,
        December 1971 (Newport, Rhode Island).

387 "Refusing to Look Through Galileo's Telescope/ The Contrivance
        of Religion." Crawdaddy, IV:10, 6 July 1970, part 2, sec-
        tion 2, p. 26-28.
        "In last fortnight's installment, Alan Watts and Allen Gins-
berg were cut off as they talked about acid's effects on U.S. social
patterns. Here they fade in again on the subject of psychedelics and
the notion of 'dropping out'...." Essentially the discussion continues
on the effect of psychedelics and pot on American culture. Ginsberg
offers Gary Snyder's solution of "centers of spiritual introduction."
He also discusses the value of accomplishment and motivation and
the effect of LSD on these values. "The LSD experience is not conceptual manipulation--and if you're not interested in conceptual manipulation at that moment, then the tests don't show anything...." Last,
the expansion of psychedelic research is discussed which Watts addresses himself.

388 Robbins, Al. "Allen Ginsberg. Off to the Boneyard." Drum-
        mer, 233, 6 March 1973, p. 9 with photograph of Ginsberg
        carrying the book by Alfred McCoy, The Politics of Heroin
        in Southeast Asia, by Neil Benson.
        The introduction to this interview records the joint reading
of Allen Ginsberg and his father, Louis, at Bucks County Community
College. "The two read together in an effort to practice what the
father calls 'peaceful coexistence'... What follows is excerpted
from a tape of a press conference held prior to the reading." The
title refers to Allen's broken leg. The discussion with Allen high-

lights his thoughts on the cultural "condition of the arts," CIA involvement with heroin traffic, Leary, government repression and alternatives for the future, both personally and generally.

388a Rodman, Selden. Tongues of Fallen Angels. New York: New
       Directions, 1974.
       This is a book composed of "conversations with Jorge
Luis Borges, Robert Frost, Ernest Hemingway, Pablo Neruda,
Stanley Kunitz, Gabriel Garcia Marquez, Octavio Paz, Norman Mailer,
Allen Ginsberg, Vinicius de Moraes, Joao Cabral de Melo Neto,
Derek Walcott." The Ginsberg conversation covers pages 183-199.
According to Ginsberg, his interview with Rodman consists of "paraphrasing" and "counterfeit quotes." This is not a reliable source
of information on Ginsberg.

389 Scharfman/Mandel. "Interview with Allen Ginsberg and his
      Father." College Press, 46, 15 January 1971, p. 1.

390 Sinclair Iain. "Ginsberg: the kodak mantra diaries /Allen
      Ginsberg's london summer." Second Aeon, 14, n.d. , pp.
      84-92, with photographs by Robert Klinert. Excerpt from
      The Kodak Mantra Diaries, October 1966 to June 1971.
      London: Albion Village Press, 1971.
       The introductory piece provides a portrait of Ginsberg,
"Ginsberg walks in: characteristic flat-foot waddle. Archetypal
non athlete." On Thursday, July 27, at the Hanover Terrace there
is a conversation between Ginsberg and Geoffrey in which they discuss "LSD" and the approaching new consciousness. "In the park"
Sinclair discusses Ginsberg's work " 'The Change' a renunciation of
visions produced by drug consciousness ... current work 'Wichita
Vortex Sutra' which incorporates Ginsberg's travels throughout the
United States on tape." In the final entry, "August / The Summerhouse" Ginsberg responds in a hostile manner to Sinclair's questions
about cycles and "global erruption" because he's worried about personal problems, "Peter Orlovsky is in New York flippin out. That's
what's on my mind. I got a letter that all the windows in my house
were smashed and that Peter was in Bellevue...."

391 Stuttaford, Genevieve. 'PW Interviews: Allen Ginsberg." Publishers Weekly, 14 November 1977, pp. 6-7, with photograph.
       "Amid the purposeful clutter of his apartment, the poet
bemoans the fate of his colleagues--and rejoices in his own first
'book book.'" Genevieve Stuttaford colorfully describes her visit
to Ginsberg's Lower East Side apartment in which she finds him "at
home in the din." They talk about the publishing field and Ginsberg's commitment to younger unknown poets in the community.
"Ginsberg's vision of a culture that values its poets would have publishing be 'a totally humane communal thing, with editors who are
of the family; who are lovers and friends.' He feels it is the little
presses that meet that need, such publishers as the New York-based
Full Court, which has recently issued a collection of his poetry,
'First Blues, Rags, Ballads & Harmonium Songs, 1971-74.' He

also singles out Don Allen, an exquisite editor, at Grey Fox in
Bolinas, California, and Lawrence Ferlinghetti of City Lights, 'back-
bone of the community....'" Although, according to Publishers
Weekly, "he's clearly delighted with Grove Press and doesn't dis-
guise it as he caresses his first 'book book.'" Ginsberg and Publishers Weekly comment on the monumental job completed by his
editor in correlating his journal material. Ginsberg reveals, "My
journals are to keep an accurate record of my interior life, a repository for what goes through my mind...." In conclusion he
verifies his literary productivity with the announcement of the forthcoming publication of a new collection of poetry by City Lights,
Mind Breaths, 1972-1977, which contains a major work, "Contest
of Bards...."

392 Tedesco, Frank. "If you see anything horrible don't cling to
     it." Berkeley Barb, 12:21:303, 4-10 June 1971, pp. 2-3,
     11, with photographs and illustrations. Reprinted in Georgia
     Straight, 5:75, 15 June 1971, p. 12.
        Ginsberg discusses a conversation with His Holiness "Pud-
jum Rinpoche [the head of the Nyima Sect] in Kalempong, India,
1961.... I was talking to him about horror visions I had on LSD.
He said, 'If you see anything horrible, don't cling to it and if you
see anything beautiful, don't cling to it!'" Ginsberg found this advice "like a sword that cuts both ways, through all the heavens and
hells and left me free of all of them." He then goes on to address
Richard Nixon and Richard Helms of the CIA as "Black magicians ...
maguns manipulating concepts and imagery and language." Further
he finds "all political activity should be done on a basis of at least
one hour a day of meditation.... That kind of meditation will guar-
antee that street action is going to be coming out of the whole consciousness..." He "doubts if the large mass of longhairs believe
in the kind of formal violence that has been encouraged by underground newspapers. I think the underground newspapers are working
against the tide...." On this two-page Ginsberg spread which contains the main body of the interview, there are also the indicated
photograph and illustration, coupled with an advertisement, "Gins-
benefit! Allen Ginsberg will be giving a benefit poetry reading ...
June 6, 8 pm" and a quote under the heading "Look Neat & Clean...
Allen: 'One thing Satchidananda once said, Very important I thought--
if you are going to wear a beard and long hair--particularly in America now, ... make yourself look neat and clean with it." There are
two other boxes. The first reads "Pleonastic/Nails/Neolithic" in
which Ginsberg comments "that mechanical civilization needs more
archaic contact, contact with archaic consciousness from an ecological
point of view" and continues with a quote from Gary Snyder. The
second box is "Allen's Barb Ad," which reads "I'm also so busy, I
hardly have time for romantic dalliance even if I could break through
my shyness. Well I'm at liberty in case anybody wants to know.
I'm almost at the level of putting an ad in the Berkeley Barb for
something like that...." Following this is a collage of the conversation between Frank Tedesco and Allen Ginsberg.

393 Tytell, John. "A Conversation with Allen Ginsberg." Partisan

Review, 41:2, 1974, pp. 253-262. Reprinted in Berkeley
Barb, 20:16:481, 1-7 November 1974, pp. 12-13, with photos.
    This is a discussion with Carl Solomon, Allen Ginsberg,
and the interviewer which particularly highlights William Burroughs'
influence on Allen Ginsberg.

394 Webster, Jack. "And the capitalists ... are willing to see the
        Georgia Straight stomped /Ginsberg and Webster," Georgia
        Straight, 3:52, 4-10 April 1969, pp. 9-12, with photographs
        by Joe Ellis and R. Valentine.
    "Here is Jack Webster's March 11 interview with Allen
Ginsberg, which was broadcast in Webster's evening hot-line show
on CKNW." Webster and Ginsberg duel with one another on a variety of subjects from reading poetry, singing Blake, Allen's music,
ecology and politics. They both seem to be enjoying this verbal
match. Later Ginsberg and Peter Orlovsky sing Blake with the
harmonium accompaniment, and Ginsberg reads his poem about 1965
in Prague. One important message for the evening is Ginsberg's
thoughts on the Georgia Straight, "the one newspaper that seems to
be recording news from the heart, and ecological news is the Georgia
Straight. "

395 Westerman, Keith F. "Speaking with Ginsberg. " The Mass
        Media, XI:24, 12 April 1977, p. 16, with photograph.
    Ginsberg recently performed in Cambridge at Passims'
Coffeehouse in Harvard Square. This interview seeks to record
this reading /performance and the "impromptu press conference at
the Dharmadhatu, a Buddhist Meditation and Study Center ... in
Cambridge. " The interviewer comments on Ginsberg's aging (as
all people do). "Bald, with a middle-aged paunch (he's in his
fifties now)... " Ginsberg talks about his meditation practices, and
comments "on the current political scene ... moves on to writing ...
[and] ... defines himself as 'some kind of pacifist Jewish, anarchist,
communist, gay, mindfulness freak. '" (In closing he lays out his
future activities.) Basically, this is not an in-depth dialogue with
Mr. Ginsberg, rather it is the recording of Ginsberg at the press
conference.

396 Young, Allen. "Allen Ginsberg, An Interview and Poem. "
        Gay Sunshine, 16, January - February 1973, pp. 4-10 with
        cover caricature by D. Levine '70 and photographs on pp.
        4, 6, 7, 8.
    "The following conversation with Allen Ginsberg took place
at Ginsberg's farm in Cherry Valley, New York, on September 25,
1972. Allen Young, who rapped with Ginsberg and transcribed the
interview, is well known in the Movement.... The conversation was
edited from the original 78-page manuscript by Winston Leyland of
Gay Sunshine. " Here is the original lengthy interview (later published in book form by Grey Fox Press*, 1974) in which Ginsberg

---

*NOTE: According to Allen Young (letter dated May 22, 1978), "To
the best of my recollection, there is no difference textually between

and Young focus on: "Ginsberg's homosexuality," "sexuality" in general, the relationship of "Whitman" to all of this (includes a photograph of Whitman, p. 5), and Ginsberg on "Solomon and Leary," on "yoga," on "Burroughs," and finally on his own self acceptance." The poem "Please Master" (May 1968) is included on p. 9. This is a beautifully detailed discourse between the two men highlighting new thoughts on older ideas and topics. "As far as we know this is the first in-depth interview by a gay person, and it is, we feel, important for the consciousness of the gay liberation movement."

397 Young, Allen. "Allen Ginsberg: An Interview and Poem." Gay Sunshine, 17, March-April 1973, p. 18. Reprinted in Berkeley Barb, 17:14:399, 6-12 April 1973, pp. 19-21; 17:15:400, 13-19 April 1973, pp. 10-11; and 17:16:401, 20-26 April 1973, pp. 15-17; in College English, 36:3, November 1974, pp. 32-40; in Gay Sunshine Interview, San Francisco: Gay Sunshine Press, 1978, volume one; in Georgia Straight, 7:278, 1-8 February 1973, pp. 9, 16; 7:281, 22 February-1 March 1978, pp. 12-13, 21; and 7:282, 1-8 March 1973, pp. 12-14, 16; in Northwest Passage, 8:11, 19 March-1 April 1973, pp. 12-13, 22; Real Papers, 2:13, 28 March 1973, pp. 8-12, 14; 2:15, 11 April 1973, pp. 14-18. The interview was also printed in the International Times (London).

Completion of Allen Ginsberg interview with Allen Young from no. 16. Topic: "Ginsberg/Russia." Ginsberg talks about the absence of personal freedom in the Soviet Union and its relationship to the idealization of American intellectual anarchists regarding the Soviet Union.

398 Ziomek, Jon. "Pair Are Somewhat Offbeat/A Little Upbeat, But Still Beat." Chicago Sun-Times, 17 March 1975, p. 36. Photograph by Chuck Kirman.

Burroughs and Allen Ginsberg return for the first time together in Chicago in a somewhat more receptive environment. This interview takes place in a hotel room in the "St. Clair Hotel" and

[Cont. from p. 60] the Grey Fox Press and the Gay Sunshine, though I think the Grey Fox Press Edition is more carefully annotated and corrected with regard to quotations from Walt Whitman, etc. That's a point ... the Gay Sunshine version of the interview added the little section on the USSR in their next issue. So really, the best version of the interview, all things considered, is Grey Fox Press, and someone who really cares for detail might desire to consult the typescript of the Paterson Library. Also, the Grey Fox Press edition has an introduction written by Allen Young describing the circumstances under which the interview occurred, which I think provides an added dimension to appreciating the interview. The Real Paper version omits a few sections, but for the part they did print, it's a bit closer to the original manuscript. A copy of the tape is on deposit, with a transcript at the Paterson library...."

essentially the message is one of "cultural revolution." Ginsberg
foresees the revolution and its impact upon government and the rest
of society and concludes: "'art is a decentralized consciousness,'
which is necessary to survival."

B. FOREIGN LANGUAGE

French

399 "Conversation between Allen Ginsberg and Peter Orlovsky."
      Starscrewer (Bernard Froidefont, Place de la Halle, 24590
      Salignac-Envignes, France). n.d. , n.p.

400 "Entretien avec le même Ginsberg." ("Conversation with the
      Same Ginsberg.") Actuel, 10-11 (juillet-août, 1971): 19-
      20. With two superimposed photographs by D.R.
      This is an interview in which both poetry and contempor-
ary issues are discussed including the case of John Sinclair, ecology,
Gary Snyder, cocaine and sexuality.

401 Grondent, Michel. "Le poète Allen Ginsberg: de la génération
      sacreificé à la révolution paisible." Le Soir, 29 janvier
      1976, p. 9, with photograph.
      Allen Ginsberg is interviewed briefly in French while at
a celebration in Brussels. He talks of his Buddhist activities, the
CIA and the corruption in American government. His most recent
activities are added as a postscript: the making of the film with
Bob Dylan from the Rolling Thunder tour, inspired by Kerouac; and
the recording of Blake's "Songs of Innocence."

402 Hochman, Sandra. "Ginsberg père et fils: Retranscription
      d'une émission de Sandra Hochman intitulee: 'Les deux
      Ginsbergs et diffusée par K.P.F.A. le 11 janvier 1965.'"
      entretiens, beat generation, 1975, pp. 59-76. Interview in-
      édite, recherche, adaptation et traduction de Jacqueline Starer.
      This interview ("Ginsberg father and son.") is one from
the KPFA broadcast in 1/11/65 with editing and translation by Jacqueline Starer. In the above, Ginsberg highlights his life on the
Cherry Valley Farm. The conversation turns to ecology and concludes with a vision of cultural revolution with a combination of
energies from the Beatles, Dylan and even Mick Jagger together
with the poets.

403 Pellec, Yves. "La Nouvelle Conscience: entretien avec Allen
      Ginsberg" ["The New Consciousness: An Interview with
      Allen Ginsberg"]. entretiens, beat generation, 1975, pp.
      41-58. (French)
      This interview takes place with Allen Ginsberg (in New
York City on the Lower East Side) under the pretense of acquiring
information about Jack Kerouac. However, the dialogue which follows presents valuable insights into the character of Ginsberg and
his circle of friends. The conversation begins with a discussion

of the character of Kenneth Rexroth in Kerouac's Dharma Bums, the
relationship between Kerouac and Rexroth, Rexroth's role and place
within the San Francisco Renaissance, the role of jazz in Kerouac's
writing, and Kerouac at Columbia University. Pellec pursues Kerouac's higher education further and uncovers a crucial influence of
Professor Weaver, a Melville scholar. It seems that it is Professor
Weaver who recommends further reading in agnostic tradition and it
is he who encourages Kerouac in these directions.

Their conversation then turns to the state of academic
literary study at that time and the lack of respect attributed by the
academic community to Whitman, and others in that tradition. The
familiar Columbia anecdotes are recollected about Jack and Allen
being caught spending the night together and Allen writing on the windows of his dormitory. This prepares the way for a series of questions which are political in content. Ginsberg indicates Kerouac's
early political ties with the Communist party. Then he describes the
basic tensions between the old Left and the revolution in consciousness by the Beats. Their revolution was one of the spirit and psychedelic consciousness. The Left tried to utilize this and transform
it into political energy. The story is an old one of failure and disillusionment. The topic turns to the influence of drugs upon the Beats and
role of William Burroughs in his influence on the younger poets. These
plus the reading of Huxley, meditation, yoga, jazz, sex, all influenced
the verse form of Kerouac, Ginsberg and the others.

Ginsberg then recounts Kerouac's troubled feelings about
his homosexual relationship to Allen. Kerouac often had demonic
feelings toward Allen which Allen attributes to his mixed feelings on
homosexuality. Kerouac was fundamentally heterosexual, yet he had
had some homosexual experiences with Allen and others. He, according to Allen, did not want this to influence his literary world. One
must remember that they were living amidst the Village culture of
NYC which lent itself to a homosexual vision, and Burroughs was a
crucial influence (and his vision was also that of the homosexual).
Much time is then spent on Burroughs and the influence that he offered from his European roots, "agnostic curiosities," and psycho-
analytical orientation. The San Francisco Renaissance is discussed
and the beginning of publication of Kerouac's and Burroughs' work
in France.

404 Tytell, John. "Conversation avec Allen Ginsberg." Tel Quel
(Literature/Philosophie/Science/Politique). 60 Hiver 1974,
pp. 54-63. Traduit par Harry Blake. This appears to be
a French translation of the Tytell interview in Partisan Review, 41:2 (1974), pp. 253-262. See INTERVIEW section
of this bibliography.

This is an interview with Allen Ginsberg (in the presence
of Carl Solomon) in which Tytell questions Ginsberg's relationship to
William Burroughs, drugs (particularly morphine). They talk about
Burroughs' influence on Pound and Eliot, about agnostic tradition,
The Fall of America, "Jessore Road," Dylan and Ginsberg's movement to more musical and spontaneous poetry, the Blake experience,
and Zen. Ginsberg highlights the use of Zen riddles for decondition-
ing the mind. Pound's influence on other writers is analyzed. And

Tytell questions Ginsberg on the link to Buddhism for Burroughs.
Their talk continues with a discussion of the Democratic Convention
of 1968 at which time Burroughs, Genet and Ginsberg participated.
Solomon comments that people have often considered Burroughs the
American "Genet." The interview concludes with Burroughs, his
use of madness, his vision of CIA control and his mission to liberate consciousness from the control forces that exist.

Italian

405 Pivano, Fernanda. "Mantra Del Re Di Maggio." Allen Ginsberg Mantra Del Re Di Maggio. Italy: Arnoldo Mondadori,
1973, 1976. (Bilingual.)
This interview was conducted in New York City (November 22, 1968) and serves as the preface)pp. 9-46) to the above
listed Italian/English anthology (See ANTHOLOGY section) of Allen
Ginsberg's work. However, the preface appears only in Italian.
After this lengthy historical and literary "portrait" of the development
of his recent poetry, Ginsberg turns to the development of his own
work and that of his immediate contemporaries, Creeley, Snyder,
Whalen, McClure and Ferlinghetti. Pivano questions Ginsberg on
his own progression with the use of language from Empty Mirrors
to Howl and on to Kaddish. Ginsberg traces his development through
individual works, giving examples, which is precisely why this conversation serves its function as the introduction to an Italian version
of poems from Reality Sandwiches (1953-1960) and Planet News
(1961-1967).

Japanese

406 "Allen Ginsberg." Goru, 24 February 1977, n. 4, pp. 46-51.
This interview includes Ginsberg talking on "Bob Dylan,
Buddhism and homosexuality." It also includes a small piece, a
personal history of Allen Ginsberg, by Yu Suwa. All in Japanese.

407 Shibazaki, Hiromasa. "Allen Ginsberg." Weekly Playboy,
n. d., pp. 44-49. (Japanese.)
Shibazaki and Ginsberg for the most part discuss meditation and breathing in meditation. A partial quotation from "Howl"
is included and the talk highlights Peter Orlovsky, William Carlos
Williams and his relation to Mahayann Buddhism and Allen's admiration of an ancient Japanese Haiku poet, Issa.

Norwegian

408 Young, Allen. "Interju med Allen Ginsberg." Vinduet, 1974,
28 yr., n. 3, pp. 16-20, with photographs.
This is a Norwegian translation of Gay Sunshine
Interview. Introduction by Allen Young. San Francisco: Grey Fox
Press, 1974.

A. ENGLISH LANGUAGE

409 "Advertising Trade Publications..." Art Direction/The
Magazine of Visual Communication, January 1973, p. 41.
Reproduction of postcard statement handwritten by Gins-
berg.

410 "Ah, Wake Up!" Newsday, 27 August 1972, n. p.
"Ah, Wake Up!" written by Allen Ginsberg, records the
events prior to the Miami Republican National Convention. He speaks
out against the Vietnam War and dramatizes peaceful demonstration.
"Therefore, we sit in this street to awaken American consciousness,
to block the road of delegate participants in the selection of a mass
murderer as head of this nation whose sins we inherit.... 'Nixon
brought us together. Nixon brought us together,' we all chant in
unison from three full trucks of human bodies, as the vans, back
doors slam shut, metal on metal. Engines roar beneath the stifling
darkness, the trucks roll off to Miami City Jail."

411 "Allen Ginsberg and Richard Howard 1971 National Book Award
Poetry Judges, explain themselves." New York Times, VII
4 April 1971; includes photographs of each.
Part of this article is a long tirade of a letter to the National
Book Award Library Fellow Judges, signed "Allen Ginsberg, Your Dis-
obedient Servant," in which he skillfully throws the committee up against
the wall, in terms of principles of selection: "Disrupt the social situation as it may, I insist on my own responsibility to that politic-social-
poetic vision and our own responsibility to historically articulate genius."
The second part of this article is a letter from the committee written by R. Howard who scolds Ginsberg for being closed-
minded: "You want a poetry of ecstasy, and you will not endure,
much less endorse, a poetry of excellence."

"Allen Ginsberg Asks 44 Questions About Tim Leary." see
"Ginsberg Asks 44 Questions About Leary."

412 "Allen Ginsberg Comes Down on Speed." Los Angeles Free
Press, 17-23 April 1970, 7:16:300, p. 12.
[Editor's Note: According to Allen Ginsberg this series
of "Down on Speed" statements were excerpted from an original interview with Art Kunkin of the Los Angeles Free Press, conducted in
the late 1960's. This series re-surfaced in this format (under
various titles, in a variety of underground newspapers and one an-

thology) in the early 1970's. The series includes: Nickel Review, 9 January 1970, v. 4, n. 18, p. 5; "Allen Ginsberg Comes Down on Speed." Los Angeles Free Press, 17-23 April 1970, v. 7, n. 16, issue 300, p. 12; "Ginsberg Talks About Speed." Door to Liberation, 10 September 1970, v. 2, n. 8, p. 4; "On Speeeeeed." The Spectator, 11 February 1970, v. 10, n. 2, p. 17; "Speed Is a No-No." Harry, 5 February 1970, v. 1, n. 7, p. 10; "Speed Kills-- Ginsberg." Chinook, 1970, v. 2, n. 7, p. 4; "Spread a Little Happiness." Nola Express, 17 April 1970, v. 1, n. 53, p. 6; "Ginsberg Talks About Speed." in The Agitator; A Collection of Diverse Opinions From America's Not-So-Popular Press. Comp. by Donald L. Rice. Chicago: American Library Association, 1972. Chronologically, the Nickel Review appears to be the origin of the retrieval of this statement. As a result, see its annotation, although it is only a variation of the annotation listed below.]
        This is a statement about the negative effects of speed on the individual and consequently on the community. "Speed is anti-social paranoid making, it's a drag, bad for your body, bad for your mind, generally speaking in the long run, uncreative; and it's a plague in the whole dope industry." Ginsberg speaks from personal experience because "since 1958 it's been a plague around my house. People that I liked, or who were good artists, have gotten all screwed up on it, and come around breaking down the door, stealing." He calls for government assistance which "ideally" would establish mountain retreats for rehabilitation of these people.

        "Allen Ginsberg on Mafia and Junk." Los Angeles Free Press.
        see "Ginsberg on Junk."

413   "Allen Ginsberg on New Wave/Ginsberg SEZ." Search & Destroy: New Wave Cultural Research, 1977, n. 1, p. 13, with photograph by Judy Steccone.
        "I like the Nuns. They're like Kabuki theater. I don't think the term "new wave" has reached the East Coast yet. I've been to CBGB's 15 or 20 times--Denise Mercedes, Peter Orlovsky's girlfriend who's really a rocker, first took me there. But now I think the Mabuhay is a better scene ... CBGB's a bit tired. The main result of protest music is usually more sexual liberation. The New Wave music is protest music, but its chief concern seems to be the Mockery of television machinery, and decadence...." Ginsberg after reviewing this statement found the "conversation boilt down, edited inaccurately by Vail Hamenaba, Editor."

414   "Allen Ginsberg on San Diego/Mind Consciousness Be-In." Los Angeles Free Press, 14-20 April 1972, v. 9, no. 15, issue 404, p. 2; also published as "mind consciousness be-in--san diego." WIN, 1 April 1972, v. 8, n. 6, pp. 14-15.
        Scenario for Buddhist and political ceremony. Prose in the shape of a poem. January 1972. "Footnote: Text represents idealized imagination Feb. 1972 writing time. I hope to go to San Diego Elephant Convention, happily but not go unless everybody responsible promises ... positive energy politics yoga nonviolence ALL levels conscious and unconscious. I don't want to invite any-

one to get his head busted, on my idiot account.   These writings
are lyric formulae/open possibility. "

415   "Allen Ginsberg on the New Dylan. "   Outlaw, 7-28 May 1971,
        v. 2, n. 2, p. 12.
            "I think that Dylan has already given so much of himself
and so altered the course of poetics in America that no matter what
he does it's just gravy at this point.   Dylan has almost singlehand-
edly brought language back into its original poetic form which is
minstrelsy. "

            "Allen Ginsberg Questions About Tim Leary. "   see   "Ginsberg
        Asks 44 Questions About Leary. "

416   "Blake Notes. "   Caterpillar, 14 (January 1971): 126-132; also
        in "Songs of Innocence and of Experience by William Blake,
        Tuned by Allen Ginsberg, " by Morris Eaves, Blake News-
        letter, 4:3 (Winter 1971), pp. 90-97.
            Reprint of the prose line notes for Ginsberg's recording
of Blake's Songs of Innocence and Experience.   See "To Young or
Old Listeners: ... " in this section.

417   "Citation for 1976 N. I. A. L. Award. "   Prepared on behalf of
        Louis Zukofsky by Allen Ginsberg, March 4, 1976 for the
        National Institute of Arts and Letters.   It is available through
        the Institute in New York City (with Ginsberg's permission).
            "TO LOUIS ZUKOFSKY, Poet born 1904 Lower East Side
New York, for his sincerity, rays of the object brought into focus
through clear physical eye, and music, particularly 'A' his poem of
a life which let speech become a movement of sounds. "   Louis
Zukofsky received an award for Literature in 1976.

418   "Consciousness and Practical Action. "   Counter Culture, The
        Creation of An Alternative Society, edited by Joseph Berke.
        London: Peter Owen Limited, 1969 (with Fire Books Lim-
        ited), pp. 172-181.
            Written informally, this essay offers Ginsberg's thoughts
on the uses of consciousness for practical political action.   In the
beginning he lingers with Hindu and Buddhist thought and the use of
LSD.   Then he enters the arena of discussion of consciousness.   He
poses fragmented questions and pursues the answers.   He asserts
that "In one sense, all history is gossip; or reconditioning or detoxi-
fication. ... "

419   "Declaration of Independence for Timothy Leary/Model State-
        ment in defense of the philosopher's personal freedom pro-
        posed by San Francisco Bay Area Prose Poets' Phalanxe. "
        Los Angeles Free Press, 16-22 July 1971, v. 8, n. 29,
        issue 365, p. 3.   Reprinted in the East Village Other, 10
        August 1971, v. 6, n. 36, p. 2.
            See original pamphlet by the same title.

420   "Encounters with Ezra Pound. "   In Lawrence Ferlinghetti, (ed.),

City Lights Anthology. San Francisco: City Lights Books, 197∢
pp. 9-21. See under ANTHOLOGY Section.

421 "An Exposition of William Carlos Williams' Poetics. " Loka
2, A Journal from Naropa Institute, New York: Doubleday,
1976, pp. 123-140.
Ginsberg describes the plight of American writers who
are "trying to find an American Language, using American local
diction, trying to find the rhythms of their own talk. " Ginsberg
concludes Williams can and should be used as a "standard you can
measure your own poetry against. " For "actually Williams is the
true hero of the first half of the American Century, carrying on the
work of Whitman. "

422 "The Fall of America Wins a Prize. " New York City: Gotham
Book Mart & Gallery, 1974. folder, 4 leaves. Available
through the Gotham Book Mart & Gallery, 41 W. 47th Street,
N. Y. , N. Y.
"This is the text of Allen Ginsberg's acceptance speech
for the National Book Award in Poetry, delivered by Peter Orlovsky
on April 18, 1974, at Alice Tully Hall, Lincoln Center, New York
City," prepared by Ginsberg.

423 "First Thought Best Thought" from the Spiritual Poetics Class,
July 29, 1974, Loka 1, A Journal from Naropa Institute,
New York: Doubleday, 1975, pp. 89-95.
Here is Ginsberg talking about breathing, chanting and
their relationship to making poetry. He talks about the discipline
of keeping a notebook and meditation as a tool to arrive at the
"mind. " The rest depends upon the effort of the person involved.
"First thought, best thought" relates to a conversation with C.
Trungpa about a "spontaneous chain poem" on which Allen was work-
ing.

424 "Focus on Poetry/An Article by Allen Ginsberg. " University
Review, February 1970, p. 17, 22, with photographs of
Ginsberg by Fred W. McDarrah. Copyright Allen Gins-
berg 1970.
This is a complete reprint of Allen Ginsberg's introduc-
tion to Louis Ginsberg's Morning in Spring and Other Poems, (New
York: Morrow and Company, Inc.), 1970.

"Get High Off the People--Smack the Enemy. " Berkeley Tribe
see "Ginsberg on Junk. "

425 "Ginsberg Asks 44 Questions About Leary. " Berkeley Barb,
20-26 September 1974, v. 20, n. 10, issue 475, n. p.
[Editor's Note: This article is the first of several reprints of the original "Om Ah Hum: 44 Temporary Questions on
Dr. Leary" (prepared on March 18, 1974) which ponders Timothy
Leary's recent actions and their ramifications. The other reprints
include: "Allen Ginsberg Asks 44 Questions About Tim Leary. "

City, 2-15 October 1974, v. 7, n. 49, p. 48; "Ginsberg: 44 Questions on Leary." Georgia Straight, 3-10 October 1974, v. 8, n. 364, p. 13; "Oh Ah Hum: Temporary Questions on Dr. Leary." Soho Weekly News, 7 November 1974, p. 10; "Allen Ginsberg Questions About Tim Leary." Win, 21 November 1974, v. X, n. 39, pp. 10-11; "Om Ha Hum 44 Temporary Questions on Tim Leary." San Francisco Phoenix, v. 2, n. 26, n. d., n. p.]

"Ginsberg: 44 Questions on Leary." Georgia Straight see "Ginsberg Asks 44 Questions About Leary."

426 "Ginsberg in Newcastle." Iron, Spring 1973, n. 1, pp. 2-3, with photograph. Excerpted as "From 'Ginsberg in Newcastle,'" in Madeira & Toasts for Basil Bunting's 75th Birthday. Highlands, N. C. : The Jargon Society, 1977, unpaged.
This is a prose statement by Ginsberg about his invitation to read at Morden Tower, Newcastle, England in 1965. "Morden Tower was famed afar, appropriately English-tongue poet of the Western hemisphere knew that Basil Bunting (companion and peer of the great word masters of the century) had found companions among the young in Newcastle who had answered the great call of Poesy.... Certainly happy circumstances for a poet, and happier to hear Bunting's concern--'Too many words, condense still more.' Thus the reading at Morden Tower altered my own poetic practice slightly toward greater economy of presentation. So I learned more reading at Morden Tower than I had at a hundred universities."

"Ginsberg: Left Should Organize JUNK LIBERATION FRONT Against Mafia." Georgia Straight see "Ginsberg on Junk."

427 "Ginsberg on Junk." Good Times, 17 April 1970, v. III, n. 16, p. 11 with photograph by Ted Benhari. [Editor's note: This article on the relationship of "junk" to the Mafia was circulated among several magazines at the same time. I believe that one of the original sources of this article was Good Times, but it is difficult to discern because of the nature of the underground press syndicate which shares articles, often without the proper credits. The reprinted versions are: "Allen Ginsberg on Mafia and Junk," Los Angeles Free Press, 22 May 1970, v. 7, n. 21, pp. 9, 11; "Ginsberg: Left Should Organize JUNK LIBERATION FRONT Against Mafia," Georgia Straight, 6-13 May 1970, p. 13; "Ginsberg Raps on Junkies' Fate," Harry 1 May 1970, v. 1, n. 13, p. 6; "Opium and ... the CIA," Quicksilver, 15-31 May 1971, v. III, n. 9, pp. 26-27; "Get High Off the People--Smack the Enemy," Berkeley Tribe, n. d. , 1971, v. 6, n. 10, issue 118, pp. 10-11.]
"Allen Ginsberg invited us over to his pad last Sunday for a rap. He is an extremely friendly, warm cat and we asked him to simply talk and let us know what he was into these days. We discussed Leary's trial, paranoia, and a few other things but the main interest of Ginsberg is junk and the Mafia which he explains in

the following transcription." Ginsberg comes down hard on junk. He documents his allegations with New York Times data. He finds the junk problem in "escalation ... the other aspect of the conspiracy is that all those junkies are giving their money to the Mafia because the Mafia is supplying the junk." He concludes "that the left has got to organize for the junkies."

428 "Ginsberg on Lowell." The Poetry Project Newsletter, 1 October 1977, n. 48, p. 7 (unpaged).
　　　Ginsberg reminisces about the times he had spent with Robert Lowell and the changes he had witnessed in the man through their interactions. It had been a long friendship of sorts: "Lowell and I met originally in 1959 when Peter Orlovsky, Gregory Corso, and I read at Harvard." Only "the Thursday before Lowell died "Ginsberg considered inviting Lowell out to "teach at Naropa." According to Ginsberg this statement comes from a telephone conversation which was edited by Frances Waldman, Anne Waldman's mother.

　　"Ginsberg Raps on Junkies' Fate." Harry see "Ginsberg on Junk."

　　"Ginsberg Talks About Speed." In The Agitator; A Collection of Diverse Opinions from America's Not-So-Popular Press see "Allen Ginsberg Comes Down on Speed."

　　"Ginsberg Talks About Speed." Door to Liberation see "Allen Ginsberg Comes Down on Speed."

429 Good Times, 28 January -10 February 1972, pp. 14-15.
　　　Two page (vertical) poster. Mind-infinity illustration with quote by Ginsberg: "We're in science fiction now. All the revolutions and the old methods and techniques for changing consciousness are bankrupt. We're back to magic, to--psychic life. Don't you know that power's a hallucination? The civil rights movement, Sheriff Rainey, Time Magazine, McNamara, Mao--it's all a hallucination, no one can get away with saying that's real. All public reality's a script, and anybody can write the script the way he wants. The warfare's psychic now. Whoever controls the language, the images, controls the race."

430 "The Great Rememberer." Saturday Review, 55:49 (December 2, 1972): 60-3.
　　　[From larger The Visions of the Great Rememberer, see BOOK section.] This was copyrighted in 1972 by Allen Ginsberg as the introduction to re-issue Visions of Cody by Jack Kerouac, to be published January, 1973 by McGraw-Hill. Here Ginsberg talks about Jack's value for the twentieth century, "young American" for he "struggled in the dark with the enormity of ... (his) ... soul, trying desperately to be a great rememberer redeeming life from darkness." Ginsberg talks about the "new section of the novel," "The Tape," which is "Cody (Neal Cassady) telling Jack the story of what it was like summer 1947. ..." Ginsberg carefully evaluates the wisdom of Kerouac and presents it to the "children" of America.

431 "How Kaddish Happened. " In Poetics of the New American
     Poetry. Ed. by Donald Allen and Warren Tallman. New
     York: Grove Press, Inc. , first edition, 1973, pp. 344-347.

432 "I learned a world from each one whom I loved. " [Allen Gins-
     berg.]
          Statement under cartoon titled, "Meditation" by Peter Max
     (1972), Long Island Press, 31 July 1972, p. 17.

433 "I Love Abbie Hoffman. " WIN, 10:6 (May 2, 1974): 19.

434 "Inspired by an Attack of Bell's Palsy: For the National Insti-
     tute of Arts and Letters. " Prepared "9:45 PM April 8,
     1969. " Available from The National Institute of Arts and
     Letters.

435 "Introduction to Gasoline. " In Poetics of the New Ameri-
     can Poetry. Ed. by Donald Allen and Warren Tallman.
     New York: Grove Press, Inc. , first edition, 1973, pp. 322-
     323.

436 " 'Junky' Restored/Guest Word. " New York Times Book Re-
     view, 6 February 1977, section 7, p. 35.
          [Editor's note: "This article has been adapted from Allen
     Ginsberg's introduction to a new edition of Wm. Burroughs' 'Junky'
     which Penguin Books will publish March 31. This edition restores
     material in the Burroughs manuscript that was deleted or altered by
     the original publisher, Ace Books, in 1953. "] Allen Ginsberg in this
     short piece describes his role in the first publication of "Junky. "
     Burroughs and he were in correspondence in the 50's and it is Gins-
     berg who acted as his "literary agent. " Carl Solomon, Ginsberg's
     "companion from NY State Psychiatric Institute, was given a job by
     his uncle, Mr. A. A. Wyn of Ace Books. " So it was Solomon who
     attempted to publish Burroughs' work. Anyway, despite all the prob-
     lems including the subject itself, the book came out edited: "Cer-
     tainly a shabby package; on the other hand, given our naiveté, a kind
     of brave miracle that the text actually was printed and read over
     the next decade by a million cognoscenti--who did appreciate the
     intelligent fact, the clear perception, precise bare language, direct
     syntax and mind pictures--as well as the enormous sociologic grasp,
     culture revolutionary attitude toward bureaucracy and law, and the
     stoic cold humor'd eye on crime. "

437 "Kerouac. " Rat, Subterranean News. 29 October-12 November
     1969, p. 17. Reprinted in Georgia Straight, 26 November-3
     December 1969, v. 3, n. 35, p. 11.
          This is a whole page devoted to Kerouac with a statement
     by Ginsberg recording his funeral at Lowell, Massachusetts, pre-
     pared on October 24, 1969 (from "Memory Garden," The Fall of
     America).

438 "Leary/Leary Defense Fund. " Helix, 9 April 1970, v. 11-15,
     p. 8.

See also "Ransom" in this section. "Allen Ginsberg spent the weekend at the University of Washington Campus, reading poems, chanting mantras, singing William Blake and raising money for Tim Leary's
defense fund.... Allen Ginsberg carried a message from Tim Leary.
Tim is presently in a mental institution and wants to hear from us.
Write to him at the Tim Leary Hospital, P. O. Box 3000, Vacavilly,
Calif." Ginsberg's statement realizes that money is the answer to
freeing Leary. "Some way must be found among us to fund Dr.
Leary's constitutional appeal, or alter the entire economic structure
of the law so that citizens kidnapped by police bureaucracy need not
be ransomed to freedom by victimized families."

"Lennon-Ono: Deporting the Great Swan" see "PEN Supports
Lennon-Ono"

439 "A Manifesto for Nonviolent Revolution." Win, 15 November
1972, v. 8, n. 18, p. 4. Prepared by Allen Ginsberg and
Ed Sanders.
        The list of "current signers" to this prose statement in-
clude: Allen Ginsberg, Maris Calais, Abbie Hoffman, David McReynolds, Peter Orlovsky, Dotson Rader, Jerry Rubin, Ed Sanders,
John and Leni Sinclair, Peter Stafford, Meyer Vishner.... Later
published in Tax Talk, October 1972, p. 1 (War Tax Resistance,
339 Lafayette Street, NY, NY 10012) with an abbreviated list of
signers "to date." [Tax Talk retains the same address as Win.]

440 "Mantra Text," from "Experimental College Course in Mantra
Chants--taught by Allen Ginsberg." Buffalo University.
February ? 1968.
        Selections from the Hindu include, "Hare Krishna ...
Gopala gopala devaki nandana gopala ... Hari om namo Shivaye ...
Om aing ghring cling chamunda vei vijay." Selections from Tibetan
include, "Om ara ba tsa na de de de de ... Om raksha raksha hum
hum hum/phat svaha ... Om tare tu tare turey/shoham tare tare
tare ... Om sri maitreya." One selection from Muslim is included:
"La illaha el (Lill) Allah who."

441 "mind consciousness be-in--san diego." Win, 1 April 1972,
v. 8, n. 6, pp. 14-15.
        Scenario for Buddhist and political ceremony. Prose in
the shape of a poem. January 1972. See "Allen Ginsberg on San
Diego/Mind Consciousness Be-In." in Los Angeles Free Press, 14-
20 April 1972, v. 9, n. 15, issue 404, p. 2, for annotation.

442 "My Free Bill of Rights." Daily Planet, 24 January 1970,
1:VIII, p. 4, with cartoon of police turning off mike on
Allen Ginsberg by Conway.
        "The following article reflects the early reflections of a
poet reflecting upon his first tropical encounter with the Heavy Metal
Kids." The Ginsberg statement included the following: "Rights
which were curtailed in Miami: 1) Freedom of Religion (re: Chanting); 2) Freedom of Speech (mikes cut off); 3) Right to assemble
peacefully; 4) Right to petition the government...."

443   "N. I. A. L. Grant in Arts & Letters. " Prepared on behalf of
       William Seward Burroughs by Allen Ginsberg, February 15,
       1975, for the National Institute of Arts and Letters. It is
       available through the Institute in New York City (with Gins-
       berg's permission).
           "To William Seward Burroughs, invisible man, explorer
of souls & Cities; whose exact-prosed JUNKY showed process of
police-state chemical conditioning;... " Burroughs received the award
in literature in 1975. As a result the citation has become part of
the published records of the Institute.

444   Nickel Review, 9 January 1970, v. 4, n. 18, p. 5.
           [See also "Allen Ginsberg Comes Down on Speed. "] This
is a statement on speed arranged in the shape of a cross next to a
story (typed on a tombstone) by a girl who dies from the use of
speed. This is Ginsberg's "general declaration to the underground
community" about the negative effect of speed.

445   " 'No Fuss on Blues'/Ginsberg's Reply to the University. " West-
       port Trucker, 2 February-7 March 1972, v. 2, n. 21, (45?) p. 5.
           This is Ginsberg's Reply to the University of Missouri,
Kansas City regarding the publication of his poem, "Troust Street
Blues" (from First Blues) by Ken Kesey in the student newspaper
(Westport Trucker). According to Ginsberg, Kesey was editing this
paper while guest lecturing there. Obscenity charges were rendered
toward the publication of the poem.

446   "No Money, No War. " The East Village Other 5:7. (January 21,
       1970): 2. Reprinted in WIN VI: 4 (March 1970): back cover.
           According to the poet, this prose statement which was
made into a book was written for the War Tax Resistance (W. R. L.)
at 339 Lafayette Street, New York, New York. (Pete Seeger also
composed music for this.)

447   "Nobody publishes a word that is not the cowardly robot crav-
       ings of a depraved mentality. " Everyman, Summer 1974,
       p. 2. Quote by Ginsberg under picture by Marianne Gell-
       man.

448   "Notes for Howl and Other Poems" (Independence Day, 1959).
       In America a Prophecy, A New Reading of American Poetry
       from Pre-Columbian Times to the Present. New York:
       Random House, 1973, p. 382.

449   "Notes for Howl and Other Poems" (Prose). In Poetics
       of the New American Poetry. Ed. by Donald Allen and
       Warren Tallman. New York: Grove Press, Inc. , first
       edition, 1973, pp. 318-321.

       "Oh Ah Hum: Temporary Questions on Dr. Leary. " Soho
       Weekly News see "Ginsberg Asks 44 Questions About
       Leary"

"Om Ha Hum: 44 Temporary Questions on Tim Leary." San
Francisco Phoenix see "Ginsberg Asks 44 Questions About
Leary"

450 "On Improvised Poetics." In Poetics of the New American
Poetry. Ed. by Donald Allen and Warren Tallman. New
York: Grove Press, Inc., first edition, 1973, p. 350.

451 "On Mindfulness/Presentation to Conference on Life Cycle Planning." Part I, II, III, IV. One page statement signed and
dated by the poet, "April 21, 1977."
This is a statement outlining a meditation practice. In-
quiries regarding this should be directed c/o Washington Dharmadattu,
3220 Idaho Avenue, Washington, D. C., (202) 686-5307.
Part IV describes the entire practice as that which "is
called in Sanskrit Samatha, Mindfulness, an old and basic style of meditation." Two suggestions are offered for reference: Beginner's Mind,
Zen Mind by Suzuki Roshi and Meditation in Action by Chögyam Trungpa.

"On Speeeeeed." The Spectator see "Allen Ginsberg Comes
Down on Speed"

452 "On the New Cultural Radicalism." Partisan Review, 39:3
(1972): 423-4.
Symposium on "Art, Culture and Conservatism." Part I,
"The Idea of the Avant-Garde," Part II, "On the New Cultural Conservatism." This essay by Allen Ginsberg is Number 9 in Part II. In
January 1972, Ginsberg finds through the "Harris Poll, in the New
York Post, November 11, 1971, p. 18" that "65% of the American
Public found fighting Vietnam morally wrong". He then uses this
to indicate that the middle class in America has come around. "For
now we are all in the same boat," middle class and revolutionaries
alike. Ginsberg is hinting at joint community effort for the future.

"Opium and ... the CIA." Quicksilver see "Ginsberg on
Junk"

453 "PEN Supports Lennon-Ono." La Star (Reseda, California) 9
November 1972, n. p., from Georgia Straight(?). Reprinted
as "Lennon-Ono: Deporting The Great Swan," an introduction to an article by Jonathan Green in It, 2-16 November
1972, n. 141, p. 8.
PEN is a "prestigious international writers' organization."
The text of the PEN statement prepared by Allen Ginsberg is included
in full.

454 "Poetry, Violence, and The Trembling Lambs." In Poetics
of the New American Poetry. Ed. by Donald Allen and
Warren Tallman. New York: Grove Press, Inc., first
edition, 1973, pp. 331-333.

455 "Poets' Colloquium." Loka 2, A Journal from Naropa Institute, New York: Doubleday, 1976, p. 164.

This article is edited from the transcription of a three hour discussion with C. Trungpa which took place on June 20, 1975, at 10:30 p.m. in Boulder, Colorado. Two photographs include Allen Ginsberg, Anne Waldman, Robert Bly, William Burroughs, Gregory Corso, and Philip Whalen.

456 "Prose contribution to Cuban Revolution. " In Poetics of the New American Poetry. Ed. by Donald Allen and Warren Tallman. New York: Grove Press, Inc. , 1st ed. , 1973, pp. 334-344.

This is a long journal-like entry of Ginsberg's from Athens, Greece, October 16, 1961, which records his thoughts, ramblings and associations which lead him to thoughts on Cuba and the revolution. In conclusion he states, "I'm NOT down on the Cubans or anti their revolution, it's just that it's important to make clear in advance, in front, what I feel about life. Big statements saying Viva Fidel are / would be / meaningless and just 2-dimensional politics. Publish as much of this letter as interests you, as prose contribution to Cuban Revolution. " The essay was supposedly reprinted in a pamphlet by John Sinclair in Ann Arbor, Michigan.

457 "Ransom. " Good Times, 13 March 1970, v. III, n. 11, p. 3.

See also "Leary/Leary Defense Fund" in this section. This is Ginsberg's statement on Leary's behalf. "I guess the main thing is money so that Dr. Leary can challenge the entire constitutionality of his imprisonment.... " He cites Dr. Spock's "purchase of legal freedom for $150,000 legal costs. "

458 "Read Any Good Books Lately?" Win, 15 June 1970, v. 6, n. 11, p. 25.

"Read Any Good Books Lately?" includes the response by Ginsberg (among others) to a Win survey of "movement activists ... titled 'Communication for the Seventies. ' To this end we have requested a list of three books (or records, pamphlets, plays, etc.) which at this time the participants feel will have the most meaning for the 1970's. " Ginsberg's response: "The Job by William S. Burroughs (Grove). Essays/interviews-instructions for psychorevolutionary education and mentality. Ezra Pound Reading Cantos 3, 16, 49, 81, 92, 106 and 115 at Spoleto, 1966 (Applause Productions SP 412, 16 W. 61st St. , NYC). Perfect-vowelled human voice. Earth Household by Gary Snyder (New Directions) and Four Changes (pamphlet, anonymously printed and unsigned by Snyder--in Win ecology issue and elsewhere). Proposals and blueprints for psychosocial direction. "

459 "Remarks on Leary's Politics of Ecstasy. " Village Voice, 12 December 1968, v. XIV, n. 9, p. 8.

Although this is a 1968 publication it is included because of its reappearance (in a revised version) later as the introduction to Leary's book, Jail Notes. (See Introductions Sections.) According to Ginsberg, this and the later statement (1970) were originally prepared for Leary's Politics of Ecstasy, but were published in Jail Notes. Allen Ginsberg places Leary within the entire spectrum of agnostic thought and its resurgence in 20th-century American culture as "the new consciousness. " In fact, "Dr. Leary is a hero of American consciousness. " Ginsberg depicts Leary's mission (LSD) as "inevitable" given the state of "the whole professional civilized world. " It is a "comedy" that this "Messiah" had to face. Ginsberg continues with comments on the writing of Leary's book, The Politics of Ecstasy in which "Leary tells the tale of his tribe. "

460 Review of Speed, by William Burroughs. It, 19 May-2 June 1971, p. 21.
        "Speed shows traces of characteristic Burroughsian laconism and precision regarding genius fact. ... Senior had done his first job with the junk Universe. Where will consciousness go next generation? Out into the solar system? Transcending these, for other worlds ... "

460a Solomon, David (ed.). The Marihuana Papers. New York: Bobbs-Merrill, 1966. Introduction by Alfred R. Lindesmith.
        Although this book predates the decade under inspection, it is included because it is often referred to by Allen Ginsberg, even in his more recent essays and interviews. Aside from an acknowledgment to the poet, it contains an essay "First Manifesto to End the Bringdown" from pages 183-195. "In the following essay, written especially for this volume, Ginsberg presents an impassioned defense of marihuana based on the evidence that supports the fact that the consciousness-expanding effects of the herb constitute 'a reality kick. '" There are two parts: "the first half of the essay was written while the author was smoking marihuana. 7:30 P. M. Nov. 13, 1965, San Francisco, California, U. S. A. Kosmos.... (The second part), 2 A. M. Nov. 14, 1965. "

461 "Some Different Considerations in Mindful Arrangement of Open Verse Forms on the Page. " In City Lights Journal. San Francisco, California: City Lights Books, 1978, n. 4, p. 137.
        Prepared April 2, 1977, at Jack Kerouac School of Disembodied Poetics, Naropa Institute and originally printed in fewer than 100 copies for classroom distribution.

462 "Some Metamorphases of Personal Poetry. " In Poetics of the New American Poetry. Ed. by Donald Allen and Warren Tallman. New York: Grove Press, Inc. , first edition, 1973, pp. 348-349.

        "Speed Is a No-No. " Harry see "Allen Ginsberg Comes Down on Speed. "

        "Speed Kills--Ginsberg. " Chinook see "Allen Ginsberg Comes Down on Speed. "

        "Spread a Little Happiness. " Nola Express see "Allen Ginsberg Comes Down on Speed. "

463 "Symposium: The Writer's Situation II. " New American Re-

view, 10 (August, 1970): 212-213.
        Includes a copy of Allen Ginsberg's response to a New American Review questionnaire written with parts of sentences and word equations in the margins of the form, signed and dated, October 29, 1969. One interesting word equation in response to question 2 (Do you believe that art and politics should be kept apart?):

" arts   =   mind   =   Biology

                                =   Sacred Heart"

" politics   =   1976   =   Biology

464   "T. S. Eliot Entered My Dreams. " In City Lights Journal.
        San Francisco: City Lights Books, 1978, n. 4, pp. 61-65.

465   "Thoughts on Israeli Arguments. " Liberation, 18:6 (2/74): 14.
        "During the last days of the Yom Kippur War, Daniel Berrigan gave a speech to the Arab Student Association in Washington, D. C. The speech launched a heated controversy which is still growing and which, to date, has been mixed in the question of whether or not Dan was anti-Semitic in his criticism of Israel. " In Ginsberg's opinion "Dan Berrigan's speech began good debate, necessary debate, break up of stock-in-trade illusions, opened space to talk and think about Israel's identity in a way that space had not been opened for me by any Jewish or Arabist commentaries that I encountered. "

466   "Time: Squeezing the Most Out of It/We Asked 32 Busy,
        Successful People How They Do It. " TWA Ambassador,
        November 1977, v. 10, n. 11, p. 23, by George Sullivan.
        On page 23 there is a small photograph and quote by Ginsberg: "I write my mind on paper once, and never more revise, unless I have to, for inattention at moment of composition. That way I speak once as if at edge of grave--no time to correct what's uttered once. That's (after Kerouac) the 'secret' of time management in poetic creation. "

467   "To Young or Old Listeners: Setting Blake's SONGS to Music,
        and a Commentary on the SONGS. " Blake Newsletter, 4:3,
        Winter 1971, pp. 98-103.
        Reprint of prose liner notes for Blake record, prepared Dec. 14-15, 1969. According to the Abstracts of English Studies (v. 19, n. 10, June 1976) "Ginsberg explains how he was inspired to set Blake's Songs of Innocence and Experience to music. In his mind's outer eye, he says he heard Blake's voice pronouncing 'The Sun Flower' and 'The Sick Rose. ' He wished to articulate musically the significance of each magic syllable of Blake's poems. He then specifically analyzes his working out of many of the individual poems in the Songs. " See also "Blake Notes" in this section.

468   "Two Interesting Dreams. " IO, 8, 1971, p. 80.
        The first is dated July 8, 1970, and the second September 2, 1970. The first focuses on "Police State conditions in USA" and the second on images of "butchering. "

469 "Watergate Apocatastasis G. Gordon Liddy--From Millbrook to
  Vancouver Airport." Georgia Straight, 14-21 June 1973,
  v. 7, n. 297, pp. 12-13 with two photographs of Ginsberg.
  Reprinted in Berkeley Barb, 29 June-5 July 1973, pp. 10-11.
  "Leary is probably the number one political prisoner in
the US because he's the last of the great '60's public figures who's
still under indictment for conspiracy and in jail for his published
speeches and writings." Ginsberg concludes after questioning at the
Canadian border about his previous use of marijuana that "so a further fallout of the whole Watergate Conspiracy has been a further
restriction of civil rights at the national border crossings" because
of the "new kinds of information" ("new policies") being generated
by the Government via telex. He ties this information gathering to
Tim Leary because it was the same G. Gordon Liddy who was responsible for the "illegal raids in Leary's experimental commune in
Millbrook. Then Liddy later, working in the White House with Hunt,
Colson and others, formed a Special Narcotic Investigation Unit ...
from 71 to 72..." And so on, Ginsberg neatly ties all of this together. He concludes with the work he did on Alfred McCoy's The
Politics of Heroin in Indochina and the "booklet Leary is concluding,
NEUROL-GIC (serialized in the Straight)."

470 "Watergate Statement." Changes, 3 September 1973. Dictated
  by phone to Susan Graham (revised).
  Specifically, Ginsberg in this statement, scrutinizes our
government's involvement with the "international narcotics traffic ...
more important than the impeachment of Nixon--which would in itself
be charming were there a suitable Presidential replacement--would
be the public realization that the Watergate gang was composed of
Narcotics Agents."

471 "What Is Literary Pollution?" Camels Coming Newsletter, n. 3,
  n. p., front cover.
  "Recently, we asked a number of people what they thought
literary pollution was. This is what they said: ... (Ginsberg) ...
What is literary pollution? Immediate association, first thought, is
plethora of books mimeo mags papers arriving in mail and more in
bookstores, wherein's reprinted every body and soul's amateur celes-
tial ravings and scribblings. More than eye can read. Over-load
of poetic information. A million authors can't be read, even by
most well-meaning scholar. Space age proliferation of written papers
and conspicuous consumption of new language. Towers of Babel!
So I shut up and meditate an hour a day, silence."

472 "What Six Nice People Found In The Government's Drawers."
  Oui, February 1977, v. 6, n. 2, pp. 116-117, compiled by
  Anita Hoffman.
  Ginsberg discusses materials the FBI had in their files
concerning him.

473 "When the Mode of the Music Changes the Walls of the City
  Shake." In Poetics of the New American Poetry. Ed. by
  Donald Allen and Warren Tallman. New York: Grove Press,
  Inc., first edition, 1973, pp. 324-330.

474 "Why Is God Love, Jack?" Earth, Air, Fire and Water.
edited by Frances Monson McCullough. New York: Coward,
McCann & Geoghegan, 1971.
"If I look funny, or get up in public and say I am a homosexual, take drugs, and hear Blake's voice, then people who are
heterosexual, don't take drugs, and hear Shakespeare's voice may
feel freer to do what they want and be what they are." (Allen Ginsberg). Includes short biography of Ginsberg on p. 175.

475 "William S. Burroughs, novelist of New York." Nominations
for Membership in the Department of Literature 1977. New
York: National Institute of Arts and Letters, (unpaged),
p. 5.
The text of the nomination prepared by Allen Ginsberg
for William S. Burroughs reads: "A major common-sense theorist
and teacher to Beat Generation writers decades ago, he has continued shattering and changing laws against Word and Image thus
altering U.S. Consciousness in succeeding generations with novels
of beauty, practical genius, and innovative aesthetic: Naked Lunch,
Soft Machine, Nova Express, Ticket that Exploded, Wild Boys and
Exterminator! Some works whose very titles have become cultural
passwords, and whose texts are much memorized by myriad high
school geniuses from New Jersey to San Francisco."

476 "Writers Protest Grant." Los Angeles Free Press, 15-25
December 1972, v. 9, n. 50, issue 439, p. 8.
Allen Ginsberg is one of the "undersigned writers and
editors" who "wish strongly to protest the Ford Foundation's recent
$50,000 grant to the International Association for Cultural Freedom
in Paris as 'emergency assistance' for the publication costs of Encounter, published in England." The group sees the above as an
insult to their literary endeavors which have so often been neglected
by the Foundation. "We urge the Ford Foundation and other organizations concerned with cultural endeavors in the United States to
take seriously their responsibility to our literary magazines."

B. FRENCH TRANSLATIONS

477 "En Marge de Howl et Autres Poems." ("Notes written on
finally recording 'Howl.'") ellipse, Québec: Faculté des
Arts, Université de Sherbrooke 8/9 (1971): 124-127.
Reprinted from Fantasy, Spoken Word Series, 7006,
copyright 1959 by Fantasy Records Inc.

478 "Henry Michaux." Les Cahiers de L'Herne. Paris: Raymond
Bellour, n.d. (translation by Pierre Allen), pp. 35-38.
Les Cahiers De L'Herne offers a varied collection of
articles which are international in scope in celebration of the older
French poet, Henri Michaux. The collection opens with an essay by
the poet himself. Ginsberg's article begins with his invitation to the
French writers in the style of Michaux (Cocteau, Céline and Genet)
through Carl Solomon during 1948 (the year Ginsberg spent in an

asylum). Michaux is a French poet who experimented heavily in hallucinogenic drugs and came back to articulately speak of it. According to Ginsberg, he was a recluse, but agreed to see him each time. Ginsberg recalls his meetings with Michaux in Paris and comments upon his perspective. "The visions of those who do drugs interest me less and less, the manner in which they report their experiences and what they do following it interest me, more and more." This was quite a mature vision for 1961. The essay ends after much description of meetings with Michaux, Corso and Burroughs. Ginsberg chants in honor of the great French poet.

VI.   MISCELLANEOUS PRINT MATERIALS

A.   LETTERS AND CORRESPONDENCE

"Abbie Hoffman-Political Poet * An Open Letter from Allen
Ginsberg to Gerald Lefcourt, Abbie's Attorney." Berkeley
Barb see "Letters from Ginsberg...." Georgia Straight

"Allen Ginsberg Defends Abbie/Letters to the Movement."
Liberation see "Letters from Ginsberg...." Georgia
Straight

479   As Ever: The Collected Correspondence of Allen Ginsberg and
Neal Cassady. Edited and introduced by Barry Gifford.
Berkeley, California: Creative Arts Book Co., 1977. Fore-
ward by Carolyn Cassady. Afterword by Allen Ginsberg.
Excerpt reprinted as: "An Introductory Note To As Ever: ..."
San Francisco Review of Books, May 1977, v. 3, n. 1, pp.
19-20, with photo.
Letters of Allen Ginsberg, Neal Cassady, Carolyn Cassady, Gregory Corso and Peter Orlovsky appear through the courtesy
of the Special Collections Division of Butler Library, Columbia University, New York; The Humanities Research Center of the University of Texas at Austin; Carolyn Cassady; and Allen Ginsberg. "The
letters are printed exact to their time, one paragraph removed to
protect living sensibilities, and some typos corrected, some footnotes added. The letters speak for themselves, regarding love and
inquisitiveness and constancy." Ginsberg's "Afterword" begins on p.
219 and was written on June 3, 1977.

479a The Beat Book, Arthur W. Knight and Glee Knight (eds.).
Pennsylvania: n.p., 1974, Comprises Volume 4 of the
unspeakable visions of the individual. It includes a letter
to Peter Orlovsky, a letter to Harold Schulman, and a letter
to Mark Van Doren by Ginsberg.

480   "Dear Readers of the Georgia Straight." Georgia Straight,
20-27 September 1973, v. 7, n. 311, p. 1, letter.
"According to pacifist Chief Dave Dellinger, Mr. Tom
Fourcade (sic) in jail with him levelled finger and said we ruined
Abbey and Jerry and we'll ruin you if you don't watch out: The
tape I made is of Dellinger telling the anecdote. Despite overground
and alas! underground press disinterest in the act of purification,
Dave Dellinger, Rennie Davis, Jeff Nightbyrd, Sherri Whitehead and
others of Miami Convention Coalition did fast seven days on fruit, 7
days on fruit juice, and thirty days on water during last year's Miami

Demonstration Retrials. Om Ah Hum. Allen Ginsberg.... I'll
be in Buddhist study till Xmas. Hare Krishna. "
　　　　See also: Forcade, Tom. Open letter. Georgia
Straight, 26 July-2 August 1973, under LETTERS TO GINSBERG in
the SECONDARY WORKS section; and "Allen Ginsberg ... Rennie
Davis and the Underground Press." Georgia Straight, 21-28 June
1973 under INTERVIEWS in the PRIMARY WORKS section.

　　　"Defend Abbie Hoffman and Individual Rights/Ginsberg writes
　　　　to one and all. " Hi, young people's newspaper see "Let-
　　　　ters from Ginsberg.... " Georgia Straight

481　"Free Willie. " nelley heathen, 15 August 1973, p. 13, with
　　　　photograph of Ginsberg in devotional setting.
　　　　Letter "To The State, Re: Religion" dated June 21,
1971 for Rev. Wilbur Minzey, B35181, PO Box A-E, San Luis
Obispo, California. This letter by Ginsberg ("not submitted in
time") on behalf of Rev. W. Minzey of the Shiva Fellowship who
received a jail sentence for the use of "cannibis as part of devotional ritual in the practice of his religion... "

482　"From an Early Letter to John Hollander. " in The New Naked
　　　　Poetry, Recent American Poetry in Open Forms. Indian-
　　　　apolis: Bobbs-Merrill Co. Inc. , 1976, p. 84.
　　　　This is an excerpt from a letter to John Hollander about
"Howl" and its poetic "construction. "

　　　"Ginsberg Makes Plea for Hoffman Defense. " CPS (College
　　　　Press Service) see "Letters from Ginsberg.... " Georgia
　　　　Straight

483　"Ginsberg on Trantino. " Liberation, February 1975, v. 19,
　　　　n. 2, p. 25.
　　　　"Tommy Trantino is serving a life sentence in Lees-
burg, New Jersey. His writing can be reduced to neat little statement or phrases, but it speaks an anger against authority that
reaches beyond the prison walls.... Allen Ginsberg writes on behalf of Thomas Trantino and connects him as a writer through Samuel Greenberg to Sherwood Anderson and Hart Crane. He refers to
Trantino as 'messenger from the Abyss of Light ... a caller of the
Great Call. '"
　　　　The letter is addressed "To Whom it May Concern" and
is signed and dated "1/7/73. "

484　"Ginsberg Won't Pay for Vietnam. " Chinook, 26 March 1970,
　　　　v. 2, n. 11, p. 6.
　　　　Letter to Mr. David Kennedy, Secretary of the Treasury.
Ginsberg refuses to pay his federal taxes on the grounds that it is
used for a war in which he does not believe. Ginsberg concludes,
"thus if our tax system is so unequitable that it cannot find a rea-
sonable alternative, such as payment of these taxes into a fund which
is not used in this war, then I will be relieved to go to jail rather
than pay money to that war. " A note for further information is at-

tached by an organization called War Tax Resistance in New York City.

484a   Legal Document: Before The Professional Practices Council, State of Florida, Department of Education. Case no. 70124, Cecil D. Hardesty as Superintendent of Schools, Duval County, Jacksonville, Florida vs. Kathryn F. Watson. 1970-71.
There are a total of 151 pages in this document which contains supporting materials (as appendix to motion) including letters, minutes and newspaper clippings. Amidst this compilation is a letter (pp. 121-123) dated December 22, 1970, submitted on behalf of K. Watson by Allen Ginsberg.
"Motion to Quash" investigation for said charge (pl): "You are charged with distributing to your class the Allen Ginsberg poem 'America,' the same being an act to which students and parents objected strenuously and which act may constitute personal conduct which seriously reduces your effectiveness as an employee of the school board."

485   "A letter to Claude Pélieu and his translator, Mary Beach, from Allen Ginsberg; date 'fugitive' (Ginsberg); abridged by Michael Andre." Unmuzzled Ox, February 1972, v. 1, n. 2, pp. 19-20.
This is a letter from Ginsberg recollecting an exchange he had with a man named DeRoux in Paris. Ginsberg attempts to clarify statements he made to DeRoux about contemporary literature because there is a misunderstanding of Allen's opinions used out of context.

486   "Letters from Ginsberg/Abbie Hoffman-Political Poet * An Open Letter from Allen Ginsberg to Gerald Lefcourt, Abbie's Attorney." Georgia Straight, 20-27 September 1973, v. 7, n. 311, pp. 4-5, 21. Reprinted as: "Abbie Hoffman-Political Poet...." Berkeley Barb, 5-11 October 1973, v. 18, n. 13, issue 425, pp. 4-5, 14; "Ginsberg Makes Plea for Hoffman Defense." CPS (College Press Service), 6 October 1973, n. 5, pp. 5-6; "Defend Abbie Hoffman and Individual Rights...." Hi, young people's newspaper, 4 October 1973, v. 5, n. 23, pp. 1, 7, 12; "Allen Ginsberg Defends Abbie/Letters to the Movement." Liberation, Sept.-Oct. 1973, v. 18, n. 2, pp. 7, 43; "Requests for Help/Info Inc. / Appeal on Behalf of Abbie Hoffman." Magic Ink, 14 October 1973, pp. 61-65.
This is a copy of the letter written in the defense of Abbie Hoffman who was "arrested for cocaine dealing." Ginsberg calls for a cleaning up of "the actual 'hard drug' mess in America... The real drug problem in America is that government narcotics bureaucracies and organized crime have had a status quo relationship for decades...." Ginsberg appeals to history in the name of Abbie Hoffman. "Threat of life behind bars for Hoffman over cocaine sale ... is an image of bureaucratic dictatorship and confusion, it is a misrule and chaos, National Folly.... OH AH HUM ... Recommending Hare Krishna to one and all. Allen Ginsberg."

"Requests for Help/Info Inc./Appeal on Behalf of Abbie Hoffman." Magic Ink see "Letters from Ginsberg. . . . " Georgia Straight

487 "Sisterbrother Allen Says To Say Ah!" nelley heathen, 15 August 1973, p. 15.

B. PAMPHLETS

488 "Allen Ginsberg." Translated by Simon Vinkenoog. Pamphlet of Ginsberg poems in translation with accompanying English. Rotterdam: Holland Poetry International Festival, June 19-22, 1973.
Includes "Op Neal's As" ("On Neal's Ashes"); "Proef Milarepa" ("Milarepa Taste"); "Hūm Bom!" ("Hūm Bom!"); "Al Stublieft Meester" ("Please Mister"); "Wat zou je doen als je het kwijtraakte?" ("What would you do if you lost it?"); and "Elegie voor Neal Cassady" ("Elegie for Neal Cassady").

489 Chicago Trial Testimony/Allen Ginsberg. San Francisco: City Lights Books, 1975. Cover by Pat Ryan.
Transcripts from the 1969 "Chicago Seven" trial which appears in comic book form. "City Lights Trashcan Series No. 1."

490 City Lights in North Dakota/The Poet Looks at Industry and Ecology. Introduction by John Little. 26 pp.
"This pamphlet consists of extracts taken from four openmike sessions held during the 1974 writers conference at the University of North Dakota. These writers ... were invited to campus as poets.... The open-mike sessions were just that. No format or subject was given in advance. The poets were free to talk about anything that interested them and to respond to questions that interested the audience. Nor did we inform the poets before the sessions that these comments would be used in this manner. So the result is a dialogue, not of experts, but poets and North Dakotans, expressing their concern for the relationship of industry, ecology, and the people and non-human things that are effected by that relationship. The pamphlet and video tape were made possible by a grant to the English Dept. from the North Dakota Committee for the Humanities and Public Issues."

491 Declaration of Independence For Dr. Timothy Leary, July 4, 1971/ Model Statement in Defense of the Philosophers Personal Freedom. Proposed by San Francisco Bay Area Prose Poets' Phalanx. San Francisco: Hermes Free Press, 1971 (July). Limited Ed. Pamphlet prepared by Allen Ginsberg, and signed by 29 others, "Poets, Essayists, and Novelists."
This is a statement which appeals to the Swiss government "to release Dr. Timothy Leary from provisional extraditional arrest, not cooperate in extraditing Dr. Leary to America. We recommend to Swiss and all other governments that they grant our

fellow Author Philosopher safe political asylum to complete his work--exploration of his consciousness, vocal literary expression of that unique individual Person whose presence is held sacred in all humane and gnostic democratic nations, and ever enshrined in their literary monuments, witness Whitman and Thoreau for America...."

492 "For L. N." Epitaphs for Lorine. Penland, North Carolina: The Jargon Society, 1973, unpaged, p. 15. Composed and printed at the Moneytree Press, Champaign, Illinois. 1,000 copies, privately distributed.

493 "General Purposes and Objectives." Excerpted from Naropa Institute Study Report for North Central Accreditation Committee. April, 1977. Prepared by Allen Ginsberg. "Touched up by Michael Brownstein and Anne Waldman."
   Fifteen-page document defining the purposes and objectives of Naropa.

494 May Day Speech by Jean Genet. Description by Allen Ginsberg. San Francisco: City Lights Books, 1970.
   Ginsberg describes "May Day 1970 at Yale" at which time the entire campus was shut down. At this convocation it was Genet who opened the program with his keynote on racism. Ginsberg finds "this classic discourse, a true commencement exercise marking the historic Graduation of white mentality to a 'delicacy of heart' hitherto forbidden in fear and greed...." According to a Ginsberg note, "The Appendix--Analysis of Establishment centers of hypnosis and repression was not read aloud in the Green at New Haven May Day 1970, but was added by M. Genet as a nine-paragraph'd thoughtful index of our civilization's mortal ills, a communicable diagnosis."
   Editor's note: "As the occasion for Yale's May Day Rally and Genet's speech as well as publication of this pamphlet is the series of political trials persecuting the Black Panther Party...."

495 New Year Blues. New York: The Phoenix Book Shop, 1972, unpaged. 7¼ x 5¼ (horizontal). 20 pp.
   New Year Blues consists of two poems "Christmas Blues," and "MacDougal Street Blues." Note: "These are first experiment blues lyrics, one written waiting turn in St. Mark's Church Xmas open poetry reading, and the other midnite in Feenjon's basement coffeeshop waiting to do hour's set backroom 1 A.M. Forms adapted from Richard Rabbit Brown's James Alley Blues (C-F-G Chords) as transcribed in The Blues Line by Eric Sackheim, Grossman, New York 1969 and heard on Harry Smith's Folkways American Folk Songs collection, New York 1952." (Allen Ginsberg.) "This first edition of New Year Blues is limited to twenty-six copies, lettered A to Z, not for sale, and one hundred copies, numbered and signed by the author.

496 Notes After an Evening with William Carlos Williams. Portents, 17 n.d.
   A pamphlet which is copyrighted by Allen Ginsberg. Portents is published by Samuel Charters. Cover: "Allen Ginsberg Wishing Him the Best. William Carlos Williams." March 12, 1952.

497   Sad Dust Glories, Poems During Work Summer in Woods.
Berkeley, Calif.: The Workingman's Press, 1975. (Distributed by Serendipity Books, 1790 Shattuck Avenue, Berkeley, Calif. 94709)
"Originally some of these poems appeared in KuKu and Bastard Angel." The content is divided into three sections: "Green Notebooks," "To the Dead," "For Sale."

C. CONTRIBUTIONS TO WORKS BY OTHERS

Introductions, Forewords and Afterwords

498   Brooks, Eugene. Rites of Passage. Introductions by Allen Ginsberg and Louis Ginsberg. New York: Eugene Brooks, 1973, pp. v-viii.
In Allen Ginsberg's introduction entitled, "Brother Poet" he establishes the reader's knowledge of his relationship to Eugene. He then evaluates the poetry, "So this poetry realizes mortal feeling, and that amounts to a vision, because it's not in the papers or on T.V." Onward he pushes, critically analyzing the major poems, commenting and evaluating. Conclusively he finds, "Outcry sounds agnostic leap of imagination--the citizen (lawyer in fact) poet finally makes use of his vocational language in combination with scientific temperment and poetic inspiration to state his mortal case to the Supreme Judge. Om ah Hum." The Ginsberg collection copies are inscribed by Ginsberg as gifts to "Nanda" and dated "27 July 1972."

499   Burroughs, William S. Junky. Introduction by Allen Ginsberg. New York: Penguin Books, 1977, pp. v-x. (originally, New York: A.A. Wyn, 1953).
Ginsberg's introduction provides the historical context to his relationship to Burroughs, particularly regarding the publication of Junky. "I am interested in the cultural fate of this book & curious how a later generation, perhaps uninterested in the historical shock the book created in its time among its friends, would react to the eternal qualities of prose mind that Kerouac, myself and others first were amazed by in Burroughs' early work.... Burroughs has created not only metaphors, but living generations with minds of their own."

500   Burroughs, William S., Jr. Speed. Introduction by Allen Ginsberg. New York: Olympia Press, 1970.

501   Charters, Ann. Kerouac: A Biography. Foreword by Allen Ginsberg. San Francisco: Straight Arrow Books, 1973, p. 9.
"Ann Charters loved Kerouac's art, did his first Bibliography with/for him while alive, cherished his scripture and literary soul-might, researched with dignity the interior of his novels and family, spoke many years with his friends, and applied her vast tactful scholarship as a master musician-archivist of jazz to the understanding of his musical sound as American lonely Prose Trumpeter

of drunken Buddha Sacred Heart. " Ginsberg, of course, is mentioned throughout the text.

502 Dowden, George. A Bibliography of Works by Allen Ginsberg, October 1943 to July 1, 1967. Foreword by Allen Ginsberg. San Francisco, California: City Lights Books, 1971.

503 Flanagan, Harley. Stories and Illustrations by Harley. Introduction by Allen Ginsberg. N. P. : Charlatan Press, 1976, p. 1.
    In this book of color reproductions of paintings and photographs there is an introduction prepared by Ginsberg on May 6, 1976 in NYC.

504 Gay Sunshine, Winter 1978, n. 35, p. 29.
    "Document received from the Hands of Gavin Arthur and its authenticity vouched for by Allen Ginsberg, San Francisco 1967 (previously unpublished). " To this account of a sexual encounter between Gavin Arthur and Edward Carpenter there is a short introduction written by Allen Ginsberg and dated July 1, 1972.

505/6 Ginsberg, Louis. Morning in Spring; and Other Poems. Introduction by Allen Ginsberg. New York: Morrow and Company, Inc. , 1970.
    From Ginsberg's introduction: "confronting my father's poems at the end of his life, I weep at his meekness and his reasons, at his wise entrance into his own mortality and his silent recognition of that Pitiful Immensity he records of his own life's Time, his father's life time, and the same Mercy his art lends to my own person, his son. " August 18-September 13, 1969.

507 Kerouac, Jack. Visions of Cody. Introduction by Allen Ginsberg. New York: McGraw-Hill, 1973.
    See "The Great Rememberer" under ESSAYS, STATEMENTS AND QUOTES.

508 Leary, Timothy. Jail Notes. Preface by Allen Ginsberg. New York: Grove Press, Inc. , Douglas Books, 1970.
    This preface is a combination of two previous statements by Ginsberg: "Remarks on Leary's Politics of Ecstasy," Village Voice, 12 December 1968, v. XIV, n. 9, p. 8; and "Continuation of Notes on Tim Leary's Public Career and Politics of Ecstasy," August 7, 1970. The Preface was originally intended for Leary's Politics of Ecstasy.
    "Dr. Leary's Jail Notes make a science fiction classic, Orwell come true.... Dr. Leary has taken the burden of giving honest report of LSD & Cannabis in terms more accurate & harmless than the faked science of the Government Party Hacks & therefore his imprisonment is an act of insult to Science, Liberty, Common Sense, Freedom, Academy, Philosophy, Medicine, Psychology as an Art, and Poetry as a tradition of human mind-vision. Well jail's honed him down to rib & soul. "

509 Maynard, Joe and Barry Miles. (compilers) William S. Bur-
     roughs, A Bibliography, 1953-1973/"Unlocking Inspector
     Lee's Word Hoard." Introduction by Allen Ginsberg. Char-
     lottesville, Virginia: University Press of Virginia, 1978.
     The Introduction was prepared August 11, 1976.
     "Who has the time to read such big bibliographies? Cer-
     tainly such readers are very specialized creatures in midwestern li-
     braries appreciatively washing their hands and smoking a little hash
     before opening up these dreadful tomes. On the other hand, there
     are young lads and lasses all over the century whose brains have
     been influenced by Burrough's implacable egolessness or deathly wit
     as 'twas said in the presence of Tibetan lamas."

510 Pélieu, Claude. Amphetamin Cowboy. Foreword by Allen Gins-
     berg. Bonn, Germany: Expanded Media Editions, 1976, p.
     5. In German. Back page photographs of Ginsberg among
     others. The Foreword was prepared by Ginsberg in New
     York on August 23, 1970.

511 Veitch, Tom. Death College And Other Poems (1964-1974).
     Afterword by Allen Ginsberg. Berkeley, California: Big
     Sky Books, 1976, pp. 175-183. Published in an edition of
     1500 copies, 26 of which are lettered A-Z and signed by
     the poet.
     Editor's note: "Allen Ginsberg's commentary is based on
     an early version of this book. A few of the poems quoted in Allen's
     essay were revised or excised from the final manuscript of Death
     College and Other Poems by the author." Ginsberg offers a literary
     critique of several included poems. He finds levels of comparison
     to his own work and that of his contemporaries. Conclusively he
     notes: "At the end he breaks thru to mystical transcendence bullshit
     humor. Shows the limit of poetry, except it be as Corso says 'a
     probe' into Death. Whitmanic too, and out of that early seriousness
     rawness and fun--long poems arrive. Why do I like Tom Veitch?
     He's just a typical poet that's why."

Quotes on Books and Records

512 Dylan, Bob. "Songs of Redemption." Desire. New York:
     Ram's Horn Music/Warner Bros. Publications, Inc., 1976.
     (Music to Dylan's Desire album.)
     Ginsberg statement (inside front cover) reviews and con-
     gratulates Dylan's Desire: "Dylan's Redemption Songs! If he can
     do it we can do it. America can do it.... And behind it all the
     vast one space of No God, or God, mindful conscious compassion
     lifetime awareness, we're here in America at last redeemed. O
     Generation, keep on working!"

513 Holst, Spencer. Language of Cats. New York: Avon, 1973.
          "Fast Notes Reading Cats Language." September 21,
     1970. Paragraph on book's dust jacket.

514 Holst, Spencer. Spencer Holst Stories. New York: Horizon

Press, 1972.
"Mysterious impersonality ... Patient genius ... old indian Aboriginal storyteller...." Statement among others used on inside dust jacket of the hardcover edition.

515 Leyland, Winston (ed.). Gay Sunshine Interviews. San Francisco: Gay Sunshine Press, 1978.

Printed on back cover and prepared by Ginsberg (1/20/78): "Entire series of Gay Sunshine Interviews is a monumental piece of self-revelation, unheard of in previous public centuries as far as I know. Here all the veiles are down and famous figures, transitory characters, and immortal elves dish out supreme accurate gossip on their intimate metaphysical sex lives. Has this ever been done before? Isn't this a fantastic revolution of manners? Won't it be a revelation of personal reality for later generations? Won't it lead to Frankness for Centuries? Won't it change literature and politics forever? It's supposed to, so let's see what happens with this book Right Now. "

516 McClure, Michael. Adept. New York: Delacorte Press, A Seymour Lawrence Book, 1971, hardcover edition; Berkeley, Calif. : Serendipity, 1971.

The following excerpt from the entire statement appears on the rear inside dust jacket: "... Total brain humor in NY novel detail--a biological Education to read McClure's long funny story, book on yr lap--hairgrowing yoga mutancy explained clearly as light from the eye of a wasp. " November 29, 1970.

517 Mountain, Stone. Pot Art and Marijuana Reading Matter. Apocrypha Press, 1972, (Box 12519, Tucson, Arizona 85711.)
"AG Pot Art Blurb" September 22, 1970. Used for publicity purposes on back cover. It "contains clippings from the popular and scientific press from 1926 to the present, ... is an anthology of reports ... graphically presents: PSYCHEDELIC SUPERMARKET, ..." According to Ginsberg, "this is History by feedback & cut-up, ..."

518 Plymell, Charles. Rod McKuen Reads, In Memory of My Father. Cherry Valley, N. Y. : Cherry Valley Editions, 1977 (special edition).
"One of the best elegies in the English language. " quote from Ginsberg on back page. Includes one small disc: "This recording was made live at Shriver Hall, The Johns Hopkins University, April 30, 1976. " (33 1/3 RPM-BRC 5142A/B).

519 Sackheim, Eric (comp.). The Blues Line, A Collection of Blues Lyrics from Leadbelly to Muddy Waters. New York: Schirmer Books, 1975. Illustrations by Johnathan Shahn.
This is a geographical survey of blues lyrics; from the 40's and 50's. Ginsberg reviews the work (on the back cover): "Paperback Sackheim blues astounding grace. The book shakes the bastions of all academy and should destroy old white versification and re-establish the classic oral transmission of poetics

by blacks and whites as integral to scholarly anthology and vocalization. How all that great poetry got shunted aside in America is a tale of imperial idiocy and redemption by the meek and despised, just like the Bible. "

520 Sanders, Ed. Shards of God. New York: Grove Press, 1970.
     Book blurb for Sanders' novel, fragments of which were used on the jacket cover. The original form was a card written on September 5, 1970.

Editorial Input

521 Catalog of Sexual Consciousness. New York: Grove Press, Inc. , 1975.
     In this "catalog," Ginsberg is listed as a contributor. There is no index or table of contents. As a result it is impossible to discern exactly what input Ginsberg had in this publication.

522 Henderson, Bill (editor with Pushcart Prize editors). The Pushcart Prize, II: Best of the Small Presses. Yonkers, New York: The Pushcart Press, 1977.
     One of the contributing editors for this edition is Allen Ginsberg. However, there is no Ginsberg material included.

523 The Marijuana Review. Publication of Lemar International (Box 71, Norton Hall, State University of New York at Buffalo, New York 14214).
     Ginsberg is a "consulting guru" for this publication.

D.   POSTCARDS AND BROADSIDES

524 "For the Soul of the planet is wakening..." Sante Fe, N.M. : Desert Review Press, 1970. Broadside, roll port. , 56 x 35 cm.
     Poster made of last paragraph of record liner notes to the Blake album 1.

525 "Going to San Diego. " Win, 8:6 (April 1, 1972): back cover, n. p. , lettering by Bill Crawford. Broadside.

526 "Lay Down Yr Mountain (To Bob Dylan). " (poem-hand written/ dated - October 31, 1975). A Folger Poetry Broadside/ Series 1977 © 1977 Allen Ginsberg. Broadside. (vertical 14x8"), blue with black ink.

527 "Milarepa Taste" (poem, 1971). Detroit: The Alternative Press. Postcard (vertical 4 x $6\frac{1}{2}$"), gold with brown letters red outlining.

528 "New York Blues" (poem). Cold Mountain Press Poetry Post Card Series II, Number 7, copyright 1974, Allen Ginsberg. (Cold Mountain Press, 4406 Duval, Austin, Texas 78751.) Postcard (horizontal $6\frac{1}{2}$ x 5").

529 "Rain-Wet Asphalt Heat Garbage Curbed Cans Overflowing"
(poem, dated August 2, 1969). (a free poem from The
Alternative Press, 4339 Avery, Detroit, Michigan). Broadside (vertical 12 x 8"), olive gold with brown lettering on
textured paper.

530 "Returning to the Country for a Brief Visit" (poem 4/20/73,
written by hand in black ink). Stone Press Weekly, n. 65,
ⓒ 1975 by Allen Ginsberg. G. P. Skratz, (ed.), 5399½
Bryant, Oakland Cal. 94618. Postcard (horizontal 6 x 4").
Has different verses than another card with this poem
printed on it. See entry below.

531 "Returning to the Country for a Brief Visit" (poem- April 20,
1973/written by hand in black ink). Copyright 1976, the
unspeakable visions of the individual, P.O. Box 439, California, Pennsylvania 15419. Postcard (horizontal 5½ x
3¼ ").
Has different verses than card with same poem printed
on it. See entry above.

532 "The Rune" (poem-January 17-22, 1977). Series 4, Copyright
1977 Hard Press, 340 E. 11th, NYC, numbered J6653.
Postcard (vertical 5½ x 4½ "), printed on textured peach-
colored paper.

E. MUSICAL SCORES

533 "Dream Stanza" (score). The Washington Post, 8 February
1976, p. G6.
Included in a review of First Blues.

534 "GOSPEL NOBLE TRUTHS. " Stupa, Naropa Institute Student
Magazine, v. 3, n. 9, n. p. (inside back cover). Music
score by Allen Ginsberg. Transcribed by Brian Muney,
Naropa Summer 1977.

535 "Guru Blues" (score). The Washington Post, 8 February 1976,
p. G6.
Included in a review of First Blues.

536 "Songs of Experience. " Quarterly West, Fall 1976, p. 48.
(Words: William Blake, Calligraphy: Mike Gibbons).

537 "Songs of Experience--A Divine Image. " Logos 3:1 (?1969).
Reprint from Strobe Magazine, 1969.

VII.   NON-PRINT MATERIALS

A.   RECORDS

538   "America Today!"   Phonodisc, CMS Records, CMS 617,
      1971.   (The world's great poets, v. 1.)
          According to the Chicorel Index this recording was "made
during the actual reading by the poets at the Spoleto Festival of Two
Worlds. "   It contains readings by Allen Ginsberg, G. Corso, and
Lawrence Ferlinghetti.

539   "Bates College Reading. "   33 1/3 rpm record. Lewiston, Maine,
      February, n. d.   Produced by The Robert R. Marino
      Co. , The Pequod Selected Readings, Box 86, Waterville,
      Maine.   Side 1: "Selected Poets. "   Side 2: "Allen Gins-
      berg. "

540   "Blake's Songs of Innocence and of Experience Tuned by Allen
      Ginsberg. "   MGM/Verse FTS 3083, New York, 1969; re-
      issued MGM, Archetype Series, 1974.

541   "The Dial-a-Poem Poets. "   Giorno Poetry Systems, GPS 001,
      2-12", 33 1/3 rpm.
          Ginsberg is one of the "Dial-a-Poem Poets" reciting
"Green Automobile," "Vajra Mantra," "Blake Song: Merrily We
Welcome in the Year" and "Spring" from Songs of Innocence.

542   First Blues: Songs.   New York: Vanguard Records, pending
      release, ? 1978.
          The "liner notes," written Aug. 5, 1977, focus on "New
York Youth Call Annunciation," "CIA Dope Calypso," "Put Down Yr
Cigarette Rag (Don't Smoke)," "Everybody Sing," "Broken Bone
Blues," "Stay Away from the White House," "Hard-on Blues," "Guru
Blues," "Sickness Blues" and "Gospel Noble Truths. "

543   "Pull My Daisy. "   45 rpm record, RCA SPS-45-298.   Side B:
      David Amram (Amram, Kerouac, Ginsberg), 1971.
          See no. 71S1/012 in Tape and Cassette Index.

544   "The Spoken Arts Treasury of 100 American Poets. "   Edited
      by Paul Krish.   LC 78-750876, Phonodisc.
          This volume includes James Merrill, Robert Creeley,
David Wagoner, Robert Bly, and Galway Kinnell reading.   Ginsberg
reads his works "Who Be Kind To" and "Uptown, New York City. "

545   "Yevtushenko in Reading from His New York and San Francisco

Poetry Concert. " Phonodisc, Columbia S31344, 1972.
Read in English by Barry Boys, Lawrence Ferlinghetti,
Allen Ginsberg, Viveca Lindfors, and Richard Wilbur; all except
the second, third and sixth poems also read in Russian by the
author, Yevtushenko.

B. AUDIO TAPES AND CASSETTES
(See also Tape and Cassette Index, Appendix B and
RADIO BROADCASTS section.)

American Poetry Archive and Resource Center,
San Francisco State University

[Available to "faculty and students at San Francisco
State University for a small service charge (return
inclusive) and by special arrangement with scholars,
bibliographers, poetry lovers, etc. " Items are not
for sale. Information per Gordon C. A. Craig,
Technical Director, American Poetry Archive.]

546   Allen Ginsberg: Second Edition (Audio Cass. # 871). Completed sound track of American Poetry Archive videotape
by the same title.
See under VIDEOTAPES section.

547   Allen Reads with Anne Waldman, Diane DiPrima (Audio Cass.
595). Boulder, Colorado, July 30, 1974.

548   Interview of Allen and Louis Ginsberg (Audio Cass. # 674).
City Lights Bookstore, San Francisco, May 8, 1974,
Stephen M. H. Braitman, interviewer.

549   Louis and Allen Ginsberg Reading (Audio Cass. # 585).   May 9,
1974, San Francisco State University.

550   USA Poetry Outtakes (Audiotapes # 799-801, 809, 814).   Original $\frac{1}{4}$ " production audio for videotape USA: Poetry Outtakes, 5/18/65.
       See Allen Ginsberg: Second Edition under VIDEOTAPES
section.

Paterson Free Public Library

[Tapes and cassettes available from the Paterson
Free Public Library, 250 Broadway, Paterson, New
Jersey 07501 under the direction of Leo E. Fichtel-
berg. Please contact the library for further information: (201) 881-3770.]

551   "Interview with Allen Young," Broadcast: Boston, WBCN-FM,
1974. 1 reel-to-reel tape; 2500 ft. , 3 3/4 i. p. s. , $\frac{1}{4}$ track;
both sides.
       See also under INTERVIEWS section.

552 "Poetry Reading" March 4, 1973. Louis Ginsberg, Allen
Ginsberg and Eugene Brooks. Sponsored by the Paterson
Free Public Library. 1 reel-to-reel tape; 1800 feet, 3 3/4
i. p. s. , $\frac{1}{4}$ track; both sides.

553 "Poetry Readings" October 17, 1975. Louis Ginsberg, Allen
Ginsberg, and Eugene Brooks. Sponsored by the Paterson
Free Public Library. Two (2) C-90 tape cassettes; L.
Ginsberg Tape I, side 1; E. Brooks Tape I, side 2; A.
Ginsberg Tape II, side 1, (II, 2 blank).

Cassette Curriculum Series of Everett/Edwards, Inc.

[The tapes are available from Everett/Edwards, Inc. ,
P. O. Box 1060, DeLand, Florida 32720. (904) 734-
7458.]

554 "Allen Ginsberg" (no. 161), in Contemporary American Poets
Read Their Work (General Editor: William E. Taylor).
30-45 minutes each. Cost: $9. 00 @; $100. 00 for the
complete series (12).
"The poets explain how their poems were written, how
they came into being. . . . The poetry comes alive as each poet tells
us how things are with him. "

555 "Allen Ginsberg" (no. 825), in Modern American Poetry Series
(General Editor: Richard Calhoun). Lecturer: Thomas F.
Merrill. 25-50 minutes each. Cost: $10@; $40 for the
entire series.
See also: 1975-76 Catalog of Cassette Lectures

Naropa Institute

[Available from Naropa Institute, 1345 Spruce Street,
Boulder, Colorado 80302. Check their Catalogue of
Recordings, Cassettes, Lectures for 1977 availability.]

556 Poetry Readings. Naropa Institute.
"Potpourri of Poetry, 1975-1976" includes readings by
Allen Ginsberg. "Potpourri is a provocative taste of the high
poetic energy, flowing from the Jack Kerouac School of Disembodied
Poetics. "
"Beauty and the Beast" Anne Waldman and Allen Ginsberg, 8/75. "The breathless lyricism of the Fast Speaking Woman
is teamed here with Allen Ginsberg's incredible powerhouse performance of epic 'Howl. '"
"Bard and Muse" Allen Ginsberg and Anne Waldman,
4/76. "Fresh from their tour with Rolling Thunder Review, Allen
and Anne chant and sing their paeans. A special delight is Allen's
musical self-accompaniment. "

557 "William Carlos Williams. " Naropa Institute.

Master tapes from Ginsberg series of lectures at Naropa Institute, Boulder, Colorado (Summer Series-Writing Workshops, 1974) on William Carlos Williams, produced in New York by WBAI and broadcast are now owned by Folkways Records in their unedited format. They will eventually be re-issued after editing through Folkways Records, New York. Contact Mr. Ash (212) 586-7260 for further information.

Other

558 "Allen Ginsberg Reads Kaddish. " Tape Recording number 512, 1 reel, "Poets and Poetry," American Jewish Archives, Cincinnati, 1971.
"A twentieth century American ecstatic narrative poem by Allen Ginsberg. "

559 Black Box (no. 12, 8/77). "Cassette Tapes of Poets Reading Their Works," organized as an audio literary magazine. Each cassette contains two 60 minute tapes.
Ginsberg on side C of these two cassettes reads "CIA Dope Calypso," "Don't Grow Old," "Father Death Blues," "July 9, 1976, Arriving Home," "Lay Down. " (17. 00 minutes). For copies or subscription information contact:
Black Box, PO Box 4174, Washington, D. C. 20015.

560 German cassette series. S Press, Michael Köhler, publisher. D-8 Münich / 40 Zieblandstrasse/10 Zieblandstrasse.

C. RADIO BROADCASTS

Pacifica Tape Library

[WBAI is owned and operated by the Pacifica Foundation, a non-profit corporation. The other Pacifica stations are: KPFA, 2207 Shattuck Avenue, Berkeley, Calif. 94707; KPFK, 3729 Cahuenga Blvd. , Los Angeles, Calif. 91604; KPFT, 419 Lovett Blvd. , Houston, Texas 77006; WPFW, 868 National Press Building, Washington, D. C. 20036. The following radio program/audio-tapes are available to educational organizations, schools, etc. (not individuals) from Pacifica Programs Service, 5316 Venice Blvd. , Los Angeles, California 90019 (213) 931-1625. The information was ascertained from "The Program Library Master Listing. "]

561 "Allen Ginsberg/Don McNeil Memorial" Archive Number BB3482. Interview Duration - 0. 45 min. Tape, Mono. Recorded by WBAI at station in 1969. First broadcast 10/18/70. Allen Ginsberg-Interviewer - Poet. Bill Handerson, Interviewer.
"Ginsberg talks about a project which he and McNeil

collaborated on, the documentation of police involvement in narcotics traffic. "

562 "The American Prophetic" Archive Number BC0437.05. Poetry.
    Duration 1 hour. Tape, Mono. Recorded by KPFK at
    University of Minn. in October 1971. First broadcast 11/
    29/71. For Pacifica Stations Only. Allen Ginsberg -
    Speaker - Beat Poet.
        "Ginsberg discusses the American Prophetic tradition
    described by this series and traces his inheritance from Whitman,
    Pound, and Williams in this insightful hour-long lecture on the re-
    cent history of English prosody and poetic consciousness. "

563 "Changes" Archive Number BB1849. Discussion. Duration
    1 hour, 11 min. Recorded by KPFA at Sausalito. No date.
    Alan Watts - Panelist - Philosopher; Timothy Leary - Panel-
    ist; Gary Snyder - Panelist - Poet; Allen Ginsberg - Panel-
    ist - Poet.
        "A discussion of LSD, art and life. "

564 "Ginsberg on Kerouac" Archive Number BB3463. Interview.
    Duration 35 min. Tape, Mono. Recorded by WBAI at
    Columbia University on 10/22/69. Reference only--not
    for broadcast, for Archives only.
        Allen Ginsberg reads own works and talks. Bill Schech-
ner- Interviewer-WBAI.

565 "Interview with Ginsberg" Archive Number BC3096. Inter-
    view. Tape, Stereo. Recorded in 1974. Duncan Martinez-
    Interviewer; Allen Ginsberg-Interviewee.

566 "Life Liberty and the Pursuit of Happiness" Archive Number
    BC2069.15. Discussion. Duration 1 hour, 57 min. , 18
    sec. Tape, Mono. Recorded by WBAI at station. No
    date. Allen Ginsberg-Panelist; Susan Sontag-Panelist;
    Murray Bookchin-Panelist; Ti-Grace Atkinson-Panelist.

567 "Return to Columbia" Archive Number BC2364. Discussion.
    Duration- 0.24 min. Tape, Mono. Recorded by WBAI at
    station. No date. Allen Ginsberg-Participant-Poet; William
    Burroughs-Participant-Poet.
        "The Beat poets return to Columbia... "

568 "Turn on Turn in Cop Out the Real Dope on Leary" Archive
    Number BC2064. Discussion. Tape, Mono. Recorded by
    KPFA. No date. Allen Ginsberg-Interviewee; Jerry Rubin-
    Interviewee; Eldridge Cleaver-Interviewee-Black Panther;
    Ken Kesey-Interviewee-Author; Wavy Gravy-Interviewee;
    Baba Ram Dass-Interviewee; Michael Horowitz-Interviewee;
    Adi Gevins-Producer/Kris Welch-Producer.
        "Discussion on Dr. Leary: 'Is he turning his friends into
the federal grand jury, if so why and if not what is he doing?'"

569 "Yippie Head Abbie Hoffman Comes at KPFA" Archive Number BC0279. Discussion. Duration 1 hour, 30 min. Tape, Mono. Recorded by KPFA at Station on 8/13/71. First Broadcast-8/19/71. Abbie Hoffman-Participant; Michael Rossman-Participant; Patric Mayers-Participant; Craig Pyes-Participant; Allen Ginsberg-Participant.
     "Everything was coughed up in this discussion, including Abbie's book, America, the personality in the movement, art, poetry, Judge Julius Hoffman, Berkeley, New York City, touching, dope, and more. "

Other

570 CKNW Radio, Vancouver, BC; "Hot Line Show. " March 11, 1969, interview with Jack Webster.
     See Under INTERVIEWS section: Webster, Jack, Georgia Straight, v. 3, n. 52, April 4-10, 1969, pp. 9-12.

571 KBEY (Radio-FM), Kansas City, Missouri. Sunday, February 12, 1972, 11:00 pm and Monday, February 13, 1972, 11:00 pm.
     Interview by Steve Bell and Steve Litman of KBEY, Jim Vogt, Bill Dehart, and Kevin Dowd of UMKC (University of Missouri, Kansas City) and Dennis Giangreco of The Trucker.
     See under INTERVIEWS section: Giangreco, Dennis, "An Interview with Allen Ginsberg. " Westport Trucker.

572 KDNA. Talk Show: Webster College, St. Louis, Missouri, November 1, 1972.
     Discussion of the death of Ezra Pound (recorded live).
     See under INTERVIEWS section: Castro, M. "Ezra Pound (1889-1972) 'A Noble Poet Nobly Elegized. '" Outlaw; also under BOOKS section: Allen Verbatim, pp. 179-189.

573 KRNW (a small privately-owned, 380-watt, Boulder, Colo. radio station).
     Interview of Allen Ginsberg regarding his teaching at Naropa and the recent financial triumph of the NYC based WBAI radio station.
     See: Rocky Mountain News, April 1, 1977, pp. 6-7.

574 WBAI. New York City. An interview with Allen Ginsberg done recently by Lynn Samuels about Bob Dylan's movie "Renaldo and Clara. " See no. 78E1/001a "C" in Tape and Cassette Index.

575 WBCN-FM, Boston, 1974. Allen Ginsberg Interview with Allen Young.
     Available through The Paterson Free Public Library.
See under AUDIO TAPES Section.

576 WOR. Arlene Francis Radio Broadcast (one hour talk show). December 10, 1977, Philadelphia.

"He talks and sings about lots of things. He sandwiches meditation instructions, theories of poetics and songs about death in between the commercials for coats, banks and non-dairy creamers."
See under INTERVIEWS section: Litterine, Lynn. "Allen Ginsberg: Olde garde isn't so avant anymore." The Philadelphia Inquirer; also, for tape of program, see no. 77E1/007 "C" in Tape and Cassette Index.

D. VIDEOTAPES

577 Allen Ginsberg; An American Poet, at home & at work in NYC. Kenneth P. Nimmer and Harris Schiff, co-producers. Color Videotape. Available: January 1, 1979. "For further information as to format possibilities, rental, copy purchase, please contact: Harris Schiff, 57 Second Avenue, Apt. #91, NYC 10003, (212) 245-5096; or Kenneth P. Nimmer, 158 Sunden Meadow Road, King's Park, Long Island, New York 11754, (516) 268-4314.

"An uniquely personal, color documentary portrait of the major American poet, Allen Ginsberg. Shot on location, March 17 & 18, 1978, in the poet's lower-east-side apartment in New York City, the subject is Allen Ginsberg's working environment, life-style, thought, methods & work. Mr. Ginsberg's generous cooperation & trust made it possible to spend three days lighting, wiring & shooting in his residence & around his neighborhood in order to project the poet's 'ordinary daily mind,' as well as to explore his ideas & his work."

578 Allen Ginsberg: Second Edition (V-T #147, American Poetry Archive and Resource Center, San Francisco State Univ.).
A completed American Poetry Archive videotape based on USA: Poetry Outtakes, Richard O. Moore, producer, KQED, San Francisco, original production location: basement of City Lights Bookstore, San Francisco, July 18, 1965.
With Neal Cassady, they discuss "political extremists, suppression of intellectuals in the USA, and America's role in Vietnam and other small countries. The film continues on December 14, 1965, at Ginsberg's apartment and at the studio of Robert La Vigne.... in the company of Peter Orlovsky and Neal Cassady...."
Black and White only. Rental (Videotape): $20.00/55 minutes; Source: American Poetry Archive, San Francisco State Univ., 1600 Holloway, San Francisco, Calif. 94132. See: Catalogue for Second Series, 1977/78, p. 91, photograph of Allen Ginsberg "taken by Richard Simpson from the original film footage."
Note: This videotape, although originally done in 1965, has only recently been re-arranged (1975-76) and become available for distribution (1977-78). Complete transcripts, indexed with film component/ shot inventory are available.
NET Outtake Series, "produced by the American Poetry Archive and the Poetry Center through a grant from the National Endowment for the Arts, is a series of films composed of outtakes from the series USA: Poetry, which was produced by the film unit ...

of KQED-TV, San Francisco. The outtake films preserve in actual shooting sequence all retrievable footage not used in USA: Poetry ... average 50 minutes in length, ... are titled 'Second Edition' to distinguish from the original films."

579   Louis and Allen Ginsberg Reading Together (V-T #35 a, b
       American Poetry Archive and Resource Center, San Fran-
       cisco State Univ.).   Nanos Valoaritis, Introduction.   Mc-
       Kenna Auditorium, San Francisco State University, May 9,
       1974.   Sponsored by The Poetry Center.   Color.   Rental:
       video-tapes / 3/4" cassette or $\frac{1}{2}$-in. reel-to-reel formats.
       $17.50 and $20.00 respectively.   Source: American Poetry
       Archive and Resource Center, San Francisco State Univ.,
       1600 Holloway, San Francisco, Calif.   94132.
           See: Catalogue for First Series, 1975, pp. 18-19, with
photograph of Allen and excerpt "from 'Death News'" p. 18 and
with photograph of Louis and his bibliographical and biographical
information, p. 19.

580   The Poetry of Allen Ginsberg (first recording), 1970, 60 min-
       utes; The Poetry of Allen Ginsberg (second recording, with
       Peter Orlovsky), 1973, 60 minutes.   Available through The
       Writer's Forum, Videotaped Interviews with Contemporary
       Writers, State University, College at Brockport, Brockport,
       New York 14420.
           Available in part "for as minimal cost as possible to all
colleges and secondary schools in New York State."   Tentative plans
for acquisition by the Library of Congress are in the works.   Further details are unavailable.

581   Seeds of the 60's (?Videotape).   Used at a colloquium: Univer-
       sity of California, Santa Cruz, October 14, 1977: "LSD--A
       Generation Later."   Ginsberg is included in some context.
           Contact people: Bruce Ehrlich/Peter Stafford, 1940 Kins-
ley Street, Santa Cruz, California 95062.   (408) 476-0411.

582   Suite (212): a video tape production by Nam June Paik, WNET,
       1975.
           Includes images of Ginsberg.   See articles by Grace Glueck,
"Videotape Replaces Canvas for Artists Who Use TV Technology in
New Way."   New York Times, April 14, 1975, pp. 33, 63.

E.   TELEVISION PROGRAMS

583   Conversations with Harold Hudson Channer (Teleprompter Cable
       Vision).   No. 53, Mr. Allen Ginsberg.   "Poetry, Politics
       and Consciousness."   60 minutes, November, 1974.   Inter-
       view with Allen Ginsberg in the office of McGraw-Hill the
       publisher of Allen Verbatim: Lectures on Poetry, Politics,
       Consciousness, with editor, Gordon Ball.
           This "was carried by the combined facilities of the
Time-Life (Manhattan) and the Teleprompter Cable Vision systems

in New York City. The interview was a widely ranged discussion of
the role of poetics in the broader patterns of human activity. It was,
of course, highlighting the publication of the new book. For further
information contact: 2 Pencil Hill Road, New Paltz, New York 12561,
(914) 255-8287.

584 Everyman Program, BBC/TV (British Broadcasting Corporation,
       London). "Still Crazy After All These Years," Bill Nichol-
       son, Producer, Everyman Film, 1977. Transmitted BBC-1-
       Sunday, 29 January 1978 at 10:05 pm. Part 1 was shown the
       previous Sunday, 22 January at 10:20 pm.
            This show includes a filmed interview about the 60's with
Allen Ginsberg. Presumably filmed in 1977.

585 Free Time, WNET/TV. November 1971, Fern McBride, Pro-
       ducer. 1½ hours (live).
            Allen Ginsberg reads "September on Jessore Road" (poem)
       and improvisation on CIA Dope Traffic with music. Re-
       corded with Dave Amram, Bob Dylan, Happy Traum and
       Peter Orlovsky among others.

586 "Kup's Show." Chicago, March 16, 1974. Moderator, Stanley
       Kupcinet.
            See Out There, n. 9, 1976, for a reference; and Chicago
Sun Times, 3/10/75, p. 70, for a review.

587 News Front, WNET/TV. Host: Mitchel Kraus, Spring/Sum-
       mer 1970, Studio 46, black and white.
            Allen Ginsberg appeared with his father.

588 Panorama. Interview, Channel 5, Washington, D.C., Hostess:
       Pat Mitchell.
            Ginsberg talks about his Washington appearances, and the
investigation of the CIA, reads and accompanies himself on the harmonium. See: The Washington Post, Sunday Magazine "Potomac,"
May 1, 1977, by Henry Allen (cover story).

589 Prime Time, WFSU-TV. April 21, 1975, 7 p.m.
            Source: Florida Flambeau, John Stevens. "Poet Gins-
berg here tonight." 21 April 1975, p. 1.

590 Speaking Freely, NBC. 1:00 a.m. Moderator, Edwin Newman.
       Poet Allen Ginsberg, guest. May 24, 1973; one hour.

591 Speaking Freely, NBC. 1:00 a.m. May 1975. Moderator,
       Edwin Newman. Poet, Allen Ginsberg, guest; one hour.
            See under SECONDARY WORKS: NEWSPAPER ARTICLES
section: The Poetry Project Newsletter, 1 June 1975.

592 "Take It from There," WRC-TV. ?April 30, 1974.
            On gay marriage with Allen Ginsberg and Peter Orlovsky.
See under SECONDARY WORKS: NEWSPAPER ARTICLES section:
Gilden, William, "Voices of Freedom Protesting," Washington Post.

593 Video and Television Review, WNET/TV.   VTR #102, Kaddish.
    October 11, 1977, 1 hour.
        According to WNET, "the VTR series ran approximately
$2\frac{1}{2}$ seasons (30-33 shows).   The show with Allen Ginsberg was one
of the last shows (artists-in-residence program) and was nationally
telecast.   The program was art computer-graphics coupled with
images of Ginsberg reciting from his poem "Kaddish" and dramatization from his mother's life acted out. . . .   The program was done
by Arthur Ginsberg. . . ."
        See: New York Times, Sunday, October 9, 1977, p. D41;
Thirteen, WNET/13 Member's Guide, October 1977, p. 8-9, "Evening Schedule, October"; Daily News, Sunday, October 9, 1977, p. 3;
Star Ledger, October 1, 1977, p. 15.

F. FILMS

        [Films preceded by a star (*) were made available
        through the efforts of the Staff of the Education Film
        Library Association, 43 West 61 Street, New York,
        NY   10023.   (212) 246-4533.]

594 Boulder 1977, by Gregory Corso.   Color/Black and White;
        silent; $\frac{1}{2}$ hour.   Available from Naropa Institute, 1111 Pearl
        Street, Boulder, Colorado 80302.
            Allen Ginsberg is in and out of the entire film as are
William Burroughs, Peter Orlovsky, Ed Sanders and Philip Whalen.

595 Breathing Together: Revolution of the Electric Family.   (Vivre
        ensemble: la famille électrique), Director: Morley Mark-
        son, 1971.   Produced by Morley Markson and Associates
        Ltd. , 84 minutes; Black and White.   Distributed by New
        Cinema Enterprises Corp. , Ltd. , 35 Britain Street, Toronto,
        Ontario, Canada, M5A 1R7.   (416) 862-1674.
            Ginsberg makes a brief appearance in this film.   For
further information contact: The Canadian Film Institute, 303 Rich-
mond Road, Ottawa, Ontario, Canada K1Z 6X3.   (613) 729-6193.

596 *Diaries, Notes and Sketches [also known as Walden].   185 min. ,
        color, 1969.   Director: Jonas Mekas; Distributor: Film-
        Makers' Cooperative, 175 Lexington Avenue, NYC   10016.
        (212) 889-3820.   With Allen Ginsberg.
            According to the Film-Makers' Cooperative Catalogue,
pp. 178-179, Diaries, Notes and Sketches is also known as Walden.
Jonas Mekas: "Since 1950 I have been keeping a film diary.   I
have been walking around with my Bolex and reacting to the immediate reality: situations, friends, New York, seasons of the year. . . .
The First Volume (the first four reels) contain materials from the
years 1965-1969, strung together in chronological order. . . .
            Walden: Reel Two. "Kreeping Kreplachs meet (Ginsberg,
Ed Sanders, Tuli, Warhol, Barbara Rubin, etc.)/Hare Krishna Walk;
autumn scenes; Sitney's Wedding; New Year's Evening in Times
Square; Goofing of 42nd Street; Uptown Party; Velvet Underground;

Deep of Winter; Naomi visits Ken and Flo Jacobs; Amy stops for
coffee; Coop Directors meet; Dreams of Cocteau; In Central Park;
What Leslie saw thru the Coop Window; Olmsted Hike. "

597 *Farm Diary. 64 min. Color, silent 8 mm, 1970. Director:
    Gordon Ball; Distributor: Film-Makers' Cooperative, 175
    Lexington Ave., NYC 10016. (212) 889-3820. With Allen
    Ginsberg.
        According to the Film-Makers' Cooperative Catalogue, p.
    19: "The farm's first ten months. Peter Orlovsky, Candy O'Brien,
    Allen Ginsberg, Julius Orlovsky, Gordon Ball, Ed the Hermit, Greg-
    ory Corso, Bessie, Panda Manda, Godly & Sadeyes, Myon Wiles,
    Stephen Bornstein, Papa Duck, Barbara Pionteck, Any Raccoon, Her-
    bert Huncke, Malcolm & Tyger, Brahma, Vishnu & Shiva, Jim Four-
    ratt, Sonja, Lygia, Cyril, Enrique, Louis Cartwright, Maretta, sala-
    manders, hawkeyes, timothy, yarrow, morning glories, corn, pump-
    kin, elm, maple, ash & many other energies.... Gordon Ball spent
    long patient seasons milking Bessie, tilling the earth and squinting
    through 8mm lens at home nature on mountaintop farm filled with
    ghostly strangers, and so documents an archetypal first year back
    to the land. "--Allen Ginsberg.

598 *Me and My Brother. 91 min. b&w/color, 1969. Director:
    Robert Frank; Distributor: New Yorker Films, 43 W. 61
    Street, NYC 10023 (212) 247-6110. Film-Makers' Coopera-
    tive, 175 Lexington Ave., NYC 10016 (212) 889-3820.

599 *Prologue. 87 min., b&w, 1970. Director: Robin Spry;
    Distributor: National Film Board of Canada, 1251 Avenue
    of the Americas, NYC 10020 (212) 586-2400.

600 Renaldo and Clara. 1978. Produced: Lombard Street Films;
    Distributed: Circuit Films, 550 East Butler Sq., Building,
    100 North Street, Minneapolis, Minn. 55403.
        Ginsberg had a role in the development of this film and
    is characterized in the credits as "The Father. " It includes an im-
    provised visit to Kerouac's grave (Ginsberg and Dylan with others),
    recitation of "Kaddish," and rendition of Blake's "Nurse's Song. "
        Note: Although released in 1978, this film was shot in
    1975.

601 [Untitled]. By: Mike Cassidy, LRS 212002; 8 min. b&w 212002;
    1975?
        Synchronized sound recording of Ginsberg's visit to St.
    Cloud State College, St. Cloud, Minneapolis 56301.

602 William Blake: Innocence & Experience (catalog no. NC551)
    and William Blake: Prophet (no. NC552). Producer: Aram
    Boyajian. 16mm, b&w, $12.00 each rental. Available
    from National Council of Churches of Christ, 475 Riverside
    Ave., NYC 10027. (212) 870-2249.
        "Each a half-hour film in color shown on two consecutive
    Sundays on the WABC-TV religious program Directions in Janu-

ary 1972. <u>Innocence & Experience</u> deals with Blake's early years, his visions, his printing of his first books.   In the film Allen Ginsberg reads in part, 'A Poison Tree,' 'The Fly,' 'London,' 'The Garden of Love,' 'The Tyger.'   He speaks of his own visions of Blake and sings the Blake poem 'Ah! Sun-Flower.'"

    <u>Prophet</u> deals with Blake's Prophetic Books and the later years of his life.   Allen Ginsberg reads from 'The Book of Urizen,' 'America,' 'Jerusalem.'   Ginsberg sings the Blake poem 'The Sick Rose.'

Allen Ginsberg

SECONDARY WORKS

I. BIBLIOGRAPHIES

603 A Bibliography of the Auerhahn Press and Its Successor David
      Haselwood Books. Compiled by an anonymous printer.
      Berkeley, California: Poltroon Press, 1976. "Somewhat
      less than 500 copies printed on a variety of presses: ..."
      The cover is silkscreened by Goodstuff Fabric.
          This is an alternative press bibliography which includes
      an acknowledgment to Ginsberg, plus other references to him and
      work by and about him. This compilation avoids systemization and
      is peculiar in its organization paralleling the type of material in-
      cluded. Some correspondence between Ginsberg and others is in-
      cluded from pages 39-44. Ginsberg is quoted in an advertisement
      for McClures' Dark Brown, a long poem, on page 37. Other ephe-
      mera and broadsides including Ginsberg are noted throughout this
      work. It is a documentation of a particular segment of the poetry /
      publishing /art world.

604 Dickstein, Morris, "Allen Ginsberg and the 60's." Commentary
      49 (January 1970): 64-70.
          The article offers a favorable retrospective vision of
      "Allen Ginsberg in the 60's" in relationship to traditional literature,
      poetry, politics, and society. Dickstein questions, "what happened
      in the 60's? It's all too early to say, it's still happening, but one
      can make a tentative and personal inventory." That is exactly what
      he proceeds to do in a journalistic, bibliographic essay. The cita-
      tions are minimal, although accurate, and particularly highlight arti-
      cles (secondary source material) of the middle 1960's. This essay,
      however, by no means fulfills the expectations of a full scale bibliog-
      raphy.

605 Dowden, George. Bibliography of Works by Allen Ginsberg,
      October, 1943 to July 1, 1967; with a chronology and index
      by Laurence McGilvery and a foreword by Allen Ginsberg.
      San Francisco: City Lights, 1971, 343 pp.
          The bibliography includes available primary citations in-
      cluding books, booklets, pamphlets, broadsides, periodical articles,
      recordings (records and tapes), films, paintings and drawings, trans-
      lations, anthologies, and "some mantras."

606 Kostelanetz, Richard.   Master Minds; Portraits of Contemporary
      American Artists and Intellectuals.   New York: Macmillan
      Co. , 1967, 1969.

This book contains a collection of articles and bibliographic essays on American intellectuals and artists. His annotations and listings of secondary sources are extensive until 1968.

607 Merrill, Thomas F. Allen Ginsberg. Boston: Twayne Publishers, Inc., 1969. (Twayne's United States Authors Series, 161).

Merrill's work consists of a series of critical essays on Ginsberg with a "Selected Bibliography" of primary and secondary sources with annotations (on secondary source material only). Merrill admits, "the following list is by no means exhaustive" and directs the reader to the Index to Little Magazines for more extensive listings. His annotations are evaluative and descriptive.

608 Tysh, Christine. Allen Ginsberg, étude de Christine Tysh: choix de poems, bibliographie, illustrations, (Paris: Segheis, 1974). (Poetes d'aujourd'hui 221).

II. BOOKS

A. ABOUT GINSBERG

English Language

609 Kramer, Jane. Allen Ginsberg in America. New York:
     Vintage Trade Books, Random House, 1968, 1969, 1970.
     Later published as Paterfamilias, Allen Ginsberg in America.
     London: Gollancz, 1970.
     Jane Kramer's book is a biography and contemporary nar-
rative about Ginsberg in the recent past and the present. It is written in free flowing journalistic verse and attempts to reveal Ginsberg and the life he leads.

610 Mottram, Eric. Allen Ginsberg in the Sixties. Brighton and
     Seattle: Unicorn Bookshop, 1971, 1972, pp. 40.
     According to the index, The Year's Work in English
Studies, Mottram discusses the value and subsequent achievement of
Ginsberg's work, "Wichita Vortex," "Television was a Baby Crawling
Toward That Death Chamber," Ankor Wat. " ... it is an excellent
monograph which outlines very knowledgeably and sympathetically
Ginsberg's poetic development in the 60's...." According to Gins-
berg this is "one of the few serious textual exams of what I've writ-
ten. "

Foreign Language

611 Friberg, Gösta and Gunnar Harding. Targas & Solrosor.
     Stockholm: n. p. , 1971. In Swedish.

612 Harding, Gunnar. Amerikansk Underground poesi; i urval och
     oversattning. Stockholm: W. & Wserien, 228, 1969. In
     Swedish.

613 Harding, Gunnar. Den svenske cyklistens säng. n. p. : Wahl-
     ström & Widstrand, 1968. In Swedish.

614 Kramer, Jane. Allen Ginsberg in America. New York: Vin-
     tage Books, 1970. (Traduction française: Allen Ginsberg
     en situation, traduit de l'anglais per Claude Gilbert. Paris:
     Union Générale d'Editions, Collection (10-18) 1973). In
     French.
          Includes "Laughing Gas," and "Shrouded Stranger," both
translated by Mary Beach & Claude Pélieu.

615 Suwa, Suguru. Allen Ginsberg. Tokyo: Yayoi Shobo, 1970.
     In Japanese.

616 Suwa, Suguru. Hoeru. Tokyo: Tanin Wo Machi-Sha, 1970.
     (Essays on Ginsberg's "Howl"). In Japanese.

617 Tysh, Christine. Allen Ginsberg. Paris: Poetes d'aujourd
     'hui 221/Editions Seghers, 1974. L'étude de Christine Tysh
     a été traduite par Claude Guillot. Published first in French
     and then translated into English by Mary Beach & Claude
     Pélieu.
         This book includes a series of essays by Tysh on Gins-
berg, an interview from the Paris Review (n. 37, 1966) by Thomas
Clark and a selection of poems which include: "Sakyamuni Coming
Out from the Mountain," "America," "Sather Gate Illumination,"
"Death to Van Gogh's Ear!" "Kaddish, for Naomi Ginsberg," "The
Change: Kyoto-Express," "Who Be Kind To. "

B. GENERAL OVERVIEW
    (with Discussion or Mention of Ginsberg)

English

618 Advance Token to Boardwalk. Introduction by Joel Oppenheimer.
     New Jersey: Poets & Writers of New Jersey, Inc., 1977.
         There is a reference to Ginsberg in Joel Oppenheimer's
Introduction.

619 Allen, Walter. The Urgent West: The American Dream and
     Modern Man. New York: Dutton, 1969.

620 Arguelles, Jose A. The Transformative Vision, Reflections
     on the Nature and History of Human Expression. Berkeley,
     California: Shambhala Publications, Inc., 1975.
         "The Transformative Vision combines history and myth,
psychology and art to provide a major new assessment of the role
of creativity in human behavior...." Chapter 22, "In the Shadow of
the Apocalypse," describes the "psychedelic revolution" as the merger
of "two cultural streams from the 1950's: the revitalized visionary
stream and the indigenous technological media culture. The first
had appeared full-blown in 1956, when Ginsberg's Howl was published,
with its incantatory lines...." Excerpts by Ginsberg are included to
exemplify the "counter-cultural protest" of the next decade. Ginsberg's Howl again is mentioned on p. 280 in the context of Shaman
seeking.

621 Bernard, Sidney. "A Reading and a Mourning. " Witnessing:
     The Seventies. New York: Horizon Press, 1977.
         This is a reprint of an article from the New York Times
Book Review, April 24, 1977, pp. 30, 32-33. See NEWSPAPER
section below for complete annotation.

622 Cargas, Henry J. Daniel Berrigan and Contemporary Protest
      Poetry. New Haven: College and University Press, 1972.
      Chapter IV, entitled,"Allen Ginsberg: The Shock of Des-
      pair. "
            Cargas explores the artist whose creativity is "rooted in
      the 'real world'" as opposed to the Ivory Tower. The chapters flow
      from a discussion of Richard Eberhart, Karl Shapiro, Robert Lowell,
      Allen Ginsberg, LeRoi Jones to Daniel Berrigan.

622a Charters, Samuel. Some Poems/Poets: Studies in American
      Underground Poetry Since 1945. Berkeley: Oyez, 1971.
            A "study" of underground poets of the twentieth century in
      America with background information in the introduction by Samuel
      Charters and photographs by Ann Charters. Ginsberg is examined
      in the context of other underground poets.

623 Codrescu, Andrei. The Life and Times of an Involuntary
      Genius. New York: George Braziller Books, A Venture
      Book, 1975.
            "This is the true story of a poet's childhood spent in a
      haunted castle in the hills of Transylvania, of this poet's early adult-
      hood and further struggle with Communist authority, and finally of
      his forced exile into the wide-opened and licensed America during the
      turmoil of the 1960's. "
            Ginsberg is included in Book Three, chapter 20, pp. 151-
      153, as the author seeks out Ginsberg on the Lower East Side of
      New York. Codrescu recounts his meeting with Ginsberg and Peter
      Orlovsky and later his lunch with Ginsberg "In an ancient Jewish
      place on Avenue B. "

624 Cook, Bruce. The Beat Generation. New York: Scribner,
      1971.
            Bruce Cook offers an overview to the Beats and various
      individual portraits. Cook works out a psychological analysis of
      Ginsberg and his relationship to Naomi, his mother. He feels that
      the poem "The Change" resolves much of the body conflict Ginsberg had
      toward women. According to Ginsberg this book is full of misinfor-
      mation and mistakes.

625 Cooney, Robert and Helen Michalowski (eds.). The Power of
      the People. California: Co-operatively published, 1977.
      Printed and distributed by Peace Press Inc. , 3828 Willat
      Avenue, Culver City, California 90230.
            There is reference to Allen Ginsberg on pages 186-7 and
191.

626 Dickstein, Morris. The Gates of Eden, American Culture in
      the Sixties. New York: Basic Books, Inc. , 1977.
            Autobiographically, Morris Dickstein parallels his intel-
      lectual development to the cultural development of Allen Ginsberg.
      First, he opens with the Allen Ginsberg of 1959 who set the New
      York intellectual community into turmoil. Dickstein himself did not
      go to the 1959 reading at Columbia by the Beats. Instead he went

"downtown that night to a Shakespeare production." In retrospect
Dickstein finds, "Ginsberg's reading was not only powerful and moving but it became for me another avenue into that very culture from
which Mrs. Trilling and Partisan Review had virtually ruled him
out--a culture, by the end of the sixties, that would embrace both
Shakespeare and Ginsberg, literature and movies, Beethoven and
rock. How this change came about is one of the subjects of this
book.... No one knew it at the time, but what Ginsberg stood for
was where a large part of American culture would soon be headed."
(p. 5).

627 Di Prima, Diane. Memoirs of a Beatnik. New York: Trav-
    eller's Companion, Inc. 1969 (The Traveller's Companion
    Series).
        Di Prima's Memoirs are the "nostalgic recordings of
her cohorts," which of course include Allen Ginsberg. An excerpt
highlighting Ginsberg appears in the San Diego Door to Liberation
1:46, 12 February 1970, p. 6.

628 Edmiston, Susan and Linda D. Cirino. Literary New York,
    A History and Guide. Boston: Houghton Mifflin Co., 1976.
        "It is both practical 'field guide' and peerless armchair
entertainment for the lover of books. The authors take us on a
fascinating pilgrimage--from the small downtown community of Washington Irving's day to the vast contemporary metropolis--into the
days, works, homes and haunts of prominent writers and their cir-
cles." This book carefully documents Allen Ginsberg's literary roots
in New York City, particularly "The East Village." The pictorial
documentation of Ginsberg among others is excellent.

629 Erlich, J. W. and Lawrence Ferlinghetti (eds.). Howl of the
    Censor: Lawrence Ferlinghetti, Defendant. Westport, Conn.:
    Greenwood Press, 1976; reprint of 1961 ed.
        Book of testimony, plus the poems. See Columbia Uni-
versity Rare Book Collection for a copy.

629a Faas, Ekbert (ed.). Towards A New American Poetics: Es-
    says & Interviews: Charles Olson, Robert Duncan, Gary
    Snyder, Robert Creeley, Robert Bly, Allen Ginsberg. Santa
    Barbara, California: Black Sparrow Press, 1978.
        The "Essay" (pp. 249-268) works through the development
of the socially/politically conscious poet of the Nation, Allen Ginsberg
in the 1970's. "Having come to terms with ... psycho-religious problems ... (he) ... began to devote more and more time to public issues, such as fighting the Vietnam war or the socio-political consciousness which caused it. Faas notes that "such new concerns
also demanded a new language--a language which could oppose the
rhetoric of politicians and public media." This dilemma is para-
lelled to the work of William Burroughs in his "'cutup' method."
Interestingly enough, "where previously Ginsberg had exorcised his
private demons by accepting his bodily self, his new body-mantra-
poetics was devised to dispel the public demons controlling our
present-day consciousness...." Music and the use of mantra blend
to form this new medium for Ginsberg's message.

630 Fleischman, Christa. (editor) Mark in Time, Portrait and
Poetry-San Francisco Area. San Francisco: Glide Publishers, 1971.

631 French, W. G. (ed.). The Fifties: Fiction, Prose, Drama.
De Land, Florida: Everett/Edwards, 1970, bibliography,
pp. 291-304.
Ginsberg mentioned in the article by K. Widmer, "The
Beat in the Rise of the Populist Culture."

632 Glessing, Robert J. The Underground Press in America.
Bloomington, Indiana: Indiana University Press, 1970.
The writing of Allen Ginsberg is mentioned in the chapter
on "historical perspective" of the underground press in its early
days (p. 14).

633 Goodman, Mitchell (comp.). The Movement Toward a New
America, The Beginning of a Long Revolution (A Collage).
Philadelphia: Pilgrim Press; New York: Alfred A. Knopf,
1970.
This is a compilation of "movement" material: a reprint
of the "Trees Are Our Allies," Fifth Estate interview by David Fraser on pp. 522-523 and an "abridged transcript of Allen's testimony"
at the Conspiracy Trial, Chicago, with introduction by Abe Peck
from Chicago Seed and Berkeley Tribe on pp. 566-567.

634 Harrington, Michael. Fragments of the Century, A Personal &
Social Retrospective of the 50's and 60's. New York: Simon
& Schuster, A Touchstone Book, 1972.
In Harrington's chapter entitled, "The Death of Bohemia"
we find him at the White Horse, a Greenwich Village bar and retreat
for Bohemian America. "So the Horse fulfilled a classic Bohemian
function; it was, to borrow from a French writer, 'a kind of organization of disorganization.'" Allen Ginsberg passes through these
pages because he, too, was there. However it was not until 1969
that Harrington met Ginsberg when he and Peter Orlovsky and another
friend came to his apartment to see his wife who was then on the
staff of the Voice. Harrington places him within his Bohemian world
and then passes on to other anecdotes.

635 Hodgson, Godfrey. America in Our Time, From World War II
to Nixon--What Happened and Why. New York: Doubleday,
1976.
Chapter 16, "An Invasion of Centaurs," is a chapter on
"The Great American Cultural Revolution" which stresses the transition in culture from the 1950's to the 1960's. Ginsberg is cited for
his contributions. On p. 322 excerpts from "Howl" (part I) are included. Ginsberg and his cohorts, the beat poets, are indicated as
"... the seed that fertilized the discontents of the 1960's...."
Throughout the section the development of the beat generation is
highlighted with information on Ginsberg. Excerpts from his poem,
"The Change" are included on p. 324. "... it was Allen Ginsberg
and his friends, more than anyone else, who was responsible for

the fact that many millions of young Americans joined a movement whose utopia was between the ears. He was in truth the prophet of a new consciousness." Ginsberg is again cited in the following chapter, "Triumph and Failure of a Cultural Revolution." On the whole this is an attempt at cultural history of the 1960's written by a "British reporter who covered the American scene for many years."

636 Howard, Richard. Alone with America; Essays on the Art of Poetry in the U. S. Since 1950. New York: Atheneum, 1965, 1969.
    This book contains an essay about Ginsberg by Howard entitled, "O Brothers of the Laurel, Is the World Real? Is the Laurel a Joke or a Crown of Thorns?" There are also bibliographic references on p. 589. In total there are 41 essays on many poets including "Ashbery, Bly, Dickey, Kinnel, Levertov, Merwin, O'Hara, Plath, Rich, Sexton, Snyder, Strand and Wright."
    See also Howard, Richard, in the ARTICLES AND ESSAYS Section under PERIODICALS--About Ginsberg.

637 Kando, Thomas M. Leisure and Popular Culture in Transition. St. Louis: The C. V. Mosby Company, 1975.
    This is a text on the concept of leisure and popular culture. In chapter 9, "Youth, Culture, and Social Change," Kando uses excerpts from Allen Ginsberg's Howl to illustrate the Beats' "disaffiliation from American materialism." On p. 255, Allen Ginsberg is mentioned in relationship to Paul Goodman's work in which Goodman "explicity reviews and rejects the philosophy and the existence of men like Kerouac, Ginsberg and Mailer." On page 257, in "The Counter Culture," Ginsberg is highlighted as a "case" in which "the counter culture's membership was a transfusion of former beatniks...." In the "Summary and Conclusion" Ginsberg's Howl is excerpted and he is cited as one of several of "the beats' main spokesmen."

638 Knight, Arthur W. and Glee Knight (eds.). The Beat Book. California, Pa.: The Unspeakable Visions of the Individual Press, 1974 (P. O. Box 439, California, Pa. 15419).
    "The Beat Book comprises Volume 4, of 'the unspeakable visions of the individual.'" It includes a letter to Peter Orlovsky, a letter to Harold Schulman, and a letter to Mark Van Doren by Ginsberg, plus three poems for Ginsberg by Gerard Malanga, a drawing of Ginsberg by G. Corso, and a letter to Ginsberg from Gary Snyder. Various photographs of all the Beats together and separately are included.

639 Knight, Arthur and Kit Knight (eds.). The Beat Diary. Pennsylvania: n. p., 1977.
    The Beat Diary documents a particular segment of our culture. In particular close attention is paid to the poet Allen Ginsberg for his words comprise the introductory note written on "Independence Day, 1959." Among other items two excerpts from The Journals edited by Gordon Ball are included: from pp. 31-34 an entry from "October 7, 1960, evening, on Kerouac on Ayahuasca" and from pp. 162-166 an entry from "May 1952, New York City."

"Returning to the Country for a Brief Visit", a poem is included on p. 79. There are photographs throughout of Ginsberg and by Ginsberg of his friends and contemporaries.

640 Leary, Timothy. High Priest. New York: The World Publishing Company, n. d., original art by Allen Atwell and Michael Green.
    "The events related in this history reflect the collective consciousness and collaborative behavior of several thousand people-- spiritual researchers, who have shared dark confusions and bright hopes, given their emotion, brain and risked scorn and social isolation to pursue psychedelic yoga...." Included here is "Trip 6: The Blueprint to Turn-On the World: Ecstatic Politics. December 1960. Guide: Allen Ginsberg." from pages 109-133. The trip itself is arranged in a long narrative with small side notations in the margins which key reader to the minute details of the larger text. Also on p. 129 there is a photograph of Ginsberg (with no credits).

641 Lewis, Felice Flanery. Literature, Obscenity, and Law. Carbondale, Illinois: Southern Illinois University Press, 1976.
    There are various references to Allen Ginsberg throughout this text including on p. 185 a reference to "Howl" as one of the well-known works challenged for obscenity after 1955; excerpts from "Howl" and a discussion of its style and of its obscenity hearings from pp. 197-200; a reference to Burroughs and Ginsberg, p. 214; "Using poetic devices, the author (Burroughs) assembled a montage of shocking scenes which are connected through their contribution to the whole work rather than through a direct linear interrelationship presented in what Ginsberg during the Boston trial referred to as a 'science fiction style.'"

642 Litwak, et al. The United States, A World Power. Englewood Cliffs, New Jersey: Prentice-Hall, Inc., 1976. 4th edition, part 2.
    This is a softcover textbook which contains Allen Ginsberg's perspective on the Cold War (as Beat poet questioning nation's sanity) and contains an excerpt from his poem "America."

643 Malina, Judith. The Enormous Despair, A Diary of Judith Malina, August 1968 to April 1969. New York: Random House, 1972, first edition.
    "The Enormous Despair is a record in diary form of the year 1968 when, after an extended tour of Europe, The Living Theater returned to our United States. In a style at times poetic, Judith Malina writes what they found...." References can be found to Allen Ginsberg on p. 26, 55-59, 65, 83, 87-92, 94, 98-99, 134, 167, 188-189.

644 Malkoff, Karl. Crowell's Handbook of Contemporary America. New York: Thomas Y. Crowell Company, 1973.
    There is a chapter on Allen Ginsberg from pp. 127-133 in which a short biographical sketch of Ginsberg's development as a poet is sketched. It encompasses his early work on the Lower East

Side, the influence of Whitman, Pound and Williams, and his San Francisco days. A short selected bibliography is also included which terminates in the sixties.

645 Manchester, William. The Glory and the American Dream, A Narrative History of America 1932-1972. Boston: Little Brown and Co. , 1973.

This "Narrative History of America 1932-1972" makes references to Ginsberg on the following pages: 393, 483, 727, 728, 1205, 1207; passing references are made in the first two instances. In part three a portrait of the Beat literary movement is painted, including Ginsberg's poem "America. " Ginsberg's testimony for the Chicago 8 is also highlighted.

646 Mersmann, James F. Out of the Vietnam Vortex, A Study of Poets and Poetry Against The War. Lawrence, Kansas: The University Press of Kansas, 1974.

"The Vietnam War provoked an unprecedented reaction among American poets during the sixties: poems and podiums rang with protest. This thematic and critical study of the poetry of protest focuses primarily on the works by Allen Ginsberg, Denise Levertov, Robert Bly, and Robert Duncan.... Mersmann first surveys the poetry of World War I and II and traces the changing attitudes toward the proper relation of poetry to politics. He then discusses the works of Ginsberg, Levertov, Bly and Duncan, examining the common techniques, attitudes, and images that have shaped their poetic outpouring against the war. Mersmann's observations are based in part on personal interviews and correspondence with the poets. "

The writer begins his study with Allen Ginsberg for "he seems to express the Zeitgeist, or that portion of the larger poetic spirit that is peculiar to this moment in history, unique to this time. " Critically, he examines Ginsberg's work and concludes "Ginsberg is not a great poet, but he is a great figure in the history of poetry. "

647 Peters, Robert. The Poet As Ice-Skater. San Francisco, California: Manroot Books, 1975. Edition of 1,000 copies.

This is a book of "parodies and imitations" which includes Ginsberg. On p. 34 "The Tower Toppler: Allen Ginsberg" appears and on p. 37 "Allen Ginsberg Blesses a Bride and Groom. "

648 Phillips, Robert. The Confessional Poets. With a preface by Harry T. Moore. Carbondale, Illinois: Southern Illinois University Press; London: Feffer and Simons, Inc. , 1973.

Phillips presents a series of essays on "The Confessional Mode in Modern American Poetry" which includes the early work of Allen Ginsberg. A "Selected Bibliography" is also included highlighting Allen Ginsberg's major books until 1973.

649 Raskin, Jonah. Out of the Whale, Growing Up in the American Left. New York: Links Books, A Division of Music Sales Corporation, 1974 (dist. by Quick Fox, Inc. , New York).

In Jonah Raskin's revealing narrative about growing up in the American Left, he, in passing, notes Allen Ginsberg. More importantly, he illuminates the other leaders of the cultural revolution of the 1960's: Timothy Leary, Eldridge Cleaver and Abbie Hoffman.

650 Reck, Michael. Ezra Pound, A Close-Up. New York: Mc-Graw-Hill, 1973.

According to Michael Reck "for this paperback edition, I have added an account of the poet's last years, including the very strange conversation with Pound and Ginsberg..." (p. xi). The "account" is covered between pages 150-158 in Part 3, "Back to Italy." It unfolds as Olga Rudge, the author, Pound and Ginsberg attempt to converse "that grey October day in 1967 ... two days before his (Pounds's) eighty-second birthday...." Ginsberg tries to convince Pound of his profound influence in America: "You have shown us the way.... The more I read your poetry, the more I am convinced it is the best of its time.... Ah, well prospero ... what I came here for was to give you my blessing--despite your disillusion ... unless you want to be a Messiah.... Do you accept my blessings?" Pound responded, "I do." Yet Pound refutes these words of praise for he feels that he has failed, particularly in regard to his previously anti-Semitic stance. In the end, however, there seems to be a meeting of souls as alluded to in the dialogue above.

651 Rexroth, Kenneth. American Poetry in the 20th Century. New York: Herder and Herder, 1971.

This is a series of "interpretive" essays on "American Poetry In The 20th Century" which, of course, cites Allen Ginsberg in the development of poetry.

652 Rorem, Ned. Pure Contraption, A Composer's Essays. New York: Holt Rinehart & Winston, 1974.

This is a collection of essays in which the essay, "Notes from Last Year" (p. 1-22) copyrighted 1971 by Modern Occasions (which first appeared in Modern Occasions) contains a musical criticism of Allen Ginsberg's performance of Blake's poems (set to music by Allen Ginsberg). Rorem's basic criticism is that Ginsberg is not a musician or composer. If he wants to, he should set his own poetry to music instead of Blake's.

653 Shaw, Robert B. (editor) American Poetry Since 1960; Some Cultural Perspectives. Great Britain: Carcanet Press, 1973.

This collection of edited essays "offers a multi-focused view of American poetry since 1960." Extensive notation of the Beat poets is made in the essay by Shaw, "The Poetry of Protest," and the essay by Alan Williamson, "Language Against Itself: The Middle Generation of Contemporary Poets." A reading list of work noted in each chapter is included at the end of the collection.

654 Shepard, Sam. Rolling Thunder Logbook. New York: Viking Press, 1977.

"Rolling Thunder Revue played thirty performances in 22 cities, culminating in a mammouth sold-out concert at Madison Square Garden complete with Muhammad Ali. " Rolling Thunder Logbook includes mention of friends "Joan Baez, Phil Ochs, Arlo Guthrie, Allen Ginsberg, Ronie Blakely. "

655 Sinclair, Iain. The Kodak Mantra Diaries, October 1966 to June 1971. London, England: Albion Village Press, 1971. An edition of 2000 with cover photograph of the poet and others scattered throughout the text. ("The photographs used in this book were taken by Andrew Whittuck--Anna Sinclair--Iain Sinclair--Robert Klinkert. ")
These are the "Diaries" of Iain Sinclair which record his vision of the above-listed Movement leaders, particularly Allen Ginsberg. It is a blend of word and visual images interspersed with conversations between Ginsberg and others. Ginsberg talks about his work, Kerouac, drugs, meditation. He reads "a Version of Television was a Baby Crawling Towards That Deathchamber. " Others comment on Ginsberg, including Lionel Trilling. The conversations alluded to are conducted by "Geoffrey. "

656 Spiller, et al. (ed.). Literary History of the U. S. : History; New York: Macmillan Publishing Company, Inc. , 1974, 4th edition, revised.
The pages which include references to Allen Ginsberg are pages 1425 and 1431-1432. Reference is made here to the San Francisco Poets and the Beats. Ginsberg's poems "Howl" and "Kaddish" are both cited. The obscenity acquittal of Ginsberg's poem "Howl" is held as a landmark decision: "Henceforth the diction of American literature was uninhibited, nor did subsequent works require a parade of eminent academic critics to assert their social value as happened in the 'Howl' case. "

657 Sutton, Walter. American Free Verse, The Modern Revolution in Poetry. New York: New Directions, 1973.
"This book concentrates on the origins and growth of the powerful free verse movement from its beginnings in the Romantic revolution to the present. " The Beats are mentioned and Ginsberg is highlighted.

658 Tytell, John. Naked Angels, The Lives and Literature of the Beat Generation. New York: McGraw-Hill Book Company, 1976.
"Portions of 'The Broken Circuit' (copyright © 1973 by John Tytell), were published in a somewhat different form in The American Scholar. " "The Broken Circuit" serves as the introductory essay to this "most serious and astute study of the Beat writers published to date; John Tytell explores the origins and development of the Beat generation in the cultural context of the fifties. ... This fascinating blend of literary and social criticism and biographical material serves to illuminate the writers themselves, their works and their influence on the 'new consciousness' of the sixties. " Two sections are specifically addressed to Allen Ginsberg: Part II,

First Conjunctions, "Allen Ginsberg" from pp. 79-107; Part III, The Books, "Allen Ginsberg and the Messianic Tradition" from pp. 212-257.

      In the first piece on Ginsberg, Tytell biographically presents the poet. This section is followed by a photography section (unpaged) including photos of: 1) Hal Chase, Jack Kerouac, Allen Ginsberg, William Burroughs, Riverside Drive, New York, 1944. Courtesy Marshall Clements; 2) Neal Cassady and Jack Kerouac, San Francisco, 1949. Courtesy Allen Ginsberg; 3) Herbert Huncke on Burroughs' farm in New Waverly, Texas, 1947. Courtesy Allen Ginsberg; 4) Allen Ginsberg and Jack Kerouac, East 7th Street, New York, 1953. Courtesy Allen Ginsberg; 5) William Burroughs on East 7th Street, New York, 1953. Courtesy Allen Ginsberg; 6) Jack Kerouac on fire escape, New York, 1953. Courtesy Allen Ginsberg; 7) Jack Kerouac at Villa Muniria in Tangier, 1957. Courtesy Allen Ginsberg; 8) Jack Kerouac, Allen Ginsberg, Gregory Corso, and Lafcadio Orlovsky, Mexico City, Zocalo, 1956. Courtesy Allen Ginsberg; 9) Peter Orlovsky, Allen Ginsberg, Allen Ansen, Paul Bowles (seated), Gregory Corso, and Ian Summerville, Garden of Villa Muniria, 1957. Courtesy Allen Ginsberg; 10) Jack Kerouac in last years. Courtesy Allen Ginsberg; 11) Allen Ginsberg on upstate New York farm, Labor Day, 1973. Courtesy MELLON; and 12) William Burroughs at the West End Bar, New York, 1974. Courtesy MELLON.

      In the second essay, Tytell culturally and from a literary point of view deals with Ginsberg the man and the poet: "Part of Ginsberg's gift as a poet has been his faith in vision that has been characteristically American because of its buoyance, its ability to return with hope despite disaster...."

659   Whittemore, Reed. William Carlos Williams, Poet from Jersey. Boston: Houghton Mifflin Company, 1975.
      There are multiple references to Ginsberg: first in the context of Paterson from pages 3-5, 8; next in Williams' admiration on page 25; then again in view of Paterson from pages 180-181; as a leading figure in the San Francisco Poetry revolution on pages 321-322, 325-328; in correspondence with Williams on page 331; again on page 335; and finally in the context of a writing trip on page 336.

660   Winterowd, W. Ross. The Contemporary Writer, A Practical Rhetoric. New York: Harcourt Brace Jovanovich, Inc. , 1975.
      In this textbook from pages 9-12, Indian Journals is analyzed in terms of the writer, the context, the structure, the style and the audience.

Foreign Language

661   Pivano, Fernanda. Beat hippie yippie/Dall' underground alla contro-cultura. (... from underground to the counterculture.) Rome, Italy: Arcana Editrice, 1972.
      It seems that Fernanda Pivano is a newspaper writer who covers cultural phenomena. This is a sociology book which mentions

Ginsberg in articles reprinted from Il Mondo, 30 November 1965;
Ciao, 2001, 9 April 1969; Gazzetta del Popolo, 7 June 1970; and
from Il Giorno.
        Also translated into French and Spanish; see entries be-
low.

662 Pivano, Fernanda. Beat Hippie Yippie/De l'Underground a la
        Contre-culture. (Beat Hippie Yippie/From the Underground
        to the Counter-culture.) Paris: Christian Bourgois Editeur,
        1972 (Arcana Editrice, 1972).
        French translation of Italian entry above.

663 Pivano, Fernanda. Beat hippie yippie. Madrid, Spain: Edi-
        ciones Jucar, 1975.
        Spanish edition of the Italian book (see above) with more
specialized chapters. Translation by José Palao.

664 Pivano, Fernanda and Luigi Castigliano (eds.). On the Road,
        by Jack Kerouac. Italy: School Publishing House, Edizioni
        Scholastiche Mondadori, 1974. Introduction by Fernanda
        Pivano.
        Allen Ginsberg, of course, is mentioned in the descrip-
tive introduction by Fernanda Pivano (Italian printing in English).

665 Quennelle, Gilbert and Guy et José Soret. The American
        Dream: Fichier pour le professeur. Paris: Dossiers de
        Civilisation/Classiques Hachette, 1975. (In a mixture of
        French and English.)
        This is a French lesson stencil and correlating teacher's
guide (both in soft cover). On page 41 there is reference made to
Ginsberg's "Footnote to Howl." There is also a short biography on
p. 59.

666 Starer, Jacqueline. Chronolgie Des Ecrivains Beats Jusqu'en
        1969. (Chronology of The Beat Writers and the Voyage Up
        to 1969.) Verifee par Carolyn Cassady, Gregory Corso,
        Lawrence Ferlinghetti, Allen Ginsberg, Eileen Kaufman et
        Gary Snyder. Paris: Etudes Anglaises, 69, Didier 15,
        1977. In French.
        "Avant-Propos" (Foreword) by Jacqueline Starer, Paris,
October 1975: "At the moment that I began this work which was to
become The Voyage of the Beats there did not exist a single historical study of the Beat Movement. Since such a work was indispensable to the analysis of this movement, I have undertaken to do
so...." This is an actual chronology (which begins with 1939) of
the people involved in the Beat Movement. At the conclusion of each
year there is a list of publications of the individuals involved. In
all this is an excellent research tool. Of course, Ginsberg and his
work are included.

667 Starer, Jacqueline. Les Ecrivains Beats Et Le Voyage. (The
        Beat Writers and the Voyage.) Paris: Etudes Anglaises 68,
        Didier, 15, 1977.

This is an historical text dealing with the Beat Movement which includes notes, "unedited pieces," "Table of Correspondence," and a substantial bibliography covering the major Beats. In short the "Table of Correspondence" serves as an identifying chart of the relationships of the individuals to one another. The "unedited" section includes a poem by Ginsberg "Flying Elegy" written November 17, 1973 and presented here in English. Since the bibliography covers all the major writers of the Beat Movement, its individual treatment of writers is not extensive (pp. 233-273). However, this is an excellent research tool in substance and arrangement.

III. ARTICLES AND ESSAYS

A. NEWSPAPERS

English Language

668 Aaron. "Two Eyes on Ginsberg." Berkeley Tribe, 99, 11
June 1972, p. 12.

669 Aldrich, Michael. "A Sign Is a Sword." The Marijuana Review. 1:5:21.
"Shortly after Yippie Convention Chicago '68, Allen Ginsberg returned to his New York farm to set these Blake Songs of
Innocence and Experiences to music. ...Inspiration is Conspiracy,
breathing in and out together." This is an introduction to Ginsberg's
work and its relationship to this year's activities of protests.

670 Allen, Henry. "Allen Ginsberg: Burning for the Ancient
Heavenly Connection to the Starry Dynamo of Washington."
The Washington Post, Sunday Magazine, Potomac, 1 May
1977, pp. 10-11, 22, 26-28, including large photographs on
pp. 10-11 and others on pp. 27, 28 by Bill Snead.
Allen Ginsberg is back in Washington, reading and investigating government injustices. This portrait of Ginsberg opens
with references to a Channel 5 talk show taping with Pat Mitchell at
which time he plugs his readings and investigations, plays the harmonium and reads. Henry Allen follows Ginsberg all over Washington as if to find out what makes Allen tick. This is an objective
descriptive article, yet colored with personal interaction on the part
of the interviewer. Historically, Henry Allen does his homework.
The article is carefully set amidst the Allen Ginsberg Washington
knows.

671 "Allen Ginsberg and Bethlehem Asylum in Concert at Miami
Marine Stadium." Daily Planet, 1 January 1970, 1:1, page
1, 8.
Allen Ginsberg will read at the Miami Marine Stadium in
Key Biscayne on Monday evening, December 22nd with Bethlehem
Asylum, a popular rock band. The article continues to give a biographical sketch of Ginsberg citing his written poetry, speaking
tours, awards and appearance in "3 motion pictures Pull My Daisy
(1961), Wholly Communion (1965), and Chappaqua (1966)."

672 "Allen Ginsberg Decries Arrests of Russians." Sunday New
York Times, 27 February 1977, p. 42, col. 3.

"Allen Ginsberg, the poet, denounced the recent arrest of Soviet dissidents in Moscow and Kiev. He spoke Friday at a news conference near the headquarters of the Soviet Mission to the United Nations, 136 East 67th Street." Ginsberg together with "Reza Baraheni, an Iranian poet and former political prisoner in Iran, and Boris Shragin, an exiled Soviet dissident, attempted to deliver a letter of protest to Oleg A. Troyanovsky, Soviet representative to the United Nations, but were informed by police that the Mission 'would not accept it' ... Mr. Ginsberg and Mr. Baraheni were permitted to walk past the mission."

673 "Allen Ginsberg in New Orleans/AUM MANI PADME HUM." Nola Express, 1971, 91, pp. 12-13. With six photographs which include Ginsberg and back cover poem, "HUM BOM!"

674 "Allen Ginsberg Joins Ranks of the Pedagogues." Rocky Mountain News, 22 June 1975, n. p.
This is an article about Allen Ginsberg, the "poet laureate" in which his activities at Naropa Institute, School for Disembodied Poets, are highlighted. Ginsberg also read in Denver and some review of this is given.

675 "Allen Ginsberg Participates in the New Nation Celebration Festival, Buffalo, New York, SUNY." New York Times, 22 November 1970, 53:1.

676 "Allen Ginsberg Poem 'On Jessore Road' Describes Horrors of India-Pakistani War"; with drawing. New York Times, 17 December 1971, 41:1.

677 "Allen Ginsberg, Poet in New York Hospital After Attack of Bell's Palsy, Expected to Be Released Soon." New York Times, 23 May 1975, 34:1.

678 "Allen Ginsberg Reads Poetry by Walt Whitman at Opening at Marine Stadium, Miami, Florida; Previous reading at stadium was interrupted by blasts of loud music intended to drown out use of four letter words." New York Times, 31 December 1969, 18:1.

679 "Allen Ginsberg Returns." Georgia Straight, 24-31 May 1973, 7:294, p. 1 with cover photograph of Allen Ginsberg titled "Ginsberg: New Poems."
This is an announcement of a reading and recital to be held on June 3rd at Queen Elizabeth Theatre, at 8 p. m. with venerable Kalu Rinpoche to "coincide with Ginsberg's birthday."

680 Alton, Lawrence. "Sometimes a Great Commotion/A Noninterview with Noise Attachments." Westport Trucker, 2 February-7 March 1972, 2:21 (45?), pp. 3, 9, with photograph of Allen Ginsberg in collage.
Alton reports on the "third RFK Memorial Symposium." Most of the story is based on his interaction with Ed Sanders and a

122 / Secondary Works

note in passing is made to Allen Ginsberg: "So the RFK Symposium
was over, with only the Intrepid Trips Information Service issue of
the U-News left as a coda. That paper has been suppressed by the
UMKC police because of an Allen Ginsberg poem on page nine which
is also printed in this paper on page 5...."

681 "... and the Deepest Om in the East." (The Grape) Western
      Organizer 6-19 June 1973, 2:11, pp. 16-17, center with
      photo by Alan Katowitz titled, "Ginsberg Wails" and small
      cover photo, "Inside the guru business, p. 16."
         Ginsberg performed on June 3 to a "crowd of 800" at
Eric Hamber Auditorium. "The message was mellowness and messier
than Garner Ted Armstrong, (also on campus) but basically the same:
praise the several thousand names of the 'LORD.'" The rest of the
article compares Allen Ginsberg to Garner Ted Armstrong.

682 Bacon, Leslie. "Leary's Smiling Inquisitor." Berkeley Barb,
      27 September-3 October 1974, 20:11:476, p. 6.
         "Just where is Tim Leary and why is everyone saying all
those terrible things about him? From talking with Allen Ginsberg
who has been seeking some specifics about his old friend Tim, I
learned even more curious details...."

683 Bangs, Lester. "Records/Songs of Innocence and Experience."
      Review of Songs of Innocence and Experience, by Allen Gins-
      berg. (Verse/Forecast/FTS 3083). Rolling Stone, 11 June
      1970, n. 60, p. 44 with photograph (by Annie Liebovitz).
         "This album contains a cycle of 21 of Blake's most affect-
ing (and least obscure) poems, set to simple melodies and sung by
Ginsberg himself.... The result is an oddly moving album which
manages to sound amateurish and pure at the same time.... It
sounds, rather, like a labor of love, a salute from a young visionary
to an ancient sage, executed with delicacy and charm in a vocal style
reminiscent of an Anglo-American muezzin...."

684 Barber, James. "Allen Enjoyed It All--and So Did Audience."
      Vancouver Province, 4 June 1973, n. p.
         "It was Allen Ginsberg's birthday and a special benefit
performance to finance the bringing to American of an East Indian
guru colleague." This article deals with Ginsberg's reading in Vancouver on Sunday evening and reaches a conclusion with words of
praise: "But that's the whole point of Ginsberg. Bold, and getting
old, sitting there in his blue coveralls and his black old beard, surrounded by flutes and tabla and enthusiasts, he is a priest.... The
only difference is that he isn't the priest of anybody dead."

685 Barnes, Clive. "Stage: Moving Appeal of 'Kaddish'; Ginsberg
      Work Given at Circle in Square." New York Times, 2
      April 1972, p. 47, column 1.
         "One of the Chelsea Theater Center of Brooklyn's achieve-
ments this year has been this production of Allen Ginsberg's play on
his original poem, 'Kaddish,' and this, augumented and adapted, has
now been brought off Broadway to the Circle in the Square."

686 Barnes, Clive. "The Theater: 'Kaddish'", "Play on Ginsberg
     Poem Opens at the Chelsea," Review of "Kaddish," by Allen
     Ginsberg. New York Times, 11 February 1972, p. 27,
     column 1. (For correction on this review, see NYT, 12
     Feb. 1972, p. 36, column 1.)
          This review describes the multimedia experience of "Kad-
dish." "The two main techniques used include showing film clips
of the actors on the screen; which both complements and illustrates
the action on the stage; the other major device is to reproduce on
the screen through closed-circuit television the actor on the stage,
so we see both the man and his enlarged video image simultaneously." Barnes concludes "this ... is a worthwhile dramatic experiment..."

687 Barry, Ann (ed.). "Arts and Leisure Guide. Of Special In-
     terest." New York Times, 27 February 1977, n. p.
          "On the Poetry Beat ... Allen Ginsberg, the poet whose
'Howl' was the anthem of the 1950's Beat Generation, is still very
much with us. Tomorrow evening, Mr. Ginsberg will appear at the
92nd Street Y, in a program in which he will not only read from
his works but sing to musical accompaniment. And on Wednesday,
he turns up at Queens College for another reading, this one free."

688 Bartley, Bruce M. "World-Famous Poet to 'Howl' Tonight."
     The News Record, 15 April 1977, 69:75, p. 1.
          This is an article announcing Ginsberg's reading "at the
George Amos Memorial Library" in Gillette, Wyoming, as part of
a tour of that state.

689 "'Beat' Poet to Speak." The Simpsonian, 12 November 1976,
     108:8, n. p.
          This is an announcement of Allen Ginsberg's appearance
"at Simpson College at 8 p. m. Nov. 22 in Pote Theatre. Following
the lecture, there will be a reception for him at the DU house....
Jim Lierow, committee chairman, calls Ginsberg 'one of the most
outstanding speakers' ever to come to Simpson."

690 Beck, David L. "Rock Artists Score Big in Salt Palace Show."
     Salt Lake Tribune, 26 May 1976, p. A 13.
          This is an article about the Rolling Thunder Revue which
alludes to Ginsberg.

691 Belt, Byron. "Sunday Press Radio/FM Best Bets." Long
     Island Press, 26 December 1976, p. 10.
          Under the heading "Tomorrow" the following is listed:
"10--end WBAI (99.5) Poetry course. Allen Ginsberg is heard in
a ten-week series on writing poetry. Listeners may phone in comments and questions at the end."

692 Berkeley Barb, 11-17 May 1973, 17:19:404, p. 13, with picture
     by Sam Silver and three new Ginsberg poems (listed separ-
     ately in the POETRY section of this bibliography).
          "Allen Ginsberg limped into the Barb office at press-time,

fresh from a successful benefit in Los Angeles for Tim Leary and
sporting a hip cast (what other kind?) from a fall on the ice sustained last winter at his upstate N.Y. farm. He will be staying in
the Bay Area for three weeks writing liner notes for Fantasy Records,
and spreading some of the latest work from his prolific pen, samples of
which the Barb is proud to present here for the first time."

693 Bernard, Sidney. "A Reading and a Mourning." New York
    Times Book Review, 24 April 1977, Section VII, p. 30,
    32-33, with photograph of Ginsberg on page 32. Reprinted in
    Witnessing: The Seventies, by Sidney Bernard. New York:
    Horizon Press, 1977.
        This is an article reviewing the reading of Robert Lowell
and Allen Ginsberg at St. Mark's Church. "A crowd of about 500,
with another hundred lined up outside the high-spired church in
Greenwich Village, all with anticipation befitting the odd-couple cast-
ing." The reading, indeed, was memorable: "The odd-couple reading, Bearded Paterson-East Side Hasid guru, tense ruddy history
ridden New England Brahim. One playing Tolstoyan fox, the other
Dostoyevskyan hedgehog. Lowell himself made the bridge: 'Actually, we're from two ends of the William Carlos Williams spectrum.'
St. Mark's the poetry temple, takes it all in."
        This reading is paralleled in the Bernard article to the
"reverent ... private" reading at NYU in celebration of the late
Anais Nin's 74th Birthday. In attendance was "a crowd of about 150,
and a well-scrubbed constituency of Anais fans and intimates--pub-
lishing librarian types, women's movement writers and activists."

694 "Biographical Sketches of Those Selected by Jurors for Pulitzer
    Prize for 1975." New York Times, 6 May 1975, 34:1.
        Gary Snyder is cited for Poetry and Ginsberg is mentioned
as his chanting "colleague."

695 Blum, Peter. "Two Events, Two Reactions. Three Apprecia-
    tions for Poet Allen Ginsberg Readings at Woodstock Artists
    Association this past weekend drew enthusiastic responses."
    Woodstock Times 6:51 (December 1, 1977): 18-19.
        Three individual articles on Allen's readings at the Wood-
stock Artists Association. P. 19, excerpt from "Who Be Kind To."

696 Bockris, Victor. "Burroughs & Death." Drummer, 10-17
    February 1976?, n.p.
        Allen Ginsberg relates an anecdote about Burroughs at a
dinner party with Sonia Orwell.

697 Bockris, Victor. "Dinner with Burroughs." Drummer, 17-24
    February 1976, 388, p. 7.
        "Allen Ginsberg in conversation with the author, Febru-
ary 1974." Allen Ginsberg discusses introducing (and meeting) Mar-
cel Duchamp to Burroughs. Merely one paragraph of this article
concerns Burroughs.

698 Bruchac, Joé. "The Gentlest Prophet/Ginsberg Reads at Skid-

more. " Nickel Review, 21 November 1969, 4:12, p. 5.
Joé Bruchac writes about her interactions with Allen Ginsberg when he came to upper N.Y. for a reading at Skidmore. Insightfully she colors the mood of his visit, "short weeks after the death of Jack Kerouac. " Ginsberg flies into Albany with two British friends, "Come up for the evening to hear him read, Caroline Coon (of Release) and Miles ... (who produced Allen reading Blake on MGM). " Allen started his reading with "the great Buddha mantra" which reminded him of Jack Kerouac. Then he continued with a reading from Jack's work and slowly moved on to read his own work, which dealt with his homosexual dilemma in which he described his desire to have children, "Like a homosexual capitalist afraid of the masses and that's my situation folks. " Allen, in closing, sang "the Blake song: 'Little Lamb, Who Made Thee?'" Again he revived the memory of his dead friend for the audience. A reception followed in which he chanted "Hare Krishna" and read poems from Chicago--"police state or image of Eden?"

699 Bryan, John. "Ginsberg, McClure, Bly/Bring Back the Muse. " Berkeley Barb, 20-26 May 1977, 25:19: 614, p. 4.
"The largest poetry reading seen in Berkeley during the 1970's brought over 3000 people to UC's Greek Theater last Saturday afternoon for the benefit of financially-distressed KPFA. Led off by Allen Ginsberg, Robert Bly, Ed Dorn and Michael McClure, the rambling, highly-varied program demonstrated that the poetic muse still resides on both sides of the Bay, that the voice of personal liberation and protest that Ginsberg first raised when he resided in Berkeley during the mid-1950's is still vibrant, that interest in small press publishing remains high, that KPFA took an enormous gamble and won. "
This article further comments on the change in the audience which attended this reading: "The audience--mostly under thirty--was extraordinarily passive and orderly, unpolluted by personal stashes of booze and wonder weed. They got highly resentful when a long verse was interrupted by too much movement or whispered conversation. They seemed meditative, day-dreamy, locked into themselves. "

700 Bryan, John. "Ginsberg Wants Purified Politics. " Berkeley Barb, 27 May-2 June 1977.
"Allen Ginsberg wants to correct a statement run by the Barb in last week's issue. He was quoted as saying in regard to his well-known political activism during the 1960's "I was wrong. I was wrong. " The phrase did come out of his mouth but he feels it was reported out of context. "I'm in favor of activism and politics wherever possible purified of resentment, anger, aggression and pride. Ideal street demonstration: vast meditation sit-ins. "

701 Buccino, Anthony. "Anthony Hears the Ginsbergs. " Independent Press (Bloomfield, New Jersey), 14 April 1975, n. p.
See same article below in Belleville Times, 24 April 1975, p. 5.

702 Buccino, Anthony. "In Father-Son Reading/Poet Ginsberg:
'Keep on Breathing.'" Belleville Times, 24 April 1975,
p. 5.
The two poets read at Rutgers University. Louis Ginsberg in his "regular meter," Allen in "free style" verse (Words
of Louis). Louis is portrayed as the "king of pun-liners." On the
whole Buccino was inspired by the two men.

703 Bukowski, Charles. "Notes of a Dirty Old Man/The Night
Nobody Believed I Was Allen Ginsberg." Berkeley Tribe,
19-25 September 1969, p. 12.
Ginsberg explores Venice, California "the new village of
LA" but finds only hostility. "Where were the writers, the painters,
the hippies, the bums?" Instead he met with hostile women, more
hostile men (Louie) and rain. In his own words "it was a con."

704 C. A. P. "Gallery Camera." Martha's Vineyard Gazette, 1 July
1975, p. 7.
"'What do I have to lose if America falls?' is the title
Peter Barry Chowka has chosen for his most recent photographs at
Gallery Camera in Oak Buffs. Extracted from Allen Ginsberg's
poem 'Crossing Nation,' it both accompanies Chowka's excellent
studies of Ginsberg and provides a unifying theme for the varied
selections comprising the display. Combining examples of his free-
lance photojournalism with prints of a lyrical, personal and esoteric
nature, he communicates a unique perception of the world in the
1970's, while maintaining an awareness of and sensitivity to his immediate, everyday surroundings."

705 C. E. O. "The National Book Award 'Show.'" St. Louis Post-
Dispatch, 21 April 1974, p. 4B.
This is an article which recounts the acceptance speech
presented for Allen Ginsberg by friend, Peter Orlovsky (prepared by
Ginsberg for the occasion). It was an appropriate "oratorical per-
formance."

706 Caen, Herbert. "Column." San Francisco Chronicle and
Examiner, 19 May 1977, n. p.
"Poet Allen Ginsberg is in town for a month, bunking
with Shig Murao, grand old man of City Lights Bookstore, which
helped put Allen on the literary map and vice-versa. Kerouac, Orlovsky, Corso, Ginsberg--my that was a long time ago...."

707 "Cafe Confidential." Soho Con/Fidential, 12 March 1977, 6,
pp. 2-3.
There is a brief reference to Allen Ginsberg in this
informal column, "Why did Allen Ginsberg make his rock'n roll
debut at a Village club whose manager is notorious for his rip-off
attitude towards the artists who appear there (usually for nothing)?"

708 Caffery, Bethia. "Ginsberg Sing-Chants." St. Petersburg Independent, 4 October 1972, p. 1B, with two photographs, one
with students, the other alone.

This article records Allen Ginsberg's appearance at the University of South Florida in a "poetry reading with student Christopher Horrell on the guitar."

709 Caldwell, Nancy. "For Arts Sake Nation's Small Presses/ Prefer Literary Values/To Commercial Success/Vehicle for Poets, Novelists/Gets Washington's Aid; Mulch HAS Earthy Goal, Hoping for Next Ezra Pound." The Wall Street Journal 24 Feb. 1976, n. p.

Caldwell's detailed article deals with the progress of Mulch Press of Chicopee, Mass. There is a reference to their publication of "The Visions of the Great Rememberer" in the context of paperback marketability. This book is by Allen Ginsberg.

710 Campbell, Mark. "Means and Meditation." Colorado Daily, 14 April 1976, pp. 9-10.

Campbell reports on Boulder and its Jack Kerouac School of Disembodied Poetics at Naropa Institute in which Allen Ginsberg participates. The article is actually a comment upon poetry, "still the nigger of the art world" because of "media hype" and the economic manipulation of these poets by the "system." Yet, Campbell chastises Ginsberg for his recent activities as "front man for a small-time Buddhist dictator like Chögyam Rinpoche," and playing "groupie to a half-assed lyricist like Dylan.... Has Ginsberg lost faith in his outlaw energy as he's gotten older? Is Buddhism an elephant's graveyard for poets? ... I feel betrayed. One of the 'best minds of our generation' is rotting."

711 Carroll, Paul. "Ginsberg and Burroughs ... The Beat Goes On." Chicago Daily News, 8-9 March 1975, p. 6, with photographs, one of which concerns Ginsberg, "Poet Allen Ginsberg showed up in the Uncle Sam hat for a peace demonstration in New York's Central Park in 1966. The photo was taken by Fred W. McDarrah."

Carroll provides a retrospective article about the years he has known Allen Ginsberg and William Burroughs which prepares the reader for "the Ginsberg-Burroughs schedule of readings" in the Chicago student area.

712 Castro, M. "Alan [sic] Ginsberg at Webster College." Outlaw, 17 November-14 December 1972, III:11, p. 13, with photograph of Ginsberg.

"Alan [sic] Ginsberg visited St. Louis Nov. 1st and 2nd to give a poetry reading at Webster College and make himself available to interested citizenry.... Ginsberg started the Webster reading about twenty minutes early ... he led the chanting of the Buddhist mantra OM AH HUM VAJRA GURU PADDMA SIDDHI HUM. This is intended to arouse in the chanter a sense of the 3 mysteries: OM, body/head; AH, the purified voice; and HUM, mind/heart. The rest of the mantra might be interpreted as an appeal to the VAJRA GURU (diamond teacher) for PADDMA SIDDHI (lotus power/power of yogic accomplishment that leads to enlightenment) through dedication to HUM (the mind/heart, which are one).... Ginsberg's Webster reading reflected his two overriding concerns: the need for the highest possible spiritual aspiration and attainment, coupled with moral and responsible actions in a social plane."

713 Charters, Ann. "Jack and Neal and Allen and Luanne and
     Carolyn: In Which Jack Hits the Road." Rolling Stone,
     131 (29 March 1973): 31-34.
     Excerpts from Kerouac a biography was published by
Straight Arrow Books in 1973.

714 Chibeau, Edmond. "UCSB Poetry Reading/Ferlinghetti, Gins-
     berg to Honor Rexroth." Santa Barbara News & Review,
     18 May 1973, II:10 (34), p. 18 with photograph of Ginsberg
     with Lawrence Ferlinghetti, titled "Allen Ginsberg in a medi-
     tative movement during one of his poetry readings."
          Ferlinghetti and Ginsberg come together for the first
time in years to read at UCSB on behalf of Kenneth Rexroth on
May 29th. "They're coming together this time in honor of Kenneth
Rexroth, USCB poet, whose contract renewal is under question....
The poetry reading is a demonstration of solidarity of students and
the artistic community in their desire to keep Rexroth at UCSB. If
the poet leaves, there is a possibility he will move to Japan." The
rest of the article highlights all three poets including their participation in the "San Francisco Renaissance."

715 Chronicle, 10 February 1976?, p. 8.
          "'Ginsberg has done LSD experiments: he was well known
during the Vietnam War. He is outspoken and controversial,' said
Tim Johnson, chairperson of the Festival of the Arts Committee.
Ginsberg will give a lecture in Steward Hall, Thursday at 8 p. m."

716 Cincinnati Enquirer, 2 February 1975, n. p.
          This is a short announcement of Allen Ginsberg's reading
at 7:30 p. m. in Seiler Commons at Thomas More College that day.

717 Cleaver, Eldridge. "Outside Algiers." Village Voice, 1971.
          Ginsberg responded to comments made by Cleaver in the
Village Voice article in another article in the Partisan Review, 38:3
(1971): 307-308, "I think his reasons for putting down acid ... (are)
... that you are left vulnerable."

718 "Colorado Authors to Discuss Work." Rocky Mountain News,
     2 August 1977, p. 37 with reproductions of three drawings,
     "Denver artist Tom Fowler's conception of three Colorado
     authors at right, poet Allen Ginsberg, and novelist Joanne
     Greenberg, center, and John Williams."
          This is a brief announcement of the discussion sponsored
by Learning for Living of the above-mentioned three on "Saturday,
August 6, from 1 to 5 p. m. at the Humphrey Mansion, 770 Pennsylvania St."

719 Cook, Bonnie L. "Celebration: Allen Ginsberg--Bhagavan
     Das." Drummer, 2 April 1974, 289, p. 5 with photograph

by Kim Sokoloff of Allen Ginsberg, Bhagavan Das and Peter Orlovsky.

"After three months meditating with Chögyam Trungpa in Wyoming, Allen Ginsberg, Bhagavan Das and Peter Orlovsky went on the road last week ... they had to offer the 600 people who gathered at the Asbury Ministry Church in Philadelphia ... a spiritual celebration ... a sharing of experiences of song, poetry, and meditation ... a simple 'being here now' of three personalities who have come to live within and around such truths."

720 Cook, Bonnie L. "Happy Birthday, Walt. --Love, Allen." Drummer, 28 May 1974, 297, cover story, p. 5, with cover photo collage by Mindy Bronson, reprinted on page 5.

Allen Ginsberg stood on the steps of Cooper School a "stately brick building in Camden" and read on behalf of Walt Whitman who read the dedication to the school 100 years ago. In part the reading offered a protest against the planned demolition of the building. More importantly, it was an occasion for Allen Ginsberg to read from Walt Whitman and his own works, thereby allowing their spirits to mingle with the crowd and each other.

721 Cooper, Claire. "Court OK's Board's Right to Bar." Rocky Mountain News, 5 March 1977, n. p.

Allen Ginsberg's books, Kaddish and Other Poems and The Yage Letters (with William Burroughs) were among the 10 books banned in the Aurora schools by its board "largely on grounds of alleged immorality." This article documents the federal court decision which legitimates the Aurora school board's "right to bar the use of 10 popular novels and poetry books in high school English classes."

722 Courtney, Marian. "Pott Operates Luncheonette." Herald News, 28 December 1976, 105:300, n. p.

This is an article about Herschel Silverman, a local poet, who runs a Bayonne luncheonette. A reference is made to Ginsberg among others: "He's (Herschel Silverman) pleased to have been included with Ginsberg in literary magazines."

723 Crandell, Ellen. "Ginsberg B'ham '74." Northwest Passage, 22 April-6 May 1974, 10:10, p. 24.

"About two weeks ago, Allen Ginsberg was in town visiting the college and gave two evening 'talks.' He shared the limelight with Bhagavan Das ..." The change in Ginsberg is noted. There is an air of spiritualism. As Ginsberg stated, "I came out of Chicago tear-gassed and old and went home and sat down at the organ and started to learn music." Ginsberg is now focusing on the political reality of the heroin traffic in Southeast Asia through collaboration, in part, with Alfred W. McCoy who published The Politics of Heroin in Southeast Asia in 1972."

724 Cusack, Anne. "Enjoying Flights of Fancy at Oakton's Spring Ritual." Herald, 8 May 1976, section 1, p. 4, with photograph titled, "Counter-culture poet Allen Ginsberg."

At a celebration of "the Rites of Spring" on the Oakton Community College campus Allen Ginsberg reads.

725 Dawson, Ilona. "Allen Ginsberg Sees Hopelessness for the
       Country. " Patriot Ledger "Limelight/Arts, Leisure, Enter-
       tainment Section" (Thursday, January 5, 1978): 32. Photo-
       graph of Allen Ginsberg by Ilona Dawson.
            Allen Ginsberg reads at "Passim Coffeehouse in Cam-
   bridge ... Kaddish, written for his mother in 1958. " This is an
   article about the brief encounter the reporter had with Allen Ginsberg and his friend Peter Orlovsky as they "spoke of their present
   attitudes and lifestyle. "

726 Della-Pietra, May. "Center Hosts Events; Poet to Recite
       Works. " The College Reporter, 1 May 1977, p. 3.
            This is an article announcing Allen Ginsberg and Charles
   Plymell's joint reading on March 6, 1977 at 8 p. m. in Nevin Chapel
   in Old Main, following a "poetry writing workshop. " These appearances are part of the College's "Values and Issues Series. "

727 Detro, Gene. "Feminist Poet Draws 500 Here. " Oregon
       Journal, 24 April 1974, n. p.
            Adrienne Rich's reading is reviewed. In passing there
   is a reference to Ginsberg as the co-recipient of the National Book
   Award for Poetry.

728 Detro, Gene. "Poet Ginsberg Shares Spotlight with Music. "
       Oregon Journal, 4 May 1974, n. p.
            Detro records Allen Ginsberg's unconventional appearance
   in Portland at which "Sufi dancers whirled happily and barefoot,
   children padded about as Allen chanted, led group mantras, played
   his funky merry harmonium, sang (if that is the proper word for
   what came out), and read occasionally from recent notebooks. "
   Again he was accompanied by his "musician friend Bhagavan Das. "

729 Diser, Phil. "Ginsberg Still Active, but No Longer Activist. "
       St. Paul Sunday Pioneer Press, 1 May 1977, p. 4, Wiscon-
       sin, with picture titled, "Allen Ginsberg, reciting poetry
       in Menomonie, Wis. last week. "
            At this reading in Wisconsin "He did not read his best
   known poems. Instead, he focused on more recent works of poetry
   and songs.... 'It's polite of me to read what I'm interested in....
   and polite of students to listen to what I'm doing now....' The performance included a five-minute period of meditation for standing-
   room-only crowd, and the only sound that could be heard was the
   fussing of a child. "

730 Doar, Harriet. "A-h-h, Say A-h-h. " Charlotte Observer, 24
       October 1972, p. 1C, 3C (col. 1), with three photographs,
       two of Ginsberg titled, "Poet Allen Ginsberg at Davidson
       College to kick off '50's Celebration ... he brought more
       politics than poetry to the campus" and "Allen Ginsberg:
       America is on a monstrous ego trip. " All of the above are
       Observer photos by Don Aldridge.
            Doar's article records Ginsberg's visit to Davidson Col-
   lege. "Ginsberg, bringing more politics than poetry to Davidson, is

spending two days on the campus, talking, reading, singing and asking the students what happened to the campus revolution and to student support of McGovern. He kicked off a month-long student celebration of the Fifties, with a public talk in Love Auditorium Monday night. "

731 Eaves, Morris. "Songs of Innocence and of Experience by William Blake, tuned by Allen Ginsberg." Blake Newsletter, 4:3 (Winter 1971), pp. 90-97.

Review includes the text for prose liner notes accompanying this record. See "Blake Notes" under ESSAYS, STATEMENTS AND QUOTES in Primary Works.

732 Edelson, Morris. "Allen Ginsberg in Madison/The War on His Mind." Wisconsin Patriot, Voice of the Wisconsin Alliance, May 1972, 2:4, pp. 6-7 with cover photograph titled, "Ginsberg oms with alliance & friends/Madison Vietnam Blues/ (Sung by Ginsberg on the Capitol steps)." On page 6 there is another photograph, titled, "OM," and in the center of pages 6-7 there is a third photograph of the Capitol with Allen Ginsberg.

Allen Ginsberg spends three days in Madison, Wisconsin aiding the political movement with words and chants, readings, talks with students and suggestions. His plans for peaceful demonstration preceded by chanting for purification reflect his motivation (now, in 1972): "His theory as well as his later acts in the next three days pushed non-violence, spiritual awareness, hope and optimism."

733 Eder, Richard. "4 Shorts at Film Forum a Blend of Charm and Naivete." New York Times, 17 October 1975, 24:3.

Four 1950's films are shown at the Vandham Theater in Soho, the "new premises" for Film Forum. "Pull My Daisy" is one of the four shown, which cites Allen Ginsberg's "participation" with Gregory Corso and Peter Orlovsky.

734 "Effeministrike." Berkeley Barb, 11-17 June 1971, 12:22:304, p. 2, with picture of Allen Ginsberg.

" 'Allen's Barb Ad' was the subject of commentary on a leaflet handed out by 3 gay men Sunday at the Ginsberg benefit reading at the Berkeley Community Theatre." Ginsberg is attacked for his "sexism" by this group signed "The Effemist." They find him guilty of falling into the same heterosexual male dominance game of looking for a "wife in a male body." The leaflet handed out "reproduced the Barb letter" and included the sexism commentary below it.

735 Ehrmann, Eric. "Angels Free Cabaret." Berkeley Barb, 13-19 August 1971, 13:5:313, p. 9, with photograph by Gregory Pickup/Interzone titled "My Son the Jewish Mother (Allen Ginsberg)." This is Allen dressed up as "the Jewish Mother."

"The Angels of Light Free Cabaret was ... held at the United Projects warehouse, 330 Grove St. , under the auspices of In-

132 / Secondary Works

terzone Collective, ... Allen Ginsberg sang beautiful Songs of Innocence which he played on his Benares Harmonium, while dressed
convincingly as a Yiddishe Momma, in what can only be termed
acute drag--."

736 Elliot, Gerald A. "A Pride of Poets/For 10 Days in June,
     Grand Valley State College Was Alive with the Concerns
     and Cadences of Modern American Poetry." The Grand
     Rapids Press, "Wonderland"/The Sun Press Magazine, 29
     July 1973, pp. 3-7, with cover photograph titled, "Allen
     Ginsberg and other word magicians at Grand Valley State
     College" (p. 3), p. 5 there is a second photograph titled,
     "Allen Ginsberg advising a student."
        Ginsberg was one of the poets in residence in the Grand
     Valley State College Poetry Festival at which "28 nationally-recog-
     nized poets" participated (Charles Rexnikoff, Rochelle Owens, Victor
     Hernandez Cruz, George Economu, Edward Dorn, David Meltzer,
     Allen Ginsberg, George Oppen, Carl Rakosi, Robert Duncan, Kenneth
     Rexroth, Diane di Prima, Theodore Enslin, among others). This is
     a lengthy photo-documented article describing the events of the Festi-
     val. Ginsberg is referred to as "possibly the most loquacious." An
     excerpt from "September on Jessore Road" from The Fall of America
     is included on page 4.

737 Epstein, J. "Chicago Conspiracy Trial." New York Review of
     Books, 14:03 (2/12/70): 25.

738 "Evening of Song and Verse Held at St. George's Church, New
     York City to Raise Funds for Bengalis in E. Pakistan.
     U.S.S.R. Poet A. Voznesensky Read Poetry in Russian and
     Ginsberg Translates." New York Times, 21 November 1971,
     55:7.

739 "Excerpts from Dialogue Between Allen Ginsberg and Louis,
     That Grew out of Joint Poetry Reading at California Univon
     Occasion of Father's Day." New York Times, 16 June 1974,
     IV: 21:5.

740 Felstiner, John. "'Psychologically, We Are Still in the Half-
     Life of the War' Remembering the Poetry of the Vietnam
     Years." Stanford Observer, May 1976, p. 3.
        "The following is adapted from the 1976 Founder's Day
     Address given by Felstiner," includes an excerpt from Ginsberg's
     The Fall of America and conclusively finds that "In this year of
     reckoning, the first time in 25 years that America has not been en-
     gaged in Vietnam, Casey, Ginsberg, Levertov, Kinnell are vital to
     us. Unlike our actual experience of the war, their poems still stand
     in front of us."

741 Fenton, David and John Collins, kfp. "John Sinclair Freedom
     Rally." Ann Arbor Sun, 17-30 December 1971, p. 11 with
     David Fenton photograph of Allen Ginsberg (see "Shots" [in

same issue] within photograph section of bibliography).
"Allen Ginsberg started out the show, howling and ooming
and vibrating his message for John's freedom; followed by Bobby
Seale" at the Chrisler Arena on December 10th.

742 Flander, Judy. "Ginsberg's Poetry--Mafia and Meditation...."
     Washington Star, 10 February 1976, pp. D1-2, with photo-
     graph on page D1 "Allen Ginsberg: Has his own guru" by
     Walter Oates, Washington Star Photographer.
        Judy Flander reviews Ginsberg's reading at Corcoran
Gallery of Art with William Burroughs. Allen is not portrayed as
an embellishment to Burroughs, but as a central figure. This differs
seriously from other reviews of the same event. Ginsberg insists
he is "a poet not a guru." In fact he explains, "I've got my own
guru, Chögyam Trungpa Rimpoche." Flander continues on to highlight
Allen's feelings on the connection between the government and organized crime (the Mafia) and comments upon his lifestyle and his poetry.

743 Fleming, John. "Allen Ginsberg in Minneapolis/The 45th
     Parallel." Metropolis, The Weekly Newspaper of the Twin
     Cities, 10 May 1977, 1:29, p. 3 with photograph by Paul
     Shambroom of the Metropolis.
        This is an article recording Ginsberg's reading "last
Friday night" for "The Loft (a benefit reading that raised nearly
$2,000)" and his later appearance at a party, including a "Ginsberg
Verbatim" section in which he talks on "American poetry ... on his
goals ... on LSD ... and on cocaine."

744 Flippo, Chet. "Rubin Carter Benefit/Hurricane's Night: Thun-
     der in the Garden." Rolling Stone, 15 January 1976, 204
     pp. 9-10, 18.
        "Allen Ginsberg's presence on stage" is mentioned at the
Rolling Thunder Revue held at Madison Square Garden, December 8th,
at the benefit for "imprisoned boxer Rubin 'Hurricane' Carter...."
Rather than use a new verse Allen Ginsberg wrote on tour for "This
Land Is Your Land," the words of Neuwrith were added because they
"touched on both the revue's travels and the campaign to free Rubin
Carter."

745 "The 4:40 Ferry to S.I. Becomes Poetry Passage." New York
     Times, 11 November 1977, p. B2.
        This article records the poetry reading of the Russian
poet Andrei Vosnesensky on "the 4:40 P.M. ferryboat to Staten Island." Allen Ginsberg stood next to him translating "his words into
English to the cheers of an eager--if a bit perplexed--crowd.... Mr.
Ginsberg summed up the afternoon this way: 'It was a poetry party
passing the Statue of Liberty.'"

746 Frick, Charles. "Two Parties/Two Worlds." Aquarian, 19
     November 1975, 10:103, p. 20-21, centerfold, there are
     three photographs which include Ginsberg among others.
     Photographs by Charles Frick. Also there is a cover photo

referring to all of this which includes Ginsberg with the
headline, "Centerfold EXTRAVAGANZA! THE BEATS ARE
BACK/GINSBERG, SANDERS & CO./PARTYING IN THE VIL-
LAGE."
Frick quickly describes the first "soire" held after the
screening of "David 'Rock On' Essex's new flick." Then, "the very
next day, a thousand cultural light years away, there was another
party downtown at the local ... (for) Ed Sanders on the release of
his new book, 'The Tales of Beatnik Glory....'" The old Beatniks
were there. Among them Ginsberg read and chanted.

747 Friedman, J. D. "Disembodied Poetry." Berkeley Barb, 15-
21 August 1975, 522, p. 11 with photograph of Ginsberg by
Bruce Bryson. Reprinted as "Disembodied Tribute to Jack
Kerouac," in Drummer, 26 August 1975, 363, p. 4, with
photo.
Ginsberg's involvement with the establishment of Naropa,
a degree granting institution of learning which mixes "Western intel-
lectualism" with "Eastern intuitiveness" is explored. The creative
writing section of Naropa is named after Jack Kerouac and dedicated
to his style of creation: "The idea of total spontaneity and acceptance
of fast mind reveries, first thought, best thought, not revising because revising is always a question of shame, trying to obliterate
traces of nakedness."
The other poets present included Burroughs, Whalen,
Waldman, Sanders, DiPrima, Corso and Lewis MacAdams, Ted Berrigan and Michael Brownstein. Apprenticeships as well as classes
have been established. It is Ginsberg who supplies the link to the
Buddhist teachings.

748 Friedman, J. D. "Disembodied Tribute to Jack Kerouac."
See entry above by Friedman.

749 Fulton, Ashby. "Poet Tsongas Hears Yevtushenko Read."
Berkeley Barb, 18-24 February 1972, 14:7:340, p. 11.
At Project Artaud Soviet Poet Yevtushenko reads. "The
reading consists of English translations read alternatively by Gins-
berg, Ferlinghetti and Yevtushenko's regular English reader Bary
Bruce...."

750 Garcia, Bob. "How Braden Delivers/A Singer Who Echoes
N. Y." Open City, 3-9 January 1969, 85, p. 5.
Braden's ("A Singer") development is paralleled to Diane
DiPrima's natural childbirth, for through this imagery Braden comes
into his own being. First he meets "the rebellious older elements
of the once rebellious established Village, DiPrima, Ginsberg, all
the beyond-tomorrow thinkers." This all influences Braden's music
and is mirrored in his work.

751 "Gay Poetry/Sing Out-Come Out." Gay News, 26 July-8 August 1973?, 28, p. 8.
"The celebrated American poet Allen Ginsberg kindly sent
us the poem/songs that appeared in a California publication called

the Berkeley Barb. Gay News sends its sincerest love and thanks to Allen for allowing us to reproduce them. " Included here are the poems "Everybody Sing," "Troust Street Blues," "The House of the Rising Sun," plus a sketch of Allen Ginsberg in an Uncle Sam hat (no credits listed).

752 Georgia Straight, 21-27 March 1969, 3:50, page 3 with photograph of Ginsberg with Phil Ochs by Joe Ellis, titled "Allen Ginsberg and Phil Ochs pooled their talents last week to raise money at the Free Press Benefit for the Straight at the Garden Auditorium. Some of the tapes for that week still have to be picked up and transcribed and will appear in next week's issue." Next to this appears the Program Budget which lists Allen Ginsberg.

753 Gilden, William. "Voices of Freedom Protesting. " Washington Post, 30 April 1974, p. B1, B9 (col. 1). Photograph of Ginsberg on page B1 by Larry Morris, Wash. Post. A second picture appears on page B9 by the same photographer. Gilden presents Ginsberg reading at the Library of Congress with Ishmael Reed, as well as appearing on "the WRC-TV (channel 4) talk show, 'Take It from Here'" which centered on "gay marriage, featuring two couples, one of which was Ginsberg and Peter Orlovsky, who held hands during parts of the show." The title on page B9 "Verse: Voices of Freedom" refers to the event at the Library of Congress at which time both poets presented their works: "Daniel Hoffman, consultant in poetry to the Library declared that 'each in his own way has a vividness that complements the other; each in his own way is the voice of freedom protesting, mocking, and excoriating the forces of oppression. "

754 "Ginsberg Activities. " PENewsletter, April 1974, n. p. "Allan [sic] Ginsberg has asked the Executive Board of P. E. N. American Center to support the defense drive for Hoffman. Ginsberg has also written to individuals and other organizations for support...."

755 "Ginsberg and Traum in Concert. " Woodstock Times, 8 December 1977, p. 22. "Ginsberg and Traum in Concert" is an announcement of Friday and Saturday, December 16 and 17, 1977 concert appearances of the two. Traum is "the well-known folksinger and Woodstock resident since the early sixties (who) has recorded and toured with Allen Ginsberg on several occasions." The concert will take place at The Woodstock Artist's Association, at which time Allen Ginsberg will read from "a major new work, 'The Contest of Bards,' as well as excerpts from 'Kaddish,' shorter poems and songs. His longtime friend, banjo-farmer-poet, Peter Orlovsky, will appear also. "

756 "Ginsberg Concentrates on Buddhism, Blues. " Rocky Mountain News, 1 April 1977, pp. 6-7, with photograph, "Allen Ginsberg ... faculty of his Jack Kerouac School for Disembodied Poetics has expanded by four. "

Re: Broadcast (radio) station, KRNW, "A small privately
owned 380-watt Boulder station. " This is an interview of Allen Ginsberg, at which time he referred to his teaching at Naropa and the
recent financial triumph of the NYC based WBAI radio station.

757   "Ginsberg for Aid. " Octopus, 21 November 1969, 2:15, II, p.
1, with photos (3) by Serge Lefebure.
Ginsberg was "brought by the English dept. of Carlton to
raise money for AID (Assistance to the Immigration and Draft). Despite the fact that the reviewer repeatedly misspells Allen's name
('Allan'), the account of the reading is written well.   First the poet
is biographically introduced.   Then the myths perpetuated by the
media (about Ginsberg) are cited and then discounted.   Ginsberg read
poems from the past "and then coming as close as any poet can to
the present he read a poem inspired/resulting from Jack Kerouac's
recent death. "

758   "Ginsberg, Stafford to Speak. " Oregon Journal, 30 April 1974,
p. 3.
The "William Stafford, Oregon's poet laureate" lecture is
announced, as is Allen Ginsberg's appearance with musician Bhagavan
Das at the Neighbors of Woodcraft Auditorium, SW 14th Avenue and
SW Morrison Street on Friday at 8 p. m.   The sponsor of the Ginsberg appearance is the Center for Truth.   The evening performance
will be preceded by a 3 p. m. "rap session. "

759   "The Ginsberg Testimony at Chicago Conspiracy Trial. " Rolling Stone, 2 April 1970, n. 55, pp. 52-53, 58.
This is a partial transcript of Allen Ginsberg's testimony
in the Chicago conspiracy trial.   Kunstler and Weinglass are defense
attorneys, Forman is the prosecutor.   Ginsberg ends his testimony
by reciting part of "Howl. "

760   "Ginsberg to Speak. " Cincinnati Enquirer, 31 January 1975,
with photograph without title.
This is a short announcement of Allen Ginsberg's participation in "Thomas More College's Humanities Enrichment Program
and Lecture Series. "

761   "Ginsberg to Spotlight SCSU Festival. " St. Cloud Daily Times,
6 February 1976, p. 21, with photograph of Allen Ginsberg
titled with his name.
"Poet Allen Ginsberg will highlight the February 10 through
February 13 'Festival of the Arts Week' at St. Cloud State University. "

762   "The Ginsbergs/An Interesting Contrast. " Nightwatch, 17 March
1975, p. 2 with photograph titled, "The Ginsbergs will be
reading their poetry at open house, April 13. "
"Louis and Allen Ginsberg, the father and son team of
poets, will present a reading of their own poetry Sunday, April 13,
3 p. m. at Rutgers Robeson Center, 350 High St. "   This was "the
highlight of Rutgers Newark Open House. "

763 "Ginsbergs Draw Attentive Crowd. " <u>Nightwatch</u> 21 April 1975,
1:7, n. p. , with two pictures.
Louis Ginsberg and Allen were participants in the Rutgers Newark Open House, Sunday April 13, 1975 where they were
introduced to read by "Professor Virginia Cremen-Rudd, longtime
friend of the Ginsbergs. " Louis Ginsberg is "a RU alumnus, a
professor of English at University College for 25 years and a native
Newarker. " Father and son read and were received with "an ova-
tion. "

764 Glueck, Grace. "Videotape Replaces Canvas for Artists Who
Use TV Technology in New Way. " <u>New York Times</u>, 14
April 1975, pp. 33, 63.
Mr. Frank Gillette is the artist interviewed, "whose new
work is part of a 12-piece cycle with an ecological theme, is one
of a growing breed of video artists, for whom the TV screen has
become an esthetic medium. " This includes "a video image of the
poet, Allen Ginsberg from Nam June Paik's 'Suite (212): Allen Ginsberg. ' credit--Davidson Gigliotti. " According to Ginsberg this was
taped while Paik was teaching at the California Institute of the Arts
for a NET broadcast. The videotape includes some Ginsberg footage
of chanting paralleled to distorted images of him.

765 Glusman, Paul. "Chicago 8 Trial/Beauty vs. Beast. " <u>Ber-
keley Tribe</u>, 19-26 December 1969, 1:24, p. 7.
These are the testimonies of Phil Ochs, folk singer;
William Styron, novelist; Dick Gregory, comedian; Allen Ginsberg,
poet and Linda Morse, Tribal sister. In the writer's opinion "Ginsberg ... (was) ... the high point of the case" because he opened the
trial up culturally.

766 "Going Out Guide/To Each His Own. " <u>New York Times</u>, 6
May 1975, n. p.
This is an announcement of Allen Ginsberg and Louis Ginsberg's joint reading at the Greenwich House, 27 Barrow Street, at
1:30 p. m.

767 Golden, Gerald. "Earth Days. " <u>Distant Drummer</u>, 30 April
1970, 83, p. 3, with picture of Ginsberg titled "Poet Allen
Ginsberg at Earth Day Rally. "
"Earth Day 1970 drew an estimated crowd of 30,000 to
Fairmount Park, to culminate the week of teach-ins and ecology ac-
tivities. "

768 Gornick, Vivian. "Jack Kerouac: The Night and What It Does
to You. " <u>Village Voice</u>, 14:55, 30 October 1969, pp. 1,
27, 30.
According to the Abstract of English Studies for 1969 the
article was about the funeral of Jack Kerouac in Lowell, Massachusetts, October 24, 1969. Ginsberg, Orlovsky, Corso were all there.

769 Gray, Francine du Plessix. "The Literary View/Black Mountain, An American Place. " <u>New York Times Book Review</u>,

31 July 1977, pp. 3, 25-26.
Francine du Plessix Gray's article highlights the Black
Mountain literary movement. It all began with the foundation of
Black Mountain College in "the foothills of North Carolina" in 1933.
Gray perceives it as "one of the most visionary communities of the
century" and offers it as historical precedent to the innovations of
the 1960's. Even in it's earlier more structured years, writers and
artists flocked to its doors. In reaction to the New Criticism of
the 1950's the Black Mountain Review was started. "In its last
number, dated 1957, one finds Allen Ginsberg's America . . . among
other beats!"

770 Greenwald, Jeff. "Ginsberg Gives SC His Heart," Santa Cruz
     Independent, 20-26 May 1977, 1:44, pp. 1, 9, with cover
     picture "Ginsberg and Leary Recall Those '60's Moldy
     Oldies," by Steve Gladstone.
        Despite the evening's billing as one of "Oratorical En-
lightenment" the reviewer finds it one with "a rather scattered program which relied heavily on gratuitous periods of silence and the
strangely fixated poetry of Orlovsky. . . . In the many, many years
of his growth as a poet, Ginsberg has experimented with countless
facets of the poetic experience. He did read several outstanding
pieces Sunday evening: a very moving hymn about the death of his
father, an extraction from an epic-in-progress, and a bluesy lament
accompanied by Orlovsky on banjo and Bhagavan Das on guitar and
vocals."

771 Grimes, Paul. "80 Americans Appeal to India to Restore
     Fundamental Rights." New York Times, 5 March 1976,
     6:4.
        Allen Ginsberg is included among the groups of Americans
who issued the "joint appeal today expressing distress at the repression in India and calling for the restoration of fundamental human
rights there." Accordingly, "the signers represent a spectrum of
political, academic and other opinion."

772 Grossberger, Lewis. "Return of the 'Beatnik Dope Fiends.'"
     New York Post, 18 April 1975, p. 40, with three photo-
     graphs by Vernon Shibla of the Post.
        The paragraph below one picture explains the entire event
at which Ginsberg offered "a sort of Ginsberg's Greatest Hits." The
evening marked the return of the Beats after 16 years.

773 Guenther, John. "The Spoken Poem Can Be a Kind of Theater."
     New York Times, II, 30 March 1975, p. 5, column 1.
        This article highlights the New York City poetry readings
in terms of places, poets, and atmosphere. It also speculates upon
the spoken genre: "Today's poets are writing primarily for expression and contact with an audience . . . they are not writing for pos-
terity but for the living present. . . ." The article includes some locations and addresses, and a picture of Ginsberg entitled, "Ginsberg--
reading for contact."

774 Halberstram, David, Francis Gary Powers, Andrew Young,
Wavy Gravy. "The Sixties." Rolling Stone 253, 1 December 1977, p. 51. Photograph by Jim Marshall, p. 51.
"Personal account of the Sixties by people who helped
change the world, excerpted from the New Rolling Stone Press
Book ..." (The Sixties, edited by Lynda Rosen Obst). "... the
book is a compilation of personal stories and memories by many
who had participated in the major events of the decade. Seventy-one
people including Julie and David Eisenhower, Abbie Hoffman, Dick
Clark, James Meredith, Benjamin Bradlee, Ralph Abernathy, Daniel
Ellsberg, Allen Ginsberg, Eldridge Cleaver, Bill Graham, Eugene
McCarthy, John Dean and Gloria Steinem were interviewed about
their contributions and recollections.... The intent was oral history;
the effect is, as one reader put it, a yearbook for every one who
graduated from the Sixties."

775 Haldane, David. "Visions of Neal Cassady." Berkeley Barb,
25 April-1 May 1975, pp. 14, 20.
Pierre Delattre, an old friend of Neal Cassady and resident of San Miguel de Allende, Mexico, the site of Cassady's death,
discusses his past relationship with Neal in the form of a dialogue
with Haldane of the Barb. In background information supplied by
Haldane for Delattre, Allen Ginsberg and the Beats are mentioned.

776 Hallock, Steve. "Allen Ginsberg/Ginsberg Carries Spirit of
Kerouac, Cassady." Denver Post, 20 July 1975, pp. 3,
16-17, with photograph by Ellen Pearlman. Reprinted in
Biography News, 2:764-5, July 1975.
This is a portrait of Ginsberg in 1975. Retrospectively
it speaks of his days at Columbia with Kerouac ("It was Kerouac,
with William Burroughs and others, who took over Ginsberg's education when he was expelled from Columbia in 1946 ...") and pinpoints
the pivotal point in his life when, "in 1955 he met up with a psychia-
trist who encouraged him to live the life he wanted." The picture
is one of perpetual motion, "Like the changing self, Ginsberg is
forever expanding his poetry, expansion in this case meaning a re-
gression to older times, when the spoken word was the dominant
form of story telling, poetry, and communication." Ginsberg speaks
of this oral tradition, the use of the mantra and his teaching at
Naropa Institute. More importantly, "writing poetry is a form of
discovering who I am, and getting beyond who I am to free awake-
ness of consciousness, to a self that ISN'T who I am.... It's a
form of discovering my own nature, and my own identity, or my
own ego, or outlining my own ego, and also seeing what part of
me is beyond that."

777 Hammond. "Tax Resistance in Kansas City." WIN 10:18,
23 May 1974, p. 16.

778 Harris, Art. "Allen Ginsberg: Nearly out of the Underground."
San Francisco Examiner, May 1977, p. 25 with two photo-
graphs by Bob McLead for the Examiner. The first is titled,
"Poet Allen Ginsberg: 'I've had a good time and an easy

role.'" The second, "Fellow Poet Peter Orlovsky and
Ginsberg at City Lights Bookstore: 'Like any happily
adjusted homosexual couple.'"
Harris presents this portrait of Ginsberg "jacketed in
green seersucker over a white shirt, gray slacks and red socks" in
the basement of City Lights Bookstore. Ginsberg talks about his
work, activities, his father who recently died, Bob Dylan with
whom he has collaborated and published. "Ginsberg admits he could
pull down bigger bucks by signing with a major publishing house,
but he says it's more important to bolster small presses like City
Lights with his reputation. It keeps me a little underground and
gives my work a little glamour,... It's a community I have a relationship with. I'd hate to break off that comfortable pattern, though
some day time will surely turn it to ash. I'm grateful it's lasted
this long."

779 Henderson, Ranni. "Ginsberg Wonders Why It's Worse." Bal-
timore Sun, October 1973, n. p.
Henderson recounts Ginsberg's appearance at Maryland
Institute at Johns Hopkins University. He addresses himself to the
rhetorical question: "What did we do wrong these past 10 years?
How come everything is worse than ever?"

780 Henneberry, Jay. "Ginsberg Alive, Well at Passims." Tufts
Observer, 25 May 1977, II:19, p. 7, with two photographs
of Ginsberg by Elsa Dorfman.
"Allen Ginsberg and friends are playing at Passims tonight and tomorrow night." Henneberry comments on his "doing
gigs these days," "Buddhist" tone of his current work. They chat
about the CIA and drug manipulation.

781 Hentoff, Nat. "Can Someone Please Find the Thread? Is It
Rolling, Zeus?" Rolling Stone, 15 January 1976, 204, pp.
34-38, photographs by Ken Regan (Camera 5).
Nat Hentoff weaves the threads of the Rolling Thunder
Revue together in this lengthy tale of their travels. The central
threads include Bob Dylan, Joan Baez and Allen Ginsberg who lend
their thoughts about the tour, each other and the world to the author.
Ginsberg and Baez disagree on Dylan's state of ego. Ginsberg believes "Bob's attitude is very similar to the Buddhist view of non-
attachment. The belief that seeking pleasure, clinging to pleasure,
evokes pain ..." Joan for obvious reasons feels otherwise. After
all it has been Joan Baez who has been Dylan's cohort in performances throughout the tour.
The reason Ginsberg feels that he was invited on tour
was a letter he wrote to Dylan after listening to the album "Blood
on the Tracks." Allen's part in the Springfield, Massachusetts,
appearance is described as he is named, "Ginsberg-the-keeper-of-the-
vision." Kerouac's influence on Dylan is indicated as he, Ginsberg
and Peter Orlovsky go off to visit Jack Kerouac's grave in Lowell,
Massachusetts. "Ginsberg had brought a copy of Mexico City Blues
and Dylan read a poem from it. The three then sat on the grave,
Dylan picking up Ginsberg's harmonium and making up a tune. When

Dylan pulled out his guitar, Ginsberg began to improvise a long, slow, 12-bar blues about Kerouac sitting up on the clouds looking down on these kindly wanderers putting music to his grave. Dylan is much moved, much involved, a state of introspection closely captured by the camera crew that has come along."

Ginsberg in an exchange with poet Muriel Rukeyser in New York summarizes his thoughts about the long range effect of the Rolling Thunder Revue, "now, the Rolling Thunder Revue will be one of the signal gestures characterizing the working cultural community that will make the Seventies ... Rolling Thunder, with its sense of community, is saying we should get our act together. And do it properly--well."

782 Himes, Geoffrey. "Allen Ginsberg: Custodian in a Museum." Columbia Flier, 24 November 1977, p. 44, with photograph.
    This article records Ginsberg's reading with host, Reza Baraheni, at a "Sunday afternoon" reading at the Oakland Mills Village Center, sponsored by "the Howard County Poetry and Literature Society" in Columbia, Maryland. "A highlight ... was 'Don't Grow Old,' a series of seven poems on the death of his father-poet Louis Ginsberg--last year dead at 80 from cancer.... After the reading, Ginsberg talked about how getting old was affecting him: 'I'm getting smarter. All my dreams are coming true. When you get old is when all your dreams come true--if you got the right dreams.'"
    In reply to a question about how it felt to have "been around so long" Ginsberg said: "Well, it feels like being the custodian of a museum.... I try to make it a good museum. I try to present all the cases nicely so people can see clearly what's there. I give passes to anyone who wants to go in the basement and in the attic. I try to label all the exhibits properly so no one gets confused. And I close down on Sundays for meditation."

783 Himes, Geoffrey. "Inter Media." Sunrise, n. d. 3:7, copyrighted 1975, pp. 16-17. "A Ginsberg appreciation" with photograph "Allen Ginsberg, a holy man" by Western Courier.
    This article by Himes recollects seeing Ginsberg "read at the Baird Auditorium at the Museum of Natural History in Washington, D. C. Himes's orientation is cultural and historical. As a result, he places Ginsberg in a recent historical context. "Just as Richard Nixon has been a part of one history since the early fifties, so Allen Ginsberg has been a part of another history from the same time."

784 "History of the Movement." Inquisition, 17 September 1969, III: 4, p. 5.
    There is a "1963" reference to Ginsberg among others: "April. Tim Leary and Richard Albert dismissed from Harvard for experimenting with hallucinogenic drugs. 'Psychedelic Left' emerges with Ken Kesey, Allen Ginsberg, Dylan and the Beatles."

785 Hodenfield, Jan. "Dylan And Friends: A Night for Hurricane." New York Post, 9 December 1975, pp. 5, 22.
    At the Madison Square Garden the Rolling Thunder Revue

spoke out and performed for Rubin (Hurricane) Carter. They are
expected to make "some $100,000 for the defense fund. Ginsberg
is mentioned in reference to the October 31st gathering of Rolling
Thunder Revue in Plymouth, Massachusetts, for "off-stage tone."
In closing Ginsberg is quoted in describing the performance ("at the
Felt Forum party afterwards") as "good clean energy." Perhaps
Neuwirth sums it up in calling the Felt Forum appearance "a go-for-
broke finale at the Garden."

786 Hunter, Bob. "Bob Hunter Column." Vancouver Sun, 4 June
        1973, n.p.
        Allen Ginsberg recounts "his arrival at customs Saturday
on his way into Vancouver to do a benefit concert for a Tibetan
religious sect...."

787 The Independent Florida Alligator, 21 April 1975, p. 3, with
        photograph of Ginsberg among others, by Eric Estrin, titled
        "Poets (from l. to r.) Allen Ginsberg, Gary Snyder, and
        Michael McClure kicked off Energy and Consciousness Week
        Sat. Night at Grahm Pond."
        "The presentation, 'Energy and Poetry' was an effort to
raise ecology consciousness by linking poetry and energy. Energy
and Consciousness Week will last until Thursday."

788 Ingram, Bob. "Allen Ginsberg's University of Awareness."
        Drummer, 13-20 December 1977, p. 12, with two photo-
        graphs.
        Allen Ginsberg reads, chants and later leads a discussion
at the YMHA, "last Saturday night" in Philadelphia in which he
"didn't exactly tell them what they wanted to hear; rather, he told
them what he wanted to talk about.... Probably the audience was
more interested in the singing than in the song, more interested in
Ginsberg the legend than the man, and I think he realizes this and
plays right through it in that friendly, fresh way of his--voice changing roles like Lenny Bruce--to jolt them a little, perhaps even to
disappoint them a little, but not to give them what they want, because Allen Ginsberg is a poet, not a guru; he is a teaching student,
not a master." Essentially, Ingram has some shrewd observations
to record about Ginsberg. I am not sure that I agree with them
all; yet the central emphasis of his thoughts are included above.
During the discussion two students of "the Philadelphia poet, C.K.
Williams, who was on the stage with Ginsberg," addressed Ginsberg
with earnest questions about poetics. Their dialogue is included.

789 Johnston, David and Janet Fries. "Dr. Hip Revisited." Berke-
        ley Barb, 25-31 October 1971, 20:15:480, p. 15.
        "Dr. Eugene Schoenfeld, Dr. Hip Pocrates began his
career ... as the medicine man of the underground ... with medical
column in the Berkeley Barb in 1967.... Tim Leary was a patient.
Dr. Schoenfeld debates with Jerry Rubin, Ram Dass and Allen Ginsberg who have "teamed up to damn Leary for his reported 'snitching'
on his former friends. At the past conference Schoenfeld staged a
frisky bit of guerrilla theatre. Dressed in a kangaroo suit, Schoen-

feld attempted, unsuccessfully, to push a custard pie into the face of Mr. Rubin. "

789a Johnston, David. "The Bitter Pill. " Berkeley Barb, 20-26
       September 1974, 20:10:475, pp. 3, 13, with three photo-
       graphs one of which includes Ginsberg among others. Re-
       printed in Georgia Straight, 3-10 October 1974, 364, pp. 1,
       12.
           "San Francisco ... and among those gathered there were
       cabinet level members of the counterculture--Rubin, Ginsberg and
       Ram Dass. Their purpose was to react publicly for the first time
       to Dr. Timothy Leary's recent disclosures that have staggered the ...
       Left. Leary has, of course, not only denounced the Left, but also,
       in testimony before Chicago Grand Jury, implicated his friends, his
       lawyers, his wife and daughter in an apparent attempt to cut short
       his time in prison. The Wednesday 'symposium' moderated by one-
       time Barb editor Ken Kelly was sponsored by People Investigating
       Leary's Lies (P. I. L. L.).... "
           Rubin spoke first and indicated the "straight line between
       Watergate and Tim Leary. " This is "the government's attempt to
       use Leary to take attention off Watergate and related matters" and
       to wreak havoc in the Movement. Ram Dass spoke for Leary and
       said, "but I still love Tim Leary. " Ginsberg chanted for Tim Leary,
       posed "forty-four questions that the Leary case presented" and dis-
       cussed his original distrust of Leary's new female companion, Jo-
       anna. Tim Leary's son, Jack, "attacks his father's actions. " Gins-
       berg concluded with a chant. Collectively they discussed Leary's
       actions in an attempt to understand his motivation.

790 Jones, Marta. "Birthday Party in the Village. " Aquarian, 19
       November 1975, 10:103, p. 15.
           "Bob Dylan and Joan Baez made an unexpected appear-
       ance at Gerde's Folk City on October 23rd, the night of a surprise
       birthday party for the club's owner, Mike Porco.... Allen Ginsberg
       on harmonium with Denise Mercedes on guitar drew the assemblage
       into a truly spirited singalong of a William Blake poem 'The Nurse's
       Song. '"

791 Kelley, Ken. "Judge raps tap. " Fifth Estate, 4-17 February
       1971, p. 5, with photograph, "Poet Allen Ginsberg and de-
       fense attorney Wm. Kunstler. "
           Kelley's article is about "an historic decision curbing the
       self-appointed power of the U. S. Attorney General to use illegally
       obtained wiretap evidence against defendants" in the state of Michigan
       (re: White Panther Party Trial). Poet Allen Ginsberg was on hand
       as the expert on young people, "a distinct group of people. " The
       judge's decision on this was not favorable, although quite a show was
       put on.

792 Kepner. "Ginsberg Blows Sacramento Minds. " J. Advocate,
       60, 26 May 1971, p. 15.

793 Kerr, Peter. "Poet Allen Ginsberg Returns to Berkeley. "

Daily Californian, 16 May 1977, p. 3, with photograph,
"Allen Ginsberg in the early 1970's."
Allen returns to Berkeley for a benefit reading for KPFA.
"In many ways it was Ginsberg who was the father of the afternoon's
verse. It was he who strung together pained images of poverty and
alienation while living in Berkeley in the mid-1950's. It was his
one-sentence, eight-page poem 'Howl' that sparked the Beat Poetry
movement, from that which the '60's counter-culture grew. Twenty-
two years later he was back on stage in Berkeley, the last poet of
an afternoon, a middle-aged man in a well-pressed white suit." Material from the poems written on his father's dying are excerpted
here.

794 Kimball. "Ginsberg at Harvard." Phoenix, 3:13, 30 March
1971, p. 27.

795 "King of May." Good Times, 30 April 1969, 11:17, p. 2.
Text which accompanies poem, "King of May": "On
May Day, 1964, Czech students fought Prague police in the streets
for the right to hold traditional May Day festivals. The authorities
relented, and allowed them to elect their own King of the May the
following year. On May Day, 1965, Allen Ginsberg was elected
King of the May. A week later, police arrested him and expelled
him from Czechoslovakia. He wrote this poem on the plane" (May 7,
1965).

796 Kleinhaus, Charles. "Allen Ginsberg, Part I." Spectator, 18
March 1969, VIII:7 pp. 14-16 with one photograph.
Although ostensibly a book review of Planet News 1961-
1967 by Allen Ginsberg (City Lights Books), this article is more of
a collage of Ginsberg vis à vis an individual, a generation, and
fellow artists. Divided into eight sections (and continued next week),
entitled: 1) "Ginsberg in the All American House"; 2) "Survival in
the 60's"; 3) "An Important Poem"; 4) "Body Politic/Body Poetic";
5) "Why some Modern Poetry Is as Dense as the Rock of Gibralter";
6) "The Poetic Politic"; 7) "The Poet and the Peasant"; and 8) "Why
Some Modern Literature and Criticism Is as Realistic as 19th Century Socialism."

797 Kleinhaus, Charles. "Allen Ginsberg, Part II." Spectator,
25 March 1969, VIII:8, pp. 14-17.
We begin where Part I left off with 9) "Killing Viet Cong
in Kansas"; 10) "Poet/Shaman"; 11) "The Politics of Metadissent";
12) "Aesthetic ... "; 13) "Up Against the Mother Wallfucker"; 14) "A
Vision of Man for Man." ("The counterculture is replacing this
shoddy view of man with a new vision ... visions are not programs
... Programs without visions are meaningless..." As is Mr. Kleinhaus' literary criticism.)

798 Knight, Hans. "The Howl of Allen Ginsberg." Philadelphia
Bulletin. 19 May 1974, n.p. with photographs. Reprinted
in Biography News, 1:751-3, July 1974.
The occasion is one of celebration of the fifth annual Walt

Whitman Day program at Rutgers University (Camden, New Jersey). Appropriately he has been invited to take part in this day's festivities, for he would like to be remembered "as someone in the tradition of the oldtime American transcendentalist individualism ... from that old gnostic tradition ... Thoreau, Emerson ... Whitman ... just carrying it on into the 20th Century. For having been fortunate making connections with the Orient and swamis, and finding practical applications for things that were just ideas of the 19th Century."

799 "Knocking on Hurricane's Door." Rolling Stone 204: (1/15/76) 11.

The Rolling Thunder Revue, including Allen Ginsberg, on December 7th, goes to the Clinton Prison facility at which time they entertain the inmates. "'Hurricane' aside, the greatest response was reserved for Allen Ginsberg's poem 'Kiss Ass.' The prisoners clapped and cheered as Allen, dressed in a conservative brown suit and narrow fifties-style tie, delivered the poem...."

800 Kopkind, Andrew. "In a Comtemptible Court." Great Speckled Bird, 9 March 1970, 3:10, pp. 8-9, with cartoon by Skip/ Williamson on p. 9. (excerpt from Hard Times).

In Kopkind's article regarding the trial of the Chicago defendants, there is a passing remark to Ginsberg: "A large part of the defense consisted of responses to the judge's antics. He baited the culture heroes which the defendants called as witnesses and even feigned a mild bemusement to Ginsberg's 'OM.'"

801 Kovarik, Lisa. "Poet Chants Beatnik Lore." Utopian, 14 February 1975, 7:5, p. 1, with photograph "Allen Ginsberg chants to an overwhelming crowd in Seiler Commons."

Ginsberg attends Thomas More College's lecture series in conjunction with the Individuality courses sponsored by the National Endowment for the Humanities.

802 Kramer, Hilton. "Literary View/Trashing the Fifties." New York Times Book Review. 10 April 1977, VII, pp. 3, 31, with a separate photograph of Ginsberg among others.

Kramer asserts, "trashing the 50's a 'radical' stance in the 60's, has become in the 70's something of an academic industry-- a fixed item in the college curriculum, and a convenient refuge for conventional minds." In this vein he takes up Morris Dickstein and his theory "that the 50's 'will surely be known for its ultimate moral cowardice.'" In this context "the great literary--and moral--hero of the '50's turns out in this scenerio, to be Allen Ginsberg."

Ginsberg is merely cited in this fashion because this is actually a critique of Dickstein and the school of thought which he represents. "Professor Dickstein offers up an academic rehash of the radical illusions of the 60's...." He is attacked for his omissions, "crude political treatment" of material included and lack of "standards of intellectual seriousness."

803 Kramer, Sylvia. "Poet's Inspiration/A Tribute to Louis Ginsberg." Jewish News, 29 July 1976, p. 19.

This is a retrospective article on Louis Ginsberg. Allen Ginsberg is mentioned briefly.

804 Kundus, Bob. "Electric Kool." Ann Arbor Argus, n. d. (follows mid March #38, 1971), pp. 20-21, with photograph. "Ch. 7 News 11 PM 3-15-71/ 'Breathing Together: Revolution in the Electric Family.'" This article highlights Ginsberg, Rubin, Buckminster Fuller, Fred Hampton and John Sinclair among others.

805 Kupcinet, "Kup's column." Chicago Sun-Times, 10 March 75, p. 70.
This lists Ginsberg's week-long visit to Chicago.

806 L. E. J. "Ginsberg: The Materialism of Spiritualism." Ann Arbor Sun, 19 April-3 May 1974, 2:8, pp. 4-5, with photograph of Allen Ginsberg by Barbara Weinberg. Second photograph by David Knapp.
Ginsberg was to preview the "Festival of Life" that took place in Ann Arbor. The reporter comments on the historical disparity between Ginsberg's past and his present actions vis à vis meditation. Ginsberg denies "the contradiction.... The idea is that meditation is a way to prepare ourselves to take more effective political action." Ginsberg and Bob Dylan perform together, leading meditations. Ginsberg reads from his gay poems and presents selections from his songs and blues.

807 Landry, Donna. "A Ginsberg Recitation: Barbs Tipped with Mirth." Washington Post, 8 March 1977, p. B2 with one photograph.
This Post article reviews Ginsberg's reading at Folger Shakespeare Library (March 7, 1977), "an appropriate setting for the peerless performer." Landry finds Ginsberg "has gained his audience not through strident polemic or outraged denunciation, but through that of a self-styled Hasidic leprechaun, a jester-provacateur whose sharpest barbs are tipped with mirth." Conclusively, she decides "At mid-life this black-haired but grey-bearded poet of the counter-culture and perpetual youth straddles Janus-like, two generations looking back in fondness and having lost none of his rancorous mirthful vision." A reading is advertised for Friday evening (March 11) at George Washington University with William Burroughs.

808 Lask, Thomas. "Publishing: What Makes Sheldon Run?" New York Times, 7 May 1976, III:16, p. 3.
A poetry reading was held at "NYU's Loeb Student Center" for the "Eighth Street Bookshop, recently burned out." Contributing to the reading were Allen Ginsberg, Joel Oppenheimer, M. L. Rosenthal and Harvey Shapiro. The shop owner Eli Wilentz comments.

809 Lask, Thomas. "Voznesensky: 'A Poet Poses Questions.'" New York Times, 21 October 1977, p. 54.
Russian poet, Andrei Voznesensky in an interview parallels the division in American poetry as "exemplified" by the work of

Robert Lowell and Allen Ginsberg to that between "Russian poetry" which "has its open, bardic, or public poets and its more formal and difficult ones ('hermetic' is the word he likes to use)." The point being that "the split between the two is not as great as it is here (America).... He exemplified that point of view by saying that he still enjoyed both Allen Ginsberg and Robert Lowell. 'They are like apples and vodka, but I like them both.'"

810 Lee, Richard. "Interview with Fuller, Assist from Ginsberg." Florida Flambeau, 23 April 1975, p. 3.
"Fuller ... fielded questions yesterday at a news conference attended by the Flambeau and Tallahassee Democrat. Fuller also answered questions posed by a bearded free-lance journalist named Allen Ginsberg." Fuller imparted his thoughts on the media "I find reporting a myth to sell advertising" and then continues on to respond to questions about his life style. When asked what he thought of Ginsberg's poetry he admitted he hadn't read enough to comment.

811 Lester, Elenore. "Drama Mailbag--Cheers for 'Kaddish'." Letter in response to the Novick Review. New York Times, 12 March 1972, p. 6, column 7.

Elenore Lester challenges J. Novick's "put-down" of the production of "Kaddish." She admits "the Chelsea Theater Center production is not perfect...." Yet "'Kaddish' stands up well as a highly evocative theater piece and may point to some new interesting directions for the theater of the 70's."
See also Elenore Lester's interview in Primary Works Section.

812 "Let's Hear It for Those Time-honored North American Institutions: Mother, Old Glory, Apple Pie, Bob Dylan." New Musical Express, 25 September 1976, pp. 5-6.
There is a reference to Allen Ginsberg in the context of Bob Dylan's "Rolling Thunder tour" as Dylan's "own On the Road odyssey across America, complete with Allen Ginsberg...."

813 Levinson, Ivy. "Ginsberg to Appear at Awards." Phoenix, 29 April 1975, p. 2.
Allen Ginsberg will present college writing awards for the year. "The awards ceremony is being held on May 8 at 3:00 p.m. on the fourth floor of the College Union."

814 Levy, Steven. "Allen Ginsberg, Love Thy Mugger." Drummer, 25 March 1975, p. 8, with cover photograph titled, "Allen Ginsberg Mugs the Main Point," p. 8.
This is an article which parallels Ginsberg's mugging in NYC to that of his followers after a reading at "Main Point."

815 Levy, Steve. "Long After Lunch, It's Almost Like Dessert." Drummer, 15 April 1975, 344, p. 10.
In this article on William Burroughs, there is a reference to Ginsberg among others on the "dial-a-poem" project in NYC, in

the context of the "Giorno Poetry System, a non-profit organization that sponsors projects to promote poetry."

816 Lhamon, W. T., Jr. "Ginsberg in Florida." New Republic, 5 & 12 July 1975, p. 29.
Lhamon reviews Ginsberg's appearance at Florida State University in Tallahassee, by recalling his message, "that the good people are winning: have stopped the funds for the war, have booted the war-mongering President, have begun the attack on the police state, have successfully carried over the cultural revolution...."

817 Liming, Robert G. "Antiwar Protestors Rally in City." State, 23 April 1972, with photograph which includes Ginsberg (by Vic Tutle).
Ginsberg appeared and read at this rally organized by the Earth Day Coalition from "an original poem dealing with the recent bombing of North Vietnam." This rally concluded "a week-long march from Greenville to Columbia by an organization calling itself Clergy and Laity Concerned."

818 Lipton. "Radio Free America." Los Angeles Free Press, 22-28 January 1971?, 8:4:346, p. 4.
"Put not your trust in princes" Lipton comments on Leary and the party re-alliances of the Weathermen. "Apparently news of change in the party line had not yet reached Leary when he wrote his open letter to Allen Ginsberg (Shoot to Live." Lipton "commends the Weatherman for their about-face." This is a regular commentary column by Lipton which appears in the Los Angeles Free Press.

819 "Literature and Revolution." Spectator, 11 February 1969, p. 14.
"... Poetry has a limited audience, though Ginsberg (sometimes financed by capitalist foundations) will pack any college auditorium...."

820 "Living Benefits." Berkeley Barb, 13-19 August 1971, 13:5:313, p. 9.
"On Friday the 13th and Thursday the 19th there will be a benefit poetry and theatrical presentation to help raise $30,000 needed by the Living Theatre Defense Fund to free them in ... Brazil." Allen Ginsberg and Lawrence Ferlinghetti among others will appear.

821 Lomas, Michele. "The Ginsberg Generations Reveal Their Poetic Gap." San Francisco Examiner, 10 May 1974, p. 25 with a photograph by Bob Jones (for the Examiner) of Ginsberg, "Father Louis Ginsberg at the podium, son Allen reverently on the floor."
At San Francisco State's McKenna Theater, a joint "lunchtime reading" is presented by Allen and Louis Ginsberg. Louis's "poetry is lyric ... a heightened response to the life around him ... he's a humanist in view of man's superiority over the rest of creation in his consciousness of his own existence...." Allen Ginsberg chants and plays his harmonium.

822 Long, Steve. "Saxbe Grilled Leary in Vain." Georgia Straight,
16-23 January 1975, 9:377, p. 4. [Reprint from Berkeley
Barb, original article not located].
Allen Ginsberg is mentioned as part of the defense group
backing Tim Leary.

823 Loquidis, John. "Concave." Chinook, 29 January 1970, 2:4,
p. 8.
Just a passing reference by Ginsberg about Beefheart
(as in Captain from the musical group): "As Allen Ginsberg would
say, Beefheart is a 'freakbrain original.'"

824 Loquidis, John. "Concave." Chinook, 9 April 1970, 2:13, p.
9.
The re-reading of Ginsberg's "Howl" is used as an introduction to Loquidis' thoughts on jazz: "It occurred to me again that
one could not enjoy this particular poem, or most of the genre, if
a knowledge and enchantment of jazz had not been established."

825 Lore, Diane C. "Russian Poet Captivates Ferry Commuters."
Staten Island Advance, 11 November 1977, p. A12, with
photograph by Irving Silverstein for the S.I. Advance.
Allen Ginsberg accompanies Russian poet, Andrei Voznesensky, in his voyage and reading on the 4:40 p.m. Staten Island
Ferry: Andrei Voznesensky read in Russian and English from his
work. "Ginsberg read an English translation of the poem 'Goya,'
from Voznesensky's book, Anti-worlds and the Fifth Ace...." The
two were off to a reading and a reception at the St. George campus
of the College of Staten Island. "Among his favorite American poets,
he includes William Carlos Williams, Allen Ginsberg, William Jay
Smith, Stanley Kunity, Richard Wilbur and Robert Lowell. Each of
these poets has also translated Voznesensky's work into English."

826 "Louis Ginsberg Dies." Village Voice, 19 July 1976, p. 36.

827 "Louis Ginsberg, 80, Dies; Read Poems with Son." New York
Times, obituary, 9 July 1976, IV, p. 11, column 1, with
photograph by the NYT.
"Louis Ginsberg, a much-anthologized poet and father of
Allen Ginsberg, died yesterday morning at his home, 480 Park Avenue, Paterson, New Jersey, after an illness of six months. He was
80 years old.... He was the author of three books: The Attic of
the Past, The Everlasting Moment, and Morning Spring."

828 Lukas, J. Anthony. "Allen Ginsberg Meets a Judge and Is
Clearly Misunderstood." New York Times, 12 December
1969, p. 33, column 7.
Ginsberg meets with Judge Julius Hoffman. The article
speaks to the total lack of understanding between Ginsberg and the
Judge.

829 Lukas, J. Anthony. "'Om', Ginsberg's Hindu Chant, Fails to
Charm a Judge in Chicago." New York Times, 13 Decem-

ber 1969, p. 19, column 4.
"From Chicago December 12." This article includes an
incident in the courtroom when "Ginsberg tries to calm the Chicago
conspiracy trial today with "a melodious 'om.'"

830 McCarthy, Colman. "The Inner Ginsberg." Washington Post,
22 April 1975, p. A18, with photograph.
McCarthy illustrates the nature of the perpetuated public
image of Allen Ginsberg. "Only a few days ago, The New York
Times ran an artist's portrait of Ginsberg at the top of its second
section, but in the accompanying text not a line appeared about the
poet on his thought." Instead of adding to this symbolic image
McCarthy turns to what Ginsberg really thinks. He cites an interview in "The Craft of Poetry," edited by William Packard, for Ginsberg on the act of writing, and continues with Ginsberg's words
from Allen Verbatim in which he "discusses the uselessness of repe-
titious condemnations of the system." Ginsberg states, "generaliza-
tions about the ... behavior of the American populace made no sense
unless one can begin with oneself and dredge one's own harbors."
Commending Ginsberg, McCarthy concludes "Ginsberg is a poet who
is repeating in contemporary ways what Whitman said a century ago:
that the nation's work has to start from within."

831 McHarry, Charles. "On the Town/Weekend Special." Daily
News, 22 February 1975, n. p.
This column opens with the question, "Is Allen Ginsberg
going square?"

832 Mackeral, Wholly. "Symposium News Confiscated/Ripped Off
Papers in 'Bad Taste.'" Westport Trucker, 2 February-
7 March 1972, 2:21 (45?), p. 5.
"An Allen Ginsberg poem not acceptable to good taste!--
prompted the UMKC police Tuesday afternoon to seize the remaining
copies of the Symposium News, edited by Ken Kesey and friends."

833 McNay, Michael. (Photograph.) Guardian, 29 June 1973, p.
6. Titled: "Poetic License: Allen Ginsberg the American
Poet, with boiler suit and crutches--he broke his leg in
January--met Farida Majid from Bangladesh at a reception
yesterday to mark Poetry International, a gathering of the
worlds' leading poets being held in London this week.

834 McTaggart, Lynne. "Poetry up from the Underground." Daily
News, 6 March 1977, pp. 5, 10.
McTaggart's article is a Daily News feature on Allen
Ginsberg on the 1970's: "In fact, too many people--who have witnessed Ginsberg's contribution in the shaping of two decades of culture, believe he represents a kind of prophet who is going to tell us
what the '70's are all about." Highlighted is a reading at the West
End Cafe which "represented a kind of homecoming for Ginsberg,"
a reading at St. Mark's Church with Robert Lowell and his current
work. Ginsberg concludes "The present for me is probably more
creative and more powerful than any other period in terms of my

getting into music. As far as I'm concerned, I'm famous for the
'80's." Previewed are an upcoming "LP of Ginsberg's music produced by John Hammond ... (and) ... a new book of poetry titled
'Mind Breaths' (City Lights)."

835 "Magical Mystery Tour of England in the Sixties." Drummer,
    19 February 1974, 283, pp. 9-11 with three pictures, one
    of Ginsberg, without identifications or credits.
        This article is without identification regarding the author.
However, it is an article about the relationship of Allen Ginsberg to
Miles (founder of International Times in England) and the rest of the
vanguard of the "cultural revolution" of the 1960's in the U.S. and
London. More specifically, this is an article about Miles's role in
this movement which was motivated by the author meeting Allen Ginsberg at a concert at Barnard in November and being introduced to
Miles. After all "it was Miles who introduced Allen Ginsberg to
Mick Jagger and to Paul McCartney" and it was "He who rescued
[him] from disintegration at Columbia University and spent a summer at Allen's farm working on the tapes." It was Miles who was
influenced by these young poets in 1958 and he who serves as archi-
vist for both Allen Ginsberg and William Burroughs.

836 Mamrak, Bob. "Allen Ginsberg/Recording His First Blues."
    Happy Times, 23 June 1976, p. 5 with a photograph.
        Bob Mamrak refers to Ginsberg's recent appearance at
Glassboro State College at which time he "performed some of his
songs." In fact, he is currently "putting together a record of songs
for Columbia Records.... It'll probably be called 'First Blues,'
that's the title of a book I've got out. It's a book of song lyrics
and lead sheets ... blues, rags, ballads and harmonium songs...."

837 Mason, Michael. "Poetry and Politics." Gay News, 12-25
    July 1973, 27, n.p. with picture of Ginsberg titled "Allen
    Ginsberg: an aura of positivity" by Stephen MacLean for
    Camera Press, London.
        This brief note cites Ginsberg's appearance in Amsterdam
at the Poetry International Festival. Ginsberg spoke on a panel
"Poetry and Politics" on June 28th which in part supplied "odd insights into the political attitudes of prominent poets."

838 Micheline, Jack. "An Old Comrade Speaks Up for the Kerouac
    He Knew." San Francisco Phoenix, 3 May 1977, 1:17, pp.
    6-7.
        Editor's note (John Bryan): "Beat street poet Jack
Micheline whose work first appeared nationally during the 'beat'
period and who was a good friend of Kerouac, dropped by the Phoenix
a few days ago to talk about the Jack Kerouac he knew and to voice
his anger over the 'fucking over' Kerouac is now taking in some of
the published material now appearing on him--most especially the
recollections from Allen Ginsberg which were first published in 'Gay
Sunshine....'"
        Jack Micheline attacks Ginsberg for attempting to "re-
write history" in his recollections of Jack Kerouac. As he continues

on, however, it appears that the attack on Ginsberg occurs because
of Ginsberg's fame and acceptance into the literary establishment
which rejected Kerouac.

839 "Michigan White Panther Trial." Outlaw, 14 April-6 May 1971,
2:1, p. 13.
"The Defense argued that their membership in the Youth
Culture had deprived them of a trial by a jury of their peers....
When the prosecution argued that no such thing as Youth Culture
exists the defense produced a number of expert witnesses including
Jack Vaughn, Chairman of the Youth Committee of the Michigan
State legislature, Julian Bond and Allen Ginsberg.... Allen Gins-
berg proved to be the defense's most controversial witness."

840 Miles. "Allen Ginsberg: Full circle." Berkeley Barb, 25-31
May 1973, 17:21:406, p. 18 with photograph of Ginsberg,
"1965: Allen Ginsberg, 'Village' poet, ousted from Czechoslovakia."
"Well, we've done it again, Miles has worked with Ginsberg for several years and below assesses the old fairy's artistic
growth." Miles muses over his relationship to Allen and traces
Allen's path from "Howl" in 1959 to his current reading at The New
School in Manhattan. "Through all the public surface his message
still gets through, it maybe made a few detours but he's back on
course again only this time it's not as part of new left, counter-culture, religious freaks, the best part of it is again coming from him
alone as always."

841 Miller, Cindy. "Beat poet is on-again off-again showman."
Tallahassee Democrat, 27 April 1975, n. p.
Ginsberg's appearance in Ruby Diamond Auditorium as a
participant of Earth Week and the Center for Participant Education
poetry series is reviewed in this carefully researched article which
is laden with insightful Ginsberg thoughts. Ginsberg, of course,
comments on government conspiracy, the Vietnam War, Tim Leary
and meditation. He sees his current "Eastern focus" as a "ripen-
ing."

842 Miller, Cindy. "Ginsberg: Poems, Chants." Tallahassee
Democrat, 22 April 1975, p. 11 with picture by Ray Stan-
yard for the Democrat, "Joyful Ginsberg at FSU...'poet's
role is frankness.'"
Cindy Miller reports on Ginsberg's reading at Florida
State University "last night" which consisted of a "juxtaposition of
holy mantras, political and imagist poems and bawdy lyrics."

843 Miller, Steve. "Ginsberg Remains Paradox/Poet Still Unortho-
dox." Retriever, 21 November 1977, 12:12, pp. 7, 10,
with photograph of Ginsberg, "Allen Ginsberg greets the
audience before his poetry reading" by Pearson.
A portrait of "paradoxes" is presented: the use of the
"harmonium: a paradoxical musical instrument," the words of Reza
Baraheni, "an Iranian teaching English at UMBC" and Allen Gins-

berg in "business suit and a tie," as Steve Miller introduces his article on the Allen Ginsberg reading from his "recent" work. Ginsberg has given them no mantras this day, worn no beads, broken no new taboos. Instead the poet has affirmed his debt to other poets, acknowledged his sources, approved of the possibilities of life."

844 Morris, Bruce. "Famous Poets Part of Symposium Featuring Energy, Consciousness." Independent Florida Alligator, n. d., n. p., with photograph, "Allen Ginsberg ... to speak at symposium."
    "Poets Allen Ginsberg, 1974 National Book Award winner for 'Fall of America,' Gary Snyder and Michael McClure will participate with University of Florida's Howard Odum and nuclear physicist Henry Gomberg in a panel discussion Sunday at 8 p. m. in University Auditorium ... for an 'Energy and Consciousness 'symposium...."

845 Moser, Norman. "Ginsberg in Performance, 1959." San Francisco Sunday Examiner and Chronicle. 7 December 1975, pp. 9-10.
    Moser recaptures Ginsberg in 1959 in California as he read "Howl" before an audience of "a lot of tough cats, worst of the Beatnik element" at "R. G. Davis' Mime Troupe's rickety old Seventeenth Street church-become-theatre, sight off Mission Street...." Ginsberg has just received national attention as the "high priest of the Beats." As Moser states, the audience was hostile, "Ain't my high priest." Well Allen waited for silence and only then began to read. "He had something--even the worst of them admitted, though many of them could not say what it was.... staying power was the minimal something a few claimed he had. Courage said others. Plain damn guts, said one guy as he cleaned his blade. He had them all, too, and a bit more besides."

846 Moser, Norm. "Watching as the Poets Break Out of the Corral." Gar, June-July 1974, 3:5:24, pp. 26-29.

847 N. R. "Write On." Village Voice, 8 March 1976, p. 56.
    This is a discussion of the establishment of Full Court Press in New York City by Ron Padgett, Anne Waldman and Joan Simon and their "first three books ... Allen Ginsberg's First Blues; Rags, Ballads and Harmonium Songs ... is one.

848 Narod, Susan. "At OCC Poetry Reading/Ginsberg: Today's Youth 'More Aware.'" Lerner Newspapers, 9 May 1976, n. p.
    This is an article regarding the Oakton Community College, Morton Grove (outside of Chicago), Wednesday, May 5, 1976 reading and presentation of ideas on political activism and current student awareness.

849 Nelson, Erik. "Outside, Looking In." City on a Hill, 11:4 October 1977, p. 4 with photograph "Ginsberg, Gaskin,

Hofmann, Ram Dass and Leary talk over at a private dinner. " Photo credits Paul Martin.
"On Friday night in a large, white antiseptically imposing house with a commanding view of Santa Cruz and the University, the 50's shook hands with the 60's and pronounced the 70's spiritually fit. Around the dinner table, Allen Ginsberg, Timothy Leary, Baba Ram Dass and a whole assortment of other midwives to the birth of American spiritual awareness had a homecoming reunion with Albert Hofmann, the 70-year-old Swiss chemist who first derived LSD...."

850 Nemo, Fred. "Ram Jai Boogalooi. " Portland Scribe, 11-17 May 1974, pp. 6, 19.
"Ram Jai Boogalooi" is a poetic response to Allen Ginsberg's appearance and the chanting of "Sri Ram Jai/Ram Jai Jai/ Ram Om. "

851 "New Jersey/This Week. " New York Times, 20 February 1977, n. p. , with 3 photographs, 1 of Allen Ginsberg.
"Allen Ginsberg reads at YM-YWHA, Wayne and Montclair State College. "

852 "New Light on Leary. " Georgia Straight, 29 May-5 June 1975, 9:396, pp. 12-13. Reprint from Berkeley Barb/APS (Alternative Press Syndicate).
Ginsberg's support of Tim Leary, "a political prisoner of war" is indicated here. Ginsberg and Ken Kesey stand behind Tim Leary in light of the "recent series of articles by the LA Freep" (Los Angeles Free Press) regarding Leary's cooperation with the CIA and Drug Enforcement Administration (DEA) to "win his freedom. " Ginsberg feels that Leary is caught in a negative situation with few options. Instead of directing negative energy at Tim Leary, Ginsberg feels that the government should be the recipient, "The government is obviously using him to browbeat any moral idealism that exists in America. "

853 "News. " Chinook, 16 July 1970, 2:26, p. 3, with 3 pictures, 1 of Allen Ginsberg (from Boulder Intermind).
"Plans continue to develop for the Community Free School's whole Earth Fair and Festival of Peace (formerly the Whole World Festival), the Free School announced recently. " The 3 pictured individuals above (Ginsberg, Steve Gaskin, Swami Satchinanda) will attend.

854 The Newsletter, on the State of the Culture, n. d. , p. 1.
"Allen Ginsberg--poetry salmon of all our U. S. rivers-- comes back to Columbia U hatchery: old West End Bar where he spawns the Sunday afternoon reading away with newborn wriggly lines, swift and frolicking.... " This is a story about Allen's West End reading and the subsequent events.

855 Newton, Peter. "No More/No Less. " Takeover Newspaper, n. d. , p. 13, with two photographs of Ginsberg, the top by Art Pollock and the bottom by Lesy.

These are the thoughts of Peter Newton on Ginsberg, arranged in free form verse which included the following information: "For the first time since his 1967 appearance with the late great Fugs, Allen Ginsberg blew into Madison for a two-day session of chanting, singing and poetry punctuated by an exorcism rite on the capitol steps...."

856 "Notes on People." New York Times, 20 July 1971, p. 38, column 3, includes a picture.
"Italian officials have decided that Ginsberg should stand trial on an obscenity charge in Terni. A court ruling overturned a previous one that determined Ginsberg's poetry reading at the Spoleto Festival of Two Worlds in 1967 'did not constitute a crime'."

857 "Notes on People." New York Times, 23 May 1975, p. 34.
Note number two concerns Allen Ginsberg who "has been in a New York Hospital since May 10, when he entered for a checkup because of an attack of Bell's palsy on the right side of his face."

858 O'Connor, John. "Television: A Night with the Video Freaks." New York Times, 5 March 1972, II, p. 17, column 1.
This is an article about "a group called Video Free America ..." who were "formed by Arthur Ginsberg and Skip Sweeney." The group then describes their recent video experience with Allen Ginsberg's production of "Kaddish."

859 "Options/Radio Free New York." Village Voice, 14 March 1977, p. 50.
"Radio Free New York: A special benefit has been organized to aid the staff union of temporarily silenced radio station WBAI. The many performers include Allen Ginsberg, Meredith Monk, Charlotte Moorman, the Talking Band, Robert Wilson, among others...."

860 Ouroussof, Alessandro. "Rattling Radical Bones." Daily Californian, 9 April 1974, p. 11.

861 "Outrageous." Advocate, 28 January 1976, p. 43, with picture of Ginsberg and Whitman titled "Montage: with apologies to Richard Avedon."
A link between Allen Ginsberg and Walt Whitman (via sleeping companions) is established in this gossip column for the gay community.

862 Palmer, George. "Mugging Bugging/So Ginsberg, Poet, Lets Us Know It." Cincinnati Enquirer, 6 February 1975, n.p., with photograph, "Allen Ginsberg ... mellowed fellow."
The Palmer article records "sessions" conducted by Ginsberg at Thomas More College and the dialogue from a "press conference" held there. In short, Ginsberg comments on his work, lifestyle, non-use of nicotine and alcohol, use of marijuana, the CIA and drug traffic, past politics and today's students. In closing he states, "I'm not much the poet laureate now. I got mugged the other day."

863 Palmer, Robert. "Friends Perform in Ochs Concert/Late
    Singer of '60's Honored at Felt Forum Tribute." New York
    Times, 30 May 1976, n. p.
        Palmer reviews the performance, "The concert's musical
highlights were a heartfelt rendition of Mr. Ochs's 'Pleasure of the
Harbor' by Tim Hardin and Rob Stoner's energetic Elvis Presley imi-
tation of 'Heartbreak Hotel,' with Allen Ginsberg, the poet, on finger
cymbals."

864 Palmer, Robert. "The Pop Life/Friends of Phil Ochs/Sing
    a Tribute to Him/Tonight at Felt Forum." New York
    Times, 28 May 1976, n. p.
        The lead article in "The Pop Life" column announces
"the concert in honor of the late folk singer Phil Ochs, scheduled
to begin at 7:30 tonight in the Felt Forum...." Listed among the
participants in a reading of a "narrative of Mr. Ochs's life" (written
by Ed Sanders) is Allen Ginsberg.

865 "Panel Set On Censorship, Pornography." Los Angeles Times,
    2 May 1974, IV, p. 18.
        "Contemporary literature week continues at USC with a
panel on pornography and censorship scheduled for 11 a. m. today
in Heritage Hall Auditorium.... Moderators will be Arthur Knight,
film critic-historian and professor of cinema at USC.... Poet Allen
Ginsberg and his father, Louis, will read from their works Monday
at noon in Bovard Auditorium."

866 "Poet Allen Ginsberg to Read at CWC Wed." Riverton Ranger,
    12 April 1977, 71:31, p. 1, with photograph of Allen Gins-
    berg.
        This is a feature story on Allen Ginsberg's reading at
Central Wyoming College in Riverton on "Wednesday, April 13, at
8 p. m. in the Dobler Room.... Ginsberg's appearance at CWC
is part of the Wyoming Poetry Circuit program."

867 "Poet Ginsbert at TMC." Kentucky Post, 4 February 1975,
    n. p.
        This is a short article referring to scheduled "poetry
reading at 4 p. m., Wednesday, at Seiler Commons, Thomas More
College. He will give a lecture and reading at 7:30 p. m., same
day and place."

868 "Poet Ginsberg Speaks Tonight." UMBC Retriever, 14 Novem-
    ber 1977, 12:11, p. 20.
        This is an announcement: "World-travelling poet Allen
Ginsberg will read from his recent poetry tonight at 8 p. m. in the
UMBC theatre.... The reading, being presented by the Depart-
ment, is free."

869 "Poetry International." London Times, 3 July 1973, n. p.
        This article records the reading of Allen Ginsberg
in London, the first in seven years since his reading with Ungaretti.
It also records the change in Allen Ginsberg physically for he's got-

ten older and has put on some weight. Nonetheless, the article continues with a review of the events at The Poetry International Festival.

870 The Poetry Project Newsletter, 1 July 1974, 17 unpaged.
    On page 2 Allen Ginsberg is mentioned with "Peter Orlovsky doing 'zen carpentry in Kitkitdizzie. '" Page 3 includes Allen Ginsberg in a reprint description of The Floating Bear (#1-37) available from Box 852, La Jolla, California.

871 The Poetry Project Newsletter, 1 February 1975, n. 22, unpaged.
    Page 1 reference to Allen Ginsberg reading, chanting and closing the evening at the January 1, 1975, New Year's Day group reading at St. Mark's Church. Page 7 reference to Naropa Institute plans for a summer "School of Disembodied Poetics. " Faculty staff includes Allen Ginsberg.

872 The Poetry Project Newsletter, 1 April 1975, n. 24, unpaged.
    There are two reference to Allen Ginsberg. The first is on page 1 in an announcement of the William Burroughs, Gregory Corso, Allen Ginsberg, and Peter Orlovsky reading April 17, 1975, at Columbia University, MacMillian Hall. The second is on page 5 in a listing of guest Naropa Institute faculty which also cites "full professors Allen Ginsberg and Anne Waldman. "

873 The Poetry Project Newsletter, 1 June 1975, 26, unpaged.
    There are numerous references to Ginsberg through-out the newsletter: page 1 "Allen Ginsberg suggests you beg, bor-row or photocopy the May 30th issue of New Times, which offers inspiring examples of government and big business working hand and glove.... " Page 2 refers to The Coldspring Journal, no. 6 with inside photographs of Allen Ginsberg. Page 3 refers to Naropa Poetics School Summer Session Reading Agenda which includes "Philip Whalen and Allen Ginsberg (June 18).... " On page 7 a reference is made to Allen Ginsberg's appearance on "Speaking Freely" on NBC-TV: "Al-len Ginsberg learned that 'Speaking Freely' with Edwin Newman is sometimes a very private affair. First, NBC-TV slotted the tape broadcast at 1 a.m. Saturday morning, hardly prime time, to pro-tect non-insomniacs from Allen's list of pleasurable psychedelics. Then, the network denuded the show of Ginsberg's references to C.I.A. spiderman Lucien Conein, mention of William Colby's leader-ship of homicidal Operation Phoenix; even clipped the entire last stanza from his poem, 'CIA Dope Calipso.... '" Page 7 reference to "happy birthdays to ... Allen Ginsberg (June 3) ... " among others.

874 The Poetry Project Newsletter, 4 July 1975, n. 27, unpaged.
    On page 2 there is reference to Allen Ginsberg (Poetics Academy professor) busy and teaching at Naropa Institute. A second reference is to a poetry reading by Ginsberg on August 9th. On page 4, "Milk Quarterly 8 arrives, sizzling from Chicago, bearing unambiguous gifts, wonderful poems from ... Allen Ginsberg ... " On page 5 "Allen Ginsberg ... and others invite you to read their work in Adventures in Poetry 12, just published.

875 The Poetry Project Newsletter, 1 October 1977, no. 48, un-
       paged.
          Ginsberg is mentioned several times throughout the mim-
eographed newsletter of The Poetry Project. Primarily in the context of a first reading given on February 23, 1977, with Robert
Lowell at St. Mark's: "The Times had referred to the reading advance as a historic event that would bring together two poets 'from
opposite ends of the spectrum,' and Lowell mentioned this with the
comment that they were rather 'from opposite ends of William Carlos Williams.'" Robert Lowell suddenly died on September 12 at
the age of 60. The course Allen Ginsberg taught in "history of his
own beat generation" at Naropa is mentioned, as is his new book,
Journals, Early Fifties/Early Sixties.

876 Poliat, Frank. "Ram Jai Boogaloo II." Portland Scribe, 11-17
       May 1974, p. 19.
          "Ram Jai Boogaloo II" is "a supplement and clarification
hopefully, to Fred's boogaloo review ("Ram Jai Boogaloo I"); to
clarify some aspects which may seem obscure if you weren't there
and maybe add some disorder of my own." Both articles are responses to Ginsberg's appearance in that area. See entry 850.

877 Peck, Abe. "Allen Ginsberg meets Julius Hoffman; Distant
       Drummer, 25 December-1 January 1970, v. 65, pp. 3-4
       with photograph by Alex Bouwer, LNS.
          See entries 879 and 880, below.

878 Peck, Abe. "Allen Ginsberg Testimony at Trial." Seed (Chi-
       cago), n.d., v. 4, n. 10, pp. 4-5, 23, 25.
          See entries 879 and 880, below.

879 Peck, Abe. "& If The Law Is Absurd ... What Then?/Because
       I Don't Know-Understand...." (J. Hoffman). Berkeley
       Tribe, 19-26 December 1969, v. 1, n. 24, pp. 14-15.
          See also entry 880 below.
          "The trial of the conspiracy is a trial of one conscious-
ness by another. On Thursday, Dec. 11, Allen Ginsberg, poet and
man of the planet, came to Julius Hoffman's courtroom to speak in
behalf of Abbie Hoffman, Jerry Rubin and the Yippie Festival of Life
that fell before police clubs in Lincoln Park and on Michigan Avenue
last August. The following is an abridged transcript of Allen's testimony. It testifies to a meeting between an ancient life-force strug-
gling to be born again and a decaying America that cannot understand
anything we believe in--from Black Panthers to White Magic."

880 Peck, Abe (Liberation News Service). "The Defense Goes on
       the Offensive in the Chicago Conspiracy Trial." Georgia
       Straight, 17-24 December 1969, v. 3, n. 38, pp. 5-6, with
       photograph "Allen Ginsberg ... on the offensive last week at
       Conspiracy trial."
          See also entries 879 above, and 881 below.
          "Ginsberg blew everyone's mind in the courtroom, includ-
ing the Judge's. He chanted. He prayed. He played his harmonium.

He recited 'Howl' and pointed to the Judge when he recited the lines: 'Moloch, the vast stone war/Moloch, the stunned government." This is a copy of the testimonies from the trial, edited with an introduction by Abe Peck.

881 Peck, Abe. "Allen Ginsberg Meets Julius Hoffman." Georgia Straight, 24-31 December 1969, pp. 6-9, with photographs. This is a continuation of the trial transcripts with editing and introduction by Abe Peck.

882 Peck, Abe. "I Don't Understand It." Helix, 2 January 1970, pp. 6-7, with photograph " 'Allen Ginsberg and Tim Leary at Human Be-In, San Francisco 1967' from the archives of Joe Cain."
See entries 879 and 880, above.

883 Peck, Abe. "Om." Ann Arbor Argus. 14-31 January 1970, pp. 7, 9, 16-18 with photograph.
See entries 879 and 880, above.

884 Pélieu, Claude. "He Answers from His New Home/A Home of the Word & Dance/A Week at Allen Ginsberg's Farm." Nola Express, 7 August 1970, 61, p. 17.
Claude Pélieu ruminates on his stay at the Ginsberg farm while working on the "French proofs of Planet News" with friends Mary and Miles (to whom this is dedicated) Allen and Peter and Gordon and Ray and Chas. Words are exchanged between the friends present and those from far away.

885 Persky, Stan. "The Other World/A Conversation with Warren Tallman, about Allen Ginsberg." Georgia Straight, 7-13 March 1969, 3:48, pp. 12-13, with photograph by Karen Tallman.
Tallman speaks of Allen as a poet dedicated to another world. He sees him in line with the "otherness" of the "Dada-Surreal-Charlie Chaplin-conglomerate world," and discusses him in relationship to the other new poets and Walt Whitman. Tallman weaves an intriguing argument for Ginsberg's "other worldliness" in concluding with his thoughts on Planet News, "News from the other world. Which is not otherwhere. Heaven exists and is everywhere about us."

886 Plamondon, Pun. "Ann Arbor Culture: Mecca of the Midwest." Ann Arbor Sun, 4-20 September 1974, 2:17, pp. 4-5, including a photograph by Barbara Weinberg.
"As many as 2,000 attended the Festival [Festival of Life], an all day affair that begins with a sunrise meditation in the Arb. There are feasts, music workshops on meditation, tai-chi, yoga, dance, astrology, palmistry, tarot, and much more. Allen Ginsberg and other prophets of the new age have participated in this festival."

887 Pollak, Michael C. "Ginsbergs Share Both Love & Poetry." Sunday Record, 8 February 1976, pp. 1B, 12B, with photo-

graph by W. Peter Monsees of the Ginsbergs "Poets Allen (foreground) and Louis Ginsberg with Edith."
This is a touching portrait of the relationships of Allen Ginsberg, Louis Ginsberg and Edith (Allen's stepmother) to one another.

888   Pomada, Elizabeth. "The Bay Area's Best Sellers." San Francisco Chronicle, 1 July 1975, n. p.
Allen Ginsberg's Howl heads the list for "all-time Bay area best sellers" at 2. 5 million.

889   "Rabbi A. W. Miller scores New York Times omission of 'four letter word describing human excrement,' from Ginsberg's 'On Jessore Road,' December 17 in light of December 20 publication of photographs showing Bengalis being humiliated, tortured...." New York Times, 28 December 1971, 28:5.

890   "Random Notes." Rolling Stone, 3 November 1977, pp. 56, 59, with photograph of Allen Ginsberg.
In the "Random Notes" column Allen Ginsberg's search "for a record company after completing an album, First Blues,... an album of original blues ballads produced by John Hammond" is described.

891   Rauch, Berna. "Poets Sing of Visions." Berkeley Barb, 19-25 July 1974, 20:1:466, p. 11 with photographs, one of Allen Ginsberg by Carlos Casal-Calvete: "Allen Ginsberg: Filling in the Deletions."
"We came to hear Allen Ginsberg, Gary Snyder, Michael McClure, and Nanao Sakaki read poetry at Berkeley.... What was it all about? About Yamaha's proposed 'development' of Suwano-se Island, a tiny, unspoiled wilderness belonging to Japan. Yamaha plans to turn the island into a plastic resort ... for rich people. If Yamaha has its way, they'll dispossess native farmers and fishermen, as well as Banyau Ashram, a spiritual community.... So Fred Brunkel organized an evening of poetry and song for the Suwano-se Defense Fund. In return for our $2 donations, each of us was given a ticket of admission, in the form of a picture post card addressed to Yamaha.... Ginsberg the magician, the energy center ... started off the evening with an improvised song.... Poet Nanao Sakaki, a native of Suwano-se, read a number of beautiful, simple poems.... Almost three hours of magic drew to a close with color slides of Suwano-se, accompanied by haunting, beautiful sung native songs...."

892   "Recipes for Happiness." Stylus, 18 October 1973, XLVII:7, page 13.
The schedule of events for October 18-24, 1973, includes a reading by Allen Ginsberg on October 19 and admission is free.

893   Reed, Jim. "A Divine Wind Blows into Town/Three Appreciations for Poet Allen Ginsberg/Readings at Woodstock Artists

Association this past weekend drew enthusiastic responses."
Woodstock Times, 6:51 (December 22, 1977): 18-19.
Three individual articles on Allen's reading at the Wood-
stock Artists Association. Page 19, excerpt from "Who Be Kind
To. "

894 Rehert, Isaac. "You Can't Do Anything About/Anything, but
Try--Ginsberg. " Sun, 14 February 1976, p. A8, with
sketch of Allen Ginsberg "Evan Keehn, a Maryland Institute
student, made this sketch of Allen Ginsberg. Mr. Ginsberg
autographed the sketch and drew the 'ah. '" It is dated "10
February 1976" by Ginsberg.
This article springs from Ginsberg's reading at the Maryland Institute. "To the newcomer on the Ginsberg scene, what is as
striking as the poet's performance are the changes--in both the poet
and in the society he confronts.... "

895 Reynolds, Ric. "Partying with the Poets. " Berkeley Barb,
6-12 December 1974, 20:486, p. 5, with cover caricature
by William Johnson.
Ric Reynolds writes about the meeting of the "American
poets at a party to end all after a reading at the 2nd Annual Santa
Cruz Poetry Reading. " Bukowski, Ginsberg, Ferlinghetti, Snyder
and others had read. Much of the party is described from Bukowski's interactions with people.

896 Richard, Paul. "Great Gray Ghost, The Invisible Man. "
Washington Post, 11 February 1976, p. C1, C3, column 2
with a photograph by Ken Feil for Washington Post, "Allen
Ginsberg and William Burroughs" followed by a quote from
Burroughs' Naked Lunch.
Allen Ginsberg appears with William S. Burroughs in
his Georgetown reading at the Corcoran on Monday, February 9,
1976. Ginsberg's chants are met with much "approval," as Burroughs' work is welcomed. Ginsberg acts as the stimulus for Burroughs throughout, "Ginsberg sits beside him, offering good quotes,
answering all questions. "

897 Ritchings, Gene. "Ginsberg, Burroughs, Corso, Orlovsky:
Alive in the Age of the Nouveau Geek. " Aquarian, 5-18
June 1975, 10:93, pp. 8-9, with photograph of Ginsberg.
This article "is an account of a recent gathering of poets
at the Dharmadatu Meditation Center at Columbia College. Ritchings
sets the tone for his thoughts with the words of Kerouac, "everyone
is becoming a geek!" For Ritchings terms our era one of "nouveau geekdom of the post-industrial 1970's in preparation to discuss
the monumental reading of the Beats at MacMillan Hall 16 years after that initial reading (when Ginsberg first read "Howl"). "It was
as if 'the triumph of poetry over the tricking of the world' Ginsberg
called for in his last reading ... was already well on its way to being true for a while at least. "

898 Rodriquez, Juan. "Rolling Thunder Spirits in Peak Form. "

Gazette, 6 December 1975, p. 49.

This is a review of Rolling Thunder Revue at its Montreal appearance which mentions Ginsberg: "The great beat poet, Allen Ginsberg drifted out of the audience to add his finger-bells to the entire troupe's finale of 'This Land Is Your Land'. "

899 "Rolling Thunder." Toy Sun, 1 January 1976, 1, p. 3.

This is an article which is an excerpt covering a dialogue between "Ginsberg as 'the emperor' and Dylan as 'the alchemist. '" It begins with an incomplete sentence and appears to be from a larger article. (Perhaps this is some sort of printing error.)

900 Ross, Cissy Steinfort. "Poet and Scientists Discuss Man's Energy Consciousness. " Gainesville Sun, 21 April 1975, p. 8B, with photograph of Ginsberg.

This article refers to the symposium, "Energy and Consciousness" held at the University of Florida at which time Odum and Ginsberg spoke among others.

901 Rossiter, Sean. "Crippled Poet Ginsberg Bruised but Still Vital. " Vancouver Sun, 4 June 1973, p. 33.

Rossiter records Ginsberg's reading and appearance "at Sunday night's benefit performance for the Tibetan Buddhist Centre" in Vancouver. "It is possible that Ginsberg, the poet, will be remembered less for his poetry than because, as it has been written, 'more than any other person Ginsberg was the spiritual godfather of the counter-culture. '"

902 Rubin, Jerry. "The Freeing of John Sinclair. " Underground Press Syndicate, 24 December 1971, 2:26, unpaged, pp. 9-12.

Rubin indicates the cultural/social/political ramifications of the Ann Arbor rally for John Sinclair, "The people on stage reflected the seed of the new cultural and political renaissance about to hit Amerika--the second cultural revolution.... This is the year for everyone to come back and start again, to come together again, in new ways, to build our culture without male chauvinism, bad drugs and crazy freakouts. We should build our culture once more, only this time with more self-awareness and self-control. We need more public events, even a huge political Woodstock at the Republican National Convention next August in San Diego. 1-2-3-4-, many more Ann Arbors! And it's only the beginning.... " Of course throughout this discourse Allen Ginsberg is mentioned.

903 Ryan, Jeanine. "Committees Come Together. " Chronicle, 10 February 1976?, n. p.

This is an article regarding the "Major Event Council's Festival of Arts" which features Allen Ginsberg as one of the individuals in residence.

904 The San Francisco Phoenix, 29 June 1973, 1:21, p. 2, with a picture of Allen Ginsberg by Alvan Meyerowitz.

"Poet Allen Ginsberg led off the May 31 benefit for Tim Leary in the Telegraph Hill Neighborhood House. More than 1,000 Leary well-wishers came and heard Allen, Barry Melton, Joanna Leary, Michael McClure and the Sufi choir. More donations can be sent to All Out Changes, Barclay's Bank, Market Street."

905 Savasana. "The Difficulty Is Really Compassion." (Milwaukee) Kaleidoscope, 28 October-11 November 1971, 5:22 (105), p. 9 with five photographs.

On October 18th, 1971 Allen Ginsberg visited Marquette. In this article he is criticized for making money by speaking out against money. Ginsberg responds in a non response, "So it's difficult to feel joyful in America except by realizing that actually the fabric of reality is an illusion ... making love with young men is what gives me the most intense joy.... The difficulty is really compassion...." He advocates political action through voting and remembers 1967 when he was forbidden to appear in Marquette.

906 "Scenery." Columbia University Press, 31 March 1974, n. p. This is an announcement of a reading by Allen Ginsberg, Peter Orlovsky, Gregory Corso and William Burroughs at Macmillan Hall, 8 p. m., April 17, 1974, at Columbia University.

907 Schourup, Larry. "Ginsberg in A^2." Ann Arbor Sun, 5-19 April 1974, 2:7, p. 7 with photograph collage.

Schourup's article serves as an introduction to Ginsberg's visit to the University of Michigan. The event is "entitled, 'An Evening with Allen Ginsberg and Bhagavan Das' promise to be a memorable one, filled with poetry, chanting to the tune of Ginsberg's harmonium, and the song and sitar music of Bhagavan Das. It is a benefit for the building of a gay community Center." Schourup fails to note Ginsberg's most recent publications, instead commenting upon Reality Sandwiches, Airplane Dreams and Planet News. Substantial information on his companion Bhagavan Das, with whom he is touring the country, is included. "Bhagavan Das is the Hindu name of the young Californian who was the pedagogue of Baba Ram Dass ... while Ram Dass was in India...."

908 Shenker, Israel. "The Life and Rhymes of Ginsberg the Elder." New York Times, 13 February 1972, p. 86, column 1, with three pictures of Louis Ginsberg.

Louis Ginsberg talks about poetry and his son Allen, and the recent production of "Kaddish." He describes their relationship as "poetic co-existence."

909 Shively, Charles. "Ginsberg Triumphant." Gay Community News, 9 April 1977, 41:4, p. 1, 12.

This article records Ginsberg's appearance at Passim's Coffeehouse in Cambridge. "Gay males in the audience cheered (while several straights squirmed) when Allen read his beautiful contemplation of sweet-young-boy asses spreading their cheeks.... The poem was dedicated to Fag Rag and the Boston gay community generally."

910 Silver, Sam. "After Bucks to the Prisoners." Berkeley Barb,
        6-12 December 1974, 486, p. 5.
        "Thirty American prisoners in one of Mexico's most no-
torious prisons are going to get some 'getting by' money as a direct
result of AIM-J poetry benefit held in Santa Cruz Monday Nov. 25."
Ginsberg, Bukowski, Linda King, Ferlinghetti, Snyder all participated.

911 Simpson, Louis. "Poetry in the Sixties--Long Live Blake!
        Down with Donne!" New York Times, VII, 28 December
        1969, p. 1, includes a picture of Ginsberg.
        "In the 1960's poetry got off the page and onto the plat-
form." Simpson attributed the catalyst of such to Ginsberg who ...
"single-handed ... changed things." Simpson then analyzes Ginsberg
as this catalyst and subsequent social figure, and highlights a network
of other poets which include William Carlos Williams, Jim Harrison,
Charles Olson, Robert Duncan, Gary Snyder, Galway Kinnell, and
others. Simpson then makes the connection between poetry and politics and concludes that "with poets such as these we have come a
long way from the timid silent fifties."

912 "Sinclair Rally Draws 15,000." Underground Press Syndicate,
        10 December 1971, pp. 1-2.
        This is a story covering the "super-rally" held for John
Sinclair which "drew 15,000 people to the giant Chrisler Auditorium
to listen to speakers and music" (in Ann Arbor, Michigan). Ginsberg is cited for opening the program "by doing some very enter-
taining songs which he sang with animated enthusiasm and surprisingly
good voice."

913 "Sit Down, Shut up." Kentucky Post, 6 February 1975, n. p.
        This is a brief note concerning Allen Ginsberg's reading
at Thomas More College, Wednesday, and his words of wisdom on
the "transcendental meditation movement." As Ginsberg said, "Anything that will get people to sit down and shut up is a good thing."

914 "Six Writers Named to Share $34,000 Worth of Grants." New
        York Times, 10 April 1969, p. 15, column 1.
        "From the American Academy and the National Institute
of Arts and Letters ... Ginsberg will receive a grant of $5,000."

915 "Sixth Free Lecture." Dixie News, 6 February 1975, n. p.
        This is a short announcement: "Thomas More College
announces its sixth free lecture of its 1974-75 Humanities Lecture
Series. 'Beat Generation' poet Allen Ginsberg will read and lecture
on the Thomas More College campus Wednesday February 5, 1975...."

916 Skir. "Listening to Allen Ginsberg." Gay Sunshine, 2:65, 9
        October 1971, p. 6.

917 Smilow, David. "Ginsberg Dialogue Compelling/Chapel Poetry
        Reading Mediocre." Wellesley News, 12 April 1973, LXVII:
        8, pp. 1, 4, with photograph by Eric Levenson.
        "Allen Ginsberg sings and chants his poetry with the au-

dience at the Chapel. Participation was disappointing, according to students and faculty members alike. " Yet "the afternoon 'conversation with Allen Ginsberg' was engrossing hours of apparent opposites; his genius vs. our general mediocrity, his Big Name vs. our anonymity, his meditation vs. his breathtaking and unflinching social consciousness, his total involvement with the world vs. our apathy, Davis Lounge on a sunnyday vs. a crowd hearing of the terrors of police states. " Poet Gregory Corso showed up later at the performance "totally wrecked" and abrasive. The entire performance was "unfortunate" because of the setting coupled with Corso's disruptive impulses.

918 Smith, R. T. "Views and Reviews/The Fall of America and
      other awards. " Appalachian, n. d. , p. 9.
          "Ginsberg's award is a long-awaited kick in the ass to
      the Apollonian mean. " This article recounts the "ceremony" of the
      National Book Awards at which Ginsberg's The Fall of America re-
      ceived an award.

919 "Some 3,000 Students of Western Michigan University, Kala-
      mazoo Pay $1. 00 to Hear Ginsberg Recite Poetry. " New
      York Times, 17 January 1971, 49:1.

920 Sorenson, Tom. "Poet Chants On/Ginsberg Captivating. " St.
      Cloud Daily Times, 6 February 1976, p. 21 with photograph
      by Myron Hall "Poet Allen Ginsberg reads a selection dur-
      ing an appearance at St. Cloud State University Thursday
      night. "
          The Sorenson article records Ginsberg's appearance at
      St. Cloud State University where he chanted, read, spoke and sang
      the blues at the Festival of the Arts.

921 Spengler, David. "Poet Provides a Touch of Mystery. " Record,
      16 February 1972, p. B10.
          A reference is made to Allen Ginsberg in this review of
      a reading by poet Stanley Kunitz at the Poetry Roundtable series,
      sponsored by the YM-YWHA and Bergen Community College: "Once
      more I thought of Allen Ginsberg's 'Oom'--becoming a major pre-
      occupation of mine--and I hungered for a chant and a howl. "

922 Starr, Carol and Frank Widder. "Poet Chants, Sings and
      Reads/Ginsberg Leads Buddhist Fest. " UCLA Daily Bruin,
      21 April 1976, XCVIII:13, pp. 2, 5, with photograph by
      Maria Levine, "Poet Allen Ginsberg: 'Existence includes
      suffering; suffering is caused by ignorance. '"
          Ginsberg offers his "contribution to the Buddha-Dharma
      festival called Tse-Ong" with his chanting, singing and reading at the
      Grand Ballroom, April 19, 1976. In this article he "explained his
      philosophies on Zen, writing and drugs. "

923 Stevens, John. "Poet Ginsberg Here Tonight. " Florida Flam-
      beau, 21 April 1975, p. 1, with photograph "Allen Gins-
      berg ... prophet-poet.... "

This announces Ginsberg's planned reading "tonight at 8:30 in Ruby Diamond Auditorium" as "the first poet to be invited ... by the Center for Participant Education (CPE) Poet series.... He will also appear on WFSU-TV's 'Prime Time' tonight at 7."

924 Stevens, Joseph. "Poor Paranoid's Almanac." East Village Other, 19 May 1970, v. 5, n. 25, pp. 4, 11, with photograph of Alan Watts and Ginsberg.
    "Everybody was there except Tim Leary" at the benefit for him (he is in jail pending appeal--Chino, California). This is a long list of those that participated: Allen Ginsberg, Alan Watts, Abbie Hoffman, Jerry Rubin, Rosemary Leary, Johnny Winters, Bob Fass, Paul Krassner, Ed Sanders and the EVO Staff among others. Abbie Hoffman alienates the audience and Ginsberg tries to calm him down. Hoffman "departs from the stage, accessing Allen Ginsberg and the rest of being another form of 'CIA Pig.'"

925 Stone, Richard. "New Leery Leary." Santa Cruz Independent, 20-26 May 1977, 1:44, pp. 9, 17.
    There is merely a passing reference to Allen Ginsberg who Leary finds "totally involved in the past. He is freaked out by the possibility that the future could be really different than the past...."

926 Stovall, Steve. "Experience Decade Ending." Star-Tribune, 15 April 1977, p. 5 with photograph.
    "Blues Poet--Poet Allen Ginsberg says the 1970's are culmination of a decade of experience. The poet appeared at Casper College on the first leg of a four-stop tour of the state."

927 "SUNY Conference on Drugs." New York Times, 28 February 1969, 18:1; New York Times, 2 March, 1969, 62:3.
    "Allen Ginsberg and Dr. Leary were present."

928 Thomas, Jack. "At Large/Times Change, So Has Dylan." Boston Globe, 24 March 1976, n. p.
    This is a critical article about the poet Bob Dylan based upon his recent appearances in the Rolling Thunder Revue and album, "Blood on the Tracks" in which he creates a song glorifying the gangster Joey Gallo. "Who else could get away with writing a song as bad as 'Joey,' a dreary dirge that attempts to mythologize the late Joey Gallo, a cruel, greedy, psychopathic Brooklyn monster to whom human life was cheap...." The article is more a comment upon the state of our culture and its heroes than anything else. There is something wrong when we idealize the lives of monsters and fail to cut through the mystique created by Dylan. Allen Ginsberg is criticized for his praise of this Dylan album. According to Ginsberg, "This is the great moment of Dylan taking off his mask. He's accepted the myth created around him and is transmitting it into artistic energy. He's alchemizing it into gold." Rather, Jack Thomas concludes, "Sure. But a short while ago, Dylan would have described that as an Idiot Wind."

929 Thompson, Howard. "Going Out 'Guide.'" New York Times, 14 March 1976, n. p.

Under "Potpourri" in this column, a Ginsberg reading is listed: "An afternoon of poetry reading by Allen Ginsberg and Peter Orlovsky is scheduled for 3 P. M. tomorrow in Egyptian Gallery No. 8 of the Brooklyn Museum, Eastern Parkway and Washington Avenue. Admission is free. "

930 Throne, Geri. "Eat Lit. " Sun Herald, 5 August 1976, p. 9.
This article records the event of a "conference call" between Allen Ginsberg and "Rollin's Beat Literature class" in the format of an informal lecture in which "each student was able to talk with Ginsberg personally. " The article provides the background information to the call and the teacher of the course, Ed Riley. Some of Ginsberg's responses are recounted as he responds to questions on "a shift in consciousness," "the death penalty," "his personal philosophy," "drugs" and his writing. Riley, the instructor, met Ginsberg at a symposium he organized over a year ago at the University of Florida at Gainesville.

931 "Thru a Looking-glass Darkly. " Logos, March 1970, 3:1, n. p. , with assorted photographs.
This is an "Alice in Wonderland" approach to the Conspiracy Trial of the Chicago 7 which ends with William Kunstler questioning Ginsberg. Ginsberg replies, "Om m m m m m m. "

932 "The Times Diary. " London Times, 29 June 1973, p. 18, with photograph on page 3.
With sarcasm Ginsberg's appearance at the Poetry International festivities is recorded. Critically the reviewer notes that most of those in attendance didn't speak about poetry. In any event "Poetry Intl. ends tomorrow night at the Queen Elizabeth Hall where Ginsberg will be appearing with Basil Bunting, Hugh MacDiarmid and Richard Eberhart. " He comments "There was some doubt as to whether Allen Ginsberg had fallen over his porch, his Porsche or his paunch as he appeared on crutches at a reception for Poetry International '73 yesterday. "

933 Topor, Tom. "Groucho Awards Obies and Insults. " New York Post, 9 May 1972, n. p.
The Obies are awards given by the Village Voice "for work off Broadway. " Marilyn Chris is cited for "Distinguished Performance" in "Kaddish. " Under the category "Visual Effects" Video Free America is cited for "Kaddish. "

934 Tripper, T. "Free John Sinclair Rally--Political and Cultural Energy Come Together. " Great Speckled Bird, 10 January 1972, 5:1, p. 13, with photograph of Ginsberg by David Fenton/Liberation News Service.
This is a story regarding the event held in Ann Arbor: "The night began when the sonorous voice of poet Allen Ginsberg chanted and moaned a lengthy invocation for the death of the culture that put John in jail, and then loosed a haunting half-beautiful drone about his recent visit to India where he saw streams of refugees fleeing from East Pakistan. The mood of the evening was set. "

935 Tripper, T. "Radical Poet John Sinclair Gets Out of Jail After
Massive Michigan Youth Rally." Liberation News Service,
18 December 1971, 400, pp. 15-16, with photograph of Ginsberg with John and Yoko.
Tripper, a correspondent from Ann Arbor, Michigan, reports on the "John Sinclair Freedom Rally" staged in Ann Arbor in
Chrisler Arena. Sinclair was released from prison "after serving
28 months of a 10-year sentence for possessing two joints of marijuana." The crowd at the rally is compared to George Harrison's
Bangladesh concert in terms of "cultural and political energy on
stage."

936 Trescott, Jacqueline. "Poets Among Poets, Just Like Ordinary
Folks." Washington Star-News, 30 April 1974, C, pp. C1-2.
Poets "Allen Ginsberg and Ishmael Reed" together at the
Library of Congress and afterwards at a party in their honor. They
are credited with "the acute ability of putting a universal experience--
blackness, Jewishness, war, death--into words understandable to
the 'common people.'"

937 Troelstrup, Glenn. "Colorado's Pride at Metro State." Denver Post, 8 August 1977, p. 10, with Denver Post photographs by Ernie Leybe, one of Ginsberg, "Writers Discuss
Their Metro State College Gathering."
"The three, termed 'Colorado's Pride,' were there to
talk about their beginnings, dreams and life work,... For the most
part, they did. Except for life work.... Ginsberg said his greatest
interest is in how the mind operates. He made fun of the 'myth'
perpetuated by the CIA and psychiatrists ... that all writers are
supposed to be neurotic and dreamers." John Williams, a Colorado
novelist, Joanne Greenberg, a Denver novelist and poet Allen Ginsberg were all present at this "three-hour dialogue" at the Metropolitan State College's Learning for Living session.

938 "Two Authors Share Fiction Book Award." Louisville "Courier
Journal." 21 April 1974, n. p.
This Associated Press article documents Allen Ginsberg's
award by the National Book Committee for his work The Fall of
America: Poems of These States, 1965-1971.

939 Upjohn, Marshall. "Poet Blasts Nixon, Military, FBI." Oklahoma Daily, 26 April 1974, p. 16, with photograph.
The Upjohn article records Allen Ginsberg's informal
sessions at the University of Oklahoma (Norman, Oklahoma) and
provides some background information on Ginsberg's recent three-
month Wyoming meditation "trip." Ginsberg comments upon his
meditative stage of being and its relationship to his poetry, as well
as criticizing the American government's recent activities in Indochina and Watergate. "He equated the perspective of history taught
in American secondary schools with Walt Disney fiction."

940 Valente, Judith. "Yank in Paris/Finds a Home/In Book Shop/
On Left Bank." Sunday Daily News, 28 March 1976, p. 1.

"Paris--Shakespeare and Company, Paris's most famous bookstore for English texts, has stood on its site at 37 rue de la Bucherie--across from Notre Dame Cathedral--since 1951. And everyday somebody new discovers it." The Valente article is about the "Bostoner" George Whitman who established it. A reference is made to Ginsberg in the context of Whitman's plans: "He wants to revive his Paris Magazine, which published once in 1966 with manuscripts from author Lawrence Durrell and poet Allen Ginsberg...."

941 Victor, Thomas. "Allen Ginsberg at the West End." New York Times, 4 February 1977, III, col. 1, p. 22, with photograph.
      Allen Ginsberg "will be reading some new poetry this Sunday at 2:30 p.m. at the West End, the bar on Broadway and 114th Street frequented by generations of students." Ginsberg will read parts of a new long epic poem "tentatively titled, 'Contest of Bards' ... and from portions of 'Mind Breaths' a collection of his most recent poetry." Also, "he will be joined by his brother, Eugene, who will also read his poetry."

942 "WRL Peace Award." WIN, 10:11, 28 March 1974, p. 11.

943 Walbye, Phyllis. "Ginsberg's Howl Changed to Mantra." Loveland Reporter Herald, April 23, 24, 1977, p. 3B. Three photographs of Ginsberg, one by the author of the article, two by Rick Thompson.
      Ginsberg's "howl has been replaced by his mantra. Ginsberg is into Buddhism, the Naropa Institute in Boulder, blues and Dylan style music, and the poetic muse of a middle-aged man." A poetry reading is recalled which initiated this historical commentary on Ginsberg. No specifics are provided about the reading.

944 Watson, Penny. "Allen Ginsberg/We Need a Lot Less Stone and a Lot More Tree Tenderness." N.C. Anvil, A Weekly Newspaper of Politics and the Arts, 17 January 1970, 3:138, pp. 6-7, with photograph.
      This is the story of Ginsberg's stay in Durham--at Duke--which comments on his new life style, need to unify with the landscape, the death of his friends and the relationship of his literary work to the world. It closes with the recollection of a visit to a Duke student's home where Ginsberg washed dishes and taught the people there to say "Om."

945 Waugh, Dexter. "Morning Devotion/Ginsberg Sings the Blues." San Francisco Examiner, 4 June 1973, p. 32 with photograph of Ginsberg," 'Dylan Gave Me Lessons on Blues' poet Allen Ginsberg."
      Dexter tells of Allen Ginsberg's activities in San Francisco with "fellow poet Gary Snyder" as the two sit "on a floor of a small, second-story room in North Beach, singing their morning devotions to Buddha." Allen Ginsberg is in town to work with City Lights on "his new books" and on "some tapes that will be issued as record albums by Fantasy."

946 Weaver, Helen. "Nay, A Household Necessity/Three Appre-
ciations for Poet Allen Ginsberg/Readings at Woodstock
Artists Association This Past Weekend Drew Enthusiastic
Responses." Woodstock Times, 6:51 (December 22,
1977): 18-19.
Three individual articles on Allen's reading at the
Woodstock Artists Association. Page 19, excerpt from "Who Be
Kind To."

947 "Weekender Guide." New York Times, 9 December 1977, p.
C26.
Under "Sunday-Reading for Children" a benefit program
for the Children's Storefront, "a free nursery school . . . for chil-
dren with special problems at 57 W. 129th Street" run by poet Ned
O'Gorman. "Mr. O'Gorman has lined up about two dozen literary
friends--John Ashbery, Allen Ginsberg, Robert Penn Warren, John
Cheever, Stanley Kunitz, Wilfred Sheed, Bernard Malamud and
others--to give readings of their work Sunday at 8 p. m. at Alice
Tully Hall. The other half of the program 'last year's Naumberg
Prize Winners for piano and violin will give a recital of Bach and
Liszt. '"

948 Weiner, Rex. "Trepidation and Disgust in Miami." Georgia
Straight, 27 July-3 August 1972, 6:252, pp. 12-13, photographs including one of Ginsberg are by Sharkie.
"Rex Weiner, the editor of the NY Ace Underground
newspaper, prepared this exclusive report for publication in the
Georgia Straight." A reference is made to Ginsberg: "Allen Ginsberg stood nearby, chanting a special Watermelon Mantra and looked
hungry for watermelon."

949 Wells, Michael. "The Second Coming/The Strange Tale of How
Miami Earned the Privilege of Becoming the Site of the
World's Longest Intermission." Daily Planet, 24 January
1970, 1:VII, p. 3, 4, 5, 7, 19.
Wells's article described Ginsberg's visit to Miami in
December 1970. Originally Allen and his father, Louis, were to
read at Temple Israel under the title, "Avant-Garde Son and Square
Father Attempt to Bridge the Generation Gap." The publisher of
Daily Planet found out about this reading and asked Ginsberg if he
would do a benefit (proceeds would go to the publisher to cover obscenity charges). This reading was billed as "Last Intellectual Happening of the Sixties." In Miami there is an ordinance called the
"Morrison Ordinance (in which any performer to appear in a city
facility must first undergo an intensive screening at least two weeks
prior to his scheduled appearance. . . . "). The rock band scheduled
and Allen's father were denied the right to appear due to their late
application.
Allen began to read that evening from "Howl." Supposedly,
the Miami Police got upset. The stadium manager claims the police
turned the mikes off and put the lights on. It turns out that Manny
Costa, the stadium manager, was responsible for the abrupt halt of
the reading and it was found, "while Costa's actions may have been

taken with the best of motives, they were legally impermissible. "
Ginsberg was not found "obscene within the constitutional standards
laid down by the Supreme Court...." Free facilities were made
available to Allen and his father was permitted to join him. On
January 2, the "First Intellectual Happening of the Seventies" com-
menced (without Allen's dad because he had to return home).

950 Westport Trucker, 1972?, 2:20, V(44), n. p.
        "Next weeks Trucker will contain an interview with Allen
Ginsberg. The same interview will also be broadcast, in part,
over KBEY fm at noon, Sunday, February 12, and 11:00 p. m. the
following day. " See volume 2, number 22 (46) 1972.

951 "What's On. " Village Voice, 5 May 1975, XX:18, n. p. , with
        photograph by NY Daily News titled, "Son and Father, Allen
        and Louis Ginsberg at Greenwich House. "
        Within this list of activities the following is included:
"Tues. (May 6) Poetry reading also discussion. Allen and Louis
Ginsberg. Greenwich House--Senior Ctr. , 27 Barrow, 1:30 p. m.
(free). "

952 " 'When Can I Go to the Supermarket and Buy What I Need with
        My Good Looks' from 'America. '" Stylus, 18 October
        1973, XLVII:7, page 11, with photograph titled, "Allen Gins-
        berg to appear at Brockport on Friday, October 19, at 8:30
        P. M. "
        "This is the first of a two-part article on Ginsberg, a
brief biographical sketch," as well as an announcement of Allen Ginsberg's reading at Seymour College Union, Friday, October 19, at
8:30 p. m. This is an informational article on Ginsberg in the form
of "a brief autobiographical sketch" introduced with a quote from the
poet: "Everything I write is one way or another autobiographical
or present consciousness at the time of writing. "

953 Wicker. "Straights Flee Cities. " Gay Sunshine, 2:51, 24 May
        1971, p. 4.

954 Widder, Frank. "Asian-American Festival: 'A Creative Union'. "
        UCLA Daily Bruin, University of California, Los Angeles
        XCVIII:11 (April 19, 1976): 1. Photograph of Allen Gins-
        berg "Allen Ginsberg (above) will be among the featured
        slate of performers in the five day TSE-ONG festival
        here.... "
        "Events for Tse-Ong, a spring festival dedicated to Amer-
ica's birthday, will also include an address given by Ginsberg in the
Ackerman Grand Ballroom tonight from 7:30 to 10 entitled, 'A Life
Empowerment'.... The purpose of the festival is to act as a link
of Asian culture and American culture, termed 'applied Buddhism. '"

955 Wilcock, John. "Other Scenes/Potpourri. " Daily Planet, 24
        January 1970, 1:VII, p. 20.
        "Potpourri" includes a quote from Ginsberg: "The trees
are the only ones who are getting the world straight.... If the

enemy is the materialistic society which is consuming all our re-
sources ... then our natural allies in this battle for survival are
the trees and the grass."

956 Williamson, Mitch. "Ginsberg: Poet, Teacher, Learner,"
        Rutgers Daily Targum, 5 May 1976, p. 18. Photograph
        by Mitch Williamson, "Poet Allen Ginsberg found time to
        converse with Rutgers students while he dined at Bower
        Commons." With manuscript reprint (handwritten) "To
        Louis Ginsberg Rutgers 1917. Allen Ginsberg May 3,
        1976."
            "This poem was written by Allen Ginsberg some time
after dinner at the Commons. Ginsberg's father Louis was a Tar-
gum editor." Mitch Williamson reviews Allen Ginsberg's visit to
Rutgers on May 3, 1976, at which time he read with the assistance
of "guitarist Jon Sholle, poet and long time friend Peter Orlovsky"
and "Miguel Algarin, Assistant Professor of English at Livingston and
published poet" from the audience. Ginsberg spent the entire day
with the student body: he ate at the student dining hall, "The Commons," read in the evening, and attended a later reception in the
Student Center. At the reading, he read, chanted and spoke about
Buddhism. In fact, he performed "A Western Style Mantra Chant
featuring a gospel form of Buddhist Noble Truth."

957 Wilner, Paul. "'Flossie's' Death Ends an Era." New York
        Times (May 30, 1976): 10-12.
            This New Jersey article pays tribute to Flossie Williams,
the wife of the late Dr. William Carlos Williams of Rutherford, who
had died recently at age 85. Allen Ginsberg was among those who
are listed on the guest list often at the Williams' home in Rutherford.

958 Winer, Linda. "It's a Home Coming for Beat Generation's
        Mellow Fellows." Chicago Tribune, n. d. , n. p. , with photo-
        graph "William Burroughs and Allen Ginsberg: A mellow
        feeling in Chicago" by Art Walker.
            This is a "mellow" article about the return of the two
artists to Chicago after the chaos of the past years.

959 "Winning Poets Due in Oregon." Oregon Journal, 23 April,
        1974, p. 4.
            This is an announcement of readings by "both winners in
the poetry category of the National Book Awards...." Adrienne Rich
and Allen Ginsberg.

960 "Words About the Man with No Words." Williamette Bridge,
        4:17 (4/29/71): 12.

961 "Writers Revealed in Photo Essay." Aquarian, 13-27 July
        1977, p. 2.
            A photography exhibit, "Tribute to Writers and Others"
by Alan Caruba, "a novelist, poet and freelance journalist" contains
one photograph of Allen Ginsberg. The exhibit "will be shown through

July 25 at the Overseas Press Club of America in the Hotel Biltmore located at 55 East 43rd Street in Manhattan. . . . Throughout the 70's Caruba photographed many of the famous writers he has met, the result being 'a unique gathering of personalities . . . all caught in what photographers call grab shots, that is candid and being themselves.'"

962 "Yip Founders." (Milwaukee) Kaleidoscope (Liberation News Service), 1-14 March 19 ?, 9, p. 12, col. 3.
  "A group of 25 artists, writers and musicians have agreed to participate in the founding of the Youth International Party or YIP today." Allen Ginsberg is among "the initial founders."

963 Young, Allen. "Concert/Rolling Thunder Revue." Win, XI:40 (Nov. 27, 1975): 19.
  Joan Baez and Bob Dylan performed together for the Rolling Thunder Revue. "The Revue has been playing in a series of special concerts to large and small audiences in several New England Cities." At the Springfield show "even Allen Ginsberg appeared on stage for the finale Woody Guthrie's 'This Land Is Your Land' singing along and ringing his Buddhist bells." However, Young's article is more a comment upon a relationship between culture and politics, between consciousness and action than a review of Rolling Thunder Revue. Indeed he did attend the November 6th show in Springfield, Massachusetts with Michael Meeropol, "son of Julius & Ethel Rosenberg" and enjoyed the "reunion" which even included Arlo Guthrie and Allen Ginsberg. "Gerald Ford was going to be in Springfield the very next morning and . . . a protest rally was planned." As one can assume from Young's association with Michael Meeropol, he is political in terms of action. He wonders why Dylan fails to promote the next day's rally when "the turnout at the next day's demonstration . . . was strikingly disappointing, given the high energy of the night before." Young ponders "the alternatives," and calls for: "some creative introspection, for some analysis, for some re-definitions about politics, and for some innovation."

964 Ziegler, Alan. "Allen Ginsberg Sees His Father Through." Village Voice, 5 July 1976, p. 120, 79-80, with two pictures.
  Father and son have come to terms with one another personally and professionally in this descriptive article about their relationship.

965 Zodiac. "Leary Interrogated by Atty. Gen. Saxbe." Sunrise, n.d., 3:7, p. 19.
  This article is based upon reports by "Michael Horowitz, the researcher who runs Leary's archives, who reportedly learned the details from a crime reporter for the Chicago Tribune," regarding Leary's interrogation by Atty. Gen. Saxbe and Special US Attorney Guy Goodwin. Allen Ginsberg is mentioned in regards to "a suit being filed by his [Leary's] daughter, Susan, and poet Allen Ginsberg, which demands that he [Leary] be produced in court so that his physical and mental well-being can be checked."

966   Zyn. "Ginsberg at Gonzaga University. " Spokane Natural,
          3:10, 9-23 May 1969, p. 5.   Photograph "Allen Ginsberg
       at Gonzaga University on Friday, April 25," by Russ Nobbs.
       Zyn adequately reviews the Ginsberg reading in a cynical
tone: "but Ginsberg is obviously still with it, even if he is a New
York Buddhist Jew intellectual.   He is one of those perennial figures
who made the change from beat generation to hip generation without
any trouble. "   Peter Orlovsky is there as well and participates in
the chanting.   The information is all there in the article: program
and details, but there is something lost in the writer's approach to
prose.

Foreign Language

967   Alvarenga, Teresa.   "Allen Ginsberg/El Llamado 'Pope' de la
          Poesia Beatnik Llega a los Cincuenta. "   ("Allen Ginsberg/
          The Recognized 'Pope' of Beatnik Poetry Reaches Fifty").
          El Nacional, 3/6/76, p. 16.   (Caracas, Venezuela), with
          photograph (Reproducción Germán González).   (In Spanish).
       In this article the author views Ginsberg at the crucial
age of 50 and places him within the poetry of the "Beat Generation,"
and the context of his times.   Other poets, Rafael Pineda and Vin-
cente Gerbasi comment.

968   "The Avantguard [sic] in Orvieto. "   Expresso, 1976, n. 15,
          p. 55 (In Italian).
       This is an article about the avant-garde in Italy.   Next
to it is a poem by Ginsberg "Hadda Be Playing on the Jukebox"
which was submitted in Ginsberg's absence from a conference of the
avant-garde in Orvieto.

969   Barberis, Robert.   "A la Rencontre internationale/Les contre-
          culturels. "   Le Jour, 28 April 1975, p. 11.   (At the Inter-
          national Conference/The Counter-Culturals. ")   (In French).
       "Les Americains" includes the thoughts of William Bur-
roughs and quotes from Allen Ginsberg: " 'Objectively, the world
situation is probably without hope.   I am entirely disillusioned, ' he
said in French.   'One cannot form a community on the basis of
anger at our suffering, ' he added as a good Buddhist.   'It is necessary to recognize and accept the existence of suffering. ' After that,
'relaxation' is possible, as is friendship, tenderness (the mellow
tone of his voice is a sign), and the confidence which is the trea-
sure of the peoples. '"

970   C. I. S.   "Blumen des Bosen. "   ("Flowers of Evil. ")   Der
          Abend, 25 September 1976, n. p.   (In German).
       In this article on William Burroughs there is a reference
to Allen Ginsberg.

971   "Chronologie parallele/1918--Premier manifeste Dada. "   Actuel,
          10-11 (Juillet-Août 1971):   3-5.   (In French).
       Mentions "Howl" is condemned for obscenity.

972 Giachetti, Romano. "Il Boom Della Poesia in America/Il porta e una farfella con lo stomaco di ferro." ("The Poetry Boom in America/The Poet is a Butterfly with an iron stomach.") Expresso, n. d. , pp. 74-94, 192. (In Italian).

This is an article in Italian about a conference in Brooklyn, New York, "Festival of the Avant-Garde." Basically, the article presents the internal debates of the avant-garde poets and provides an American historical context for discussion. Paralleled to the development of poetry is work in music, cinema and prose. Feminist, Black, ecological, "family lyricists" and new form poetry are discussed. For historical flavor the development of the Black Mountain College, the San Francisco Renaissance, Beat and New York School poets are discussed. Ginsberg is highlighted as a Beat poet with a one paragraph portrait on page 77. Essentially the article concludes that there has been no actual revolution in poetry, but some significant changes.

973 Hanck, Frauke. "Ginsberg singsang auf A/Der Amerikanische Lyriker bei einer Nachtlesung im Ari." ("Ginsberg sing song in A/The American Lyricist at a Reading at Night in Arri.") Tages-Zeitung, 2. /3. October 1976, Feuilleton 9 (Newspaper n. 9), n. p. , with photograph.

This is a description of the Beat Lyricist Allen Ginsberg in an unspecified book of authors published in Munich, September 30, 1976.

974 Joris, Pierre. "Propos recuèillis." Actuel, 10-11 (Juillet-Août 1971): 20-22. (In French).
Conversation evaluated.

975 Lubo. "Richard Lindner Bilder: Leben als Reklame." ("Life as Advertisement.") Berliner Morgenpost, 23 September 1976, n. p. , with reproduction of picture of Ginsberg by Lindner (Foto: Will). (In German).

Allen Ginsberg in this article about the German born artist Lindner, who now works and lives in NYC, is called "The Prince of the Beat Generation." This announces a gallery showing of Lindner's work. Although not indicated, the picture noted above was later used on a post card series for Ginsberg.

976 Lubowski, Bernd. "Festwochen-Lesungen Met Allen Ginsberg, Susan Sontag and William Burroughs/Die Beat-Generation erwies sich als kritisches Gewissen Amerikas." ("Festival-Reading ... the Beat Generation Has Proven Itself to Be the Critical Conscience of America.") Berliner Morgenpost, 23 September 1976, n. p. , with photographs of the three authors, individually (Foto: BM). (In German).

The introduction to this article is painted in an historical context with parallels to the expatriates of the 1920's. Ginsberg and "Howl" are mentioned. Today's lecture by Allen Ginsberg is announced at the Academy of the Arts at 8:00 p. m. , to be followed first by a film and then by a discussion led by Fred Jordan of Grove

Press. Tomorrow Sontag will speak and on Friday William Burroughs will conclude.

977 Rohde, Hedwig. "Heiliger and Maienkönig/Allen Ginsberg in der Akademie der Kunste." ("The Holy One and the King of May/Allen Ginsberg at the Academy of the Arts.") Der Tagesspiegel, 24 September 1976, nr. 9424, p. 4. (In German).
"We are legends" said Ginsberg thirty years ago. Ginsberg who has outlived his legend is now in his late Buddhist phase. His visit to the Academy is described in this article.

978 Sinhuber, Bartel F. "AZ-Gespräch mit dem U. S. -Poeten Allen Ginsberg/Die Polizei sol jeden Tag mediteren." ("AZ-Conversations with the U. S. Poet Allen Ginsberg/The Police Should Meditate Daily.") Arbeiter-Zeitung, 1 October 1976, page 19, with photograph.
Ginsberg and Miehe met during Ginsberg's visit to Munich. They discuss music and individual freedom among other topics. Ginsberg is quoted in this discussion: "If somebody writes a poem about forbidding certain careers then he must be clear for all to understand. In 1965 in Prague, Czechoslovakia, I was forbidden occupations which later provided difficulties in America with the FBI and Narcotics Bureau. In this regard East and West are of the same opinion. My solution for this problem, will be to have the police meditate one hour daily. If someone wishes to become a policeman, he must be disciplined, meditation leads to discipline and that's also true for all radicals."

979 Superlove, January 1969, n. 15. (In Danish).
This is a Danish underground newspaper (Larsbjoernstraede 13, 1454 Copenhagen K, Denmark). Page 15 mentions Janis Joplin, Eric Clapton, Allen Ginsberg and Motown.

980 Thériault, Jacques. "Semaine de la contre-culture/Un bilan positif et ouvert...." ("Counter-culture week/An open and positive evaluation....") Le Devoir, 28 April 1976, p. 12. (In French).
At Saturday's assembly after a week of activities on the counter-culture, criticism was offered for inviting the "establishment" of the counter-culture, namely William Burroughs and Allen Ginsberg. "Only the white majority was represented.... It seems the minority groups, the chicanos and blacks, are forgotten."

B. PERIODICALS

Articles About Ginsberg in English

981 Alexander, Floyce. "Allen Ginsberg's Metapolitics: From Moloch to the Millenium." Research Studies of Washington State University 38, pp. 157-73.

982 Alkabutazolidan. "Witness in Naropa." NewsArt The New
York Smith 1:4, n. d. , pp. 1, 31, 50.
"In Naropa, the latest hotbed of Eastern exotica, high
near Denver, William Burroughs, Allen Ginsberg, Anne Waldman,
W. S. Merwin, Phillip Whalen, Ed Sanders and other literary lu-
minaries discuss the kosmos with Guru Chögyam Trungpa, Rinpoche."
The article from there becomes very critical of the activities at
this center, and its Buddhist orientation to writing: "One danger of
any such practice of religion is that the norms and forms assume
primacy, and the devotee dogs the footsteps of dogma, often more
in enchanted narcissism than in truthseeking. Americans are stronger
on knowhow than know. They seek prescriptions, formulae, a meth-
odology to buy, a gameplan or program for life.... Contemplating
spiritual 'experts' and their dogma, the Buddha said, 'The unheeding
sage ignores what others toil to learn.'"

983 "Artists on Watergate." Changes, A Metropolitan Monthly of
Art & Trends, September/October 1973, 84, pp. 22-24, 43.
Allen Ginsberg comments on the relationship of the
"Watergate gang" and that which they represent to the distributors
of narcotics He believes "that further investigation of the Watergate
culprits in their role as a White House Special Narcotics Investigation Team would reveal scandals much more shocking than already
revealed in Watergate investigation, namely high-level White House
working relationships with high-level international heroin traffic
capitalists ... the impeachment of Nixon might only result in the
replacement of Nixon with another Nixon...."

984 "At Gate Three." The Mystery Gate, 1976, unpaged.
In soliciting "People's Poems" there is a reference to
Allen Ginsberg: "Allen Ginsberg, Jack Kerouac, Gregory Corso,
and the rest of the 'Beat' poets have laid down the Western Foundation of Prose."

985 Ball, Gordon. "Ginsberg and Duncan." American Poetry
Review, 3:3, May/June 1974, pp. 52-57.
Excerpts from Allen Verbatim, particularly two chapters,
"Words and Consciousness" and "Early Poetic Community." The
first is from an "Epistemology Class, Wisconsin State University
April 13, 1971" and the second from "Kent State April 7, 1971."

986 Berkson, Bill. "Comment." Poetry, 114:4, July 1969, pp.
251-6.
"Comment on Fourteen Books," the first of which is
Ginsberg's Planet News. This article is just that, a "comment" on
an overview of Ginsberg and more precisely on his book Planet
News.

987 Bernard, Sidney. "On Uses and Abuses of the 'Movement.'"
New American Review II Smith (NADA Review Special Is-
sue), 22-23, July 1973, pp. 56-60.
According to the criticism offered by Abstracts of
English Studies, "Allen Ginsberg's 'From These States' (1966),...

(is) ... included perhaps, because of 'technical need,' rather than of 'poetics'. " The collection is assessed as representationally "acceptable," however, " 'Movement' writing" on the whole is criticized as "bad writing, taken over from the word-creators by the codifiers and ecclesiastes. "

988 Bertlet, Chip and Henry Doering. "The Other Miami Story. "
     Straight Creek Journal, 1:30, 31 August 1972, pp. 1-7.
     In this story of chaos at the Miami Republican Convention, under the heading, "The Conflict" covering Wednesday's activities, "Allen Ginsberg and Zippie leader Jeff Nightbird were among the first arrested when police moved in on the march as it neared the Doral.... "

989 Bradley, John and Joel Goldstein. "Journalism Shaping the
     World. " Athos, 20 June 1970, p. 3. Photograph of Allen
     Ginsberg by Silverstein.
     Allen Ginsberg attended the third annual national conference at SUNY at Buffalo of the Committee of Small Magazine Editors and Publishers at which he presented an address. "In an interview before his formal speech, Mr. Ginsberg stated that he's 'primarily interested in the organizing of material about repression of small papers and magazines...: I want to present this information to the United Nations. I want to ask the U.N. to intervene in the persecution of writers merely for their literary texts, such as Leary, Cleaver and John Sinclair. ' "

990 Brownstein, Michael. "Robert Stone. " Changes, April 1975,
     pp. 31-36, within a larger article "Three Generations of
     American Tough-Guys Writers: Robert Stone (by Michael Brownstein), Richard Price (by Adam Haridopolos) and Charles Bukowski (by Bruce Wagner).
     In the piece on Robert Stone on page 33, Brownstein refers to Allen Ginsberg when speaking to Stone. "Well, I used the word 'rumor' but it's considerably more than that. People like Allen Ginsberg have compiled quite a dossier of CIA involvement over the years. The theory is not simply one of individuals making money off of heroin as they would off of anything else, but of a plan--in a ghastly science fiction sense to undermine the troublemaking element of the American population; in other words, to keep people down on heroin as an element in some sort of wide-ranging plot. ... "

991 Burroughs, William, Jr. "Creemedia. Just Because Allen
     Ginsberg Meditates Doesn't Make Him Stupid. " Creem,
     America's Only Rock 'n' Roll Magazine, 7:11, April 1976,
     pp. 54-56. Photograph: "Dylan and Ginsberg at Jack Kerouac's grave, Lowell, Mass.: But it's all over now, fellas. " Photo by Ken Regan p. 54. Photograph: "The gay bars were closed so he climbed a mountain. " Photo by Joe Stevens p. 56.
     Editor's note: "... Here is an intimate off the cuff portrait of the man, written by someone who has known him for years ...

the son of ... William Seward Burroughs...." William Burroughs, Jr., turns to Allen Ginsberg with admiration and fascination: "Allen was my Godfather and sooner or later I would go to New York and join the heroes of my bookstores...."

992 Burroughs, William S. "Time of the Assassins." Crawdaddy, September 1975, pp. 12-13.
        In William S. Burroughs' column written "from Boulder, Colorado," he debates his "general theory ... that the word is virtually a virus.... But the word clearly bears the single identifying feature of virus: it is an organism with no internal function other than to replicate itself." Burroughs discusses this with Allen Ginsberg among others and paraphrases his response to "this simple question: 'Who are you talking to when you are talking to yourself?'"

993 Case, Brian. "Side Swipe. Brian Case Chronicles the Rise and Fall of the Movement...." New Musical Express, 8 January 1977, pp. 22-23. Photograph "Ginsberg reading on the '50's: 'I saw the best minds of my generation destroyed by madness.'" p. 22
        "The beats were the most exciting literary movement since World War II, prophets of the Rock Culture that sprang up in their wake...." Brian Case in his "chronicles" refers to Ginsberg's catalyst effect on the movement when he arrived in San Francisco and read "Howl." On p. 23 in a "Selected Bibliography" Allen Ginsberg's Howl and Other Poems is listed among others.

994 "Charles Olson, Robert Creeley, Allen Ginsberg, Robert Duncan, Gary Snyder, Lawrence Ferlinghetti." American Literary Scholarship (1975): n. p.
        This merely is a brief encounter with all of the above poets. A passing reference is made to Allen Ginsberg when the author talks about the Olson archives which contain "unpublished poems and a taped discussion from Vancouver (Olson, Creeley, Duncan and Ginsberg)."

995 Charters, Ann. "Allen Ginsberg and Jack Kerouac, Columbia Undergraduates." Columbia Library Columns, 20:1, November 1970, pp. 10-17.
        This article briefly describes Allen Ginsberg's relationship to Jack Kerouac, a fellow "Columbia undergraduate," and their individual relationships to the formal education offered to them at Columbia. "Now completing the circle, he (Allen) has made his alma mater the depository of his papers. In them is written the fullest account of the remarkable careers of Ginsberg and Kerouac both in and out of Columbia."

996 "Chatter." People, 24 November 1975, p. 80.
        In this column subtitled "Package Tour" there is an amusing report of the surprise performance of Allen Ginsberg, Bob Dylan and Joan Baez of the Rolling Thunder Revue tour at the Sea Crest Hotel in North Falmouth, Massachusetts. Instead of the usual "borscht-belt entertainment, ... a lush bearded man appeared and

began to read poetry. He was joined by a disheveled male folk
singer, and then a slender female balladeer. "

997 "A Chopped Beard. " Time, 34. Photograph of Allen
        Ginsberg by Beth Bagby.
            Regarding Allen Ginsberg after he shaved: "Last week
the once furry-faced arch beatnik appeared before a flock of followers in Berkeley without a beard and without his old vigor. Denying
that he had even said he would not shave until the Viet Nam War
was over, Ginsberg insisted that 'it had nothing to do with anything
conceptual. '"

998 Crawdaddy, 20 February 1972, section 2, p. 37.
            "The following is a discussion between John Wilcock
(who helped found the Village Voice and East Village Other and now
edits Other Scenes) and Paul Krassner, editor of The Realist, taped
in 1970. " There is a reference here to Allen Ginsberg, "What about
kids who have never heard of Paul Krassner, Allen Ginsberg, Jack
Kerouac, Lenny Bruce, or Tim Leary? Or these other people?"

999 Dickey, R. P. Sewanee Review, n. p. , n. d.
            In the article according to The Year's Work in English
Studies, he "attacks what he calls 'The New Genteel Tradition in
American Poetry' in a manifesto which divides contemporary poets
into what he calls 'good guys' who are bad, and 'good /bad guys' who
are good. The list of those anathematized includes Ginsberg, Bly,
Snyder and Creeley; the admired group brackets Leonard Cohen and
James Dickey with Robert Lowell, Allen Tate. "

1000 Dullea, Gerald J. "Ginsberg and Corso: Image and Imagina-
          tion. " Thoth, II:2, Winter 1971, pp. 17-27.
            This article explores the use of image and imagination
in the poetry of Ginsberg and Corso from the standpoint of New
Criticism. "The imagination is the source of the art, which rests
primarily in the image" states Dullea. However, after weaving a
careful analytical framework for discussion, Dullea sinks to the con-
descending voice of a New Critic up against the inexplicable word of
the "Beats. "

1001 "Education /A Sad, Solemn Sweetness. " Time, 17 November
          1975, pp. 74, 76.
            This is an article recording the death of critic Lionel
Trilling in which Allen Ginsberg is quoted: "He had a sweet heart,
a sad solemn sweetness. "

1002 Eron, Carol. "The Book Awards. " Book World, 28 April
          1974, pp. 3-4.
            This Book World article announces the winners of the
25th National Book Awards and recounts some of the events. "Accepting the Award for poetry shared by Allen Ginsberg and Adrienne
Rich, Peter Orlovsky spoke on behalf of Allen Ginsberg in a prophetic
message from the poet. "

1003 Gertmenian, Donald. "Remembering and Rereading 'Howl.'"
Ploughshares, 2:4, 1975, pp. 151-163.

1004 "Ginsberg--Alive." Athos, 19 November 1970, 4:17, p. 12,
with cover drawing of Allen Ginsberg and photos (2) of
Ginsberg by Graley (bug) on page 6, part of a whole set
of others from pages 6-7, titled "getting into living,"
plus another photo by the same person on p. 12 by the
article.
        Ginsberg reads at SUNY/Buffalo "from his break-neck
machine gun-style poetry." He chanted "Hare Krishna," used a
"tape from Timothy Leary in Algiers," and closed with "Om."
Gregory Corso introduced him. The article was written by a student who refers to Ginsberg as "the father and brother of us all.
From the 'beat' days to now. Ever growing. Ginsberg the poet,
the revolutionary."

1005 Goodman, Paul. "The Politics of Being Queer." Unmuzzled
Ox, 4:3, n.d., 48-57.
        "A version of this essay titled 'Memoirs of an Ancient
Activist' was published in Win, 15, November 1969. Goodman revised the essay considerably and put it among his papers--where it
was found at his death." Mention of Allen Ginsberg to illustrate
that "In essential ways, my homosexual needs have made me a
nigger." The point made is "Allen Ginsberg and I once pointed out
to Stokely Carmichael how we were niggers, but he blandly put us
down by saying that we would always conceal our disposition and
pass."

1006 Hahn, Stephen. "The Prophetic Voice of Allen Ginsberg."
Prospects, An Annual of American Cultural Studies, New
York: Burt Franklin and Company, Inc. and Jack Salzman (dist. by Lenox Hills), 1976, volume two, edited by
Jack Salzman.
        Hahn offers a social and literary critique of Allen Gins-
berg and his work, which successfully links Ginsberg with his literary (poetic) past. A traditional literary analysis of crucial Ginsberg writing is included. The social and cultural analysis is limited,
often not venturing beyond mere reference: "By uniting the formal
innovations, the visionary content, and the social dissent of the early
poems in one great cry, 'Howl' becomes Ginsberg's single most
formidable poem." There, however, are glimmers of insight, as
Hahn continues later: "It presents a condensed panoramic vision of
America and a sustained lyrical response to the travail of body and
soul in a decade dedicated to grey flannel, technology, and the cold
war. Here Ginsberg fully assumes the prophetic mantle." Hahn
skillfully unites the process of creativity with the poetic process.
I disagree with his conclusions that "the death of Neal Cassady in
1968 and of Jack Kerouac in 1969 in many ways signal the end of
an era of Ginsberg" because in 1972 Ginsberg publishes his monumental work in The Fall of America. Perhaps Hahn should be more
precise in defining the chronological patterns in Ginsberg's work.
Admittedly, he concludes "indeed, whatever may eventually be de-

cided about the literary value of his work--it is clear that Ginsberg is an important cultural figure. For in a time when our public accolade has been 'taxed by war,' when political figures mouth the words of biblical prophets, Ginsberg has taken the role of prophet seriously."

1007   Harding, Gunnar. "Allen Ginsberg Meets with the Swedish
       Cyclist." Evergreen Review. 74:14, January 1970, pp.
       23-36, translated by Gordon Brotherston.
       Story: stream of consciousness passage in and out of
Ginsberg's poetry reality, bits and pieces of visions are revealed,
social criticism surfaces and ends in optimism for "poetry is on the
way."

1008   Harding, W. "Allen Ginsberg on Thoreau." Thoreau
       Society Bulletin, 112, 1970, p. 7.
       Harding wrote to Ginsberg omqioromg about his
feelings regarding Henry David Thoreau. Here is printed the letter
from Allen Ginsberg, dated August 24, 1970.

1009   Horowitz, Michael. "Foreword." New Departures, 7/8
       and 10/11, n.d., pp. 8-9.
       There is a mention of Ginsberg's maturation as a poet
in this essay which also includes an excerpt from "his acceptance
speech for the National Book Award of 1974 for The Fall of America."

1010   Howard, Richard. "Allen Ginsberg: 'O Brothers of the Lau-
       rel, Is the World Real? Is the Laurel A Joke or a
       Crown of Thorns?'." Minnesota Review, 9:1, 1969,
       pp. 50-6.
       Howard skillfully explores the psyche of the poet through
his past words in interviews, past and present poems, and dedications. He realizes that "it is Ginsberg's presence ... which allows
his prophecy its full function." He denotes the important process
of discovery for Ginsberg and speculates upon the prophecy of Ginsberg and his work.

1011   Jennings, C. Robert. "Cultsville, U.S.A." Playboy, 16:3,
       March 1969, pp. 86-88, 151-154, 156-7.

1012   Kinkead, Linda. "Allen Ginsberg Living Legend." Queen's
       Jester, 21 February 1975, p. 21. Photograph of Allen
       Ginsberg.
       Kinkead refers to Allen Ginsberg as "that gentle, wave-
making poet" in her article, written after the St. Thomas More
College appearance, which stresses his political and literary contributions. Ginsberg refers to himself as a "Jewish, Buddhist, faggot,
anarchist, poet, singer, bard."

1013   Kinnell, Galway. "Whitman's Indicative Words." American
       Poetry Review, 2:2, March/April 1973, pp. 9-12.
       "Whitman knew that in its own time Leaves of Grass
was a failure ... Whitman's return to American poetry, if we can

set a date, did not come until one hundred and one years after the appearance of <u>Leaves of Grass</u> with the publication of Ginsberg's <u>Howl</u> in 1956.... Only now is Whitman fully accepted as our greatest and native master...." With this introduction Kinnell then launches an encounter with the rhythm of Whitman's words, leaving Ginsberg far behind.

1014 Knight, H. "Howl of Allen Ginsberg." <u>Biography News</u> 1, July 1974, pp. 751-3. Reprinted in <u>Authors in the News</u>, ed. by Barbara Nykoruk. Detroit: Gale, 1976, pp. 181-3.

1015 Krim, Seymour. "We Were the Early Band of the Insane." <u>Crawdaddy</u>, 20 February 1972, section 2, pp. 34-35.
    In this article on the death of Bohemia, there is a reference made to the Beats and, of course, Allen Ginsberg.

1016 Kronsky, Betty. "Allen Ginsberg in India: Therapy, Buddhism and the Myth of Happiness." <u>Humanist</u>, 35:1, January/February 1975, pp. 32-35.
    Kronsky begins her article with an overview of her path to Gestalt therapy and its relationship to the myth of happiness, a common abstraction of American Society. She highlights Ginsberg's <u>Indian Journals</u> as the end result of his "drive for happiness." She finds "it is only through suffering and deprivation that we can arrive at true openness to experience beyond the ego's machinations to attain happiness." Kronsky concludes that Gestalt theory coupled with "Buddhist psychology" seem to offer a plausible solution.

1017 Lamantia, Philip. "Poetic Matters." <u>Arsenal</u>, (Surrealist Magazine, Chicago), n. d. , pp. 6-10.
    The author appears to be making an argument for surrealism in poetry and art by critiquing the work of recent poets, in particular that of Allen Ginsberg: "But the fact remains, we have reached the point in 1975 that the act of reading Ginsberg and Olson or any of their epigones is interchangeable with the scanning of <u>Time</u> and <u>Newsweek</u>. I maintain this is no 'accident' but clearly delineates the <u>false consciousness of poetry</u> proliferating within the shifting gears of decadent capitalism." That is, to conclude, "--most established American poets of this century have given us a massive literature of sensibility, self-narration, virtuosity and literal confessions signed very energetically by the stylus of the death-wish."

1018 Latham, Aaron. "The Columbia Murder That Gave Birth to the Beats." <u>New York</u>, 9:16, 19 April 1976, p. 41.
    "The father of the Beat Generation was not Jack Kerouac or Allen Ginsberg or William Burroughs. It was Lucien Carr. He was the one who brought the others together. He was the one the others revered. He was the one the others expected to change America. And he might have if he had not killed a friend in 1944, when he was a sophomore at Columbia College. Reading Dostoevsky, Carr had come to believe in what he called 'the New Vision' to the point where he seemed ready to live <u>Crime and Punishment</u>." Aaron Latham weaves this tale of comaraderie which pivots around Lucien

Carr who killed his scout master David Kammerer who followed him
everywhere from school to school. However, throughout the text in
Allen Ginsberg's personal copy, there are remarks contesting the
validity of comments involving the author. As a result, it is satis-
factory only to note that Allen Ginsberg is included in this interpretation of the development of "The Beats."

1019 Lhamon, W. T. , Jr.   "Ginsberg in Florida." New Republic,
      173, 5 July 1975, n. p.
         Lhamon talks about the Ginsberg of the 1970's who is
"continuously matching his rhythms to America's only authentic art
form--jazz, rock and blues." After highlighting his performance
in Florida, he concludes that Ginsberg "mixes them (jazz, rock and
blues) with his charismatic, electric alchemy to fuse a national resource all of his own still in 1975."

1020 Luster, Helen.   "Allen Ginsberg: The Green Man Is Alive and
      Thrives." St. Andrews Review, 2:1, Fall/Winter 1972,
      pp. 35-41.
         According to the Abstract of English Studies: "This
article is a tribute to Ginsberg and the sources of his energy."

1021 Lyon, George W. , Jr.   "Allen Ginsberg: Angel Headed Hip-
      ster." Journal of Popular Culture, Winter 1969, III:3,
      pp. 391-403 with notes.
         Lyon through example has "attempted to show in this
paper [that] Ginsberg has found in mythology and mysticism a feeling
of oneness with the universe, with God, which has enabled him to
live freely and sanely and personally in a world that is cruel, bru-
tal and impersonal. His unifying vision is a personal one, modified
by factors that are not relevant to all men of his time, but he has
attempted to circumvent that problem by revealing himself as completely as is painfully possible, thereby allowing what is personal to
the poet to show itself as such, while the archetype remains pure.
Thus the poet hopes to transmit his myth."

1022 Malanga, Gerard.   "In Memory of the Poets of the Beat
      Generation." Crawdaddy, 2, 20 February 1977, p. 38.
         This is a poem written "for Allen" by Gerard Malanga
which is introduced by lines from William Burroughs, "All past is
fiction."

1023 Mazzocco, R.   "Between Thunder and Lightening." New York
      Review, 22:6, 17 April 1975, p. 24.

1024 Merril, Sam.   "The Hollywood Laugh Track/For Young Sit-
      Com Writers, 'the money's too good to worry about minor
      details like integrity.'" New Times, 9 January 1978, pp.
      27-32, 36-37, 84-90.
         A passing reference is made to Ginsberg and his cohorts
in this New Times article about comedy writers, television and the
state of culture. The theory which includes this reference is as

follows: "The American counterculture, circa 1969, sprang not from the writings of Kerouac, Ginsberg and Burroughs, but from the television sit-coms of the late fifties and early sixties. Whatever craziness might have been going on in our own homes, we could always tune to <u>Father Knows Best</u>, <u>Make Room for Daddy</u> and <u>Leave It to Beaver</u>, hear Jim Anderson, <u>Danny Thomas and Ward</u> Cleaver dispense the kind of solid McCarthy-era advice a growing child could depend on. Then the Vietnam War arrived and brought with it the ultimate disillusionment: Jim Anderson and Ward Cleaver were full of shit. TV was our literature, our babysitter, our make-believe friend. The TV families were our families and I have come to look upon The Revolution as a pan-generational, electric-speed decision not to grow up to be Robert Young. But the values of The Revolution have slid so far back into our cultural history that today they wait only for the right promoter to come along and market them as nostalgia.... Being American means never having to remember your past."

1025 Molesworth, Charles. " 'We Have Come This Far': Audience and Form in Contemporary American Poetry." <u>Soundings: An Interdisciplinary Journal</u> 59, 2, 1976, pp. 204-225.
    Molesworth delivers a long creative, yet literary examination of contemporary American poetry and its relationship to its audience, specifically highlighting that of post World War II. Conclusively, he surmises that: "No simple scheme, even one that grips both audience and the status accorded the world of objects, fully conveys the variety of voices and complexity of desire in poetry since 1950. What we can see, however, is an emerging tradition of catholicity among our poets, a willingness to remain open not only to experience, long an American poetic dream, but also open to one another, now a possibility more proximate.... Perhaps a new awareness of whom to address and what to lift to consciousness will be an important shaping force in the new ideas of form." Skillfully he places Ginsberg's work in the tradition of Pound, Whitman and Romanticism; and critically analyzes the form and content of the last lines of "Sunflower Sutra." Interestingly enough, he proceeds beyond the literary analytical levels to the cultural in that he finds: "The variety of poetic styles in America results from several causes, among them social heterogeneity--a heterogeneity experienced as a lack of social forms rather than an abundance of possibilities-- that has increased since the end of World War II in almost exponential measure. To this we should add at least two other causes: the monetization of relationships and the uprooting of language by the media."

1026 Montgomery, George. "The Tourists Were Too Much with Their Fingers Snapping, Instead...." <u>Crawdaddy</u>, 20 February 1972, section 2, p. 37.
    Montgomery paints the picture of the time with references to the cultural and artistic heroes. In referring to Allen Ginsberg, "The Beats seemed to stick together more than the kids of today.... We all knew each other. We all knew Ginsberg said things we went along with yet we would think them over. Argue over them. Give them thought...."

1027 Mooney, Jack. "Seminar '71 to Cover Poetry from A to Z."
      Alabama Journal, 14 June 1971, p. 7. Photograph (Jour-
      nal Staff Photo): "Famous Poets Correspondence Work
      Seminar '71 Includes Letters, Poems and Autographed
      Pictures."
         "Another pair of poets have sent holograph verses,
written under most poetic and coincidental circumstances. Allen
Ginsberg, the aging 'enfant terrible' of the Beat (or Hippy) School
of Poetry, wrote in a covering letter of May 4: 'Sitting in a pine
wood with Gary Snyder--here are some little poems for your coffee
house--mouth or wall--Good luck with Poesy--' And signed it with
full signature and a bold daisy-like motif. The coincidence is that
both Ginsberg and Gary Snyder, a younger poet of the 'school,' had
been written but the Snyder letter had been returned as no longer
at the indicated address. In one envelope were letters and verse
(both quite printable, even in Montgomery!) by the bearded Ginsberg
and a verse, 'Original Vows,' signed Gary Snyder and a stick figure
of a horned Pan playing his pipe."

1028 Moraes, Dom. "Somewhere Else with Allen and Gregory."
      Horizon, II:1, Winter 1969, pp. 66-67.
         "It all started in Paris in the Spring of 1958, when the
young British poet Dom Moraes invited Allen Ginsberg and Gregory
Corso to visit Oxford. They did." Free flowing description of
Dom Moraes' encounters with Allen and Gregory in Paris and then
in Oxford. Whimsical encounters with the established poetry world
of Oxford.

1029 Mortimer, Peter. "Ginsberg-Master of the Universe." Jour-
      nal, 7 August 1973, n. p., with photograph of Ginsberg
      coupled with two poems: "from 'Iron Horse'" and "Sun-
      flower Sutra."
         Ginsberg talks to Mortimer before his reading at the
Mining Institute in Westgate Road, Newcastle (the last time he
was here was 1965) about the Movement, politics and sex.

1030 Murray, Charles S. "Rolling Down Thunder Road/Bob Dylan's
      on Fire." New Musical Express (based on material assem-
      bled by Lisa Robinson), 15 November 1975, pp. 6-7, with
      photograph.
         "More famous people per square inch than anywhere
else in this issue ... Allen Ginsberg, Joan Baez, Roger McGuinn,
Ramblin' Jack Elliott, Ronee Blakeley, Bobby Neuwirth, Mick Ron-
son and hordes of others, all captured in Springfield (Massachusetts)
by the covert camera of Mandy Brady...." The Rolling Thunder
Revue performs in Plymouth, Massachusetts on November 4, 1975.
The Revue is described and Allen Ginsberg is cited as a cohort.
By the way the Rolling Thunder Revue was "named, incidentally,
after a Cherokee Indian Medicine man who's a friend of Ramblin'
Jack Elliott's and who gave the opening date his personal benedic-
tion."

1031 "Music and Dance/The Masked Man." Time, 17 November
      1975, pp. 69-70.

The Rolling Thunder Revue is reviewed: "The 'group' is a comfortable array of friends, mostly old, with a few new--Folksinger Joan Baez, ex-byrd Roger McGuinn, Nashville star Ronee Blakeley and even poet Allen Ginsberg."

1032   Notley, Alice.   "The Gorgeous Week."   Out There, 9, 16, March 1975, pp. 78-80.
        In Alice Notley's journal entry, she records the Ginsberg and Burroughs week of appearances in the Chicago area.   In particular, she notes "the week finished Sunday night with Ginsberg on 'Kup's Show' on TV.   His conversational partners were a group of bright-seeming TV and movie actors who knew nothing about contemporary poetry and were trying to sound interested in it only to see if they would wing it through the conversation with Allen Ginsberg.   He used a few shock techniques on them and won the show-- they couldn't even keep Timothy Leary's name straight--but our gorgeous week was over, and we were back in that place that feels a little like wandering around in the Northwestern parking lots."

1033   "On Tour with Bob Dylan."   Modern Screen, April 1976, pp. 40, 42.
        Rolling Thunder Revue is found "at the plush Seacrest Resort Hotel on Cape Cod."   Allen Ginsberg was introduced by the emcee and "read from his best known work, 'Kaddish.'"   Secrecy of the tour's whereabouts and schedule was of primary importance. Dylan "was checked into each hotel as 'Phil Bender,' Joan Baez was 'O. Tannenbaum,' Ginsberg, 'William Carlos Williams.'"

1034   Orth, Maureen, "Music: 'It's Me, Babe.'"   Newsweek, 17 November 1975, p. 94.
        "It's Me, Babe" is a one-page feature article on Bob Dylan's Rolling Thunder Revue.   Their ceremonious beginnings are described as the sun rose over Newport, Rhode Island and Rolling Thunder, the Cherokee Medicine Man officiated the circle around the fire which included Allen Ginsberg: "'Music comes from the earth to fill our souls,' Rolling Thunder intoned.   One by one, each of the celebrants sprinkled some tobacco into the smoldering fire and when it was Dylan's turn, he stepped forward and whispered: 'We are of one soul.'   At the ceremony's end, he had a tear in his eye."   Allen Ginsberg is quoted in the demasking of Dylan: "This is the great moment of Dylan taking off his mask....   Bob, Joan, myself, we've all transcended our hangups,..."

1035   Parkinson, Thomas.   "Reflections on Allen Ginsberg as a Poet."   Concerning Poetry, 21:1, Spring 1969, pp. 21-24.

1036   Parsons, Tony.   "Side Swipe While Tony Parsons Examines the Legend of Jack Kerouac, Beat Chronicles Supreme." New Musical Express, 8 January 1977, p. 23.
        Tony Parsons in this retrospective on Kerouac mentions Allen Ginsberg in the context of "Kerouac and his Beat Generation Buddies."
        See also Brian Case article above.

1037 "People." Time, 104:52, 18 November 1974.

1038 Peters, Rachael and Eero Ruuttila. Sitting Frog, Poetry of
Naropa Institute. 1976. (unpaged, arranged alphabetically).
In this "book" of poetry which includes Allen Ginsberg's
"Sickness Blues" written on July 19, 1975, in the introduction there
is a reference to Ginsberg as a co-founder of the Kerouac School of
Disembodied Poetics with Anne Waldman.

1039 Peters, Robert. "Funky Poetry: Allen Ginsberg's The Fall of
America." New: American and Canadian Poetry, 22:23,
Fall/Winter 1973-74, pp. 69-75.
"'Funky Poetry' is my invention for a genre of poem
best executed by Allen Ginsberg." Peters continues on "'towards
a definition' of this genre in his disc of 'The Fall of America.'"
He takes argument with Ginsberg's use of "Western Unionism Style"
which is "monotonous in the extreme." Point two of funk is "Ginsberg's culture-figures are for the most part funky people, in heroes
of (of) counter-culture movements:..." Point three is "The numerous elisions where articles are omitted...." Point four is "language ... takes the form of Zap Comix language...." Leaving
Funk for a while, Peters criticizes Ginsberg's failure "to transform
the wisdom of the east into any fresh vision for the west." However critical Peters has been, in the end, he praises Ginsberg's
"tremendous power and beauty." Yet critically he returns, "selfish-
ly, I do not want to see him settle for less than his best."

1040 Podhoretz, Norman. "The Culture of Appeasement. A Naive
Pacifism Is the Dangerous Legacy of Vietnam." Harper's,
255:1529, October 1977, pp. 25-32.
There is a reference to Allen Ginsberg in the context
of "homosexual writers ... in whose work we find the same combination of pacifism (with Vietnam naturally standing in for World
War I)... to one's own country and its putatively dreary middle
class way of life, and derision of the idea that it stands for anything
worth defending or that it is threatened by anything but its own
stupidity and wickedness...." Podhoretz parallels the culture in
the United States to that of "England in 1937" and concludes: "Mean-
while, the parallels with England in 1937 are here, and this revival
of the culture of appeasement ought to be troubling our sleep."

1041 A New Conservative Strategy. "Podhoretz's Kolturkampf,"
p. 4.
This criticism which appears to be on the magazine's
editorial page finds Podhoretz's articles "a rather boring polemic
against the decline of the military spirit in the United States."
Reference is made to Podhoretz's point on the "homosexual writers
as Allen Ginsberg, James Baldwin, and Gore Vidal." The argument
of this article is that "Podhoretz ... missed the point. War is a
tragedy for homosexuals, but it is a tragedy for heterosexuals also.
In particular, it is a tragedy for the wives, the parents, and the
children who have lost one of their family to the war. And when a
war is utterly without reason the tragedy becomes unbearable. That

is what happened in the United States between 1965 and 1975, and these simple facts make unnecessary Podhoretz's 'theory' of what produces aversion to war."

1042   "Poetry." Metropolis, 3 May 1977, p. 19, with photograph of Allen Ginsberg (no credit).
        This article concerns itself with Allen Ginsberg's spiritual "eclecticism" and compares this with his "unlikely fusions" in poetry.

1043   Potts, Charles. "The Yellow Christ ... Shit Crackers" (two pieces of prose by Potts) Valga Krusa (1977): n. p.
        In "The Yellow Christ" section "Laffing Water Drops Out" mentions Allen Ginsberg in reviving the Grass Prophetic Review with others. Thoughts from back cover indicate the strangeness of this "schizophrenic" selection of writings, neither fiction nor nonfiction.

1044   Radcliffe, Rich. "The Other Ginsberg: Not Ralph, Not Ralph!" Venue, 18 May 1976, p. 9. Photograph of Ginsberg by Cavallini.
        Steve Taylor, a student, accompanies Allen Ginsberg on guitar in his performance at Glassboro State College. "He sat at the mike, comfortable, enthused, reading selections of Charles Reznikoff. Discussed 20th-century poetics. The mindfulness of poetry/meditation (stressing the importance of breath) dropped names of any other notorious beings from Burroughs and Leary to J. Edgar Hoover and Rockefeller...."

1045   "Roots, Bohemia & The Ancestry of Hip/The Early Underground Looks Around." Crawdaddy, 20 February 1977, section 2, pp. 34-47.
        This is a compilation of articles and photographs with illustrations on Bohemia, its offshoots in New York City a "Post script--1967-1972--NOW!"
        The major articles concerning Ginsberg have been annotated separately (See in this section: Crawdaddy, Seymour Krim, Gerard Malanga, Carl W. Solomon, and George Montgomery), but the others which include brief references to him are as follows: Mornaghan, Brigid, "Faces and Horses and the San Remo on McDougal Street," pp. 41-43; McReynolds, David, "What Roots?" pp. 43-46, with bottom photograph by David Gahr, titled "Allen Ginsberg and long time friend Peter Orlovsky"; and Jaffee, Lenore, "Their Politics Was in Their Art," p. 47. Also, on page 39 a reproduction of the book cover from Howl and Other Poems is included.

1046   Schechner, Mark. "Down in the Mouth with Saul Bellow." American Review, 23, n. d. , pp. 40-77.
        According to James H. Justus in American Literary Scholarship (1975): "Unlike the influence on Paul Goodman, Allen Ginsberg, Mailer and Kerouac, Reich's political dimensions (the 'bio-energetic program') are resisted by Bellow, who refuses to ascribe public virtue to therapeutic radicalism."

1047 Schulke, Paul. "In Your Own Backyard, Beat Generation
Poets Behind Energy Consciousness Week. " New Look
Magazine, 2:10, 15 April 1975, pp. 6-8. Photograph on
page 7 titled, "Poets Gary Snyder, left; Allen Ginsberg
above; Michael McClure.
    This article provides the background information which
led to the planning of the nation-wide Energy Conference at the University of Florida, April 19-23. "Back in November '74, Lawrence
Ferlinghetti.... Admonished an attentive literature class ("Literature of the Beat Generation") for wasting their time talking to him
(long distance) when they could be learning more important and useful information from Howard T. Odum, who worked 'in your own
back yard,' in Gainesville. "
    It seems that this literature class called Lawrence
Ferlinghetti in San Francisco for the learning experience and here
was this important research associate at the University of Florida
who was receiving network publicity for his energy theories, a topic
of much concern of the underground culture. According to Schulke's
article, no one in the class knew of Professor Odum, even though
he appeared recently in the "January 13 Newsweek magazine for his
theories about 'net energy. ' Because it takes energy to produce
energy, Odum has devised a rating system for energy sources in
order to develop the most efficient methods of energy reclamation. "
The ideas for the conference began to mesh after an article about
all of this appeared in the campus newspaper (The Independent
Florida Alligator, Thursday, November 7, 1974, p. 4, " 'Beat'
Class via phone to Frisco" by Cathy Callahan, Alligator staff writer).
    Lawrence Ferlinghetti was invited "to Gainesville to
meet Odum. " He agreed to come with Allen Ginsberg and Gary
Snyder. Lawrence Ferlinghetti later cancelled but Michael McClure
was added. All four writers" ... have perennially expressed a personal consciousness contrary to that of mass society since the fifties, and this counter-consciousness has presently centered on ecological concerns. " In any event "Energy Consciousness Week"
which consists of five days of activities including Earth Day and
Energy Day was planned. Allen Ginsberg is cited as "America's
best known poet. " It also seems that Gary Snyder and Michael
McClure have both quoted from Odum in their publications. Conclusively". . . "a prime impetus for organizing Energy Week ... (was) ...
The need for 'Poets publicizing energy consciousness,' " according
to Robertson, the coordinator of the Energy Center on Campus.

1048 Shively, Charles. "Notes on the Poem 'Please Master. ' "
The Eulenspiegel Society, PRO-ME-THEE-US (Sexual
Minorities Report). n. d. , pp. 17-32.
    This is a reprint of part of an article about Allen Gins-
berg which "appeared in Gay Sunshine Issue No. 17, 1973. It included remarks on the poem ... (Ginsberg): This poem is much
more than a Bondage/Discipline fantasy, it is an exorcism--a prayer,
a magic formula to encompass the beautiful memory/body of Neal
Cassady and all the young blue jeaned blond lovers of fantasy.... "

1049 Slaughter, William. "Eating Poetry. " Chicago Review, n. d. ,
n. p.

According to volume 55, 1974 of The Year's Work in English Studies: "Starting from Eliot's remark that in seeking to go beyond the visual and auditory imagination, 'one must look into the cerebral cortex, the nervous system, the digestive tracts.' Slaughter identifies the gustatory imagination drawing our attention to a striking poem by Mark Strand and bringing together references to Eve Merriam, Peter Michaelson and Allen Ginsberg."

1050 Solomon, Carl W. "'Howl' Written in Parting Gesture to Me, Evidently Touched Off Big Movement Dubbed 'Beat.'" Crawdaddy, 20 February 1977, section 2, p. 38.
Carl Solomon presents his perceptions of the Bohemian movement. The title describes the main Ginsberg reference.

1051 Spencer, Robert H. "The Spirit of Jefferson Keeps Renewing Us." Creative Living, The Magazine of Life, 5:1, Winter 1976, pp. 18-25.
Spencer presents an introduction to comments by Ginsberg among others on the attempt by the "New Jefferson" to facilitate "the work started two hundred years ago which remains unfinished." On p. 23 Ginsberg addresses the issue of "power" in America: "Though the conception of 'America' proposed decentralization of power, our economic and industrial set-up seems to have centralized power in relatively few hands or heads, none of them sufficiently egoless to decentralize the power glory and material super-structure in a way wholesome to earth by stability for diverse cultures." (In particular the "oil" situation).

1052 Stafford, Peter. "The Contriving of a Religion." Crawdaddy, 4:9, 22 June 1970, pp. 29-31.
Peter, Alan Watts and Allen Ginsberg discuss the formation of this religion of new consciousness which encompasses the use of LSD and the work of Tim Leary. Ginsberg in particular speaks to the mission of Leary and his doctrine, "Drop Out!"

1053 Starer, Jacqueline. "'Beatology' and Other Things ... Gathered ... in August 1972 ... Near London...." Soft Need, No. 9, Spring 1976, pp. 7-9.
In this magazine which is dedicated to Claude (Pélieu) there is a conversation among Jacqueline Starer, Claude Pélieu and Mary Beach which refers to Ginsberg. Claude in describing his involvement with the Beats refers to Allen Ginsberg, but only briefly. According to Mary: " ... The stuff that's in 'Howl' Carl (Solomon) had told it to Ginsberg, in confidence, modestly. Allen used it all, repeated it all. If Carl Solomon hadn't been in hospital Allen Ginsberg could never have written 'Howl'...."

1054 Stupa, Naropa Institute Student Magazine, v. 3, n. 7, unpaged.
The back page lists "Aug. 3rd" joint poetry reading Allen Ginsberg and Anne Waldman.

1055 Tallman, Warren. "Wonder Merchants: Modernist Poetry in Vancouver During the 1960's." In Boundary, 3:1, Fall 1974, pp. 57-89.

The influence of Allen Ginsberg, among other U.S. Modernists, on the Canadian West is cited by the review of this article in Abstracts in English Studies (V. 20, N 4, 12/76).

1056 "Teacher in Her Own Words." People, 18 August 1975, pp. 22-24, with photograph of Waldman and Allen Ginsberg along with Corso and Burroughs.

This is a feature article on poet, Anne Waldman, which includes a few comments on Allen Ginsberg. In particular, the article spotlights Waldman as the "queen" of the St. Mark's Church Poetry Project and as the co-founder (with poet Allen Ginsberg) and chief administrator of the poetry program at Naropa Institute.

1057 "A Touch of Form/Allen Ginsberg." Focus, The Sunday Camera's Magazine, 17 July 1977, pp. 23-25, with 2 photographs of Allen Ginsberg, one on page 24, the other on page 25.

"Different area artists are represented weekly in 'A Touch of Form.'" Allen Ginsberg's poems "Hearing 'Lenore' read aloud at 203 Amity Street," "War Profit Litany (To Ezra Pound)," "V," "VI," "Easter Sunday," "Describe: the rain on Dasaswamedh," "Galilee Shore," and an excerpt from "Indian Journals/December 13, 1962" are included here.

See titles of individual poems within the Poetry Section under Primary Works.

1058 Tytell, John. "The Beat Generation and the Continuing American Revolution." The American Scholar: A Quarterly for the Independent Thinker (Phi Beta Kappa), Spring 1973, pp. 308-317.

This essay serves as the basis for Tytell's introductory essay "The Broken Circuit" in his book on the Beats, Naked Angels, The Lives and Literature of the Beat Generation (New York: McGraw-Hill, 1976).

1059 Veatch, Henry B. "The What and the Why of the Humanities...." The Key Reporter, Phi Beta Kappa Newsletter, XXXVII: 4, Summer 1972, pp. 2-4, back cover.

Veatch offers a scholarly article "based on a talk he delivered before the Chapter at Marquette University on the "humanities" which refers "to three primary disciplines: history, literature, and philosophy." He refers to a "Sunday New York Times Book Review entitled "Poetry in the Sixties--Long Live Blake! Down with Donne." He uses the reviewer's comments on Allen Ginsberg and his cultural ramifications to illustrate: " ... that a choice between poets is no less than an ethical choice, a choice between lives. Moreover, if such a choice is not to be blind and arbitrary, it had better be made in the light of something like a genuine ethical knowledge and understanding, just such knowledge that the true humanist aims at, and that the humanities as a pedagogical and scholarly discipline are intended to convey."

1060 Vespa, Mary. "The 1960's Come Alive on a New York Stage

at a Memorial for the Tragic Phil Ochs. " People, 14
June 1974, pp. 24-26.
        Tribute is paid to Phil Ochs from members of his
community. Allen Ginsberg is noted as a participant with a picture
on page 25 titled "Poet Allen Ginsberg hit the boards with cymbals
and the gold lame suit Ochs wore at a 1970 rock 'n' roll concert in
Carnegie Hall. "

1061   "Village Arts/the Poets Ginsberg Debut a Deux. " Villager,
        1 May 1975, p. 5, with a photograph of Allen Ginsberg
        titled "Poet Allen Ginsberg will join his father, poet Louis
        Ginsberg, for a reading and discussion at 1:30 p. m. Tues-
        day, May 6, at Greenwich House. "
        Allen and Louis Ginsberg will read together at the above
listed location on 27 Barrow Street. "Their visit is sponsored by
Greenwich House Senior Citizen's Literary Group. "

1062   Vogel, George (class of '48 reporter). Alumnae Bulletin,
        (Columbia University), 1971?, p. 27.
        "Allen Ginsberg and some of his friends took advantage
of WNET-TV's 'Free Time' in Nov. to take Channel 13's audience
on a 90-minute trip in which poetry, music, the songs of William
Blake, a phantom poet, and discussions on the CIA and Bangladesh were
on live, unrehearsed, spontaneous television. "

1063   Wallace, Kevin. "Louis and Allen--The Filial Poetry Show. "
        San Francisco Chronicle, 10 May 1974, p. 5. Photograph
        Allen Ginsberg and Louis Ginsberg, "Two generations of
        Ginsberg poets--Allen and his father Louis--at San Fran-
        cisco State. " Photograph of Allen Ginsberg, "Papa Gins-
        berg read in a traditional style--and Allen chanted mantras
        and exclaimed his poetry while seated. "
        This is an article which reviews the joint reading of
Allen and Louis Ginsberg at San Francisco State on May 9th, 1974.
Comparisons are indicated between the father and son team. Yet
Louis muses, "People have said these readings bridge the generation
gap, but I doubt that. But I do think we transcend it. "

1064   Washam, Veronica. "A Glimpse of Ginsberg, Establishment
        Honors Go to Anti-Establishment Poet. " Villager, XLI:5,
        10 May 1973, p. 5.
        Photograph "Allen Ginsberg ringing the bell at Nixon
campaign headquarters on Madison Avenue and 53rd Street during
last year's Presidential election" by Bill McLatchie. Ginsberg is
interviewed in "his third floor tenement walkup on E. 10th Street.
He is on crutches due to a fall three months ago. " Basically this
is an informative article bringing us up to date on Allen Ginsberg's
professional accomplishments: the publication of books of poetry,
The Fall of America, The Gates of Wrath, Iron Horse, Poetics
Improvised; University readings; election to the National Academy of
Arts and Sciences; intended trip to International Poetry Conference
in Rotterdam and International Poetry Festival in England. Ginsberg
is portrayed in "a monk-like existence. Thoreau style. "

1065   Weatherhead, A. Kingsley. "Poetry: The 1930's to the
         Present." American Literary Scholarship (Duke Univer-
         sity, Durham, North Carolina) 9, 1973, n. p.
            Abstracts of English Studies (20, n. 1, September
1976) cites the work of Allen Ginsberg included in "this evaluative
survey."

1066   Webb, Marilyn. "Meditation and the Arts at Naropa." East
         West Journal, 6:5, May 1976, pp. 18-21. Photograph
         Allen Ginsberg, William Burroughs, Philip Whalen. p. 19.
            Naropa Institute offers a Buddhist approach to living,
"writing, dance, theater, what have you." In describing Naropa,
Marilyn Webb offers a warm portrait of Allen Ginsberg at a reading
as he "accompanies himself with himself in voice and harmonium
on Sony cassette, having a grand old time. It reminds me of singing 'Hatikvah' at a Jewish wedding, everyone loud and slightly off
key, together. It's the naive rhythm that's so contagious, making
the beat of the words the universally felt image-speaking itself of
the ebb and flow quality of life. It's not great art; but it's not
bad...."
            Her first encounter with Ginsberg is worth repeating:
"I first noticed Ginsberg not as Ginsberg but as middle-aged Allen,
someone who made a lot of noise when he ate, sitting for a week of
meditation on the Zafu next to mine at Karmê Chöling, Rinpoche's
Vermont retreat center. This Allen annoyed me. He farted, wig-
gled, picked his teeth, but he also impressed me. There are not
many middle-aged folks willing to sit. And he did dishes silently
in a flowered apron, and he sat and sat and sat...."

1067   Wilcock, John. "Un´dèr ● ground, n." Countdown, A Sub-
         terranean Magazine, 1970, pp. 186-175 (numbered back-
         wards).
            John Wilcock mentions Allen Ginsberg on p. 186 as
"Anarchist" in describing heroes and poets within the Movement.
On p. 180, "The Underground Press is the loving product of the
best minds of my generation...." Of course citing Ginsberg.

1068   Yost, George. "The Romantic Movement of Today, and
         Earlier." FORUM (Houston) 10:2, Summer-Fall, 1972,
         pp. 16-21.
            According to Abstracts in English Studies (v. 19, n.
10, June 1976) "Three avant-garde poets of the San Francisco Ren-
aissance--Allen Ginsberg, Brother Antoninus and Lawrence Ferling-
hetti--have much in common with the Romantic Poets and illustrate
the parallels between our age and the Romantic Period (1770-1830):
The endorsement of nature because it is not man-made; sensitivity
to nature, often enhanced by drugs; a movement back to nature; a
longing for the past; a love of the primitive; a professed interest in
mysticism; a turning inward to the world of the imagination; the
cult of emotion, of love; racial and sexual protest; and despair, the
cult of emotion for its own sake."

Foreign Articles About Ginsberg

Czech

1069 Pivano, Fernanda. "Vodíková Hrací Skříň. " Světová Literatura 1969. Prague, Czechoslovakia, n. p. , 5-6, pp. 117-
139.
    This is an article on poetry which includes a reference
to Allen Ginsberg. Czechoslovak periodical--translation of article
by Zdeněk Frýbort. Text by publikován ve Světové literatuře.

1070 Williams, William Carlos. "Kvílení pro Carla Solomona. "
("Howl for Carl Solomon"/Introduction). Sešity pro litera-
turu a diskusi. Duben 30 (1969): 8.
Czechoslovak magazine.

1071 Zábrana, Jan. "Uvodem ke Ginsbergovu kvílení. " (Article
about "Howl. ") Sešity pro literaturu a ídskusi. Duben
30 (1969): 7.
Czechoslovak magazine.

1072 Zacio, Mircea. "Searăcu tigri si Allen Ginsberg. " Steaua
24, IV: 16-17.

French

1073 Bowering, George. "Ce Hurlement que j'entends. " ("How I
Hear Howl?") ellipse, Québec: Faculté des Arts, Université de Sherbrooke. 8/9 (1971): 128-140. Traduit
par Marc Lebel.
    "How I Hear Howl?" which first appeared in Beaver
Kosmos, folio I (1964, 1965, 1968, 1969) offers a critical response
to the spoken "Howl" as recorded by Fantasy Records. Bowering,
in so doing, places Ginsberg within the framework of agnostic oral
poetic tradition.

1074 Izoard, Jacques. "J'ai renontre Allen Ginsberg a Rotterdam. "
("I Met Allen Ginsberg at Rotterdam. ") le journal des
poetes, 43:6 (Aout 1973): 4 (including an excerpt from a
Ginsberg poem in English without a source).
    Topic: Poetry International held in June 1973 in Hol-
land. Jacques Izoard describes his meeting with the poet at a small
cãfe in Rotterdam and the experience of his readings. Peculiarly,
he comments on the Belgium media and how they ignored the entire
event (Poetry International). There is an editor's response that
states they were not even aware that such an event was taking place;
"The poetic life is so intense that one cannot be everywhere. ... "

1075 Ouimet, P. "Deux bibites dans le système ports. Le Maclean,
15:46, October 1975, pp. 42-4.

1076 "Poètes Américains d'aujourd'hui. " Les Lettres Nouvelles,
December 1970-January 1971, n. 41.
    Section "After the Beat Generation" includes Ginsberg.

1077 "Quand s'eveilla l'Amerique ... Ginsberg temoigne. " ("When
America Wakes Up ... Ginsberg Testimony. ") Bretagnes,
Revue Littéraire et Politique. (Automne 1976): 24-29.
This is an edition of this magazine dedicated to the study
of Kerouac, published from Morlaix which is located in Brittany
(which is where Jack Kerouac believed his family originated). It
contains this excerpt from a long interview between Allen Ginsberg
and Yves Le Pellec published in the special edition of Entretiens,
(1975). Ginsberg is included as the "theoretian" of the Beats and
the excerpt from the lengthy interview highlights Jack Kerouac and
the years he spent at Columbia.

German

1078 "Allen Ginsberg über The Fugs. " ("Allen Ginsberg About
The Fugs. ") Götter, ("Twilight of the Gods" from Wagner), 1 (Juni 1977): 17.
Ginsberg's words describe the cultural and psychedelic
revolution and the Fugs. The text is from the record jacket LP
"The Fugs" which appeared in January 1966. (Translated into German by T. Schroeder.)

1079 Burns, Glen. "Indian Madness. " Sonderdruck aus Amerika-
studien. Stuttgart: J. B. Metzlersche Verlagsbuchhand-
lung, Jahrgang 22 (vol. 22), Heft 11 (No. 11): 89-106.
(In English).
In this scholarly article delving into the concepts Burns
terms "Indian Madness" which encompass the confrontation arche-
typically and historically between man and "geographical and psycho-
logical frontiers," he presents the contrasting theories of Leslie
Fiedler and Richard Slotkin. According to Burns's interpretation of
Fiedler, "The 'madness' of the frontiersman, both as archetype and
resistance--paradigm to The Institution, seemed to represent an es-
cape from history; but his sanity, within history, has been described
by Richard Slotkin as a mythopoesis which produced a hero precari-
ously balanced between Europe and Indian: myth becomes ideology,
directly transferred into imperialist power structures ranging from
economic exploitation to genocide. "
The character of Allen Ginsberg is introduced as Burns
begins to discuss "The anarchist ... renegade. " Indeed after reviewing his work he finds "It was a leap into Indian Madness which
has made him (Allen Ginsberg) into a clearing-house for all the
diverse streams flooding our ego-consciousness.... " Playing upon
an analogy between the Wobblies and poets, Allen Ginsberg and Gary
Snyder, "One strand of Indian Madness is unalienated labor, another
is a democracy of workers based on a native comradery. American
history can also be studied as its suppression of its own meaning. "
Continually he draws Ginsberg into his argument. Conclusively he again uses Ginsberg in his suggestion of "the alignment
of old and new frontier strategies which would come together in opposition to the goal-oriented fetishism of WASP-America. " This
theory is footnoted as a "Favorite" of Ginsberg's otherwise known
as "The 'tip of the iceberg,' ie. the 'great subculture....'"

1080 Burns, Glen. "Ist ein deutsches 'Geheul' möglich?" (Is It
Possible to Have a German 'Howl'?") Exempla, Eine
Tübinger, Literaturzeitschrift Texte Aus Nordamerika,
3:1 (1977): 17-19. Translator Jörg Ross.
Burns is convinced that Ginsberg's pseudo hip language
loses in translation, despite the efforts of the translator.

1081 C. I. "Berg--und Talfahrt/Reise in die Vergangenheit: Allen
Ginsberg las in der Akademie." ("Up and Down/A Trip
into the Past.") Der Abend, 23 September 1976, n. p.
This article provides a poetic description of meditation
and Allen Ginsberg's reading at the Academy. Walter Höllerer was
the moderator.

1082 Combecker, Hans. "Allen Ginsberg 'In Back of the Real':
Ein Stück Beat Poetry." Die Neueren Sprachen 22: 74-
76.

1083 F. M. (Berlin). "Gruss an Ginsberg." ("Greetings to Ginsberg.") gesprachsfetzen, ein rundbrief für freunde erscheint, wenn es sich ergibt (Remnants of Language, a
round letter to friends which appears whenever it is possible), VI: 3/4 (Mitte 1969): 28-30.
This is a poem to Ginsberg.

1084 Rahlens, Holly-Jane. "William Burroughs--Allen Ginsberg."
Rias Quartral, 5 (January 1977): 23.
Holly-Jane Rahlens questions William Burroughs on the
Beat Generation. (In her opening words she introduces Burroughs
as one whose views are skeptical toward the authority of government,
laws and good and evil.) A brief exchange between Burroughs and
Ginsberg follows in which they discuss authority, law and the value
system taught in schools.

1085 Vietta, Susanne. "Allen Ginsberg." (F 128): 581-601.
In Christadler, Martin (ed.). Amerikanische Literatureder
Gegenwart, Stuttgart: Alfred Kröner, 660 pp.

Italian

1086 Santi, Roberto. "Allen Ginsberg: Un Poeta." Il rinnovamento, 20 November-20 December 1977, anno VII, pp.
48-57.
Roberto Santi has dedicated this text to the subject matter. Il rinnovamento is a local religious review.

1087 Ungaretti, Giuseppi. Presentation of Allen Ginsberg's Poems
(Naples 1966), Books Abroad, 44:4 (Autumn, 1970): 559-
63. (Italian).
According to The Abstract of English Studies, Ginsberg
"is a founding member of the Beat Generation--whom one must not
confuse with the inferior poets, such as Bob Dylan, of the next generation, the Vietnicks.... This article is taken from the steno-
graphic transcript of a speech translated into English by Italo Romano."

Japanese

1088 "Allen Ginsberg." Play Map (Monthly Town Magazine). May
1972, n. 5, pp. 23-49.
A series of six articles by Japanese writers on Allen
Ginsberg which includes a translation of "Howl." Old and new photographs of the poet are interspersed throughout the text. The first
article is "Singing Ginsberg" by T. Iimura. Others not able to be
translated.

Norwegian

1089 "Creeley, Ginsberg, O'Hara, Bly--4 Poeter født 1926." Vinduet, 1974, 28 yr., n. 3, p. 22.
Introduction to translation of poetry with photographs.

Russian

1090 Voznesensky, A. Foreword to translation of Ginsberg's "Jessore Road" 15 Literature Gazeta (Moscow), (December 9,
1971). (Russian).

Spanish

1091 Fox, Hugo. "Mistica Norteamericana del Siglo XX." ("North
American Mystic in the 20th Century.") Eco contempor-
aneo ("Vida Total"), 12 (1969): 10-15.
There is a reference to Ginsberg in this political criticism in an Argentine periodical of the hippie movement as an off-
shoot of capitalism.

General Overview Articles
(with Discussion or Mention of Ginsberg)

1092 "Acid Return." Good Times, Interview, 3 July 1969, v. II,
n. 25, pp. 2-7.
Timothy Leary and Good Times discuss the ensuing
cultural revolution and the Aquarian Age. Allen Ginsberg (on p. 6)
is mentioned as the proselytizer of this New Age. "Can't you see
Allen Ginsberg running around the country doing it all the time."

1093 Amram, David. "In Memory of Jack Kerouac." Evergreen
Review, 14:74 (January 1970): 41, 76-78.
"The story of a friendship and a farewell salute" to
Jack Kerouac which highlights Ginsberg along the way since he was
part of this circle of friends.

1094 André, Michael. "Warhol Interview." Small Press Review,
Interview, November 1976, n. 46, v. 8, n. 11, p. 6.
Andy Warhol inquires about Allen Ginsberg's health.
Michael André tells him about Ginsberg's having pneumonia, break-
ing his leg and passing a kidney stone.

1095 Antin, David. "Modernism and Post Modernism: Approaching the Present American Poetry. " Boundary 2, 1, 1972, 98-146.

    According to The American Literary Scholarship from 1973, "David Antin sees Schwartz, Lowell, Snodgrass and others at the end of the moderns; and Olson, Creeley, Ignatow, Zukofsky, and Ginsberg as the beginning of the post moderns. "

1096 Ardinger, Rick and Rosemary P. Ardinger and Judy Morency. "Interview with Carolyn Cassady. " Limberlost Review, v. 1, n. 3, June 1977, pp. 43-51.

    The Limberlost Review, a magazine of poetry contains this interview with Carolyn Cassady in which she discusses her book, The Third Word about Jack Kerouac and Neal Cassady among others. It seems that "Heart Beat" is an excerpt from this longer manuscript. There is a specific reference to Ginsberg when she is questioned (on page 51) about "the past intense involvement with Neal, Jack and Allen Ginsberg...." and its influence on her current activities.

1097 Bockris-Wylie. "Interview with Claude Pélieu and Mary Beach. " Soft Need 9, (Spring 1976): 19-23, with introduction by Miles.

    In this magazine which is dedicated to "Claude" there is an introduction to an interview (noted above) by Miles which refers to works Mary Beach and Claude have translated into French of Allen Ginsberg among others.

1098 Bowering, George. "Kerouac's 'Big Book of Love. '" Review of Visions of Cody, by Jack Kerouac. Georgia Straight, 19-26 April 1973, v. 7, n. 289, pp. 16, 20.

    Ginsberg wrote the introduction to this "the most famous unpublished book in America, a legend always referred to by Allen Ginsberg, etc. "

1099 Cary, Richard. "Bern Porter's Friends in Books. " Colby Library Quarterly, 9:2 (June 1970): 114-219, includes inscription by Allen Ginsberg dated 1963.

    "Bern Porter's friends including "Henry Miller Anaïs Nin, Karl Shapiro, Eli Siegel, Walter Lowenfels, Allen Ginsberg, and Kenneth Patches ... from the bulk of inscriptions in Porter's collection. "

1100 Chowka, Peter Barry. "The Original Mind of Gary Snyder. " East West Journal, July 77, v. 7, n. 7, pp. 34-40, 42, 44. Photographs by Peter Barry Chowka. Part two of three.

    In this lengthy interview on Snyder, a photograph of him "in Allen Ginsberg's apartment" is included as are references to Ginsberg in the context of the "confessional mode" of "Howl, " and the comradery of the poets "in the San Francisco Bay area in the middle and late '50's.... "

1101   Chowka, Peter Barry.   "The Original Mind of Gary Snyder."
East West Journal, August 77, v. 7, n. 8, pp. 18-30.
"This is the third and final installment of an interview with
Gary Snyder conducted during ten days in April 1977 in
NYC." Photograph "Snyder in his Berkeley Cottage, 1955,
p. 18 by Allen Ginsberg. Photograph, "Allen Ginsberg
and Gary Snyder, NY, 1971" on p. 20. On p. 22,
"Gary Snyder at Allen Ginsberg's apartment."
This final installment to the Snyder interview is inter-
spersed with comments about Allen Ginsberg and photographs by and
including the poet. For as Chowka indicates in his introduction
there has been a long association between Gary Snyder and Allen
Ginsberg of the "Beats."

1102   Christy, Jim.   Review of Visions of Cody, by Jack Kerouac.
Globe and Mail, 20 January 1973, pp. 1-3.
"In the wave of nostalgia which overtook the media,
people remembered Jack Kerouac and criticized him for not being
what they wanted him to be. They wanted another Allen Ginsberg.
It wasn't Kerouac that had changed but America."

1103   Clancy, Laurie; Bramwell, Murry; and Altman, Dennis.
"Notes on the Counter Culture." Southern Review (Adelaide) 6:3, September 1973, pp. 239-51.
According to The Abstracts of English Studies, 1975,
the effect of "Richard Brautigan, Allen Ginsberg and Gary Snyder"
on language and its relationship to the counter culture is discussed.
"These brief commentaries were presented at a symposium on the
counter culture (5th Conference of the Australian and New Zealand
American Studies Association, 1972, Flinders University)."

1104   Dowling   College.   "Confessions of an American Guru." New
York Times, 4 December 1977, section 6, pp. 41-43, 136-
149.
This is a long detailed interview/portrait of Baba Ram
Dass (Dr. Richard Albert), which is the cover story of the magazine section. There is a passing reference to Ginsberg (p. 139,
col. 2).

1105   Fitzgerald, Gregory, and Ferguson, Paul.   "'The Frost
Tradition': A Conversation with William Meredith." South
west Review, 57:2 (Spring 1972): 108-116.
Ferguson questions Meredith about his seemingly "negative" response to Ginsberg's "To a Western Bard." Meredith then
discusses his opposition to the school of free verse (of which Ginsberg is part) in light of the school he leans to of "iambic penta-
meter."

1106   Grossman, Richard.   "Jack Kerouac: His Myth and the Reality." Review of Visions of Cody, by Jack Kerouac. The
San Francisco Phoenix, 3 May 1973, v. 1, n. 17, pp. 6-7.
Grossman mentions articles by Allen Ginsberg on Kerouac's Visions of Cody which can be found in the Berkeley Barb and

other Underground Press Syndicate papers. Apparently with the publication of this book, previously untold parts of the "On the Road Legend" are revealed.

1107 Gussow, Mel. " 'Kerouac' by Duberman One Side of the Beat Generation. " New York Times, 7 December 1976, p. 56. Review of Visions of Kerouac, a play by Martin Duberman.
Allen Ginsberg is mentioned in the context of the content of the play in the above review.

1108 Holmes, John Clellon. "Gone in October. " Playboy Magazine, 20:2, (February 1973): 96-98, 140.
"For raucous Jack, eager Jack, Jack of the tender eyes-- the end of the night. " The article commences with a journal entry recording the death of Jack Kerouac. Holmes creates a valuable article by "writing an account" of the entire situation involving friends, relatives, etc. " He places Kerouac in a recent historical context and concludes: "that Kerouac was a true and magnificent ORIGINAL whose vision of America was a true and magnificent one.... "

1109 Leyland, Winston. "Gerard Malanga: An Interview. " Gay Sunshine, January-February 1974, n. 20, pp. 4-8, including photograph by Finklestein (Black Star) "Allen Ginsberg & Gerard Malanga at the Village Vanguard, NYC Winter 1968. "
Questions referring to Gerard Malanga's thoughts on Allen Ginsberg appear in this interview (page 8). In particular, Ginsberg's possible direct influence on his writing is questioned. Although Malanga admits they "both come from the streets ... the street poetry-nature comes from different areas of our imagination as an extension of body as form is an extension of content. Allen has never been a direct literary influence to any extent on my writing. " Yet, Allen's "motherly instincts" toward younger poets are not neglected.

1110 Leyland, Winston. "John Giorno the Poet in New York. " Gay Sunshine, Spring 1975, n. 24, pp. 7-8 with photograph of Ginsberg among John Giorno and Peter Orlovsky "outside the Republican Convention, Miami Beach 1972, " by Les Levine.
There are references to staying on Ginsberg's farm in Cherry Valley, his hernia operation and his trip to the Republican Convention in Miami. Ginsberg's quality as a poet is discussed. According to Giorno, "Allen Ginsberg hasn't written a good poem in years, and hasn't written a great poem in 20 years. When he wrote 'Howl,' he was the voice of the moment, mirroring what everyone felt, the moment in a larger sense. Now he's more or less a bad poet and everyone listens to him because he's famous.... " There is an allusion to Ginsberg as "entertainer. " Giorno feels this is a negative relationship to poetry because "poetry is not entertainment. " Ginsberg's recent experiences with meditation and his use of mantra in readings are both discussed.

1111 McMurtry, Larry. "A Still Silenced Voice." Review of
         Heart Beat: My Life With Jack & Neal, by Carolyn Cas-
         sady. The Washington Post, 16 August 1976, n. p.
         In the introduction to this review, McMurtry evokes the
spirit of the Beat Movement. "At the center of the movement was
what has come to seem an immortal triad ... Jack Kerouac, the
novelist, Allen Ginsberg, the poet, and Neal Cassady, the what?
The driver? The talker? The energizer? The adonis?...
         Heart Beat is a fragment of an apparently longer work,
an excerpt dealing with a few years in the '50s when Kerouac lived
intermittently with the Cassadys. It's interesting for its portrait of
Kerouac, but adds little to what we know of Cassady, which is after
all, hard to add to. Two writers of some genius devoted some of
their best gifts to him--others, even wives would do just as well
not to apply."

1112 Mark, J. "The New Humor." Esquire, 72:6, December 1969,
         pp. 218-220, 329, 330.
         Mark's article is about "the first wave of the American
social and cultural revolution" and its relationship to the humor of
youth. Passing remarks are made about the possibility of Ginsberg's
and others' roles in this matter.

1113 Messing, Gordon M. "The Linguistic Analysis of Some Con-
         temporary Nonformal Poetry." Language and Style, II:4,
         Fall 1969, pp. 323-329.
         Stylolinguistics and the problem it faces in relationship
to nonformal poetry are discussed. After citing work by Creeley,
Ginsberg, and Marianne Moore, Messing concludes "it would seem,
then, that stylolinguistics must yield to stylobehavioristics whenever
there are insufficient formal features for the linguist to analyze.
When surrounded by such poetry, what can we linguists do against
it, or shall we, and why not, turn it over to the goddam literary
critics."

1114 Mishra, Ajit Kumar. "The Beatnik Vision of Life." Literary
         Criterion, 9:4, Summer 1971, pp. 51-58.
         Mishra has presented here an overview of "the beatnik
vision of life" with allusions to contemporary sociological jargon,
i. e. "inner and outer directed," "negation and self-analysis," "The
Organization Man." The Beat Work is characterized by that of Kerouac, Ginsberg, Carl Solomon, and Lee who issue a violent response to society which they see in decay. There is a glimmer of
hope in the end, "since it is only the beginning of the end we must
wait for the beginning of the beginning."

1115 Poulin, A. , Jr. "Contemporary American Poetry: The Radi-
         cal Tradition." Concerning Poetry, 3:2, Fall 1970, pp. 5-
         21.

1116 Raidy, William A. "First Nighter/Very Strong Portrait."
         Long Island Press, 9 December 1976, p. 12.
         This is a review of "Martin Duberman's half-documen-

tary play, 'Visions of Kerouac' at the off-Broadway Lion Theatre"
which introduces his comments with the first lines from Allen Ginsberg's "Howl." Ginsberg is also mentioned throughout in context
and is called "Irwin Goldbook in this play...."

1117 Rissover, Fredric. "Beat Poetry, 'The American Dream'
and the Alienation Effects." Speech Teacher, 20 January
1971, pp. 36-43.
Beat poetry was selected to accompany a performance
of Edward Albee's "The American Dream." "Using the poetry as a
kind of commentary on the play, almost an annotation on it, we
hoped we could call particular attention to the problems which both
Albee and the Beats had observed. There was a complement 'in
subject and tone' as well as 'in style.'"

1118 Robinson, J. T. "Authors and Editors." Publishers Weekly,
195, 23 June 1969, p. 18, including a picture of Ginsberg.
The article begins with a comment by Ginsberg on Jane
Kramer's "version of reality" which "is not quite the full reality"
and continues with a discussion of poetry and publishing, highlighting
the work of Ferlinghetti. Ginsberg feels "the scene for publishing
poetry is getting better and better but the real action is occurring
in mimeographed magazines."

1119 Rockwell, John. "The Pop Life/Bob Dylan and his 'Desire.'"
New York Times, 9 January 1976, n. p.
Rockwell reviews Dylan's album Desire and in describing
"the back and inner jacket cover" he mentions the "messianic notes
from Allen Ginsberg." The praise for the album is straightforward:
"The album also contains some of the most wonderful music Mr.
Dylan has ever made...." He disagrees with the dissatisfaction
rendered by others and praises the parts taken by two women, Em-
mylou Harris on vocal and Scarlet Rivera on violin.

1120 Sainer, Arthur. "Kerouac Plays the Politics of Ecstasy."
Review of Visions of Kerouac, a play by Martin Duberman.
Village Voice, 20 December 1976, pp. 109-110.
Allen Ginsberg is mentioned throughout this review in
the context of the play.

1121 Shepperd, R. Z. "Sweet Jack Gone." Review of Kerouac, by
Ann Charters, and Visions of Cody, by Jack Kerouac.
Time, 22 January 1973, pp. 71-72.
In this review there is an anecdotal reference to Allen
Ginsberg.

1122 Sienicka, Marta. "William Carlos Williams and some Younger
Poets." Studia Anglica Posnanlensia, An International Re-
view of English Studies, 4 (1972): 182-193.
The article according to the MLA Index highlights
Charles Olson, Robert Duncan, Robert Creeley, and Allen Ginsberg.

1123 Simpson, Louis. "The California Poets." London Magazine,
11:6, February/March 1972, pp. 56-63.

Simpson talks about urges to communicate with the landscape in the Whitmanesque style. He then speculates about the California Poets from the "San Francisco Renaissance" and concludes that these poets are not for him. Their poetry is a "social activity" and their "words were like the sound track of a movie, an accompaniment to pictures of life rather than the thing itself."

1124 Tytell, John. "The Beat Generation and the Continuing American Revolution." The American Scholar, 42:2, Spring 1973, pp. 308-317.
John Tytell's article involves a perspective of the Beats in a modern context. It ties the Beats to the Dadaists, Surrealists and older American poets and writers. Individually he treats the Beats with accuracy and precision. He creates an overview which is brimming with optimism.

1125 Zweig, Paul. "The New Surrealism." Salmagundi, 22-23, Spring/Summer 1973, pp. 269-284.
Zweig finds traces of surrealism in the later part of the twentieth century. "It was inevitable that the techniques of Surrealist language should appeal to poets like Ginsberg, O'Hara, Koch, Bly, Lamantia." He concludes "having long since come to an end as a 'movement' surrealism has become the language our poets speak."

1126 Zwerin, Michael. "Tim's Letter, Interview with Eldridge." Berkeley Tribe, 5-12 February 1971, v. 3, n. 3, issue 81, p. 13.
This is part of the coverage of the Eldridge Cleaver/ Tim Leary situation in the 1970's. Within the Cleaver interview there is a reference made to Allen Ginsberg among others (Jerry Rubin, Abbie Hoffman and Stew Albert). It is not a crucial reference, merely one in passing.

IV.   REVIEWS AND CRITICISM

A.   BOOKS BY GINSBERG

Airplane Dreams

1127   Durgnat, R. Review of Airplane Dreams, by Allen Ginsberg.
       Poetry Review, (London), Winter 70/71, p. 366.

Allen Verbatim

1128   American Literature, Review of Allen Verbatim, March 1975,
       v. 47, p. 143.
           "Transcriptions from tapes of Mr. Ginsberg talking,
       more typically in question and answer situations on college campuses
       than 'lecturing' situations. "

1129   Best Sellers, Review of Allen Verbatim, 15 December 1974,
       v. 34, p. 409.

1130   Book World, (Washington Post), Review of Allen Verbatim, 1
       December 1974, p. 2.

1131   Booklist, Review of Allen Verbatim, 1 February 1975, v. 71,
       p. 542.
           "Most interesting here are the insights from Ginsberg's
       garrulous comments on his writing methods and influences and his
       informed evaluation of modern poetry; the material on other subjects
       tends to be rather muddled philosophically and rhetorically due to
       the manner of presentation and Ginsberg's idiosyncrasies. "

1132   Brinkmeyer, Robert. "Ginsberg Weathers Test of Time Bet-
           ter Than Passive Types. " Review of Allen Verbatim, by
           Allen Ginsberg. Herald, (Durham, North Carolina) 26
           January 1975, n. p.
           "Overall, this is an important book for anyone who
       wants to understand Ginsberg, or indeed, the entire Beat generation.
       Moreover, it is highly recommended to all those people who think
       that Ginsberg writes his poetry the way he does because he does not
       understand meter, rhythm, word choice, etc....   This assumption
       of Ginsberg's literary ineptitude could not be further from the truth,
       as this book, 'Allen Verbatim,' abundantly testifies. "

1133   Brinnin, John Malcolm. "The Theory and Practice of Poetry. "
           Review of Allen Verbatim, by Allen Ginsberg. New York
           Times Book Review, 2 March 1975, pp. 4-5, including a photo-

graph of Ginsberg among the collage on page 5.

Ginsberg's book is reviewed in a lengthy article on "the theory and practice of poetry" which illuminates Ginsberg's work because of its survival over the past poetic battles of the last decades.

1134 Choice, Review of Allen Verbatim, March 1975, v. 12, p. 72.
"A collection of edited transcriptions of informal lectures and conventions recorded on Ginsberg's cross-country reading tours in the spring of 1971 ... one section is devoted to Ginsberg's researches into the drug traffic and 'addiction politics.' The freshest material, however, is his conversations on poetry with Robert Duncan, his keen analysis of Kerouac's prose style, and his paeans to Ezra Pound...."

1135 Crosby, K. P. "The Beat Generation Poet in Prose." Review of Allen Verbatim, by Allen Ginsberg. 9 January 1975, p. 13.
Crosby heralds Allen Verbatim as "an engaging hotchpotch" which "will delight Ginsberg fans, students of 20th-century poetry and anyone interested in a solid, idiosyncratic view of the American condition."

1136 Dandridge, Ned. "On the Road with Allen, 'Verbatim.'" Review of Allen Verbatim, by Allen Ginsberg, News & Observer, (Raleigh, N. C.), 26 January 1975, n. p., with photograph from the book jacket of Allen Ginsberg.
"This collection should appeal to the admirers for the semi-bald genial-looking guru photographed for the jacket. But many others who prefer to have their consciousness and their meditation stimulated less by William Buckley than by Art Buchwald will pass this one by." Descriptively Dandridge evaluates Allen Verbatim chapter by chapter. In the end he also supplies biographical information about the editor.

1137 Ford, Michael C. "Ginsberg: Tapes of Satori and a Guru on the Run." Review of Allen Verbatim, by Allen Ginsberg. Los Angeles Free Press, 28 February 1975, n. p.
The reviewer lauds the achievements of this collection because it is "a really heavyweight resource for Ginsberg's own awareness of himself as projector of clips ranging from dimensions of classical poetics ... to alternate levels with systems of speech in modern poetry ... and a whole hell of a lot more than the usual bullshit guru image that Madison Avenue, old tired Playboy magazine hype had us blimped on."

1138 "Ginsberg Comments." Review of Allen Verbatim, by Allen Ginsberg, Times-Picayune, 23 March 1975, n. p.
"Whatever subject Allen Ginsberg happens to be talking on, his extraordinary intellect commands our attention."

1139 Kirkus. Review of Allen Verbatim, 1 July 1974, v. 42, p. 716; 1 August 1974, p. 818.

1140   Library Journal. Review of Allen Verbatim, September 1974,
            v. 99, p. 2067.

1141   Metro, Jim. Review of Allen Verbatim, by Allen Ginsberg.
            Advertiser and Alabama Journal, 19 January 1975, n. p.
                "Ginsberg has progressed from outraged and outrageous
        outsider to a respected critic and opinion leader of our times. "

1142   N. "Today's Books. " Review of Allen Verbatim, by Allen
            Ginsberg. Independent/Press-Telegram, 25 March 1975,
            p. B3.
                This is a single descriptive paragraph on the book
        which closes evaluatively, "wise, serene, occasional anger tempered
        by wit. "

1143   Offen, Ron. "Poetry Beat. " Review of Allen Verbatim, by
            Allen Ginsberg. Chicago Daily News, 28 December 1974,
            n. p.
                This reviewer names Allen Ginsberg "America's great
        Wizard of Om.... " and finds "This compilation of taped student
        talk sessions and extemporaneous lectures from a 1971 college-cir-
        cuit tour reveal the spontaneous freshness of his language, the way
        he constantly plays with words and ideas and the depth of his knowl-
        edge about his art. "

1144   Publishers Weekly. Review of Allen Verbatim, 13 October
            1975, v. 208.

1145   Schoen, John E. Review of Allen Verbatim, by Allen Gins-
            berg. The Literary Tabloid, April 1975, v. 1, n. 2, p.
            27.
                "On Burroughs' work" (Reality Sandwiches, 1954) is in-
        cluded to describe Allen Verbatim which the reviewer finds "impos-
        sible" to conform to "a 'standard' review. " In fact, "let's just say
        that this is the kind of a book in which a radical undergrad who's
        into Zen and who sees Ginsberg as the leader of a cause can make
        discoveries. But it's also a book in which a retired professor who's
        still learning can do the same. " Yet Schoen is critical of the editing
        completed by Gordon Ball.

1146   Seelye, John. "The Sum of '48. " Review of Allen Verbatim,
            by Allen Ginsberg. New Republic, 12 October 1974, v.
            171, n. 15, issue 3118, pp. 23-24. The photograph in-
            cluded is a reproduction of a painting by Raphael Soyer.
                "This collection of lectures and conversations is a
        pocket epitome of the Beat genesis, for it too begins in hope, in
        1971, and ends two years later in sadness and a sense of defeat.... "

1147   Village Voice. Review of Allen Verbatim, 2 December 1974,
            v. 19, p. 41.

1148   Williams, Richard. Review of Allen Verbatim, Carolina
            Quarterly, Spring/Summer 1975, v. 2, n. 2, p. 113.

"It is therefore a great pleasure to see in print a book that illuminates the systematic nature of Ginsberg's intellect in a wide range of topics...."

Ankor Wat

1149 Brownjohn, A. Review of Ankor Wat, by Allen Ginsberg. Newstatesman (London), 10 January 1969, p. 52.

1150 Hayman, R. Review of Ankor Wat, by Allen Ginsberg. Encounter (London), February 1970, v. 34, p. 89.

1151 Lask, Thomas. "Books of the Times; Guru and Faculty Advisor." Review of Allen Ginsberg in America, by Jane Kramer, Planet News, Ankor Wat and T.V. Baby Poems, by Allen Ginsberg. New York Times, 17 May 1969, p. 31, column 1.
    The opening of the article is an overview to Allen Ginsberg, "the most integrated writer in America" for "he's made it," his own way. This serves as a good lead into Jane Kramer's book and then onto some words about Ginsberg's most recent books, Planet News, Ankor Wat, and T.V. Baby Poems.

1152 Lehman, D. Review of Ankor Wat, by Allen Ginsberg. Poetry, September 1969, v. 114, pp. 403-405.
    "When the Sun Tries to Go On," comment on four books, the second of which is Ginsberg's Ankor Wat. It describes Ankor Wat as a "retrospective ... long poem from his journals written in Siemreip, Cambodia, in 1963." Lehman sees it as "a marvelous book ... the poem should be read straight through ... the non-stop movement from scene to scene, voice-to-voice, so vitally builds and sustains an undercurrent of urgency and dread."

1153 Shapiro, K. Review of Ankor Wat, by Allen Ginsberg. Book World, 25 May 1969, p. 6.

1154 Times Literary Supplement, Review of Ankor Wat, (London), 30 January 1969, p. 107.

As Ever

1155 Curley, Arthur. Review of As Ever, by Allen Ginsberg and Neal Cassady. Library Journal, n. d. , n. p.
    This is a brief descriptive review of As Ever which indicates the importance of the included Ginsberg letters, "but more valuable are the intimate, generous, poetic letters of Ginsberg tracing his personal struggles, flamboyant travels, artistic development, and perpetual search for transcendence...." In the end, the book is viewed as "a fascinating and important literary document."

1156 Hershman, Marcia. "Short Takes." Review of As Ever, by Allen Ginsberg and Neal Cassady. Boston Sunday Globe, 1 January 1978, n. p.

The second review in this threesome is that of As Ever which the reviewer depicts as more effective than "straight biography" because it "is a good way to go to the source of what made the Beat Poets tick. The result is that, except for the few times things get too bluntly rambunctious, the emotional concerns of the vocal alienated generation were not so different from those of the Silent Majority."

Bixby Canyon

1157 Shively, Charles. Review of The Fall of America, Iron Horse, Bixby Canyon/Ocean Path/Word Breeze, The Gates of Wrath, by Allen Ginsberg. Gay Sunshine, June-July 1973, n. 18, pp. 14-15, with picture of "Allen Ginsberg 1968, at Kerouac's funeral." p. 1.

The Fall of America

1158 Abramson, Neal. Review of The Fall of America, by Allen Ginsberg. Footnotes, magazine of Lehman College, n.d., pp. 7-10 with two photographs to illustrate points on pp. 7, 9-10.
"Allen Ginsberg has taken the job of literary historian of the 1960's ... the last sections of this book, 'Ecologues of These States 1969-1971' and 'Bixby Canyon to Jessore Road' are a mixture of memories, flashbacks, Oms, graffiti, and ponderances on America's condition.... These poems are an expression of life in the 1970's through a human language, a language that is able to penetrate the heart.... Allen's poetry comes directly from the newsprint, radio broadcasts, and graffiti scribbled on a bathroom in a Syracuse airport. It is a language of the 70's with a message from the 70's. It is the poetry that confronts everyone of us today. And it is the poetry that we must confront."

1159 Albert, Stew. "Comedians, Folksingers, and Lovers." (editorial) Review of The Fall of America, by Allen Ginsberg. University Review, April 1973, n. 28, n.p.
In this third section of the Albert editorial, he concludes "it is six years of American history: of genocide, wiretapping, and pollution; of MyLai, Bach Mai, blood-baths in our streets, of personal tragedy for Allen."

1160 America. Review of The Fall of America, 9 June 1973, v. 128, p. 553.

1161 Andrews, Lyman. "Tones of Voices." Review of The Fall of America, by Allen Ginsberg. Sunday Times (London), 15 April 1973, p. 38.
Three other books are mentioned, Funland and Other Poems by D. Abse; The Rough Field by J. Montague and A Sense of Measure by R. Creeley. "The Fall of America contains some of Ginsberg's best writing for a long time. Subtitled 'Poems of These States, 1965-1971,' it confirms Ginsberg's status as the true successor to Whitman."

1162 Booklist. Review of The Fall of America, 15 December 1972,
v. 72, p. 562.

1163 Choice. Review of The Fall of America, June 1973, v. 10,
p. 618.
"Ginsberg is by now an authentic institution, more interesting to many than his verse. His verse is not uninteresting,
but is often undisciplined.... Ginsberg throws in the kitchen sink,
reveling in verbal histrionics but rarely refining them.... At its
worst Ginsberg's poetry is like that angry undergraduate verse which
surfaces annually in college lit mags; and like Huck, the reader is
apt to feel that he has been there before. But at its occasional
best, The Fall of America is as outrageous and funny and disturbing
as Ginsberg himself."

1164 Fried, Jerome. Review of The Fall of America, by Allen
Ginsberg. San Francisco Phoenix, n.d., p. 25.
The review by Fried finds the work included uneven in
quality, "there are two basic kinds of poems in Ginsberg: the
aural/oral type that needs to be read aloud and the more traditional
sort that comes across to the reader from the printed page. Un-
fortunately, Ginsberg the live performer prevails over Allen the
quiet reader and as a book, this one consists about 80% of banality."
Despite this sharp criticism, he finds "the remaining 20% of the
book, on the other hand, reinforces my feeling that Ginsberg is our
best true poet living today." Cited as noteworthy are "War Profit
Litany," the Neal Cassady Elegies, the Kerouac memorial, and the
death poems. "Yet the Cassady piece beginning on page 75 is also
a good example of what's lacking throughout the book: a pause for
reflection, either on Ginsberg's part or on his publisher's. That
poem and numbers of others throughout could have used a firm editorial hand."

1165 Gaines, Jacob. "The HIP World Poet Laureate." Review of
The Fall of America, by Allen Ginsberg, Independent
Journal, 10 March 1973, p. M31, with photograph titled,
"Voice of the Young."
"This is hard-core Americana and its author Allen
Ginsberg, is an important American poet." This is more personal
reminiscing than a review.

1166 Grant, Barry. Review of The Fall of America, by Allen Ginsberg. Ethos, n.d., v. 8, n. 2, pp. 15-17, with photographs by Jim Johnson of Allen Ginsberg.
Barry Grant presents a long thoughtful review of Allen
Ginsberg and his most recent work. He separates Ginsberg from
the others of the Beat Generation because he is "the only one still
alive who has managed to create a body of work which has changed
and remained relevant and urgent." With careful social and historical perspective, Grant portrays Ginsberg's poetry which "extends
beyond the social movements of post World War II America to embrace the very center of the nation's experience and therefore its
literature." The comparisons with Walt Whitman cannot be ignored

for "the book is dedicated to Whitman" and plays upon the verse and word form of Whitman's writing. Descriptively and critically the book is analyzed: "the book contains some powerful and fine verse, but its vision is overwhelmingly black. If we can achieve only periodic glimmers of intimacy, as expressed by the rare poems in this book, rather than create an intense bisexual love 'carried to degrees unknown' then this is, indeed, The Fall of America."

1167 Hall, Donald. "Knock Knock." (A Regular Column.) Review of The Fall of America, by Allen Ginsberg. The American Poetry Review. July/August 1973, v. 2, n. 4, p. 37.
    In this brief review of The Fall of America, the work is compared to Howl and found to be "better poetry, images instead of rhetoric."

1168 Henry, G. Review of The Fall of America, by Allen Ginsberg. Poetry, August 1974, v. 124, pp. 292-3.
    "Starting from Scratch" (the title of the old "Comment" column of Poetry magazine) is a review of four books, the first of which is Ginsberg's The Fall of America. This is a thought-provoking critique because Henry is not quite sure what to do with Ginsberg. He concludes "the poems ... aren't much as poems, but there's a whale of a mensch behind them." In Henry's terms a "mensch" equals an "engaging and likeable culture hero."

1169 Library Journal. Review of The Fall of America, 1 June 1973, v. 98, p. 1823.

1170 Martin, Sam. Review of The Fall of America. door, 22 March-12 April 1973, v. 4, issue 18, p. 14.
    "The Fall of America is an excellent book of poetry and a review of American tragedy. It's a long poem, a lot of short poems, a continuation of Planet News, another ride through the dying nation. Fall of America is a brief history of these states between 1965-1971. It is a tale of deceit, of a senseless war, of a dying or already dead environment.... Allen Ginsberg is the grand poet of our time and The Fall of America is the best book of American poetry of our time...." Selections included are "Crossing Nation," "Death on All Fronts," and "The Planet Is Finished."

1171 Middlebrook, Diane. "Bound Each to Each." Criticism of Allen Ginsberg's The Gates of Wrath and The Fall of America; Poems of These States, Parnassus II, (Spring/ Summer, 1974), pp. 128-135.

1172 Moon, Byron. "Literata." Review of The Fall of America, by Allen Ginsberg. Minnesota Daily, 29 January 1973, v. 74, n. 89, pp. 13, 16, with a caricature of Ginsberg (unsigned).
    Moon's article is a review in the form of a dialogue between "three voices: Anopheles, a scribe; Mingus, a scarab; Anilingus, a scab; "interspersed with bits of poems from the collection.

1173 Moser, Norm. "Books, Arts in Review." Review of The
Fall of America, by Allen Ginsberg. GAR, February-
March 1974, v. 3, n. 3, pp. 26-27.
"The Fall of America is in its way, a contribution of
the powerful and magical work he was writing earlier in his career."
Moser explains his past remarks on homosexuality and art clearly
excluding Ginsberg's work: "When I said in a poem in Jumpsongs
that homosexuality in art is 'art at its adolescent stage' and that in
life it is 'sexual life/at its most adolescent,' I had reference
mainly to those persons unable to transcend their limitations in art
(or life). But these arguments, in a poem or out, do not refer to
Ginsberg, Whitman or the actor Sir John Gielgud in his work."

1174 Murray, Michele. "Leafing Through/Poets Buck the Coca
Cola Syndrome." Review of The Fall of America, by
Allen Ginsberg. National Observer, 9 June 1973,
n. p., including Ginsberg's "Easter Sunday."
"Easter Sunday" is lauded as a "very fine poem" within
this "newest collection by an authentic son of Whitman who remains
an American no matter how much he draws his inspiration from In-
dia--for he draws his language from America."

1175 National Observer. Review of The Fall of America, 9 June
1973, v. 12, p. 23.

1176 New York Times Book Review. Review of The Fall of America, 10 June 1973, p. 41.

1177 New York Times Book Review. Review of The Fall of America, 2 December 1973, p. 79.

1178 Niederman, Fred. "Shaman a Showman." Review of The
Fall of America, by Allen Ginsberg. Daily Nexus, 3 May
1973, v. 53, n. 119, pp. 3, 4, col. 2.
"Through the whole book there is ... a frantic energy
matching in intensity the beat poets, yet differing from them in the
clarity of outrage and the despair at politics and political events....
In this book we see the grim autumn of the dissolving America, as
we look through the various states of both the country and Ginsberg
himself."

1179 Norris, Ruth. "Allen Ginsberg's Euphoria Transcends Social
Solutions." Review of The Fall of America, Daily World,
15 June 1973, p. 8.
Ruth Norris, in reviewing Allen Ginsberg's new book,
skillfully presents Allen Ginsberg ... "an American phenomenon"
whose "poems are as formless and undisciplined as the landscapes
he describes...." Norris possesses the ability to historically and
culturally place Ginsberg and his poetry in American civilization.

1180 Pritchard, W. H. Review of The Fall of America, Hudson
Review, Autumn 1973. p. 592.

1181 Rogers, Michael. "Kerouac and Ginsberg: On the Road
        Again." Review of The Fall of America, by Allen Gins-
        berg and Visions of Cody, by Jack Kerouac. Rolling
        Stone, 12 April 1973, n. 132, p. 68.
            "We're back on the road again; one last time with the
    travel worn ghosts of Jack Kerouac and Neal Cassady, and one
    more time with the undeniably lively presence of Allen Ginsberg.
    Kerouac and Ginsberg, two long-time buddies who have managed
    together to put a considerable twist into the literary and social con-
    sciousness of the last two decades, and here they are represented
    by long work that reflects both the best and the worst of each."

1182 Shively, Charles. Review of The Fall of America, Iron
        Horse, Bixby Canyon/Ocean Path/Word Breeze, The
        Gates of Wrath, by Allen Ginsberg. Gay Sunshine, June-
        July 1973, n. 18, pp. 14-15, with picture of "Allen Gins-
        berg 1968, at Kerouac's funeral."

1183 Slater, George Dillon. "Ginsberg Is Angry, Allen Sees All
        Sorts of Creeping, Crawling Perils in 'The Fall of Amer-
        ica.'" Review of The Fall of America, San Francisco
        Chronicle, 23 June 1973, n. p., with a photograph of Gins-
        berg.
            Slater justly names Ginsberg "the undisputed effusive
    sidewalk bard of America" and compares his work and cataloguing
    techniques to Whitman. "Ginsberg tries desperately to map out
    some cohesive order from our incomprehensible lives." Though he
    admits "I must confess I don't care for at least half the poems in
    the book--some of the sexual ones are as tedious as 'Deep Throat'--
    but the ones I do like pierce my inner ear like pins. 'Car Crash,'
    is a soft and sad biopsy performed on a fatigued and thoroughly in-
    spected soul. 'Easter Sunday,' opening with 'Slopes Woods snows
    melt,' is verse as elegant and evocative as will be found. 'Sep-
    tember on Jessore Road,' is a staggering journey into authentic
    anguish written in rhyme pacing with pain. Ginsberg's poetry mir-
    rors our accelerating contemporary reality, of which half is always
    unbearable."

1184 Times Literary Supplement. Review of The Fall of America,
        (London), 27 April 1973, p. 474.

1185 Vendler, H. Review of The Fall of America, New York Times,
        15 April 1973, p. 1.

1186 Village Voice. Review of The Fall of America, 18 April
        1974, v. 19, p. 27.

1187 Yenne, Bill. "Viewing the Apocalypse." Review of The Fall
        of America, City Magazine, July-August 1973, v. 2, n.
        10, p. 41.
            The "sensitive subjectivity" (Ginsberg's own words) with
    which Ginsberg "tells the story of America" is recognized as "...
    the basis of his poetry, his 'taperecorded scribed by hand or sung

condensed' poetry. This is the element that separates the present
work from journalistic/history book images of America.... All the
acid visions and sweaty moments no history book would dare to
record. In attempting subjectivity, Ginsberg has created a universal
vision. "

First Blues

1188 Kissel, Howard. "Book Making, Edwin Denby's Poems."
      Review of Collected Poems, Women's Wear Daily, 16
      January 1976, n. p.
           This is a brief review by Howard Kissel of Denby's
Collected Poems which mentions "'First Blues,' recent poems by
Allen Ginsberg; and 'I Remember,' delightful, touching sentences
and photographs by the painter Joe Brainard, describing poignant,
funny, erotic memories of his youth. "

1189 Lally, Michael. "Ginsberg's Songs and Other Delights. " Re-
      view of First Blues: Rags, Ballads, and Harmonium
      Songs, 1971-74, The Washington Post, 8 February 1976,
      p. G6 with score from First Blues of "Guru Blues, " and
      "Dream Stanza, April 24, 1975. "
           The reviewer finds fault in "calling Ginsberg's book of
songs poetry.... There's an implied prejudice ... that's based on
a conception of songs as inferior to poems. " He finds the collection of "song-writing by a poet" important for its own value. In
total this is a review of the first three publications of Full Court
Press in NYC: I Remember, Joe Brainard; Collected Poems, Edwin Denby; and First Blues.

1190 Ratner, Rochelle. "Christmas Poetry. " Review of First
      Blues, Soho Weekly News, 25 December 1975, n. p.
           This review column deals with Allen Ginsberg's First
Blues in its acknowledgement of "Dylan and Blues" on the product
which is "pure Ginsberg. The songs came at a time when perhaps
the poetry was starting to lose its power, and in the end they extended the total range. The voice is less personal here, more of
a reaching out to give everyone foothold. Simple music notation is
included for many songs. "

1191 Saroyan, Aram. "New Collections by Allen Ginsberg, Edwin
      Denby and Joe Brainard lend prestige to little-known
      press. " Review of First Blues, Village Voice, 16 August
      1975, p. 30, photographs by Fred McDarrah.
           Saroyan comments on the valuable service provided by
"small, independent publishers" to the "most endangered of literary
species, the American poet. " Briefly he describes Ginsberg's new
book and includes an excerpt. Instead he dwells on the economic
virtue of "an Allen Ginsberg title" for Full Court Press.

1192 "Scoop/CIA Takes Its Licks... / Telephone Polling Tricks... /
      Here Comes Another Sequel Flick. " Village Voice, 29
      September 1975, p. 34 with a photograph "Ginsberg as
      songwriter. "

In this column under "CIA capers" the following reference is made: "and if that's not enough, Full Court Press is about
to publish poet Allen Ginsberg's song 'CIA Dope Calypso,' a little
ditty which tunes into the CIA's role in drug traffic in southeast
Asia."

1193 "Soho's/Hot Spots." Review of First Blues, Soho Weekly
News, 15 January 1976, n. p.
"Some of the most enjoyable Ginsberg since his 'Howl'
days. In the Fifties, we all chanted along with him. Now he encourages us to sing. Children enjoy these songs. So will adults."

The Gates of Wrath

1194 Brodey, Jim. "Ginsberg in His Twenties: A Thrilling Precision." Review of The Gates of Wrath, City Magazine,
July-August 1973, v. 2, n. 10, with illustration including
Ginsberg by Bill Yenne.
"The Gates of Wrath presents Ginsberg's early poems
of his Blakean youth. All of his rhymed poems (1948-1952) are included. These were the first works of Ginsberg's that William
Burroughs saw; these are the works that drove Jack Kerouac into
friendship with this mad young Jewish poet at Columbia University;
they show the original powers which Ginsberg had to draw on....
This book is a chain of truths from a poet who has given us (and
continues to give us) words from boundaries beyond the conscious
stream we have sought to enter ... at its lowest ebb. It is a
must for a full sense of who Allen Ginsberg is, and how much one
can be thrilled by his words."

1195 Choice, Review of The Gates of Wrath, September 1973, v.
10, p. 975.

1196 Middlebrook, Diane. "Bound Each to Each." Criticism of
Allen Ginsberg's The Gates of Wrath and The Fall of
America; Poems of These States, 1971-1974, Parnassus
II, (Spring/Summer, 1974), pp. 128-135.

1197 Shively, Charles. Review of The Fall of America, Iron
Horse, Bixby Canyon/Ocean Path/Word Breeze, The Gates
of Wrath, by Allen Ginsberg. Gay Sunshine, June-July
1973, n. 18, pp. 14-15, with picture of "Allen Ginsberg
1968, at Kerouac's funeral." (p. 14).

Gay Sunshine Interview

1198 Scott, Andrew. "A Little Tenderness." Review of Gay
Sunshine Interview, with Allen Young. Georgia Straight,
6-13 June 1974, v. 8, n. 347, p. 11, with caricature of
Allen Ginsberg's profile by FINART.
"Allen Young conducted this lengthy interview with Ginsberg at a farm in Cherry Valley, N.Y. in September 1972. It was
originally published in Gay Sunshine in January, 1973 and parts of

the interview also appeared in other periodicals including the Georgia Straight. "
      The reviewer first begins to struggle with his own heterosexuality regarding the review of Allen's thoughts on homosexuality. Getting over that hurdle, the reviewer moves on to descriptively analyze the text and compare it to Passages About Earth by William Irwin Thompson. Ginsberg not only talks about homosexuality, but the entire realm of human relationships. He highlights his relationship to Peter Orlovsky, William Burroughs and others. He talks about Buddhism and his trip to Cuba. Nonetheless, the reviewer has difficulty with Ginsberg. First it is his homosexuality which makes it difficult to deal with him, and then it is the reviewer's "out-of-touch Canadian eyes" which make it difficult to view the poet.

Howl and Other Poems

1199 New York Times Book Review. Review of Howl, 13 February 1972, pp. 2-3.

Indian Journals

1200 "Des Livres pour Voyager." Review of Journaux Indiens, by Allen Ginsberg [and Le Livre des Rêves by Jack Kérouac.] Cosmose, 4 (1977).
      This is a review of Indian Journals by Allen Ginsberg and The Book of Dreams by Jack Kerouac, with a notation to the publication of the above listed two works, followed by a brief discussion of Ginsberg's work.

1201 Ginsberg, Louis. Review of Indian Journals, Win, 1 September 1970, v. VI, n. 14, pp. 28-29.

1202 Guardian Weekly, Review of Indian Journals, 3 October 1970, v. 103, p. 18.

1203 Library Journal, Review of Indian Journals, 1 September 1970, v. 95, p. 2801.

1204 Whittemore, Reed. "From Howl to Om." Review of Indian Journals, New Republic, 25 July 1970, v. 163, pp. 17-18.
      The reviewer sees two stages and then a third stage in Ginsberg's writing. The first encompasses "Howl" which he respects for it was "descriptive of a vast socio-spiritual death." However, he sees the "Om Stage" as a "cheaply acquired religious experience" and concludes that with Allen Ginsberg's introduction to his father's book, Morning in Spring, in which Allen "prophesizes ambiguously the country's return to his father's kind of verse," Allen goes "beyond Om." Cynically the reviewer agrees "it would be grand to go beyond Om almost anywhere."

Iron Horse

1205 Grant, Barry. "The Machine in the Desert." Review of

Iron Horse, Ethos, 18 July 1974, v. 8, n. 6, pp. 9-10, with photograph of Ginsberg by Elsa Dorfman (p. 10) titled, "The whirling neutrons and protons which are these various levels of consciousness and diction are kept from spinning off into formlessness or incoherence by the adroitly handled image of the iron horse."

The reviewer finds "Allen Ginsberg's Iron Horse is a long poem which is chronologically a sequel to the trips and resulting poems in The Fall of America which through ... free association, bits of personal history, self-reflection, cultural analysis, and poetic intellectualizing all blend in a poem of impressive complexity."

1206   Kliatt (Paperback Book Guide). Review of Iron Horse, September 1974, n. p.

"Iron Horse will be widely read because it fits the Ginsberg pattern of power and controversy.... Through it all Ginsberg wonders at the America he sees and compares it to the mythical one of Hart Crane and Walt Whitman. There is a haunting question effectively raised here. What happened to that direction of our past?"

1207   Shively, Charles. Review of The Fall of America, Iron Horse, Bixby Canyon/Ocean Path/Word Breeze, The Gates of Wrath, by Allen Ginsberg. Gay Sunshine, June-July 1973, n. 18, pp. 14-15, with picture of "Allen Ginsberg 1968, at Kerouac's funeral." (p. 14)

Journals: Early Fifties, Early Sixties

1208   Abhishaker, M.J. "Allen Ginsberg and the 'Middle Way of the Buddha.'" Review of Journals, Minneapolis Tribune, 27 November 1977, p. 180, with photograph of Allen Ginsberg.

Abhishaker dispels more traditional criticism of Ginsberg's Journals for "if one evaluates his work as a whole--dreams, ravings and celebrations coupled with action--one will recognize the literal and metamorphic map of a poet's progress. Ginsberg is an unflagging quester--always probing forever seeking. His is a search for self-knowledge which is simultaneously a search on behalf of his generation. This is the Middle Way of the Buddha whose example he emulates so we learn from his recent interview with Kenneth Koch. For this reason the Journals are indispensable for a fuller understanding of a man who symbolizes today's changing lifestyles and emerging aesthetic."

1209   Bender, Donald. "The bookshelf 'Journals' has 'gems' among the 'tedious.'" The Independent and Gazette, 9 September 1977, p. 13 with photograph.

"The quality of 'Journals' is extremely uneven. The poetic gems are buried deep within a mire of the self-indulgent and the tedious. Nothing is more boring to read than the detailed recounting of someone else's dreams. But the book is worth reading, because the poetic gems are definitely there rising out of the mud like gleaming lotus petals."

1210/12 Booklist, Review of Journals, 1 November 1977, p. 451.
A short descriptive review of Journals complete with cataloguing information.

1213 Craig, Paul. "Poetry/Memory Lane Looks a Lot Like Old North Beach." Review of Journals, Sacramento Bee, 18 September 1977, n. p.
Ginsberg's work is mentioned among others in this composition called the "regular North Beach Grab Bag." Journals is "a must for Ginsberg fans and the nostalgic who wonder where the 50's and 60's went." The central focus of the commentary is that the "writers and editors are busily building the 50's-60's era into something magic that it never was. Most of it was tawdry and more than a little dog-eared."

1214 Dachslager, E. L. "Remember Moondog?" Review of Journals, The Houston Post, 20 November 1977, n. p.
Dachslager finds that Ginsberg's Journals are "a fairly full account of the 50's and early 60's from one who lived at the center--or one center--of those now slightly unreal and almost unrecognizable years just before the Beatles, Bob Dylan, the assassinations, Vietnam, Watergate, etc., etc."

1215 Davis, L. J. "A Beat Idol Past His Prime." Review of Journals, Chicago Tribune, 18 September 1977, n. p.
Davis pans The Journals for "all of Ginsberg's best work has already been published somewhere else; what we have here amounts to the laundry list of a distinctive but minor talent. The Ginsberg of the journals has outlived his time."

1216 DeGregori, Thomas R. "Ginsberg's Journals." Review of Journals, by Allen Ginsberg. Houston Chronicle, 18 September 1977, p. 17 with photograph of Ginsberg.
DeGregori who teaches economics at the University of Houston critically offers: "Ginsberg seems to grow older without growing more mature. One need not resurrect the canard of demanding that a critic of society offer something positive. Intelligent dissenters, in poetry or in politics, in the very nature of their dissent, offer in time an alternate vision of life. There seems to be little in Ginsberg beyond drugs and narcissism. His followers are legion and he has the respect of many critics. Some may find considerable merit in this volume, but this reviewer didn't."

1217 Desilets, E. Michael. "Poet Allen Ginsberg, Conjurer of Images." Review of Journals, The New Haven Register, 9 February 1978, n. p.
"Gordon Ball, who edited 'Journals' from 18 separate notebooks, has included an extremely useful Reader's Guide that highlights Ginsberg's life from his Columbia University days (1943-1948) through the years covered by the text."

1218 Elman, Richard. "Books & The Arts/Beyond Self-Absorption." Review of Journals, The Nation, 12 November 1977, pp. 500-501.

Journals is praised for its content and arrangement. "Ginsberg's friend and admirer, Gordon Ball, has provided an excellent introduction and copious, unobtrusive footnotes to these journals; they are readable, bawdy, and in places, frightening.... Gordon Ball has indicated relationships between journal notes, rants and published poems.... It is being able to do just this sort of comparing of the published works to the journals that yields one of the very special pleasures I got in reading this book; and as there are very few living poets of his stature who have made themselves as vulnerable to those who know their finished work, it's an inspiration and a joy to see how Ginsberg's art is so strongly shaped from the materials of his senses."

1219   Goshorn, Gayle. "Notes from an Original Hipster." Review of Journals, Iowan, n. d. , n. p. , with illustrations of Ginsberg by Dower.
        The editing and inclusion of the lengthy dream section are criticized in this review.

1220   Hayes, E. Nelson. "At Last, Ginsberg Flourishes." Review of Journals, Patriot Ledger, 5 January 1978, p. 32 with photograph by Ilona Dawson.
        Hayes remembers the first time he read Howl and recalls the ambivalence with which he first confronted this work. Through tracing the development of his reactions to Ginsberg's work, he parallels the actual development of this work by the poet. "I am still offended intellectually and even aesthetically by much of Ginsberg's writing. But the gut growls." In the end he finds the Journals are "astonishing, compelling reading" and urges all to confront them.

1221   Herman, Jan. " 'Journals' Juicy But Incomplete." Review of the Journals, The Burlington Free Press, 14 November 1977. Reprinted as "Beat Down ... " in Chicago Sun-Times, 4 December 1977, n. p. , and as "Book Page ... " in Poughkeepsie Journal, 15 January 1978, n. p.
        Sternly Jan Herman criticizes this work because "it is both voluminous and incomplete ... the major figures of the 'beat generation' rarely come into focus in spite of many entrances and exits. We can learn more about Neal Cassady and William Burroughs from Jack Kerouac's novels and more about Kerouac from Ann Charters' biography. Additionally, there is a mysterious gap in the journals from 1956 to 1959.... And Ginsberg's crucial Berkeley period of 1955 is virtually nonexistent."

1222   Kostelanetz, Richard. Review of Journals, by Allen Ginsberg and The Beat Diary, by Arthur and Kit Knight. The New Republic, 22 October 1977, pp. 33-35.
        Cited for his role in creating " 'poetry reading' a popular cultural fashion all over the land," Allen is lauded for his "literary-political" presence and for defining writing as the "process of creation ... for Ginsberg has been a poet not of invention but of expression, not of construction but of communication, constantly revealing

his mind through language." Kostelanetz notes the publication of "secondary Ginsberg literature," and places Journals in this context. He praises Gordon Ball for his endeavors in editing and offers these words for the work itself: "What these Journals portray is the early progress of the man, from a private, insecure, self-conscious poet, learning from other poets and sampling mind-bending drugs, unsure of how he might economically survive, to a mature fulltime professional in command of his personal powers and aware of his growing eminence. The book's final line written February 11, 1962, is a testament to his self-realization: 'I'm on a trip of my own.'"

1223 Krim. "From Allen Ginsberg's Head to the Pad Beside His Bed." Review of Journals, Village Voice, 26 September 1977, p. 45, photograph by Fred W. McDarrah titled, "Beat memories: Peter Orlovsky, Gregory Corso, and Allen Ginsberg ready to do their stuff at Columbia in the late 1950's."
     This lengthy critical review finds Gordon Ball's editing at fault because of his "fastidious love" for Ginsberg and his work. "Too much inflated regard for history and not enough for the living reader is lurking in many of these pages. A more objective editor, equally admiring of Ginsberg, would have weighed his equal responsibilities to the poet and the public by a cannier, even a more hard-boiled method of selection." A key point is that his is not a "university press book." Rather it is a trade product for which "one would have hoped for a broad readership and a wide sale." The criticism notes the time gaps and the inclusion of the extensive dream section, that is, "over 60 per cent of the entire book is devoted to them."

1224 Long, Robert Emmet. "Books/Ginsberg's 'Journals' of a Voyager Life; As Much as Kerouac's 'On the Road,' the 'Journals' have a manic open-ended jazz beat." Review of Journals, Syracuse New Times, 8 January 1978, p. 6, with early photograph of Ginsberg.
     "What they do reveal is a lifestyle. As much as On the Road, the Journals have a manic, open-ended jazz beat; they show a 'voyager' life that is continually itinerant and on the move, urgent and intense. They reveal Ginsberg's youthful creative energies stretched toward their limits, which will make many readers of this book more than a little envious. Some may have to ask themselves a painful question--why did I let my youth go by in such conformity and inhibition?"

1225 "Mlle. What's Choice." Review of Journals, Mademoiselle, December 1977, p. 20.
     "Mlle. What's Choice" column includes among others a short descriptive reference to Journals.

1226 Maves, Karl. Review of Journals, The Advocate, 16 November 1977, n. 228, p. 28.
     Maves takes on the editor of the Journals, Gordon Ball. "Who is Gordon Ball and why has he done such a haphazard job?"

Thereby concluding, "we aren't really given Ginsberg's journals, ...
but a rewriting of them, a selection of highlights. Great, but let's
be more open about it, shall we?" The reviewer continues on in
the same spirit, critiquing the editing of the collection, rather than
the contents which include "a gallimaufry of autobiographical musings
and inconsequential dreams, trips on cocaine and trips to California,
the first drafts of published poems and poems that didn't make it beyond a first draft."

1227 Messerli, Douglas. "Book of the Day/Allen Ginsberg: a
      maturer voice." Review of Journals, New York Post, 12
      October 1977, n. p.
      "This is a difficult book, often rewarding, and it has a
few editorial problems--a confusion in the introductory pages, an
erratic use of footnotes and the lack of an index--but for its utterly
fascinating revelation of one of our most important poets, it is a
remarkable work."
      See following entry from the Washington Post Book
World, 2 October 1977 for a different version of the same review.

1228 Messerli, Douglas. "The Making of Allen Ginsberg." Review
      of Journals, Washington Post Book World, 2 October 1977,
      n. p. , with cover photograph from the book, "Photo of
      Allen Ginsberg in N. Y. , 1960" by Mario Jorrin.
      "And in fact these journals are ... illuminating not so
much in terms of what happened to Ginsberg in a social or political
context, but in terms of the personality behind the cultural events."
      See entry above from the New York Post, 12 October
1977 for a different version of the same review.

1229 Murphy, Avon Jack. Review of Journals, The Grand Rapids
      Press, 23 October 1977, p. 2-F.
      The Journals perhaps "valuable to Ginsberg scholars
and some aficionados ... for most readers including many who
appreciate the poet's work ... aren't worth much. Many pages are
bleary repetition of other pages, the gossip is tedious, we learn
little of Ginsberg's milieu, and the writing is nearly always bad."
His editor's efforts are valued as are the contents of Journals. But
there is some criticism for the editor. "He should have toned
down the sense of adulation in his introduction. Also, he finds
Ginsberg's very personal writing more important on its own merits
than it really is."

1230 Patnaik, Deba P. "Allen Ginsberg's Journals: The Myriad
      Mind of a Man." Review of Journals, The Courier-Jour-
      nal, 8 January 1978, p. 5 with photograph reproduction of
      a painting: "Gregory Corso and Allen Ginsberg," 1965.
      One of the illustrations in Diary of an Artist by Raphael
      Soyer.
      Patnaik values "the visual effect of these pages ... " in
which "all sorts of motifs, symbols, images and ideas dancing,
leaping, swirling" are contained. He is fascinated with the "process
of transmutation and synthetic composition" and the inclusion of
"dreams."

1231 Publishers Weekly, Review of Journals, 7 September 1977, n. p.
  Gordon Ball's editing which created "coherence of selection" is noted, as are the good and bad of the contents. In the end, one is urged to "read the book for its harvest of newly published poems, for the deep sense of his political 'ravings,' for the glimpses of Kerouac, Corso, Burroughs, Dylan Thomas, Auden, for Ginsberg's powerful and sometimes prophetic vision of the American scene."

1232 Simon, Jeff. "Ginsberg Journals Take Reader on a Wild Journey with Poet." Review of Journals, Buffalo Evening News, 8 October 1977, n. p., with photograph "Allen Ginsberg Fountain of Outrage."
  After setting the cultural context for a discussion of Allen Ginsberg during the Journal period of the 50's and 60's, by characterizing the man and the poet, and by briefly quoting from the introduction, Jeff Simon concludes "Ginsberg's Journals are both a delight and an insufferable bore. They are fascinating and silly. They are in the end, just right, eminently fitting their keeper. Greatness through being ridiculous has always been his way."

1233 Simpson, Louis. Review of Journals, New York Times Book Review, 23 October 1977, section 7, pp. 9, 46-47, with two drawings (p. 9) by Pierre LeTan, one "Allen Ginsberg in 1960," the other "Allen Ginsberg now."
  Generally, Louis Simpson finds the Journals to be a "record of his actual travels and his mental journeys." On an informational level for "serious readers of poetry" it is of "factual value." In the end, Simpson concludes after lingering on his thoughts about Howl and Kaddish, "anything the author of these poems wrote deserves to be read, including his Journals."

1234 Spearman, Walter. "'Journals' Reflects Author's Diversity." Durham Sun, Greensboro Record, Southern Pines Pilot and Roxboro Courier-Times, n. d., n. p.
  This is a local (North Carolina) literary column which deals with the activities of North Carolina writers. Gordon Ball, the editor of Journals is spotlighted for his editorship of both Journals and Allen Verbatim. He is a resident of North Carolina and graduate student at Chapel Hill (UNC).

1235 Strachan, Don. "Following in Whitman's Footsteps." Review of Journals, Los Angeles Times, 1977?, p. 18, with photograph. Reprinted as "Ginsberg Potpourri Offers Heady Feast," in The Indianapolis Star, 20 November 1977; as "Journals House Dream of Poet," in Tuscaloosa Alabama News, 16 December 1977; and as "National Bestsellers," in New Mexican, 8 January 1978.
  "The 'Journals: Early Fifties, Early Sixties,' are a heady mix of prose and poetry, a great feast of incandescent phrases and images tumbling after each other in stroboscopic flashes." One crucial point developed by this reviewer is the link between Allen's

use of dreams and prose, "Ginsberg the artist links dreaming and waking in two ways: through developing a style so imagistic and nonlinear that it makes waking observations sound dream-like and in descending so deeply into his subconscious that his dreams often yield complete poems."

1236 Stuttaford, Genevieve. "Publishers Weekly Interviews: Allen Ginsberg." Review of Journals, Publishers Weekly, 14 November 1977, pp. 6-7.

Ginsberg and PW comment on the monumental job completed by his editor in correlating his journal material. Ginsberg reveals, "My journals are to keep an accurate record of my interior life, a repository for what goes through my mind...."

1237 Thompson, Francis J. "Perhaps Discretion Would Be Better." Review of Journals, Tampa Tribune, n. d. , n. p. , with photograph, "Ginsberg/Other Poets Had Better Idea."

"Perhaps Discretion Would Be Better" epitomizes the message of this review: "Let's say the triumvirate is responsible, and had three motives: First, to shock the establishment; an easy way to make a quick buck. Grove Press would find this sufficient reason. Also, as an enfant terrible, Allen began shocking his family and friends in childhood.... Gee, maybe Oscar [Wilde] and Walt [Whitman] were smarter to be discreet. After a hundred years they remain powerful voices in world literature. In 2077 will Allen be remembered as anything except an enfant terrible?"

1238 Trexler, Connie. "Poet's Presence Obvious, Unavoidable." Review of Journals, Advertiser and Alabama Journal, 30 October 1977, n. p.

This is an opinionated review praising the Journals from the viewpoint of a voyeur. Other than assessing the book as "a gold mine for future thesis writers," Trexler states in assessing the editing of the selections, "but in other cases you will find yourself slipping into this warped, constantly sliding world and coming out a little less sure of the Outside and more familiar with the Inside of yourself. The authoritative and informative Reader's Guide puts the journal entries well into perspective, and throughout the book are wonderful historical anecdotes revealing the slimy interior and crumbling exterior of our near past."

Kaddish

1239 "Criticism." America, 126, 4 March 1972, pp. 239-240.

1240 "Criticism." Nation, 214, 28 February 1972, p. 286.

1241 "Criticism." Newsweek, 79, 21 February 1972, pp. 98-99.

1242 "Criticism." Saturday Review, 55, 22 April 1972, p. 24.

1243 Vendler, H. "Helen Vendler on Allen Ginsberg's Kaddish and Other Poems." Mademoiselle, 81: 32+, October 1975.

Planet News

1244 Berkson, B. Review of Planet News, Poetry, July 1969,
      v. 114, p. 251.

1245 Brownjohn, A. Review of Planet News, Newstatesman, 10
      January 1969, p. 52.

1246 Grissim, John, Jr. Review of Planet News, Rolling Stone,
      17 May 1969, n. 33, p. 18.
         "Allen Ginsberg is the Frank Zappa of American letters
      and older perhaps but nonetheless gloriously profane, hairy, benevo-
      lent, perverse, and without question a first rate artist.... In its
      honesty and immediacy, 'Wichita Vortex Sutra' is that cry of a gen-
      eration. As a poem it establishes Allen Ginsberg as a poet of the
      first magnitude. And as a book, Planet News, is a beautiful ex-
      perience in sharing one man's vision of humanity. "

1247 Hayman, R. Review of Planet News, Encounter (London)
      February 1970, p. 89.

1248 Lask, Thomas. "Books of the Times; Guru and Faculty Ad-
      visor. " Review of Allen Ginsberg in America, by Jane
      Kramer, Planet News, Ankor Wat and T. V. Baby Poems,
      by Allen Ginsberg. New York Times, 17 May 1969, p.
      31, column 1.
         The opening of the article is an overview to Allen Gins-
      berg, "the most integrated writer in America" for "he's made it, "
      his own way. This serves as a good lead into Jane Kramer's book
      and then onto some words about Ginsberg's most recent books,
      Planet News, Ankor Wat, and T. V. Baby Poems.

1249 Leibowitz, H. Review of Planet News, Hudson River, Autumn
      1969, pp. 500-501.

1250/58 Lipton, Lawrence. "News from Planet Earth as Reported by
      Allen Ginsberg. " Review of Planet News, Los Angeles
      Free Press, 7-13 February 1969, v. 6, issue 238, pp.
      26-27. Reprinted in Georgia Straight, 28 February-March
      1969, v. 3, n. 47, pp. 11, 14.
         "Offhand I think it is the most staggering, mind-blowing
      collection of seven years' work of any poet writing in the Western
      world.... Ginsberg's most potent weapon of guerrilla warfare is
      verbal blockbusters.... "

1259 New York Times Book Review, Review of Planet News, 31
      August 1969, p. 8.

1260 Robinson, Bill. Review of Planet News, by Allen Ginsberg.
      Great Speckled Bird, 24 March 1969, v. 2, n. 2, p. 8,
      with two photographs of Ginsberg.
         A "Ginsberg-like" review which concludes, "many
      watched, few understood. As with Ginsberg's word games. "

1261   Vendler, T.   Review of Planet News.   New York Times, 31
       August 1969, p. 8.

1262   Wirick, Richard.   Review of Planet News, Damascus Free
       Press, July 1969, v. 1, n. 6, p. 2.
              "All one hundred and forty-four pages of Planet News
       is a miraculous carnival, a modern masterpiece by a beautiful mad-
       man.   Sometimes I think we should thank that madman for giving
       us back our sanity....   Cosmic Jesus Allen ... O Great Spirit of
       Poetry. "

1263   Wolf, R.   "12 Minute Derivative Mock-Up. "   Review of
       Planet News, Common Sense, 1 October 1969, v. 1, n.
       14, p. 8, with photograph, "Allen Ginsberg and Gregory
       Corso, 1957" by Lawrence Lipton.
              "Ginsberg reveals secret talks with self and others in
       long day's journey.... "

1264   Zweig, Paul.   "Music of Angels, "   Review of Planet News by
       Allen Ginsberg.   Nation, 10 March 1969, v. 208, pp. 311-
       313.
              Paul Zweig sings of the wonder of Ginsberg's Planet
       News, for it "contains some of Ginsberg's finest poems" for "Gins-
       berg ... has given us a music of Angels. "   He reveals a universal
       nature of the poet's words and notes the link in genre with other
       such poets particularly Whitman.   This link Zweig concludes is a
       "psychic genre. "

Sad Dust Glories

1265   Miller, Brown.   "Leaving Things Alone. "   Review of Sad
       Dust Glories, by Allen Ginsberg.   Small Press Review,
       December 1977, p. 5.
              In Miller's introductory remarks, he refers to an
       interview with Charles Plymell (forthcoming issue of Nitty-Gritty) in
       which Plymell comments on Ginsberg: "Ginsberg actually believes
       that everything he got down in his notebooks is some kind of golden
       Blakean vision.   Blake babbled a lot of shit, too, come to think of
       it. "   After all of this, he praises Sad Dust Glories as "an impor-
       tant addition to his published work, one that may become pretty
       rare in a short time.   I'd say you better get hold of a copy....   The
       poems are short, finely crafted ... and reflect a calm, centered con-
       sciousness.   These may someday replace the current crop of Gins-
       berg so often anthologized; they strike me as more mature, more
       believable, and certainly tighter.   They have a haiku flavor about
       them and a punch of Snyder influence. "

1266   Weinstein.   Review of Sad Dust Glories, Western American
       Literature, n. d. , v. XI, n. 2, n. p.
              " 'Who am I wandering/in this forest...?' Allen Gins-
       berg asks an 'Energy Vampire,' the best poem in this small collec-
       tion.   It is the central question of this book and, indeed, of the best
       of Ginsberg's entire work, an attempt to define the Self, or one's

consciousness of one's Self, in relation to everything outside that
consciousness, to investigate in Emerson's terms, the relation of
the ME to the NOT ME. " Weinstein continues in this mode commenting upon the "personal and lyrical tone, a quiet humility that
one hasn't seen in Ginsberg's work in years. "

To Eberhart from Ginsberg

1267 Carruth, Hayden. "A Letter for Poets. " Review of To Eber-
       hart from Ginsberg. Bookletter, 11 October 1976, p. 7.
       Carruth describes the content of this book and excerpts
a portion of the Ginsberg letter. "Ginsberg's letter to Eberhart is
clear and brief, the most trenchant expression I have seen of his
basic propositions and hence is an indispensable document, not only
for its historic value but its many pure-hearted and clear-minded
admonitions to all poets, whatever their modal and cultural affinities
may be. "

1268 Glass, Jesse, Jr. Review of To Eberhart from Ginsberg.
       Northeast Rising Sun, July 1977, p. 19.
       "To Eberhart from Ginsberg is a historically interesting
book. It is also a beautiful book to see and feel--tastefully printed
on fine paper with original etchings of Ginsberg and Eberhart by
Jerome Kaplan.... This book is a must for the student who wants
to examine the roots of the Beat movement, and of modern culture
itself. "

1269 Library Journal. Review of To Eberhart from Ginsberg, 1
       January 1977, v. 102, p. 109.

T. V. Baby Poems

1270 Katz, Bill. Review of T. V. Baby Poems, Library Journal,
       August 1968, v. 93, p. 2882.

1271 Keyes, Mary. Review of T. V. Baby Poems, Canadian Forum,
       November 1968, v. 48, p. 182.

1272 Lask, Thomas. "Books of the Times; Guru and Faculty Ad-
       visor. " Review of Allen Ginsberg in America, by Jane
       Kramer, Planet News, Ankor Wat and T. V. Baby Poems,
       by Allen Ginsberg. New York Times 17 May 1969, p. 31,
       column 1.
       The opening of the article is an overview to Allen Gins-
berg, "the most integrated writer in America" for "he's made it,"
his own way. This serves as a good lead into Jane Kramer's book
and then onto some words about Ginsberg's most recent books,
Planet News, Ankor Wat, and T. V. Baby Poems.

1273 Potter, T. Review of T. V. Baby Poems, by Allen Ginsberg.
       Poetry Review, Summer 1968, p. 116.

1274 Revell, P. Review of T. V. Baby Poems, by Allen Ginsberg.
       Alphabet, December 1969, p. 69.

1275 Stein, C. Review of T.V. Baby Poems, Nation, 17 February
      1969, p. 217.

1276 Symons, Julian. Review of T.V. Baby Poems, by Allen Gins-
      berg. Newstatesman, 3 November 1976, v. 74, p. 595.

1277 Walsch, Chad. Review of T.V. Baby Poems, 28 July 1968,
      p. 4.

The Visions of the Great Rememberer

1278 Village Voice. Review of The Visions of the Great Remem-
      berer, 10 October 1974, v. 10, p. 33.

B. PERFORMANCES

Kaddish

1279 Aronowitz, Alfred G. "Pop Scene." Review of "Kaddish,"
      by Allen Ginsberg. New York Post, 15 August 1972, p.
      36.
          Aronowitz urges the public to see "Kaddish" which is
in financial trouble at the Circle in the Square Theater. He con-
curs with Jack Kroll, the critic of Newsweek, and his praise for
the production: "You may never again see a performance so shattering as Marilyn Chris' portrayal of Naomi, Allen Ginsberg's mother
and 'Kaddish' is no intellectual exercise, either. It is a play that
anybody can understand and Allen himself calls it 'a rock tearjerker.'
It has too much meaning to toss away in flip phrases. As an experience, it is overwhelming."

1280 Hipp, Edward S. "N.Y. Stage/Drama by Ginsberg Splendid."
      Review of "Kaddish," Newark Evening News, 14 May 1972,
      n. p.
          Hipp lauds "Kaddish" as "one of the season's more
moving programs on or off Broadway."

1281 Kroll, Jack. Review of "Kaddish," Newsweek, n. d. , n. p.
          "One of the most brilliant theatrical productions of our
time."

1282 Lebowitz, Fran. "On Stage: Allen Ginsberg's 'Kaddish.'"
      Review of "Kaddish," Changes, n. d. , p. 7.
          Indeed the goals stated in the program were achieved
in that "the production of 'Kaddish' ... (was) ... neither a play
with supplemental visual effects, or a television experience with
supplementary live actors." It was an attempt "to develop an individual form to express the poem" which utilized "film in grainy
black and white ... to show vital off-stage action and to efficaciously
mimic on-stage action."

1283 Lester, Elenore. "Allen Ginsberg Remembers Mama." Review of "Kaddish," <u>New York Times</u>, 6 February 1972, II, pp. 1, 4, with photograph by Steve Shapiro, titled "Poet Allen Ginsberg whose 'Kaddish' is at the Brooklyn Academy of Music 'Blessed daughter come to America, I long to hear your voice again. '"

1284   The Newsletter on the State of the Culture, Review of "Kaddish," 21 February 1972, pp. 2-3.
It took four years to complete this production which "is done in a series of terse, quick-shifting scenes over two long acts .... As for the production--the entire cast, as well as director Robert Kalfin, can hardly be faulted in terms of its energy, and its warm reading of the playscript. " In all, both the work and the Center (The Chelsea Theater Center of Brooklyn) are praised.

1285   Novick, Julius, "After 'Kaddish's' Poetry Goes, What Is Left?" Review of "Kaddish," New York Times, 20 February 1972, II, p. 1, column 5.
This is a review of the Chelsea Theater Center production which "includes live action coupled with video projection. " Novick critically evaluates the weaknesses of the attempt "to develop an individual form to express the poem. " He sees the downfalls of a poem brought to life and concludes "a play ... cannot and should not be the same as a poem, but in this case the poet has been expunged and nothing much has been found to take his place. "

At the "Other End"

1286   Kirb. "New Acts. " Review of Allen Ginsberg at The Other End. Variety, 9 March 1977, p. 76.
In Ginsberg's "Cabaret Room 619" he mixes poetry and song. "The poetry seg opens as Ginsberg reads a fascinating series. The repertory changes from set to set ... (the) Song program includes numbers from 'First Blues,' title of his new songbook and also of his upcoming Columbia album ... Ginsberg also plays a portable squeezebox, varies from near chanting to a dry singing, aided in the vocal department by Peter Orlovsky.... Able instrumental backup is cellist Arthur Russel of The Flying Harts, and guitarists John Sholle and Denise Mercedes, the former a studio musician also playing currently with Bonnie Koloc. " As a whole, Ginsberg's "program is a good one" because "the care is there now. "

1287   Wortsman, Peter.   "Clubs/Cosmic Imp of Verse. " Review of Allen Ginsberg at The Other End. The Villager, 10 March 1977, v. XLV, n. 10, p. 10, with photograph by Jack Beshears.
This is a descriptive review of Allen Ginsberg's "cosmic poetry and music" performance at The Other End, a nightclub. "He does one half-hour of 'plain' poetry, after which three guitarists, a cellist and back up vocalist Peter Orlovsky join in.... " He sings of "Sickness Blues," chants "from William Blake's 'Nurse's Song. '"

C. SECONDARY WORKS

Allen Ginsberg in America, by Jane Kramer

1288 Lask, Thomas. "Books of the Times; Guru and Faculty Advisor." Review of Allen Ginsberg in America, by Jane Kramer, Planet News, Ankor Wat and T. V. Baby Poems, by Allen Ginsberg. New York Times, 17 May 1969, p. 31, column 1.
The opening of the article is an overview to Allen Ginsberg, "the most integrated writer in America" for "he's made it," his own way. This serves as a good lead into Jane Kramer's book and then onto some words about Ginsberg's most recent books, Planet News, Ankor Wat, and T. V. Baby Poems.

1289 Lipton, Lawrence. "The Very Groovy Life and Times of Allen Ginsberg." Review of Allen Ginsberg in America, by Jane Kramer. Los Angeles Free Press, 13-20 June 1969, v. 6, n. 256, pp. 50, 68-69, with photograph of Ginsberg with Gregory Corso in Venice West, 1957 by Lawrence Lipton, plus a reproduction of the cover photograph from the book.
Lipton criticizes the Kramer book and the review of it by Kenneth Rexroth in the New York Times. "It may have served the purpose of the New Yorker profile ... to commission somebody whose acquaintance with the Beat and Hip movement was nil and who hadn't even met Ginsberg.... The pity of it is that with such trivia in print and Ginsberg's unedited verbalizations, the fine prophetic anger of such poems of his as 'Howl' and 'America'--yes loving, laughing, weeping anger--tend to be forgotten." True it is the best thing written about Ginsberg and "yes, there are passages in this book that, taken together with Ginsberg's poems, suggest the depth of his prophetic commitment, but there is hardly a hint in it that suggests how such a man could have written poems like 'Howl' or 'Wales Visitation...'"

1290 Rexroth, Kenneth. Review of Allen Ginsberg in America, by Jane Kramer. New York Times, 11 May 1969, VII, p. 8, 41.

1291 Shapiro, Karl. Review of Allen Ginsberg in America, by Jane Kramer, Book World, 25 May 1969, p. 6.

1292 Time, Review of Allen Ginsberg in America, by Jane Kramer. 8 August 1975, p. 6.

American Review 16, by Theodore Solotaroff

1293 Allen, Bruce. Review of American Review 16, edited by Theodore Solotaroff. Library Journal, 15 April 1973, n. p.
Praise is offered for the inclusion of Ginsberg's "Ecologue" which is included in the selection of the American Review.

1294 Hayes, Brian. "A Stage for the Folies-Litteraire: The
American Revue. " Review of the American Review 16,
edited by Theodore Solotaroff. The Sun, 25 February
1973, n. p.
This is a critical analysis of American Review 16 and
its content. It is described as "a magazine almost entirely without
personality. It possesses only austerity. " The included Ginsberg
poem is described as "a bucolic poem. "

1295 Henderson, Mike. "Rising Above a Low Watermark. " Review of American Review 16, edited by Theodore Solotaroff.
Post-Intelligencer Book World, 18 March 1973, p. 19.
This review criticizes the included Ginsberg work for
"Ginsberg's contribution is yet another catch-all indictment of our
ever-Americanized world (haven't we for Christ's sake had enough
of these already?) in which everything has gone wrong; but none of
the fault is shared by Ginsberg and his pals. " The work of Carolyn
Kizer which is included is praised.

1296 Indianapolis News. Review of American Review 16, edited by
Theodore Solotaroff. 3 March 1973, n. p.
This review cites the inclusion of work by Allen Gins-
berg.

1297 Kamstra, Jerry. "Books/New Literature. " Review of American Review 16, edited by Theodore Solotaroff. San Francisco Bay Guardian, 29 March 1973, n. p.
This is a review which praises the inclusion of Ginsberg's long poem "Ecologue" as "one of the finest poems he's
written. " Yet the anthology as a whole is criticized because "placing Ginsberg in this collection of ostensibly new writers points up
one of the fallacies of the anthology.... A lot of writing is by old
writers, and even the new writers obviously all have book contracts
(except for the poets, and nobody gives poets contracts for anything) and agents who hustle their work. You see very little writing
by writers who have had no chance of being published before. "

1298 Kisor, Henry. "The Paperback Rack. " Review of American
Review 16, edited by Theodore Solotaroff, Chicago Review, n. d. , n. p.
"American Review 16's quality remains high, energetic,
spirited and often surprising.... The mostly first-rate poetry is
led by a new offering from Allen Ginsberg. "

1299 Lothamer, Dr. Eileen. Review of American Review 16, edited
by Theodore Solotaroff, Long Beach News, n. d. , n. p.
Ginsberg's poem "Ecologue" is termed "pastoral" and
"worthy. "

Naked Angels, by John Tytell

1300 Mandel, Siegfried. "Beat Generation Given an Upbeat Treatment by Author. " Review of Naked Angels, by John Ty-

tell. Denver Post, 28 March 1976, n. p.

After voicing reservations, the reviewer admits the book "is a well written, first-rate example of systematic research into all available published and unpublished documents that provide insights into the life and work of the beats. "

1301 New York Times Book Review.   "Paperbacks: New and Noteworthy. "   Review of Naked Angels, by John Tytell, 3 July 1977, p. 19.

"A critic assesses the Beat Generation of the 50's by taking a close look at the lives and works of three of its most prominent writers--William Burroughs, Jack Kerouac and Allen Ginsberg.   Despite lapses into hagiography and blurbery, this Book Reviews appraiser concluded, the result was 'strong, urgent, ultimately thrilling. ' "

1302 New Yorker Magazine.   Review of Naked Angels, by John Tytell.   3 April 1976, n. p.

Tytell's brilliant comparison of the writings of Jack Kerouac, Allen Ginsberg and William Burroughs to "masterpieces" win over the claim to the "ludicrous" nature of the subject itself. "Placing the Beat movement against the backdrop of the fifties' fear and hysteria, he recounts the bohemian careers of these three writers, then presents sympathetic readings of their work. "

1303 Peters, Robert.   Review of Naked Angels, by John Tytell.
Gay Sunshine, Summer/Fall 1976, n. 29/30, p. 30.

Despite the fact that "Tytell expends most care and passion ... on Ginsberg" Peters is critical of the entire work. "There's no particular sparkle or shine and the pedantic moments (there are several, especially in the latter half of the work, devoted to the writing) do mar the whole. " Peters even disputes several points made by Tytell in regard to Ginsberg.   For example, "As courageous and seminal as Ginsberg is, he is not a saint: his obsessions with Eastern philosophies, his guru-trips, his fascination with drug cultures, his confusion of an oral tradition in poetry with the art of poetry, his apparent facile rejection of any kind of polishing and honing--viz. , his penchant for speaking endlessly into a tape recorder and publishing the results--all suggests that this splendid man has feet of clay and may not be the ultimate answer to the world's need for poetry Tytell seems to think he is.   Eclecticism does not necessarily produce fine art.... "

1304 Schjeldahl, Peter.   "Claiming the Beats for American Litera-
ture. "   New York Times Book Review, 9 May 1976, p. 4, with photograph from the past of "Kerouac, Ginsberg & Burroughs. "

Tytell's Naked Angels is praised for its "belief in the great worth and seriousness of his subject" but criticized for his "partisan" approach and various other "surface blemishes. " Allen Ginsberg is mentioned as the hero "of mystical experience and bardic mission. " The reviewer utilizes a skillful understanding of the type of data and social climate dealt with in Naked Angels.

Schjeldahl does not condemn Tytell for his "partisan" manner. "Is it yet possible for anyone not to be? ... the Beat eruption involved a terrific confrontation of values.... The clash of feelings occasioned by this confrontation was so momentous that serious discussions of the literature could seem practically quixotic, and that's pretty much how things have stood through two decades of tendentious defense and attack."

Rolling Thunder Logbook, by Sam Shepard

1305   Palmer, Robert. "Books of the Times/A Rock Tour Recalled." Review of Rolling Thunder Logbook, by Sam Shepard. New York Times, 17 September 1977, p. 21, section 1.
       "It is interesting primarily because the Rolling Thunder tour in 1976 was interesting--it was organized by Bob Dylan and featured an assortment of poets and folkies, Allen Ginsberg and Ramblin' Jack Elliot among them--and because press coverage at the time was minimal. [Rolling Thunder] was a conscious attempt to reconsider the roots of these alliances. The tour meandered through New England on a bus, playing for small audiences in town halls as if trying to recreate the troubador era.... Mr. Dylan and Mr. Ginsberg visited Jack Kerouac's grave and Mr. Kerouac's brother's bar, both in Lowell, Mass.... 'Rolling Thunder Logbook' is in the writer's words, a 'fractured' account of the tour, designed 'just to give the reader a taste of the whole experience.'" The reviewer refers to "Mr. Ginsberg and Mr. Elliot" as Dylan's "spiritual fathers."

Other Works

1306   Bess, Donovan. Review of The Beat Generation, by Bruce Cook, Rolling Stone, 11 November 1971, p. 68.
       "Recommendation: when you visit your neighborhood bookstore, read the last six pages of this book. It's almost entirely quotes from Ginsberg at his highest energy level."

1307   Chura, David. Review of Angels of the Lyre, A Gay Poetry Anthology, edited by Winston Leyland, Gay Sunshine, Winter 1975-76, n. 26/27, p. 29.
       "This anthology is significant because its scope has reachable limits. All the poems have been written within the last twenty-five years, thus we get the seminal benefits of such people as Allen Ginsberg, John Wieners, Frank O'Hara and Jack Spicer as well as those of more recent writers...."

1308   Coyne, John R. "Coopting Kerouac." Review of The Beat Generation, by Bruce Cook. National Review, 5 November 1971, pp. 1246-7.
       Coyne critically reviews and analyzes Bruce Cook's book. The core of which "consists of a series of interviews with Beat writers, chief among them Jack Kerouac, Allen Ginsberg, William Burroughs, Gregory Corso, and Gary Snyder." So much for

the review and onto the criticism, "Cook felt it necessary to impose a thesis and by forcing the material to validate the thesis ... Cook's points too often [are] strained and overstated."

1309 Ellmann, Richard. Review of Ezra Pound: The Last Rower, A Political Profile, by C. David Heymann and The Cantos of Ezra Pound, The Lyric Mode, by Eugene Paul Nassan. New York Times Book Review, 4 April 1976, pp. 25-26.
    In this review reference is made to Allen Ginsberg in the recollection of a comment made to Ginsberg by Pound: "He had botched his life, he now felt, and he remarked to Allen Ginsberg, 'the worst mistake I made was that stupid, suburban prejudice of anti-Semitism. All along, that spoiled everything.'"

1310 Grumbach, Doris. "Fine Print--More from the Small Presses." Review of The Beat Book, published and edited by Arthur Winfield Knight and Glee Knight. The New Republic, 1 March 1975, p. 32.
    This article reviews the fourth volume published by The Unspeakable Visions of the Individual Press, edited by the Knights, called The Beat Book for it's "an indispensable compendium of writing on, about and for the beat generation...." Of course, Allen Ginsberg's work is cited.

1311 Haines, Steve. "Memoirs of a Beatnik." Review of Memoirs of a Beatnik, by Diane Di Prima. Berkeley Tribe, 15-21 August 1969, p. 20.
    The author is described as "a Bay Area poetess" who tells "a love story" on many levels. A tale involving Ginsberg and his cohorts is included.

1312 Halley, Pat. "Halley's Comment: Marcuse, Ginsberg, Di Prima & Kerouac." Review of City Lights Anthology. Fifth Estate, 6-12 February 1975, v. 10, n. 11 (245), p. 5, with anthology cover photograph including Ginsberg.
    Pat Halley critically reviews this anthology which encompasses the work of "Marcuse, Ginsberg, Di Prima, Kerouac, Bukowski, 'The' Surrealist Movement, Brautigan, Snyder." He attacks Ginsberg's work and the tendency of the anthology towards the promotion of "the old ecology/mysticism trip" which tends to become "redundant to the point of Gospel." The reviewer considers "this cheap, because the writing itself may not be new and creative, so much as the writing is about the 'new consciousness' in America (which he also supports and promotes) and is interesting only to the degree of ignorance of the reader."
    Again Halley criticizes the surrealist section of the anthology for its claim to "authoritarian thinking" which is contradictory to "Lautremont's saying, which Surrealist Franklin Rosemont is fond of repeating, 'Poetry made by all.'" Yet despite his criticism, Halley wholeheartedly recommends this anthology. Perhaps Halley is criticizing the alternative culture for becoming another part of the mass culture. If this is indeed the case, he must proceed much more cautiously, carefully documenting his argument. Be-

cause to say, "Ginsberg stinks in this book" and to compare one of his interviews to the geriatric ward is a low blow, not worthy of consideration.

1313 Kirsch, Robert. "The Book Report/The Beat Movement's Brief Candle." Review of The Beat Book, published and edited by Arthur Winfield Knight and Glee Knight. The Los Angeles Times, 12 May 1975, IV, p. 18, with photograph of Allen Ginsberg.
    Apart from collecting data, "there are scattered in these pages an anthology of Beat writing, past and present, which suggests that the movement, with its varied poets and associates, retains vitalizing and in some pieces a level of literary accomplishment which is impressive.... Ginsberg, brilliant and uneven, was hungry for celebrity and I think embarrassed by it."

1314 Lask, Thomas. "Books of the Times/Poetry in Retrospect." Review of A History of Modern Poetry, by David Perkins. New York Times, 23 July 1977, p. 17.
    This is a review and critique of Perkins' first of two volumes which spans the period from 1890 to 1959. One may guess that Allen Ginsberg and his cohorts are excluded from this volume. However, this is not true. Allen Ginsberg is mentioned twice in this review. First in reference to the quieting of previous feuding in American literary circles between "New York-Black Mountain-San Francisco axis ... Allen Ginsberg and Robert Lowell read from the same platform." Second, in a statement by Leslie Fiedler that "the best proletarian poem ... is Allen Ginsberg's 'Kaddish.'"

1315 Lenson, David. "Books Briefly." Review of The Beat Diary, published and edited by Arthur Winfield Knight and Kit Knight. The Chronicle of Higher Education, 14 March 1977, n. p.
    The reviewer applauds the publication of first The Beat Book in 1974 and now The Beat Diary by the Knights because "they are both essential documents for anyone interested in modern literature" and they collect data previously unretrievable. "Like its predecessor, the Knights' new volume, The Beat Diary, not only retrieves documents that might otherwise vanish, but also creates new documents of its own." Ginsberg's poetry, of course, is included.

1316 Leyland, Winston. "54 Books." Review of Homosexuality: Lesbians and Gay Men in Society, History and Literature. (A Collection of 54 Books and 2 Periodicals. Arno Press, NYC). Gay Sunshine, Winter, 75/76, n. 26/27, pp. 30-31.
    In this review of this collection which "is obviously aimed mainly at libraries" Leyland refers to the reprint difficulties of small presses, in particular "recent interviews ... in book form" including one by Allen Ginsberg.

1317 Lipton, Lawrence. "Poetry of the Neo Beat/'There isn't any elephant at all.'" Review of The Living Underground, A

Critical Overview, by Hugh Fox. Los Angeles Free Press, 6-12 August 1971, v. 8, n. 32, issue 368, p. 39.
"The continuity from Beat to Hip poetry is only now being recognized...."

1318 McNamara, Tom. "Memoirs of a Beatnik." Review of Memoirs of a Beatnik, by Diane Di Prima. Madison Kaleidoscope, November 1969, v. 1, n. 9, p. 5. Reprinted in Milwaukee Kaleidoscope, 13-26 February 1970, v. 2, n. 26 (52), n. p.
This reviewer includes the tale of Diane Di Prima's meeting with Ginsberg. "Her telling about her first meeting with Ginsberg and the ensuing subsequent love feast is one of the high points in current writing, a marvelous blow for sexual liberation.... It is about those times when those of us who were really isolated and scared found each other through a poem of Ginsberg's."

1319 Malone, Hank. "Books, 'Our Dreams Proved Innocent.'" Review of Jerry Rubin's Letter to the Movement, New York Review of Books, February 13, 1969; The Young American Poets, edited by Paul Carroll; Evergreen Review Reader, edited by Barney Rossett. Fifth Estate, 20 February-5 March 1969, v. 3, n. 21 (73), p. 21.
The reviewer cites Ginsberg's role in each for "in a sense we have all come down from a fantastic 'high' that started in 1957 a HOWL that turned everybody young on and off and out and over."

1320 Montgomery, George. Review of The East Side Scene, edited by Allen DeLoach. Win, 1 May 1972, v. 8, n. 8, p. 33.
"This is an anthology of poetry that came out of the East Side of NYC in the early '60's. Some very fine poets are included: Ginsberg, Carol Berge, Peter Orlovsky, Will Inman, Diane Wakowski, Ed Sanders, Tuli Kupferberg, etc...."

1321 New York Times, Review of The Gates of Eden, by Morris Dickstein. 13 March 1977, n. p.
Reference is made to Allen Ginsberg in the context of this book.

1322 Saroyan, Aram. "Prose of a New York poet/Standing Still and Walking in New York." Review of Notes and Essays by Frank O'Hara, edited by Donald Allen. New York Times Book Review, 14 December 1975, n. p.
In this review, Frank O'Hara and his work are placed in the 1950's as prominent in "the original generation of the New York School of poets" and compared to the Beats of San Francisco. "O'Hara places himself most succinctly in his most famous essay, 'Personism: A Manifesto,' perhaps the closest thing to a definitive statement of the poetics of the New York School, when he worries if he isn't 'sounding like the poor wealthy man's Allen Ginsberg.'" Saroyan concludes that this is exactly what he is. Having dealt with these ideas, Saroyan continues on with the work at hand, "a wide-

ranging collection of his notes and essays, as well as an interview with him, by Edward Lucie-Smith." In closing he refers back to his original impulse to compare O'Hara to Ginsberg, "throughout it all, he seems to be having a good time. More casual in tone than Allen Ginsberg, he is often equally as penetrating."

1323 Village Voice. "Alternative Currents/Small Press in Review." Review of The Beat Book, published and edited by Arthur Winfield Knight and Glee Knight, and Essaying Essays (Out of London Press, 12 West 17th Street, NYC 10011). 5 April 1975, p. 51.
         This review discusses two essay collections. One, Essaying Essays which in a discussion of "form" alludes to the Beats, in particular Kerouac and Ginsberg for their discard of "form." The second, The Beat Book, refers to Ginsberg among others.

V. MISCELLANEOUS

A. LETTERS TO GINSBERG

1324 Arcaini, Dan. "Viewpoints/Student Supports 'Daisy' in Con-
      tinuing Argument. " Letter. Glassboro Whit, 11 March
      1976, p. 3.
          In a letter from Dan Arcaini there is a statement of
      support for the film Pull My Daisy. There is a reference to Allen
      Ginsberg in the context of this film.

1325 Blickstein, Steve. "Letters to Lemar" (column) The Mari-
      juana Review, October-December 1969, v. 1, n. 3, p. 3.

1326 Bockris-Wylie. "Open Letter on Behalf of the Staff. 13 Febru-
      ary 1974. " Drummer, 19 February 1974, n. 283, p. 2.
          This is an open letter apologizing for "turning an inter-
      view into an article and secondly ... (for) ... making stylistic and
      factual mistakes in that article. " These comments apply to the ar-
      ticle "On Heroes" (Drummer, 12 February 1974, n. 282, pp. 3-4).
      See under INTERVIEWS in Primary Works Section.

1327 Burroughs, William, Jr. Letter to Allen Ginsberg. Bombay
      Gin, n. d. , unpaged, pp. 4-5.
          Stream of consciousness prose in the form of addressing
      Allen Ginsberg rhetorically, while recollecting events and ideas.

1328 Burroughs, William S. Letter to Allen Ginsberg, n. d. , In-
      trepid, 14/15, Fall/Winter, 1969/1970, p. 96.
          "Special Burroughs Issue" with acknowledgment to "Wil-
      liam Burroughs and to Allen Ginsberg for this issue. "

1329 Forcade, Tom. Open Letter. Georgia Straight, 26 July-2
      August 1973, v. 7, n. 303, p. 1 under title "$1000 says:
      'Ginsberg Is a Liar. '" (with reprint of check for $1100
      to Georgia Straight Legal Defense Fund).
          "In the Allen Ginsberg interview in the Georgia Straight
      of June 21-28, Ginsberg is quoted as saying: "But Forcade also,
      in addition to attacking Abbie and Jerry in jail, levelled his hand at
      David Dellinger who was on a 30-day fast, and said, 'We ruined
      Abbie and Jerry and we'll ruin you if you don't watch out!' which I
      have a record of--a tape. " Forcade point by point denounces Gins-
      berg's assertions: "First it was I who was in jail, not Abbie or
      Jerry.... Second, I did not 'ruin' Hoffman or Rubin. Their be-
      havior discredited them.... Third, I have never stated that I would
      'ruin' David Dellinger.... Fourth, as for the rock opera entitled

Eat the Rich, I am pleased to hear that the minor American poet Ginsberg considered it Burroughsian, since I have long been an ardent fan of William Burroughs' books...."

See "Dear Readers of the Georgia Straight" under LETTERS AND CORRESPONDENCE in the Primary Works Section; also see "Allen Ginsberg ... Rennie Davis and the Underground Press" under INTERVIEWS in the Primary Works Section.

1330 Leary, Timothy. Letter to Allen Ginsberg. Georgia Straight, 9-16 December 1970, v. 4, n. 139, p. 10, with photograph of Timothy Leary and Allen Ginsberg.
"My first message is to Allen Ginsberg. I want Allen to know that I am alive and well with Rosemary and that rumors to the contrary that I have been offed by the CIA are grossly exaggerated! ... In closing Rosemary has a message for our friends in Babylon: Smoke it! SMOKE IT! AND BLOW IT UP!"

1331 Leary, Timothy. Open Letter to Allen Ginsberg. 30 December 1970. Berkeley Barb, 1-7 January 1971, v. 11, n. 26, issue 281, p. 3. "Exclusive/New Year and New Life/ An Open Letter to Allen Ginsberg on the Seventh Liberation." Reprinted in East Village Other, 12 January 1971, v. 6, n. 7, p. 13; Georgia Straight 5:44, 13 January 1971, p. 5; Los Angeles Free Press, 15-21 January 1971, v. 8, n. 3, issue 339, p. 4.
"SHOOT to Live offered as Our Seventh Liberation mantra ... SHOOT to Live no longer our mantra/now being filed by archivists in Babylon Illham'dilla.... Six Revolution Liberation Cycles--Rights of Passage 1960-1970:

1. Sacrament	Acid	Energy	Om Tao
2. God	Spirit	Center	Om Man, Padma Hum
3. Mate	Tantra	Love	Come Together
4. Tribe	Brotherhood	Tolerance	Live & Let Live
5. Home	Possession	Sharing	Give & Receive
6. Freedom	Politics	Strength	Power to the People

Our loving defense of them
Having made inevitable the Seventh Liberation

7. Life	Body	Courage	Shoot to Live/Aim for Life

1332 Lenihan, Bob (film chairman). Letter to Glassboro Whit. Glassboro Whit, 26 February 1976, p. 3.
The showing of Jack Kerouac's Pull My Daisy was disrupted by the student body at Glassboro. This letter speaks to the "outlandishly childish behavior" which took place. Ginsberg is mentioned as a participant in the film.

1333 Martino, Dennis. Open letter to the Berkeley Barb. Berkeley Barb, 13-19 December 1974, issue 487.
"Tim Leary's Narc Friend Denounces Pill People.... A blistering attack on Allen Ginsberg, Jerry Rubin and other members of PILL (People Investigating Leary Lies) is made in an open letter Barb received this week from Dennis Martino, a longtime friend of

Timothy Leary and Joanne Harcourt-Smith and himself a drug in-
former for the Federal Drug Enforcement Administration. "

1334 Venceremos Brigade. Letter to Georgia Straight. Georgia
        Straight, 17-24 October 1971, v. 8, n. 366, p. 3.
        This is a letter under the title "Seery!" which addresses
itself to "Ginsberg--44 Questions on Leary" (Georgia Straight, 3-10
October 1974, v. 8, n. 364) which the writers do not feel "adequately analyzed" the situation because it "focuses too much attention on
the role of (1) Leary's latest mistress (2) the fascist character of
Amerika (3) Leary's supposed mental collapse and (4) Ginsberg himself. While these are interesting items in themselves they do not
get inside the skull of the HIGH priest of LSD. Of course maybe
only LSD can do that??"
        The alternative community rebuffs Ginsberg for his words
of woe.

1335 Young, Allen. Open Letter to John Giorno. Gay Sunshine,
        Spring 1976, n. 28, p. 26.
        "The following letter is an open letter to poet John
Giorno, commenting upon part of the Giorno interview published in
Gay Sunshine, no 24." This letter from Allen Young takes offense
with Giorno's "anti-Semitic comments directed toward Allen Ginsberg. . . . Did you say the stuff to be cute, to get Allen Ginsberg
pissed off, or to get sensitive Jews like me pissed off? Well, it
isn't funny. . . ."
        See Leyland, Winston. "John Giorno the Poet in New
York" under INTERVIEWS in the Primary Works section.

B. DISSERTATIONS

1336 Andre, Kenneth Michael. "Levertov, Creeley, Wright, Auden,
        Ginsberg, Corso, Dickey: Essays and Interviews with Con-
        temporary American Poets." Ph. D. dissertation, Colum-
        bia University, 1974.

1337 Betting, Richard A. "The Reconciliation of Spirit and Flesh
        in Allen Ginsberg's Poetry." Ph. D. dissertation, Northern
        Colorado, 1973 (DAI 34:4243A).

1338 Cargas, Harry J. "Daniel Berrigan and the Ideas Found in
        Contemporary Anti-Establishment Poetry." Ph. D. disser-
        tation St. Louis, (DAI 32:957A). Published in 1972. See
        under BOOKS--GENERAL OVERVIEW in Secondary Works
        Section.

1339 Huebel, Harry R. "A Study of the Beat Generation and Its
        Effect on American Culture." Ph. D. dissertation, Wash-
        ington State, 1971.

1340 Lin, Maurice Y. "Children of Adam: Ginsberg, Ferlinghetti,
        and Snyder in the Emerson-Whitman Tradition." Ph. D.
        dissertation, Minnesota University, 1973, (DAI 34:781A).

1341 Mersmann, James F. "Out of the Vortex: A Study of the
     Poets and Poetry Against the Vietnam War." Ph.D. dis-
     sertation, University of Kansas, 1972, (DAI 2944A).
     According to the MLA Index for 1973, the poets in-
cluded are Allen Ginsberg, Denise Levertov, Robert Bly, and Robert
Duncan.

1342 Skau, Michael W. "Themes and Movements in the Literature
     of the Beats." Ph.D. dissertation, University of Illinois;
     Urbana-Champaign, 1973, (DAI 34:5995A).
     According to the Journal of Modern Literature this dis-
sertation encompasses the work of Jack Kerouac, William Burroughs,
Lawrence Ferlinghetti, Gregory Corso, and Allen Ginsberg.

C. PAMPHLETS

English Language

1343 Fass, Ekbert. Pamphlet. "Preamble" from Towards A New
     American Poetics. (Santa Barbara, California: Black
     Sparrow Press), September 1977.
     Prophetically, Fass states, "And it may well turn out
to be one of the major tasks for present-day artistic aestheticians
and scholars to follow pioneers such as Duncan or Ginsberg in the
attempt to reformulate the new aesthetics in terms of this heritage
and to rewrite literary history surrounding such major figures as
Dante, Shakespeare, Goethe, or Yeats whose works played a crucial
role in rescuing the heretical wisdom from total suppression and in
preparing the ground for a total redefinition of art in our century. "
In this introductory note Fass indicates his reasons for compiling
the group of essays and interviews. Historically, in terms of
world civilization, he paints a picture of a new aesthetic. He quotes
from Ginsberg among others who usher in this new art, by turning
to "song forms" and "mantra chanting. "

1344 Hahn, Stephen. Pamphlet. "The Prophetic Voice of Allen
     Ginsberg" n.p. , Burt Franklin and Company, Inc. , 1976
     (reprint). Originally in An Annual of American Cultural
     Studies Prospects, volume 2, edited by Jack Salzman.
     See also under PERIODICALS--Articles About Ginsberg
in the Secondary Works Section.

1345 Poet's Conference. Pamphlet. Collection of reprints from
     local newspapers regarding the City Lights Poetry Con-
     ference held at the University of North Dakota in Grand
     Forks, North Dakota. The contact person there is John
     Little of the English Department.
     The articles included which cite Ginsberg are as follows:
Vadnie, Michael. "City Lights in North Dakota/'beat' poets appear
at 'City Lights in North Dakota.'" Grand Forks Herald, 19 March
1974, n.p. ; Smith, Stuart. "'Beat Generation' poets Lash Out
Against Dehumanization. " Grand Forks Herald, 20 March 1974,

n. p. ; Vadnie, Michael. "Beat Poets Delight Large Crowd." Grand
Forks Herald, 22 March 1974, n. p.; Vadnie, Michael and Stuart
Smith. "Poet Recalls Movement at Conference." no source; Smith,
Stuart and Michael Vadnie. "Writers Conference Ends with Reading
of Classic Poem." Grand Forks Herald, 24 March 1974, n. p. with
photograph of Ginsberg among others on p. 6; Vadnie, Michael and
Stuart Smith. "Views on the Writers' Conference." no source; "U
Writers Meet, Awarded Grants." Grand Forks Herald, 27 March
1974, n. p. , with photograph by Michael Vadnie.

Foreign Language

Dutch [Allen Ginsberg attended the Holland Poetry International
Festival held June 19-23, 1973. The following Dutch
pamphlets were included in a publicity folder at the event.]

1346 Knopselkrant. Rotterdam: Rotterdamse Kunststiching Rotterdam Arts Foundation, Livu 20-6-73, number 35.
This is a compilation (in Dutch) from various Dutch
newspapers collected in this format. The sources are rarely identi-
fiable.

1347 Löbler, Ruud (comp.). "A Concise Poets' Who's Who /The
Poetry International Rotterdam 1973 Poets with the Excep-
tion of Poets Writing in Dutch--Text. " (in English).
Allen Ginsberg is mentioned on page 2 in a biographical
commentary.

1348 "Poetry International. " 29 Dicters, C. Budding H'/Anton
Kloppers/Martin Mooij, Donia Pers Produkties, Rotter-
dam, 1973 Juni (unpaged).
P. 13: there is a photograph of Allen Ginsberg in
Uncle Sam pose; p. 14: there is biographical and bibliographical
statement; p. 15: "A Vow" (In English).

French

1349 Journal de poche 10. (Pocket Journal 10.) Periodique d'in-
formations culturelles du Theatre de Poche de Bruxelles/
Théâtre Experimental de Belgique [Cultural information
periodical of the Pocket Theatre of Brussels /Experimental
Theatre of Belgium], numero special [special issue], Ren-
contres et Colloques [Meetings and Colloquia], editor-in-
chief Robert Malengreau.
There are several references to Ginsberg.

Japanese

1350 Su-wa-no-se /The Fourth World. Pamphlet. Tokyo: Japan,
n. d. (In Japanese and English). 23 pp.
This pamphlet accompanied a documentary film by the
same title, produced by Keiichi Ueno. Allen Ginsberg is mentioned
as a member of the cast and a photograph is included among the film

clips (pp. 14-15). On page 9 he is featured in a photograph among
other poets. On page 21 he is cited for his participation in the
July 1974 "Save Su-wa-no-se Sanctuary/Berkeley Poetry Reading"
with Gary Snyder, Michael McClure and Nanao Sakaki from Su-wa-
no-se. In short, here was a move to stop Yamaha Corporation
from industrializing this special area.

Spanish

1351 De Mello, Andres Boulton Figueira. Pamphlet. A-All-Al-
      Allen Ginsberg/Aullido y otros poemas. Uruguay: Los
      Huevos Del Plata, 1969.
          This is a whole pamphlet on Ginsberg with a short text
by Andres Boulton Figueira de Mello. Included are the following:
"Howl," "Footnote to Howl," "Poem Rocket," and "Magic Psalm."

D. ACKNOWLEDGMENTS AND DEDICATIONS

1352 Ashley, Richard. Heroin: The Myth and the Facts. New
      York: St. Martins Press, 1972.
          This "comprehensive study and series of interviews
with addicts and police officials" is inscribed by hand to the poet:
"To Allen Ginsberg--Who has done what/a man should do/, Given
light to his/, brothers & sisters."

1353 A Bibliography of the Auerhahn Press & Its Successor Dave
      Haselwood Books. Berkeley, California: Poltroon Press,
      1976.
          This is an alternative press bibliography (listed in the
appropriate section of this bibliography) with an acknowledgment to
Allen Ginsberg on page 3.

1354 Bowering, George. Curious. Toronto, Canada: The Coach
      House Press, 1973.
          In the Ginsberg collection copy of this series of descrip-
tive encounters with writers (one of which is with Allen Ginsberg,
p. 1) there is an inscription to "Allen" from the author. The acknowledgment page notes "The characters in this book are all crea-
tions of the author's imagination. Any resemblances to actual people, living or dead, are coincidental."

1355 Bruno, Salvatore. Originale Nudo Respirante. Editrice "Il
      Rinnovamento" Roberto Santi, n. p., n. d. (In Italian).
          Salvatore Bruno's collection of poetry was influenced
by Allen Ginsberg's poem "Illumination of Sather Gate" for on the
title page a quote from Ginsberg is used and the poem acknowledged.

1356 Charters, Ann. Kerouac: A Biography. Foreword by Allen
      Ginsberg. San Francisco, California: Straight Arrow
      Books, 1973.
          Dedicated "To Allen Ginsberg."

1357 Christ, Carol T. The Finer Optic, The Aesthetic of Particularity in Victorian Poetry. New Haven, Connecticut: Yale University Press, 1975.
The references to Allen Ginsberg include pages 14-15, 22-23, 24. Carol Christ refers to Allen Ginsberg in her introduction: "While writing these pages, I have often recalled Allen Ginsberg's lines, 'What did I notice? Particulars! The vision of the great One is myriad.' I quote them here to prepare the reader for the many and sometimes contradictory manifestations the concept of particularity had for the Victorian world."

1358 Clausen, Andy. Shoe Be Do Be Ee-Op. n. p. (n. d.).
This is a soft cover, mimeographed, 18-page pamphlet collection of poems by Clausen (limited in distribution) with a dedication to Allen Ginsberg: "To Allen Ginsberg/whose words at depressing/times of my life, have/put wheels on my road/once again."

1359 Cosmic Consciousness Newsletter, n. p. , July 1972, n. 10.
On page 1: "This issue is dedicated to Walt Whitman, William Blake and Allen Ginsberg." This is a Philadelphia newsletter which is a selection of poems and prose by famous and not so famous individuals. No work of Ginsberg's is included.

1360 De Loach, Allen (ed.). Intrepid. Fall/Winter 1969/1970, 14/15, "Special Burroughs Issue."
Acknowledgment: "Many thanks to William Burroughs and Allen Ginsberg for this issue."

1361 Di Prima, Diane and LeRoi Jones. The Floating Bear, A Newsletter. La Jolla, California: Laurence McGilvery, 1973. n. 1-37, 1961-69.
This is a compilation of Floating Bear from 1961-1969. All references other than in the introduction (completed in 1970) refer to Allen Ginsberg in the context of issues prior to 1969.

1362 Kawin, Bruce. Telling It Again and Again/Repetition in Literature and Film. Ithaca, New York: Cornell University Press, 1972.
In Kawin's introduction to this text, on page 5, he refers to the work of Allen Ginsberg and praises him in note number 3: "Allen Ginsberg has that kind of presence in this book. I am deeply indebted to him, and can at this point only refer the reader to the title poems of his books Howl and Kaddish, and in particular to 'The Change' in Planet News (all available from City Lights Books, San Francisco)."

1363 McCoy, Alfred W. with Cathleen B. Read and Leonard P. Adams. The Politics of Heroin in Southeast Asia. New York: Harper & Row, Publishers, 1972, 1973.
This is the book referred to by Ginsberg in many of his articles, particularly to the alternative community (through the Underground Press Syndicate) on heroin and the social bureaucracy.

Within the acknowledgement section Allen Ginsberg is among those
thanked for their efforts.

1364 Norse, Harold. Carnivorous Saint, Gay Poems 1971-1976.
San Francisco, California: Gay Sunshine Press, 1977.
Carnivorous Saint is a collection of poems which reflect Harold Norse's "gay consciousness." Allen Ginsberg is mentioned in the author's introduction as one of the people whose path
crossed his in the "New York Scene."

1365 Pereira, Teresinha Alves. A Revolução das Moscas/Ensaios
de Literatura Ibero-americano. [A Revolution of the Flies,
Essays in Literature in Latin America]. Belo Horizonte,
Brazil: Livraria Sarara, 1975.
In this small, private Portuguese edition, on page 48,
there is an appreciation of Allen Ginsberg by Manuel Andujar.

1366 Peters, Rachael and Eero Ruuttila (eds.). Sitting Frog,
Poetry of Naropa Institute. (n.p.) 1976, unpaged, alpha-
betical listings.
Among the acknowledgments on page 6: "warm thanks
to Allen Ginsberg...."

E. POEMS/PROSE MENTIONING GINSBERG

1367 Ball, Gordon. "Woeful Cowboy." Sitting Frog, Poetry of
Naropa Institute, n.d., pp. 12-13.
Prose piece which refers to "working with Allen."

1368 Conkle, D. Steven. "Mémerè." Poem in the form of a
broadside ($8\frac{1}{2}$ x 11" vertical) in which Ginsberg is mentioned in line 1, "Ginsberg back at Jack's still trying to
make peace." Copyrighted 1975 by D. Steven Conkle.

1369 Lee, Jesse. "Ginsberg." Helix, 2 April 1970, v. 11, n. 14,
p. 6, with photograph.
Poem about Ginsberg's visit.

1370 Packard, William. "For Allen Ginsberg." Boxspring, Fall
1975, n.3, [p. 8].
Poem.

1371 Shanken, Zev. "Israel: After Allen Ginsberg's 'America.'"
Response: A Contemporary Jewish Review, Spring 1977,
v. XI, n. 1, cover no. 33, pp. 45-46.
Poem.

1372 Thygesen, Erik. "Ginsberg/Sorte Troldmaend." Super Love,
April 1969, n. 18, p. 14, with illustration. (In Danish).
This seems to be a poem to Ginsberg.

1373 Weiss, Betty. "Following." The University Magazine, A

Journal of Writing and Visual Art, April 1974, n. 1, p. 14.
Weiss inscribes this poem to Ginsberg. There is a
reference to him in line 28: "I whisper How's your big toe, Allen?"

F. ADVERTISEMENTS AND PUBLICITY POSTERS

English Language

1374 "Kaddish." (advertisements for the play). New York Times,
11 February 1972, p. 27, center; New York Post, 10
March 1972, n. p.; New York Times, 15 April 1972, n. p.
(Circle in the Square).

1375 Planet News (advertisement), in "Book List # 4." The Marijuana Review, January-March 1969, v. 1, n. 2, p. 16.

1376 "An Interview and Poem" (advertisement for Gay Sunshine, issue
n. 16). Georgia Straight, 7:285, 22-29 March 1973, p. 20.
"Ginsberg on Kerouac and the Beats, Peter Orlovsky,
sexuality, yoga, Walt Whitman, Burroughs, LSD, Cuba, Carl Solomon, Gay Liberation; and previously unpublished S & M poem,
'Please Master....'"

1377 Poetry reading (advertisement). Daily Planet, 1 January
1970, 1:1, page 11 (insert).
Advertisement for Ginsberg poetry reading with Bethlehem Asylum, a popular rock group at the Miami Marine Stadium
on December 22nd with a picture of Ginsberg and the rock band.
"Guess who coming to the Promised Land??? !*"

Foreign Language

French

1378 Place aux Poètes (Poet's Place). Place aux Poètes de tous
pays de tous temps (Poet's Place of all countries, of all
times) list includes Ginsberg's name.
An 8½ x 11" vertical poster advertising this reading
place: a la Casanous, 485 Ouest Sherbrooke coin aylmer, tous les
mercredis à 21. 30 h. (at the Casanous, 485 West Sherbrooke at
the corner of Aylmer, every Wednesday at 9:30 pm).

1379 "Rien Contre ça." ("Nothing Against That"). (14 x 8½" publicity
flyer).
"12 heures de poesie et de musique presenté par
l'ATEM et les productions Beau Bec dans le cadre de la rencontre
internationale 'de la contre-culture.' Apportez vos coussins.
dimanche 27 avril, de 14. 00 h. a 2. 00 h., Palais du Commence."
"12 hours of poetry and music presented by ATEM and
Beau Bec Productions in connection with the International Counter-
Culture Conference. Bring your cushions. Sunday 27 April 1977,
from 2 pm until 2 am, Palace of Commerce."

Allen Ginsberg is included among those who will appear. Second side: Calendar of events; includes at 7:00 pm (for comments) on April 25, 1977, Allen Ginsberg among others. (International Counter-Culture Conference presented by the Studio of Multidisciplinary Expression in connection with the National Library.)

German

1380 "Allen Ginsberg Live at St. Marks, N. Y. City" (advertisement for the Fall Program from S Press Publication of tapes, poster, $8\frac{1}{2}$ x 11, in German).
The tape records Ginsberg reading poetry with accompaniment on the guitar. It's 42 minutes, a 13 cm. roll, priced at 25 Marks, available from S Press (Michael Köhler/D-8 München 40/ Zieblandstrasse 10/Zieblandstrasse).

1381 Berlin Festival Weeks (color poster, 47" x 33", vertical).
"26th week Berliner Festwochen"/2 Sept. -2 October, at: Berliner Festspiele GmbH, Bundesallee 1-12, 1000 Berlin 15. Telefon 882 2081.
September 22, 23, 24 at 8:00 pm at Academy, Artistic readings from Allen Ginsberg, Susan Sontag, William Burroughs, New York.

1382 Berlin Festival (publicity/flyer). Festival "New Yorker-- Downtown Manhatten: SOHO." Akademie der Künste (Academy of the Arts), Berliner Festwochen (Berlin Festival). Ausstellungen-Performance-Video-Film-Tanz-Theater- Musik-Lesungen, 5 September-17 October 1976.
Includes: Allen Ginsberg/Mittwoch, 22. September 20 Uhr/Studio. (Wednesday ... 8:00 pm) Moderation: Fred Jordon and Walter Höllerer. Allen Ginsberg, führender Vertreter der modernen Gesellschafts kritischen Lyrik Amerikas, liest neuere, noch nicht ins Deutsche übersetzte Gedichte. (Allen Ginsberg, the leading representative of modern society, culture linguist of America, will read his new poems not yet translated into German.)
Filme mit Allen Ginsberg: Pull My Daisy, Buch: Jack Kerouac, Regie: Robert Frank und Alred Leslie; Me and My Brother, Regie: Jonas Mekas; A Film About Allen Ginsberg, Regie: Michael Cassidy.

1383 Poetry Reading: Poster, "Allen Ginsberg/Night Poetry Reading," $16\frac{1}{2}$ x $11\frac{1}{2}$, horizontal, 1976.
Held at Neues Arri-Kino, Turkenstrasse 9/ on Thursday, Sept. 30th at 10:30 p.m. Sponsored by the Cultural Committee of the Capital of the State at Munich.

Spanish

1384 "Allen Ginsberg/Planet News." El Corno emplumado (The Plumed Horn). 29 (1969): 37.
One-page advertisement for Planet News written in English as an advertisement for this literary magazine/review.

G. PHOTOGRAPHS

>   See also NEWSPAPERS in the Secondary Works
>   Section for photographs of Ginsberg.

1385 After Dark, The National Magazine of Entertainment, August
>   1974 (Special Issue: San Francisco, The People and The
>   Place), pp. 58-59. Photo by Zagaris.
>   Titled: "Lawrence Ferlinghetti smiles as Soviet poet
> Yevgeny Yevtushenko embraces him and fellow-poet Allen Ginsberg.
> Although a native of Yonkers, New York, Ferlinghetti has long been
> a resident of San Francisco where he, along with Ginsberg, first
> received attention in the mid-fifties as a strong poetic spokesman
> for the Beat Generation...."

1386 Ann Arbor Sun, 17-30 December 1971, 22, pp. 7-14. "Shots"
>   by David Fenton and LNS.
>   Photographs from the Underground to be published by
> Douglass Books and distributed by World Publishing, introduction
> by Ericka Huggins and Bobby Seale. On page 11 there is a photo-
> graph of Ginsberg.

1387 The Beat Book. Ed. by Arthur W. and Glee Knight. Cali-
>   fornia, Pa.: The Unspeakable Visions of the Individual
>   Press, 1974. Various photographs of all the Beats to-
>   gether and separately are included.

1388 Berkeley Barb, 2-8 July 1971, v. 12, n. 25, issue 307,
>   p. 3. Titled "Krishna's Little Helpers Do Their Things,"
>   by Gary Freedman.

1389 Berkeley Barb, "Living Theatre's Day in Court," 20-26
>   August 1971, 13: 6: 314, p. 7. With photo which includes
>   Allen Ginsberg by Mother Boats, titled "The Friends Really
>   Are!"

1390 Boulder Daily, 18 August 1977. Photo by Jerry Cleveland.
>   Allen Ginsberg is included (among others) in this news-
> paper photograph titled "Naropa Graduation--Wednesday was the first
> graduation day for Naropa Institute. Twenty certificates and degrees
> were awarded in subjects ranging from dance to Buddhist and West-
> ern psychology in ceremonies at Sacred Heart School. William Mc-
> Keever, Naropa's executive director, made the opening remarks."

1391 Changes: Journal of Arts & Entertainment, November 1974,
>   n. 90. Photo by Jill Krementz.
>   Photograph within interview with William Burroughs
> titled, "Jean Genet, Burroughs and Allen Ginsberg at the Chicago
> Convention in 1968."

1392 The Craft of Poetry: Interviews from the New York Quar-
>   terly. Ed. by William Packard. New York: Doubleday &
>   Co., 1974.
>   Includes photo of Ginsberg.

1393 Deciduous, n. d. , n. p. Photo by Christopher Frank. A 17" x 11½ " single sheet, folded in two with two-sided insert covered with prose, poetry, drawings and photographs. Ginsberg's photograph is amidst the collage.

1394 Diary of an Artist, by Raphael Soyer. Washington, D. C. : New Republic Books, 1977.
The Diary includes a reproduction of a painting of Allen Ginsberg titled, "Gregory Corso and Allen Ginsberg," dated 1965.

1395 Dorfman, Elsa. Allen Ginsberg's primary photographer. A complete list of photographs by Dorfman of the poet is available from The Witkin Gallery, 41 E. 57th Street, New York, New York; (212) 355-1461. Please contact them directly for further information.
See also Elsa's Housebook below.

1396 The East Village Other, volume 5, n. 16, March 24, 1970, p. 10.

1397 Elsa's Housebook: A Woman's Photojournal, by Elsa Dorfman. Boston: David R. Godine, Publisher, 1974.
Elsa's Housebook beautifully mixes visual documentation with prose in the form of journal text, both by the photographer. The book is completed with fine visual skill; each black and white photograph is outlined simply in black, titled by hand in black pen and placed carefully on the page. There is a simplicity to the accompanying journal text which matches the simple lines of the photographs. Allen Ginsberg is mentioned extensively in the "Flagg Street" section from pp. 16-21.
"Allen Ginsberg is a person dear to me in reality and important as an idea. About once a week, I'm in a situation that makes me ask myself, 'What would Allen have done?...'" Elsa recalls activities in November 1972 and then in April 1973, photographs accompany these thoughts about Allen. On page 16 there is a photograph of Allen Ginsberg seated on her couch, on page 17 is a photograph of Allen in a meditative position, on page 18 there is a photograph titled "Allen Ginsberg & Ed Sanders, 1972," on page 19 there is another titled "Allen Ginsberg on Sunday morning, 1973," on page 20 there is one "Allen Ginsberg and Gregory Corso, April 1973" and finally on page 21 there is one titled, "Allen Ginsberg and Peter Orlovsky, April 1, 1973." Incidentally the couch photograph is included as one of the three on the front cover of the book. "The November 1972 photographs are from a time Ed Sanders and Allen Ginsberg came to Cambridge to perform ... to raise money for a loose confederation of folk singers.... The pictures of Allen eating at the breakfast table, of Allen and Gregory Corso in the kitchen, of Allen and Peter Orlovsky in the living room, were all taken in April 1973. They were here for a Kerouac festival at Salem State College...."
See also Dorfman, Elsa, above.

1398 Fusion, 26 December 1969, n. 254, p. 50. Photo by Charles
       Steiner.

1399 Hartford's Other Voice, 12 May 1969, n. 1, n.p.

1400 Limberlost Review, v. 1, n. 2, 1977, n.p. Photo of Gins-
       berg with Kerouac and others by John Cohen.

1401 Liberation News Service. "Allen Ginsberg, John and Yoko,"
       18 December 1971, 400, p. 5, no credits.

1402 McDarrah, Fred. Of the Village Voice, he has also com-
       pleted major work on photographing Allen Ginsberg. For
       sale information contact him. His personal files begin
       in 1958. A list of his work with corresponding file num-
       bers is reprinted below (1969-1975). These photographs
       are for sale, not loan. Do not contact him for research
       purposes.
            (1794) At the American Academy of Arts & Letters
       party May 21, 1969. (2065) At National Book Awards with uniden-
       tified bearded man (Benjamin?) Mar. 2, 1971. (2187) Playing
       mantras in recording studio with Bob Dylan, David Amram and
       others Nov. 13, 1971. (2198) Portrait with scarf in Soho Gallery,
       December 18, 1971. (2204) Reading poetry at St. Mark's in
       Bowerie [sic] with Corso, Jan. 6, 1972. (2596) In audience at Bob
       Dylan concert with Al Aronowitz and Peter Orlovsky. Jan. 30, 1974.
       (2703) With Gordon Baer [sic] his biographer reading poetry Nov. 6,
       1974. (2814) At Columbia reading poetry with Burroughs and
       Corso on 16th anniversary of original poetry reading. April 17,
       1975.

1403 Masters of Contemporary Photography, The Photojournalist:
       Mary Ellen Mark & Annie Leibovitz. Text by Adrianne
       Marcus with the editors of Alskog, Inc. New York:
       Thomas Y. Crowell Company, Inc., Lawrence Schiller,
       1974.
            This is a softcover photojournal of "two women [who]
       explore the modern world and the emotions of individuals." The
       photographs included are in color with accompanying text about the
       two women photographers. Annie Leibovitz "concentrates on the
       United States, photographing icons of various youth cultures and
       countercultures." In the narrative about Annie and her crucial
       connection to Rolling Stone magazine, the following text is included:
       "She had asked to see the art director. She stood there, shifting
       from foot to foot, trying not to stare at the people flowing around
       her.... This can't be the place--Rolling Stone--I always read it.
       I even had it sent to me in Europe.... Half an hour later, she
       walked out in a daze: art director Robert Kinsbury not only liked
       the picture of Allen Ginsberg, he had bought it, then thanked her
       for getting it there just one day after she'd taken it...."

1404 Milwaukee Kaleidoscope, 24-30 August 1970, v. III, n. 11
       (# 63), p. 4.

Nude pose with Ginsberg's left hand covering genital area, right hand raised to take an oath.

1405 Ms. n.d., p. 105.
___ Four of Elsa Dorfman's photographs appear on pp. 104-105 as excerpts from her first book, Elsa's Housebook: A Woman's Photojournal. This is a publicity layout, not a review.

1406 Naked Angels, The Lives and Literature of the Beat Generation, by John Tytell. New York: McGraw-Hill, 1976. Includes photos.

1407 New York Quarterly, "Allen Ginsberg photographs," issue # 13.

1408 Newsweek, 24 July 1972, p. 32. Frederic Ohringer and Nancy Palmer.
Includes photo, "Sideshow: Tent City at Flamingo Park, Ginsberg and the old folks." Coincides with an article regarding the happenings at the Democratic National Convention in Miami Beach in 1972. A senior citizen holds up a book Sex and the Senior Citizen.

1409 Nola Express, 30 October-12 November 1970, n. 67, p. 9, in the context of the Sykes interview.
Photograph of Allen Ginsberg with "Roosevelt Sykes (Blues)."

1410 Nola Express, 25 December-7 January 1971, p. 2. Photo of Ginsberg with attorney Richard Sobol and Henry Baker to go with article by Shaman on the Jim DeGraff trial, "Free Yourself & Free Jim DeGraff.... Jim DeGraff goes on trial ... for possession and sale of LSD (to a Federal agent) ... LSD is a way of life and Jim DeGraff refuses to cop out...."

1411 Scenes Along the Road: Photographs of the Desolation Angels, 1944-1960. Ed. by Ann Charters. New York: Gotham Book Mart, 1971.
This book consists of a series of photographs compiled by Ann Charters, with three poems and comments by Allen Ginsberg. The book of photographs includes: 1) New York, 1944-1954; 2) On the Road, 1947-1956; 3) San Francisco and Berkeley, 1954-1959; 4) Mexico and Abroad, 1951-1960.
"Scenes Along the Road is a collection of snapshots of a group of men before they become as Jack Kerouac put it 'famous writers, more or less.'"

1412 Statesman, 8 February 1972, v. 15, n. 31, n.p. Photograph of Allen Ginsberg with Peter, Ken, Rich.
Marked as such in pen when Allen Ginsberg and Peter Orlovsky spoke to a large group at Stonybrook.

1413 Vinduet [Norwegian publication]. 1974, 28 yr., n. 3, p. 25, followed by comments on page 26.

1414 Vogue, February 1978, v. 168, n. 2, whole n. 3152, pp. 192-3. Photo by Leonid Lubianitsky of Ginsberg facing Andrei Voznesensky.
"Andrei Voznesensky (left) the noted Russian poet, has been on an extensive poetry-reading tour of the U.S.A. He met old friend Allen Ginsberg (right) in New York City, and talked with him about shifting sensibilities in America. At Max's Kansas City, a NYC club, Voznesensky was introduced to punk rock...." Coinciding with interview by Olga Carlisle, "Poets and Peace" of Andrei Voznesensky, pp. 193-4, 244.

1415 Volz, Timothy. 1912 Ward Street, Berkeley, California, 94703, (415) 548-1264. Photos of Ginsberg available.

1416 Washington Star, 10 February 1976, n. p. Photo of Ginsberg by Walter Oates.

1417 Westport Trucker, 1971, v. 2, n. 15 (24), p. 2. Photo by David Fenton (Rainbow Peoples Party /LNS).
Coincides with "Free John Rally Draws 15,000" from UPS which records the Ann Arbor, Michigan gathering in Chrisler Auditorium (Ginsberg was present).

1418 Win, 15 November 1969, p. 16. Photo by Hap Stewart.

1419 Win, 1 December 1969, n. p. back cover.
Uncle Sam pose.

APPENDIX A

ALLEN GINSBERG DEPOSIT IN THE
RARE BOOK AND MANUSCRIPT LIBRARY,
COLUMBIA UNIVERSITY*

Unpublished Material

1937-1969   Deposit (this deposit is organized):
Name file: 12 boxes
Correspondence and miscellaneous (mss. other than
A.G.; 1939-1969, arranged chronologically): 18
boxes
Drawings: 2 boxes
Manuscripts--by titles: 7 boxes
Manuscripts--untitled poems: 1 box
Manuscripts--untitled prose and miscellaneous notes:
1 box
Notebooks and journals (1937-1964): 4 boxes
Junior High and High School materials: 1 box
Columbia College: 1 box
Photographs: 7 boxes
Maps: 1 box
Clippings (1942-1972): 4 boxes
Memorabilia: 1 box

March 1970   Deposit:
11 boxes completely unidentified in envelopes from
Gotham Book Mart: approx. 1/3 printed material.

1971   Deposit:
5 boxes with no printed material, only correspondence or manuscript materials.

1972   Deposit:
7 boxes, completely unidentified. See 1970.

1973   Deposit:
Total of 21 boxes: 8 clearly identified as manuscript materials or correspondence; 13 unidentified. See 1970

1974   Deposit:
4 unidentified boxes. See 1970

---

*Compiled by Kenneth A. Lohf, Librarian for Rare Books and Manu-
scripts; Mary Bowling, Reference Librarian and Bibliographer; Bernard Crystal, Assistant Librarian for Manuscripts.

Published Works

Airplane Dreams, compositions from journals. Toronto: Anansi,
1968.

Bixby Canyon, Ocean Path Word Breeze. New York: Gotham Book
Mart, 1972. via Andreas Brown: "First publication in the
world issue no. 24, Winter 1972." No. 15 of 100 copies numbered and autographed by the poet. Inscribed by the poet to
Columbia University.

The Dream of Tibet. With William Burroughs' The Retreat Diaries.
New York: City Moon, 1976.

Empty Mirror; early poems. Introduction by William Carlos Williams. New York: Totem Press, 1961. Inscribed by author
to Philip Whalen.

"The Fall of America" Wins a Prize. New York: Gotham Book
Mart and Gallery, 1974 folder (4ℓ.) 23 cm.
"This is one of 126 special copies numbered 1-100 and lettered
A-Z and signed by the author."
This copy is no. 35 and lettered "F."

First Blues: Rags, Ballads and Harmonium Songs, 1971-1974. New
York: Full Court Press, 1975.

The Gates of Wrath; Rhymed Poems, 1948-1952. 1st edition. Bolinas, California: Grey Fox Press, 1972.

Howl and Other Poems. San Francisco: City Lights Pocket Bookshop, 1956.

Howl of the Censor. Lawrence Ferlinghetti, defendant. 1st Edition,
San Carlos, California: Nourse Publishing Company, 1961.
144 pp., 22 cm.

Howl for Carl Solomon. San Francisco, 1956. 15ℓ., 28 cm.

Howl for Carl Solomon. San Francisco: Grabhorn-Hoyem, 1971,
1959. 43 p., 30 cm. "With recent minute revisions ... and
the addition of a related fragment The Names...."
One of 275 copies autographed by the poet. Cover drawing by
Robert LaVigne. Prospectus laid in.

Improvised Poetics. Edited, with an introduction by Mark Robinson.
1st Edition, San Francisco: Anonym Press, 1971. 51ℓ.p., illus.,
17 cm. 1 of 1000 copies.
A selected bibliography: p. 52.

Indian Journals. San Francisco: Dave Haselwood Books, 1970.
210 p., illus. 21 cm.

Kaddish. 2nd Edition. San Francisco: City Lights Books, 1964, 1961. 100 p., 17 cm., n. 14. Autographed by the author.

The Moments Return. San Francisco: Grabhorn-Hoyem, 1970, 5ℓ., col., illus., 24x39 cm., with three drawings by Robert La Vigne. 1 of 200 copies autographed by the poet and the illustrator.

New York Blues. 1st Edition. New York: Phoenix Book Shop, 1972. 15 p., 14x19 cm. (Phoenix Book Shop oblong octavo series, no. 14). No. 32 of 100 copies numbered and autographed by the author.

On Huncke's Book, 1973. The Unspeakable Visions of the Individual. Herbert Huncke issue. California, Pennsylvania: Stripmine Publications, 1973. 72 p., illus., 28 cm. (v. 3, n. 1-2, 1973). Publisher from New Ser. Tit., Jan-Mar 1973. "This issue is dedicated to Herbert Huncke." Included On Huncke's Book by Allen Ginsberg and From My Last Two Thousand Years, by Herbert Gold.

Rain-wet asphalt heat, garbage curbed cans over flowing. Detroit: The Alternative Press, 1969? broadside, 13x21 cm. Copy 2 inscribed by the author to Herbert Huncke.

Scrap Leaves: tasty scribbles.... New York: Printed at Sri Ram Ashram for the Poet's press, 1968. 16 p., illus., 19 cm. Poems. "Old Poet's Extra" copy of 150 signed by the author.

T. V. Baby Poems. Series by Victorian Sardou, Allen Ginsberg and the Great Crystal, cover photograph by Malcolm Hart. London: Cape Goliard Press, 1967, 31 p., illus., 25 cm.

To Eberhart from Ginsberg. Lincoln, Massachusetts: Penmaen Press, 1976. No. 221 of 300 signed by the correspondents.

The Visions of the Great Rememberer. by Allen Ginsberg; with letters by Neal Cassady; and drawings by Basil King. Amherst, Massachusetts: Mulch Press, 1974. 71 p., 3 leaves of plates, illus, 22 cm. 'A Haystack Book.' RGM/MMF 9-30-77. Gift of Basil King.

Wichita Vortex Sutra. San Francisco: Coyte; distributed by City Lights Books, 1966. 15 p., 22 cm. Cover--title. "This edition has been limited to 500 copies."

Wichita Vortex Sutra. Berkeley, California: n.p., 1966. 4 p., illus., 40 cm. From the Berkeley Barb, v. 2., n. 21, May 17, 1966.

Published Works by Others

Brooks, Eugene. Rites of Passage. Introduction by Allen Ginsberg and Louis Ginsberg. Plainsview, New York, 1973. ix, 119 p., 22 cm.

Charters, Ann, comp. Scenes Along the Road. New York: Gotham, 1970. 56 p., illus., 26 cm. Paperback edition, inscribed by Ginsberg and Columbia University and autographed by compiler.

Charters, Ann, comp. Scenes Along the Road. New York: Gotham, 1970. One of the 200 hardbound copies.

Charters, Ann, comp. Scenes Along the Road. New York: Gotham, 1970. One of 50 specially bound copies.

Genet, Jean. May Day Speech (pamphlet). Description by Allen Ginsberg. San Francisco: City Lights, 1970. 25 p., 21 cm. $1.00.

Ginsberg, Louis. Morning in Spring and Other Poems. New York: Morrow, 1970. 125 p., 22 cm., $5.00. Inscribed by the author. Autographed by Allen Ginsberg.

Kerouac, John. Vision of Cody. Introduction by Allen Ginsberg. 1st Edition xii, 398 p., illus., 24 cm. $8.95.

Kramer, Jane. Allen Ginsberg in America. New York: Random House, 1969. xix., 202 p., 22 cm., $4.95.

Lucie-Smith, Edward. Mystery in the Universe; notes on an interview with Allen Ginsberg. London: Turret Books, 1965. 9 p., 19 cm. Number 26 of 200 copies autographed by the author. "This interview ... was originally commissioned by The Sunday Times, and some of the material first appeared in the columns."

San Francisco Bay Area Prose Poets' Phalanxe. Declaration of Independence for Dr. Timothy Leary, July 4, 1971: Model Statement in defense of the philosopher's personal freedom/proposed by San Francisco Bay Area Prose Poets' Phalanxe. San Francisco. San Francisco: Hermes Free Press, 1971. 8 p., 22 cm. Cover title. Declaration signed by Allen Ginsberg and others.

Van Buskirk, Alden. Lami. With an introductory note by Allen Ginsberg. San Francisco: The Auerhahn Society, 1965. 91 p., port. 24 cm. On cover: "The last poems of a poet who died in his early 20's.... Collected from his writings by David Rattray." Reprinted in part from various periodicals. One of 1000 copies.

APPENDIX B

INDEX TO GINSBERG TAPES AND CASSETTES*

(in the Ginsberg Deposit at Columbia University)

Key to Indexing System

1) The first two digits are the year, e.g., 68 = 1968.
2) The third element, a letter, represents the tape classification, e.g., 68A: "A" = poetry.
   A Poetry
   B Blake (usually sung)
   C Mantras
   D Taped Conversation
   E Interviews (including TV and Radio)
   F Lectures
   R Random assemblages of tapes
   S Song, Song composition, Song rehearsal
   P Club Date (mixed poetry, song, mantra etc.)
3) The fourth digit is the number of tapes containing the program, for example, 68A2 means a two-reel or cassette program.
4) The next three digits after the slash represent the identification number of each reel or cassette, e.g., 68A2/012 is the twelfth reel or cassette logged for the year 1968. Its companion tape would be 68A2/013. Recording dates are not chronological within a year.
5) A "C" in brackets or quotes indicates a cassette.
6) "5" indicates a five-inch size reel.
7) "7" indicates a seven-inch reel.
8) A "K" noted with or around an index number indicates the tape is being kept at home by Allen Ginsberg.
9) Complete date of recording follows if known.

Pre-1968 Tapes

59E1/001 WFMT Chicago 1958 "7." Studs Terkel interviews Allen Ginsberg, Peter Orlovsky and Gregory Corso. Time of Big Table Reading.

63A1/001 11/26/63 (Pacifica Tape). Allen Ginsberg Reads.

64A1/001C "C" Nov. 24, 1964. Allen Ginsberg reading "Kaddish." Brandeis Univ. Dub of Atlantic Verbum 4000 NY 1968.

64A1/002 "5" 11/23/64. Allen and Louis Ginsberg read and discuss family life in N.J. (Pacifica Tape)

*Compiled by Bob Rosenthal, Neil Hackman, and Michael Scholnick.

64A1/004 "7" 11/24/64. Ginsberg, Orlovsky, Brandeis U. Vietnam Sign, Telephone, The Charge, Whitman, My Sad Self, To an old Poet in Peru, Orlovsky reading, Ginsberg intro. to Kaddish.

65E1/001 "C" 1/11/65. Allen and Louis Ginsberg. Sandra Hochman program, KPFA--conversation and poetry.

66C1/001 (K). Anthology of best mantras '65 & '66.

66C2/001A and 66C2/001B 5/30/66. Let's Take a Trip: Acid and Sociology (Pacifica Tape)

66A1/002 "5" 5/11/66. LIU Read-In Vietnam, Professor Economou.

66C1/003 "5" 2/66. Allen Ginsberg and Peter Orlovsky. Hare Krishna Mantra, Lincoln, Nebraska.

66F4/035 Nov. 12 '66. Lecture Question and Answers, Utilitarian Church, Boston, Mass.

67D1/001 (K). Gregory Corso on Spontaneous zither.

1968

68B1/001 "5" nos. 1-14 (excluding 4). First anthology Blake dubs.

68B1/002 "5." Blake Grey Monk Rehearsal, Voice of Ancient Bard.

68A2/002A "7" 6/68. A. Ginsberg, W. Lowenfels, Dick Higgins, J. Ashbery, R. Creeley discuss National Book award. (Pacifica Tapes)

68A2/002B-68A1/003 "7" 4/8/68. A.G. in San Francisco at the "Rolling Renaissance." (Pacifica Tapes)

68A1/004 and 68A2/004 contd. "7" 1/19/68. Allen & Louis Ginsberg reading. (Pacifica Tapes)

68C1/005. Discussion of government pressure and people in underground film produced by Jim Berland for KPFK also discussion with producers D'Antonio and Lampson about the making of the film and Weather Underground. (Pacifica Tapes)

68A1/006 "7" reel 2 7/31/68. The poetry of madness (Pacifica Tapes). Essalin Meeting, Longshoreman's Hall, San Francisco.

68C1/006A "7." Julian Siberman, John Perry, Caludio Narango, Allen Ginsberg, Alan Watts in San Francisco symposium. (Pacifica Tapes) Same place as above.

68A1/007 "7" 6/8/68 (Pacifica Tapes).
Reading by Lew Welch, Phillip Whalen, M. McClure, L. Ferlinghetti, David Meltzer, John Weiners, and Allen Ginsberg.

68C1/008 "7" (Pacifica Tapes). Discussion on LSD and art and life with T. Leary, Gary Snyder, and Allen Ginsberg.

68A1/009 "C" February 13-15, 1968. A. Ginsberg reading at Union College in Schenectady, N. Y.

68B1/009A "5" August 10, 1968. First recordings of Blake w/ Dan Moore and Grey Monk, A. G. voice and harmonium. Duet w/ Moore--When God commanded this; Thousands Strong; Dan Moore solo--I Die to End; August 12, 1968--on airplane.

68S1/018 (inadvertently numbered 018) "5" Dec. 17, 1968. To Tirzah; The Schoolboy; Side B--Dub of Dub of Blake Anthology 1/31/69. A. G. , Cyril Caster, Lee Crabtree, P. Orlovsky, Charles Gokum.

68B1/019 (inadvertently numbered 019). Ginsberg Blake Intro. , Shepherd, Echoing Green, The Lamb, Little Black Boy, Blossom, Chimney Sweeper, Little Boy Lost, Little Boy Found, Laughing Song, Holy Thursday, Night Experience, Nurses Song, Sick Rose, Ah Sunflower, Garden of Love, London, Human Abstract, Tirzah, Grey Monk.

1969

69B1/001 "5. " Allen Ginsberg Apostolic Blake, mono.

69B1/002 "5" March 30, 1969. Blake--Jerusalem; crystal cabinets, improvisation.

69B1/003 "5" January 24, 1969. Blake dubs of best available Revelations; also conversation w/Carl Rakosi.

69A1/004 "7" Allen Ginsberg reading at New School, N. Y. 2/25/69. (Pacifica Tapes "Ginsberg at the New School") Archive # BB3774. 00, . 01, .02.

69B1/004A. Side 1 Songs of Innocence and Experience--Blake dub of MGM Verve FtS 3083 1969--Intro. ; The Shepherd; The Echoing Green; The Lamb: The Little Black Boy; The Blossom; The Chimney Sweeper; The Little Boy Lost; The Little Boy Found; Laughing Song; Holy Thursday Night Experience. Side 2 Intro. (Voice of Bard); Nurses Song; The Sick Rose; Ah Sunflower; The Garden of Love; also 1971 Blake Recordings in San Francisco (Album II): A Cradle Song, The Divine Image; Spring; Nurses Song; Infant Joy; Side 2 (after a tape gap continues with): A Dream; On Another's Sorrow; Holy Thursday; The Fly; The School Boy; The Voice of the Ancient Bard; Musicians: Scholle--Human Abstract; To Tirzah, The Grey Monk Band, Don Cherry, Elvin Jones, Herman Wright, Arthur Russel, John Meyers, Alan Senauke. Vocals and Tunes by Allen Ginsberg.

69A2/004 B.   Blake & Mantras 2/20/69.

69A1/005 "7."   October 22, 1969.   Allen Ginsberg talks about
Kerouac.   (Pacifica Tapes "Ginsberg on Kerouac") Archive #
BB3463.

69C1/005A "5."   Ginsberg talking to Don McNeil of Village Voice
and project to document police involvement in drug traffic.

69A1/006 "C"   Allen Ginsberg speaks of 20th-century prosody and
its cultural consequence; attends to Ezra Pound.

69E1/007 "C"   Late 1969.   Allen Ginsberg broadcast on CBC for
use in English 414 Simon Fraser University (Vancouver) opening
paragraph (1 page transcribed w/tape ... chanting articulates
the mutuality of soul ... speech making doesn't touch on ...
home from the convention I began tuning Blake.)

69D1/008 "5"   November 1, 1969.   Cherry Valley, N.Y.   Initiation
ceremony Saligram Sukla.

69B1/009 "5"   1/31/69.   Dub of dub of Blake tunes done.

69A1/010 "7."   Allen and Louis Ginsberg read new work recalling
father and son life.

1970

70D1/001 "C"   May 7, 1970.   Conversation with Carl Solomon "Odd
Bird."   Phonecall w/Sherwood Bishop of Liberation May 29, 1970.
also on tape--June 3--Harry Smith Birthday visit to E. 12th St.

70A1/002 "C" (K).   Tape of Charles Bukowski distributed by Nola
Express, Box 2342 New Orleans, L.A.   70116.

70D1/003 "C"   September 11, 1970.   Maretta Greer, Prajnaparamita,
across border Toronto Drug Conference.   Side B--stopped by
cops Canadian border Sept. 14, September 20; Maretta & Allen
Ginsberg duet; Cradle Song.

70B1/004 "C"   August 10, 1970.   Allen Ginsberg and Peter Orlovsky--
On Another's Sorrow, The Divine Image.

70B1/005 "C"   July 1970.   A.G. Blake improvisations.

70D1/006 "C"   July 4, 1970.   Gordon Ball conversation with Allen
Ginsberg & others.   Side B--July 18th, 1970, Allen Ginsberg w/
Peter Orlovsky--Human Abstract, On Another's Sorrow, Echoing
Green, Spring, Gregory Corso speaking.

70D1/007 "C"   July 10th 1970.
Allen Ginsberg conversation w/Lucien Carr in auto on way to

Albany from Cherry Valley, New York. Side B--Conversation with Robert Creeley, Gordon Ball, upon arriving in Boston for Student Strike Fund Reading (June 10?).

70D2/008A "C" same as D1 (continuation of D1 above).

70D2/008 "C" July 15th 1970. Claude Pélieu, Mary Beach, Allen Ginsberg--Revision of T.V. Baby Poem--French translation--"I Am from the Central One Come Blow the Cosmic Horn."

70B1/009 "C" August 11, 1970. Allen Ginsberg & Peter Orlovsky-- On Another's Sorrow, The Divine Image.

70D1/010 "C" July 30, 1970. Front Yard babble of Plymel, Pélieu, Ginsberg, Corso, Beach, De Loach. Side 2--On Another's Sorrow (variations).

70D1/011 "C" June 28th 1970. Louis Ginsberg talking, Newark Houses; A.G. --On Another's Sorrow, Firefly Walk, Peter drunk.

70C1/012 "C" June 11, 1970. 2AM chant in Harvard yard--Pad- masambhava, Blake's Spring w/chorus to end side 1. Side 2-- Jazzy Hare Krishna--occasion of neighborhood Cambridge strike against Harvard; car poesy w/Creeley June 16th; Nurse's song-- Cherry Valley.

70C1/013 "7" April 22, 1970. Son of Earth Day--speeches in Phila- delphia by Allen Ginsberg, Pete Seeger, Tom Stokes, George Wald. (Pacifica Tapes "Son of Earth Day")Archive # BB3960.

70A1/014 "7" December 7, 1970. Allen Ginsberg reading among others. (Pacifica Tapes "Writers and Writing") Archive # BB2919.

70C1/014 "5" February 13, 1970. Allen Ginsberg conversation with Gary Getz, Ray Bremser.

70S1/015 "5" January 21, 1970. Allen Ginsberg w/autoharp, Ray Bremser harmonica. Jerusalem, When I Died, Broken Time experiment.

70S1/016 "5" January 19, 1970. Cherry Valley, New York--Lucien Carr present. When I Died, Ballad (written A.G. 1948, music 1970), also Little Boy Lost and Little Boy Found.

70S1/017 "C" February 13, 1970. Gary Getz and Allen Ginsberg (on piano)--Youth of Delight.

70S1/018 "5" February 5, 1970. Gary Getz, Allen Ginsberg--Sound the Flute.

70S1/019 and 70S2/019 "5" February 17, 1970. Divine Image, Nurses Song, Youth of Delight-(twice), Spring Frankenstein, Tree Ode Heart of Texas Blues.

70D1/019 "5" October 18, 1970. OM orgy San Francisco distributed by Alternative Project One Media, 389 Howard St., San Francisco. Benefit for Timothy Leary with Dan Moore, Tibetan Opera Co.

70B1/020 "5" February 11, 1970. Allen Ginsberg--Blake--A Dream, also--Indian Mode, HUM and OM, G. Getz guitar, A.G. vocal, energetic voice duet (A.G. organ). Side 2--Hare Krishna.

70B1/021 "5" February 10, 1970. The Divine Image, When I Died w/Ray Bremser. Gary Getz--bass and electric guitar.

70S1/022 "5" (See 68B1/009A.) First Grey Monk experiment w/Don Moore, San Francisco--Alone Can Free the World from Fear, Angel King, War's Overthrow, I Die I Die the Mother said ... Children lack bread.

70S1/023 "5" 2/18/70 Allen Ginsberg "OK" Spring variation.

70S1/024 "5"

1971

71S1/001K "7." Holy Soul Jelly Roll. Side two--Final Mix.

71S1/002K "7." 11/19/71. Greaser Jam. Ginsberg, Dylan.

71S1/003 "7." 2/17/71. Ginsberg Song rehearsal; Dylan.

71S1/004K "7." Jessore Road--Nov. 17, '71--Final Mix.

71S1/005 "7." 11/24/71. Jessore Road, Hari Om Namo.

71BM/006 "7." Vol. II Blake Songs/Mantras Sholle/Russel/ Myers/Senanke, Summer 1971, Pacifica High Studio, San Francisco.

71B1/007 "7." 7/14/71 Blake Songs of Innocence & Experience, dub. Copyright Poetry Music Inc.

71C1/009 "C" July 1971. Allen Ginsberg--Pacific Sound, San Francisco. 1) Padmasambhava Mantra, 2) Om Mani Padme Hum, 3) Ong Namo Shivya, 4) Ragdupate Raj Hava Raja Ram.

71B1/010 "C" July-August 1971 (K). Side 1--San Francisco--Blake Holy Thursday, Infant Joy, Voice of the Ancient Bard, The Schoolboy, The Divine Image, The Fly, Cradle Song, On Another's Sorrow, Nurse's Song, Spring, A Dream. Side 2--Mantras-- Om E Ah Hum Vapuri, Guru Padme, Om Namah Shivya, Ragdupate Rajhava Raja Ram.

71D1/011 "C" March 20, 1971. Allen Ginsberg discussion with

Karnow on ICC involvement in illicit opium traffic in Southeast Asia.

71D2/011 "C" March 21.

71D3/011 "C."

71D4/011 "C."

71D5/011 "C."

71S1/012. 45 record--David Amram Quintet & Rambling Jack Elliot. Side A--Rambling Jack Elliot--"Going North" (RCA SPS-45-298). Side B--David Amram--"Pull My Daisy" (Amram, Kerouac, Ginsberg).

71B1/013 "C." Allen Ginsberg, Volume II--Blake Songs and Mantras. Human Abstract, Cradle Song, Spring, Nurses Song, Infant Joy, The Emmet Hum, On Another's Sorrow, Chimney Sweep, The Fly, The Schoolboy.

71A1/014 "C" April 13, 1971. Platteville, Wisconsin--Police Science Department Lecture. Side B--4/14 Railroad poesy, St. Paul; 4/15 conversation after reading Tyrone Guthrie Theatre, Minn.; East Dubuque Mississippi Poem.

71B1/015 "C" 8/21/71 (K). Blake/Mantras Album II recorded Pacific High Studios--Allen Ginsberg, John Sholle, J. Southie, P. Hombeck, Jigme, Solo: The Divine Image; Holy Thursday, Infant Joy; Remix: Voice of the Ancient Bard; Remix: The Schoolboy; Ragupate Rag Have (w/Jigme Cello).

71S1/016 "C" Oct. 31, 1971 (K). Side 1--Vajraguro--Dylan on organ, Amram, A. Ginsberg, Peter Orlovsky; talk pertaining to chords G♯, C♯, F♯, organ drone starts recording from other room, Infant Joy (twice) Holy Thursday, The Fly. Side 2--Amram improvising, Dylan on guitar, Spring, Merrily Dream; Amram Flute solo, Om Mani Padme Hum; Dylan lesson on chords.

71D1/017 "C" September 8, 1971. Side A--Tarapith--Sadhu Kali Bhaganon Das--smoking and prayer. Side B--September 8, refugee camps to Sept. 9, Kopo Takshe floods.

71D1/018A Sept. 9, 1971. At River Kapolal, John Giorno, Noon, Flood.

71D1/018B "C" Sept. 12, 1971. Dusk in Benares--Nagranand, and Trilochan. September 14--Rickshaw to Sarnath--circumambulation of Stupa; Dharma and John Giorno; Lama picture stand at Galugpa Temple chanting; Kirtan Pasaummedha Ghat--Benares.

71S1/019 "C" November 13, 1971. Tsaid Kogi mantra and songs of Jigme; end calm version of Jessore Road.

71D1/020 "C" October 14, 1971. Paterson, N.J., desultory conver-

sation in car to Irvington General Hospital. Side B--Louis and
Allen Ginsberg and Abe in Irvington (1/3 side).

71B1/021 "C." Blake rehearsals--Infant Joy, Holy Thursday--with
Jigme and Sholle.

71D1/022 "C" September 12, 1971. Benares--Trilochan, Allen Ginsberg, Nagranand, John Giorno--Kabir Math; Trilochan Shastra--
afternoon; Kabir Math--Sadhu Songs; w/Khanjari--drum "This
world's useless"; Nagranand singing Kabir "Renounce Worldly
Tastes, they are troublesome," "Enjoyment causes disease ...
This is whole life, death, merrymaking, trouble."

71B1/023 "C" July 1971. Blake Songs, Youth of Delight, etc.--Pad-
masambhava Mantra--recorded San Francisco.

71D1/024 "C" September 2, 1971. Calcutta, Salt lake refugee
camp. Sept. 4 w/Mustapha--guide of Bangladesh; Laxman Das,
Shanbinbetan--September 6, 1971.

71E1/024 "C" October 16, 1971. Earth's Answer--on airplane; In-
terview w/Channel 2 TV, Dayton, Ohio, October 25, 1971;
Gregory Corso, David Amram. Side B--Rag Hipate Raghava,
November 7, 1971--Jigme, Peter, Allen, Denise.

71D1/025 "C" January 27, 1971. Zogchen Sadhana, NYC--Sonum
Kaze & Saide Lama; Sheldon Cholst, M.D., on opium.

71C1/026 "C" June 8, 1971. Surya Mantras; Infant Joy with Peter
Hornbeck. Side B--Berkeley.

71D1/027 "C" February 2, 1971. Allen Ginsberg phone conversation--
illicit Southeast Asia opium.

71A1/028 "C" Sept. 28th 1971. Poetry Airplane utterances; San
Francisco, Sept. 26, 1971--Sri Ram--Jigme and friends, Ellen,
Jeff, Allen.

71D1/029 "C." Davis, Ram Das Muni, Allen Ginsberg--Blake Songs,
including Infant Joy; conversation.

1972

72E2/001 "C" March 14, 1972. KBEA-KBEY 1701 S. 55th St.,
Kansas City, Kansas. Interview w/Allen Ginsberg.
72E2/001A "C" interview continued through side 1.

72S2/002 "C" February 22, 1972. Allen Ginsberg and musicians at
Zen Center--Prajna Paramita; Padmasambhava Mantra; Dharma
Blues; Jessore Road; OM Mani Padme Hum.
72S2/002A--OM Mani Padme Hum, contd.

72D1/003 "C" June 18, 1972 (K). Auto Poesy Denver; Santa Fe June 14, June 17th and 18th--Chants. Side 2--Bhagavan Das aids Allen and chorus in tent, w/Laura, Anita, Allen Ginsberg.

72S1/004 "C" 7/72 (K). Ed Askew, 14 Sylvan Avenue, New Haven, Conn. --original Songs, harmonica and guitar.

72S2/005 "C" October 25, 1972. Davidson College, North Carolina; "Bob Dylan Blues I Guess." Side 2 blank.
72S2/005A "C." Same as 72S1/005.

72C1/006 "C." November 27th, Washington, D. C. 1) Prajnaparamita. 2) Ram Das, Om Namah Shivya.

72D1/006A "C." December 1972--January 1973. Allen, Peter, Gregory, Steven B. --New Year's Eve--Cherry Valley, N. Y. Thoughts Sitting. Side B--Allen Ginsberg and Gregory Corso argument--January 26, 1973.

72B1/007 "C." June 28, 1972. Blake--Clod and Pebble, Sunflower; July 7, Allen Ginsberg on harmonium singing Blake; July 2, Cherry Valley--Blake; August--Dellinger, Miami.

72S1/008 "C" January 1, 1972. A New Year's remembrance for Allen Ginsberg from Lawrence Ferlinghetti--San Francisco--L. Ferlinghetti sings Blake w/John Fahey on guitar.

72D1/009 "C" May 7, 1972 (K). Chögyam Trungpa--A Ah Sha Ma Ha; Snyder, Nansoi, Allen. June 10--Teton Village Mountain-- Gaté, Sambhava, IOU syllable Mantra. Discussion: Food Offering, lineage.

72S1/010 "C" Spring 1972. Peter practicing. Side B--Allen and Bhagavan Das improvise.

72A2/011A "7" April 29, 1972. Contemporary American Poetry (Pacifica Tapes, "Collage Poetry"), Archive # BC0730. Ginsberg, Ferlinghetti, Levertov, Snyder, Bly, Dylan.
72A2/011B "5."

72A1/012 "C" March 24, 1972, through March 29, 1972 (K). Voznesensky, poem and conversation; spontaneous mind rehearsals-- "can't fall off the mountain ... sorrowful Jack..."; Australian desert chants, learned & gently remembered; babble haikus, Bliss to Brian, Everywhere Always; Bliss to Flys (actual buzz; Ginsberg heard voice of Kerouac, "deep and straight" say, "Ginsberg"; Voznesensky "reading from mind" Khrushchev. See also 72E3/012.

72D1/013 "C" April 9, 1972. Side A--Alaska song ending w/corn game, 11-12 PM.

72D1/014 "C" March 7, 1972. Fiji--Ferlinghetti luncheon conversation at Iron Table; South sea songs. Side B--Adelaide, Australia.

72S1/015 "C" Post Adelaide--March 16, 1972 (K). Brian Moore Empty Bed Blues; Melbourne midnight. 2) Midnight Blues, Hotel Windsor ... "turn usefulness in different direction, transmit attention as Whitman, Kerouac did."

72D1/015A. This is your life William Burroughs, assembled by Peter Newton "5" 1/72.

72D1/016 "C" March 15, 1972. Aborginal Songmen--South Australia School of Arts.

72D1/017 "C" March 11, 12, 1972. Adelaide, Australia--Supper conversation--Mr. and Mrs. A. D. and Penelope Hope, Geoff Hutton and Lawrence Ferlinghetti.

72E1/018 "C" KITKIDIZE, February 18, 1972. Gary Snyder--Woodfish 1) Daikishion Doran (compassionate one); 2) Four Vows; 3) Turning over Merit.

72E1/019 "C" March 19, 1972 (K). Sidney, Australia. Airport interview; March 21--Brian Moore--Farewell Blues.

72D5/020. Australian Tapes, March 28, 1972. Yirkalla, Land mourning.

72D5/021 March 28, 1972. Walkabout Motel--Ginsberg, Vosnesensky, Kim Lockwood interview, Morning Ceremony.

72D5/022 March 28, 1972. Ceremony contd.

72D5/023. Australia, Alice Springs, Riverside Hotel, Public Songs & Noises, March 22, 1972.

72D5/024. Australia, April, 1972. Abascan Pottach and Dance New Minto Chant, Alaska.

72A1/015. Ukrainian Translation of Ginsberg's Poem. A Supermarket in California, Trans. by Ivan Drach.

1973

73S1/001 February 27, 1973 "C." Allen Ginsberg--Broken Leg Blues (rehearsal), Prayer Blues. Conversation with Louis Ginsberg. April 17, Cambridge, Mass. --Ram Dass regarding Leary and some music.

73E1/002 June 4, 1973 "C." Allen Ginsberg--Interview with Alice Garr, Vancouver, B. C. , KLG FM.

73S1/003 April 27, 1973 "C." Allen Ginsberg--Everybody's Queer Twice w/Peter Orlovsky and Denise Mercedes. December 21, First Blues 4AM, Come All Ye White Boys. December 23, Airplane Blues.

73S1/004 October 23, 1973 "C." Cortland, New York--Allen Ginsberg and Peter Orlovsky improvising.

73S1/005 February 10, 1973 "C." Cherry Valley, New York, Allen Ginsberg--Broken Bone Blues, Lord I'm Scared, 4 AM Prayer, Blake.

73B2/006 "5" Spring. A.G., Bob Dylan, Happy Traum, Dave Amram, Arthur Russel, March 7, '73.

73B2/007 "5" Spring. March 7, 1973.

73P1/008 "10½" July 22, 1973, London. Shaw Theatre (3 hrs.) Allen Ginsberg & Nicholas Kormen. Mantras, Blake, Poetry, Blues.

1974

74S1/000 "C" January 30, 1974. Dylan concert, Madison Square Garden, taped by Jessica Goodyear.

74F2/001A "C." Newcastle, England, Basil Bunting lecture, general senses of poetry.
74F2/001B "C." Basil Bunting--European renaissance, Campion, Wyatt, Spenser.

74S1/002 "C." Allen Ginsberg, unknown musicians--O My Soul Shalom, Holy Soul Jelly Roll.

74S1/003 "C."
74S2/003 Blues I "C."
74S3/004 Blues II "C."
74S4/005 Blues III "C."

74R1/004 "C." Jack Kerouac Blues and Haikus, Al Cohn & Zoot Sims--saxes recorded off record.

74F1/005 "C" August 1974. Naropa--Boulder, Colorado. Allen Ginsberg with Jose Arguelles--sexuality "The Feminine Class." (poor sound at beginning gets better in middle and side 2.)

74E1/006 "C" January 3, 1974. Broadcast NET. First Part Round Table.

74E1/007 "C" December 1974. Interview with Allen Ginsberg by Richard Haight--Ph.D. Asst. Prof. English, S.M.U., Dallas, Texas. Allen summarizes activities of prior 3 years.

74F1/008 "C" March 4, 1974 (K). "4 Million Lips"--Orlovsky. Neal Cassady at rock event, San Francisco. "He did nothing/I did nothing/finally there was nothing."

74S1/009 "C" February 1974. Allen Ginsberg with Jim Gruerholz. New York Youth Call, Xmas Blues, NYC Blues, improvisation. Side B--mostly blank.

74S1/009A "5" 9/15/74. Bedrock Motor--Don Scott.

74D1/010 "C" November 1, 1974. Broken tape regarding Leary.

74D2/010 "5" May 16, 1974. San Francisco--Holiday Inn Rm. 2215. Louis and Allen discussion.

74S1/011 "C" February 1974. Improvisations and rehearsals, babble, Jersey City Blues, Dylan concert aftermath.

74D2/012. Same as 74D2/010.

74F1/013 "C" Aug. 9, 1974. Naropa--On Sexuality.

74C1/014 "5" Sept. 6, 1974. Bedrock Motor, Don Scott Outlaw Ballad, Pretty Boy Floyd. B: Esmeralda 12 am.

74S1/015 "C." Allen Ginsberg, unknown musicians, Holy Soul Jelly Roll.

74P2/016 "7" 11/21/74. Ginsberg, WABE--Ahhh, Elegy Che Guevara, On Neal's Ashes.
74P2/017. Reel 2.

74P2/018 "7" 11/21/74. Allen Ginsberg, Lone Mountain College, San Francisco.
74P2/019. Reel 2.

74 P1/020 "7." The Poetry Center, McKenna Auditorium SFSU

74A2/021 "7." WRFG, Atlanta, Georgia, unmarked.
74A2/022 "7." WRFG.

74D3/023 "7." 5/3/74. Portland, Ore., Bhagavan Das and Allen Ginsberg. 3 pm discussion and chanting, Friends of Woodcraft Hall.
74D3/024 "7." Tape 2.
74D3/025 "7." Tape 3.

74A2/026 "7." 4/9/74. A.G. and (Ram Dass?), College of Marin, Kentfield, Calif.
74A2/027 "7." Tape 2.

1975

75A4/001 "C" (K). Moming, Chicago, March 11, 1975, marked 1 & 2.

75A4/002 "C" (K). Moming, Chicago, March 11, 1975, improvisation.

75A4/003 "C" (K). Moming (?), Chicago, March 11, 1975. Possibly remastered. Marked 1 & 2.

75A4/004 "C" (K). Moming (?), Chicago, March 11, 1975. End, improvisation marked 1 & 2. Plus end of Trungpa, Ginsberg, Corso taped conversation at Naropa, Summer '75.

75D2/005 "C" (K). Trungpa, Ginsberg & Corso conversation at Naropa, Summer '75.

75F1/006 "C." Boulder, June 19, 1975--Quatrains followed by introducing Corso to class. Side 2--June 12, 1975, Karma Tinly singing smells tree service, 6 pm, Naropa 1-50.

75S1/007. First Blues rehearsal, Sholle, Mansfield, N.Y.

75B1/008 "5" October 21, 1975. Gospel Noble Truths. Allen Ginsberg, Arthur Russel, Denise Mercedes. First guitar experiments.

75S2/009A "C" October 21, 1975. Come All Ye Boys, Gospel Noble Truths in two Versions. Same personnel as 75B1/008.
75S2/009B "C" December 25, 1975. Sickness Blues, Favorite Beat Quotes, Koans to Brad Gordon.

75S1/010 "C" December 9, 1975. Allen Ginsberg, John Sholle. Side 1--Gospel Noble Truths, Guru Blues (slow--one wrong chord), Come Along Vietnam, Dope Fiend Blues, Sickness Blues. Side 2--Jan. 8, 1976, Dub from original. Chelsea Hotel--Harry Smith, Allen Ginsberg, John Sholle--Blue Gossip.

75D1/011 "C" May 7, 1975. Allen Ginsberg conversation with Carl Solomon. Denise Mercedes band rehearsal--Come Along w/harmonica, I Can't Find Anyone--NY May 6, 1973; also Jack Albert poems.

75A1/012 "C" Summer 1975. From Naropa School of Disembodied Poetics, Boulder, Colorado. Anne Waldman reading, side 1-- 1. Rocky Plutonium Fantasy, 2. Notes from Rolling Stones, 3. Sun the Blonde Out, 4. Fast Speaking Woman. Side 2-- Allen Ginsberg reading Howl for Carl Solomon.

75D2/013A "C" December 31, 1975. Paterson N.J. Louis Ginsberg, Allen Ginsberg, Peter Orlovsky, Denise Mercedes, Edith Ginsberg, Gordon Ball--supper talk 2:45 PM--4 PM.
75D2/013B. Same as above.

75D2/014A "C" December 17, 1975. 437 E. 12th NYC 6-10 PM.

Supper talk including Hubert Huncke, Lewis Cartwright, Allen Ginsberg, Denise Mercedes and Peter Orlovsky.
75D2/014B "C." Same as above.

75D1/014C "C" June 5, 1975. Louis Ginsberg conversation.

75E1/015 "C" March 10, 1975. Chicago. Allen Ginsberg, William Burroughs interviewed by Linda Wiener for Chicago Tribune.

75A1/016A "C." Naropa Poetry Reading 8/9/75, Chögyam Trungpa, Rinpoche. Selections from Kerouac Records--Jack Kerouac & Steve Allen, San Francisco, 3rd St.--Neal and Stooges. 1975-- Jerry Kamstras recording dubbed by Scoop Niskern.

75S1/017 "C." Allen Ginsberg First Blues.

75E1/018 "C" March 13, 1975. Chicago. Interview with Allen Ginsberg by Robert Schwarz. Interview with William Burroughs by Barbara Barg.

75A2/019A "C" December 1975. Side 1--Louis Ginsberg reading at Paterson N.J. Library. Side 2--Eugene Brooks reading.
75A2/019B. Allen Ginsberg reading at Paterson N.J. Library.

75D3/020A "C." 10:30 PM conversation Allen & Louis Ginsberg-- Pesach Seder, Paterson, New Jersey.
75D3/020B "C." Conversation before Seder.
75D3/020C. 4:12 PM. Louis Ginsberg.

75E1/021 "C." January 23, 1975. Interview with Allen Ginsberg by Rick Waddington of Univ. of Washington Daily.

75D1/022 "C." July 10, 1975. Begins--We're talking to A.G., Poet.... Talk of CIA Colby Hitchhiking Dope verse censored by NBC, then sung; suggestions for Church committee to subpoena also censored.... From poetry classes (Naropa) basically the history of English poetry leading up to 19th and 20th century breakthroughs in consciousness ... possibly Louis Ginsberg present. Side 2--Leary in jail three years for misdeameanor....

75E1/023 "C." March 12, 1975. Chicago. Interview with Bill Burroughs and Allen Ginsberg for Chicago Sun Times by John Diomah.

75A1/024 "C." Allen Ginsberg with Michael McClure reading, NYC, spring '75, St. Marks Church, 2nd Ave. & 10th. Recorded by M. Koherls Press 3 Dusseldorf, Munich, 56 W. Germany.

75E1/024A "C" March, 1975. Interview with Allen and W.S. Burroughs by Scott Becher, Chicago.

75A1/025 "C." August 9, 1975. Naropa Institute, Boulder, Colorado. Chögyam Trungpa Rinpoche reading poetry ... Chögyam spinning....

75A1/026A "C." April 19, 1975. Energy and Consciousness Poetry
Reading--Ginsberg, Snyder, McClure reading, Florida.
75A2/026B. Ginsberg and Snyder reading--April 19, 1975.
75A3/026C "C." Panel discussion- Gomburg, Odum, Ginsberg,
McClure, and Snyder--April 19, 1975.

75D1/027 "C." June 20, 1975. Boulder, Colorado, Naropa--11 PM.
Conversation involving Chögyam, Burroughs, A. Waldman, A.
Ginsberg, P. Whalen, and W.S. Merwin.

75D1/028 "C." June 20, 1975. William Burroughs and Chögyam
Trungpa talk on meditation (Gregory Corso present)--"Well
Gregory, there's nothing wrong with dope."

75F1/029. Someone's lecture on Pound--"musical ideas from 19th
century...." Ideas picked up from Ernest Fenollosa.

75E1/030 3/11/75. Terkel w/A.G. & W.S.B.

75P1/031 "7" 3/9/75. A.G. & W.S.B. reading, University of
Chicago.

75P2/032 "7" 2/5/75. Poetry reading, Humanities Series Thomas
Moore College.
75P2/033 "7." Reel 2.

75P2/034A "7." 4/17/75. Another Night at Columbia, Part One:
Corso, Orlovsky, Burroughs.
75P2/034 Another Night at Columbia, Allen Ginsberg--Barry Chowka.
75P1/035 "7." 3/11/75. A.G., Chicago?

75A4/036 "7."
75A4/037.
75A4/038 4/21/75. A.G., Tallahassee, Florida, FSU.
75A4/039. From WFSU--FM.

75P1/040 "7." 4/23/75. University of Cincinnati--Chant & Reading.

75E1/041 "7." 4/24/75. A.G. in conversation w/Bob Stevenson
of WGUC, Univ. of Cincinnati.

1976

76A3/001, 002, 003 "5." April 19, 1976. U.C.L.A. w/Sensei,
Ken Kesey, Wavy Gravy.

76E1/004 "C." January 23, 1976. W.O.R. Radio Show. A.G.,
Peter O., B. Farber, Jne. Robbins. Ends improvised blues with
Farber, Robbins, LSD Peter reads poems.

76A2/005, 006 "C." 1976. Paterson Free Public Library--Allen & Louis Ginsberg, Eugene Brooks.

76A1/007 "C." 2/11/76. A.G. & Reza Baraheni, Hatch-Billops Archives, N.Y.C.

76A1/008 "C." 2/28/76. A.G. reads poetry of Basil Bunting at Chumley's, Greenwich Village, N.Y.C.

76S1/009 March/June 1976. First Blues--A.G., John Sholle, David Mansfield, Arthur Russel--10 songs.

76S1/010 "7." March 23, 1976. 8 songs First Blues--rough mix-- A.G., John Sholle, Arthur Russel.

76S1/011 "7." June 1, 2, 1976. Mansfield, Sholle, Russel--First Blues, rough mix.

76S1/012 "5." June 2, 1976. Ginsberg/Hammond--52nd St., Columbia Studio, with David Mansfield-Dobro and John Sholle-Guitar.

76S1/013 "5." June 26, 1976. Boulder, Colorado--Hardon Cancer Dharma Blues--Gregg Rutter, Allen Ginsberg (vocal & harmonium); OK Blues w/Scott Grooin.

76F1/014 "C." October 28, 1976. Allen Ginsberg Poetic Ground-- Vajra Dhatu Seminary, Kings Gateway Hotel & Inns, Land O' Lakes, Wisc. 54540.

76F1/015 "C" Oct. 26, 1976. Poetry Class II Vajradhatu Seminary, Land O'Lakes, Wisc. Reznikoff, texts and discussions, Comparative Buddhism, critical paragraphs from William Carlos Williams and Trungpa.

76F1/016 "C." October 30, 1976. Vajradhatu Seminary--Poetic Lecture--Reznikoff, William's "measure."

76F1/017 "C." November 12, 1976. Poetic Lecture--Reznikoff, Trungpa, Blythe, Kerouac; Ezra Pound's criticism; Haikus by students; Vajradhatu Seminary--Land O'Lakes, Wisc.

76F1/018 "C." November 24, 1976. Vajradhatu Seminary, Land O'Lakes, Wisc. --Reading Whitman; Discussion.

76F1/019 "C." November 14, 1976. Vajradhatu Seminary, Land O'Lakes, Wisc. Winter Haikus; Issa, Basho, William Carlos Williams.

76F1/020 "C." November 26, 1976. Vajradhatu Seminary, Land O'Lakes, Wisc.

76F1/021 "C." November 16, 1976. Vajradhatu Seminary--Discussion of William Carlos Williams' early poems; Prosody considerations; Discussion of Marianne Moore's syllabics--Proletarian Portrait/McLeod/Sunday/Dead Baby/Pastoral.

76F1/021A "C." December 30, 1976. Allen G. reading, discussing Changdeva, Kerouac, Rimbaud. Side 2--Trungpa's poetry read by A.G.

76S1/022 "C." February 19, 1976. Allen Ginsberg & James Grauerholz. Jam--Gospel Noble Truths, Sickness Blues etc.--kitchen, 437 E. 12th, N.Y.C.

76S1/023 "C." March 23, 1976. Hammond recording session--Lay Down, Guru Blues, Slack Key guitar, Reef Mantra, Sickness Blues, Youth Call Annunciation, Dive Apartment NYC Blues (rough mix).

76A1/024A "C." May 6, 1976. Allen G. , 8th St. Bookshop benefit reading. Improvised poem; songs by Peter Wortsman; 49 W. 8th St. , N.Y.C.

76S1/024 "C." January 4, 1976. Excerpts from rehearsal session--Sholle, Wyeth, Mansfield, Traum--Guru Blues, Sweet Oaha, Broken Bone Blues, N.Y. Blues, Don't Smoke.

76S1/025 "C." May 20, 1976. Other End rehearsal--Sholle, Mansefield, A. Ginsberg, A. Russel--Lay Down (several versions), Gospel Noble Truths, Guru Blues.

76E1/026 "C." September 23, 1976. Berlin--A. Ginsberg & W. Burroughs w/young journalists.

76E1/027 "C." January 23, 1976. A. Ginsberg, Robbins, Peter Orlovsky--last hour Barry Farber Radio Show. Side 2--Buckminster Fuller, W.S. Burroughs, A. Ginsberg--February 9, 1976, WTOP TV, Washington, D.C.

76D2/028A "C." February 14, 1976. Rose Savage supper conversation--P. Orlovsky, A. Ginsberg, Denise Mercedes--14th St. stories, 6:30 to 8:30 PM.
76D2/028B "C." February 14, 1976. Same as above plus Allen and Peter singing Blake.

76S1/029 June 1, 2, 1976. Columbia Studios--Everybody, Dope, 4 am.

76D1/030 "C." May 17, 1976. Louis Ginsberg talking about WWI Socialism, glue factory, Wordsworth quote on immortality (Paterson).

76S1/031 "C." May 1976. Steven Taylor, Allen Ginsberg--improvised duet, first stanzas of Jessore Road. Side 2--Dub of Howl & Other Poems recorded at Big Table reading, Chicago,

1959 and Fantasy Studios, San Francisco, 1959. Howl (first line missing), Sunflower Sutra, Footnote to Howl, Supermarket in California Transcription of Organ music, America, In Back of the Real, Strange View Cottage in Berkeley, Europe Europe, Kaddish Poem (incomplete).

76D2/032A "C." June 4, 1976. Side 1--Alan Ziegler, Louis Ginsberg, Allen Ginsberg, conversion--<u>Village Voice</u>.
76D2/032B. Ginsberg/Ziegler--Father Death Blues, midnight, July 8, 1976 (first recording).

76D1/033 "C." March 6, 1976. Paterson, N.J.--11 am. Louis Ginsberg on dreams, Allen Ginsberg second version of Lay Down; March 7, 1976--Sunday afternoon dinner, Louis Ginsberg monologue to Alan Brooks and Allen on different jobs (sly humor); March 8, 1976, Louis Ginsberg, Allen Ginsberg, Alan Brooks, 2 PM conversation about jobs; 8-9 PM--Louis Ginsberg, Allen G., Eugene & Alan Brooks--Louis laughing, Edith & Ellen; March 13, 1976, Allen Ginsberg--Lay Down; Louis Ginsberg talking about fourth book "Our Times."

76D1/034 "C." Party conversation after Big Reading August 8, 1976, Boulder--W.S. Burroughs, Anne Waldman, Allen Ginsberg, Chögyam Trungpa, D. Di Prima, J. Rothenberg. Alan De Loach, Tom Savage, Gordon Ball.

76D1/035 "C." January 12, 1976. Monday--Paterson, N.J., 490 Park Ave.--Eugene & Alan Brooks, Allen & Louis Ginsberg--conversation, 1930's debts, 10:30-11 am; January 13, 1976, 12-1 pm, conversation on Paul Robeson--Louis's Rutgers recollections, 1 pm--Louis talking; July 16, 1976, Paterson, tune from a dream recorded for reference.

76D1/036 April 6, 1976. Boulder, Colorado--Kent Daisey (student?) discussing his poems with Allen Ginsberg.

76A1/037 "C." August 7, 1976. Poetry Reading at Naropa in Boulder, Colorado--Anne Waldman, Allen Ginsberg, Trungpa Rinpoche.

76A1/038A "C." 8/7/76. Reading by W.S. Burroughs; Reading by Chögyam Trungpa Rinpoche w/readings in English by David Rome. Side 1--1) Victoria, 2) Memorial Song May 19th, 3) Cynical Letter 1972, 4) June 5, 1972, 5) Sheep Roam in the Meadows, 6) Glorious Bhagvad Ghetto. Side 2--1) Eating Father's Flesh, 2) Motel Poem #1, 3) Missing the Point, 4) Motel Poem (Norwegian Girl), 5) Love's Fool. August 13, 1976, A.G., P. Orlovsky, Steven Hall (guitar), Lloyd W. (saxophone), Carl Grundberg (guitar), AH, Gate, etc.

76A1/039 "C." July 4, 1976. Naropa, Boulder, Colorado--Come All Ye Brave Boys, Pussy Blues, plus improvisation; Steve Hall guitar.

76D1/040 "C." Allen Ginsberg conversation with Murray Bramwell, Dept. of English, Flanders Univ., Bedford Park, S. Australia, February 6, 1976. Questions on public role of poet; comments, reminiscences of Dylan and Rolling Thunder, on affinity w/Gary Snyder, on other contemporary influences--songmen/women that are particularly significant, the promise of the 60's continuing to be fulfilled? comment on Fall of America, relation to Whitman, what poems of his A.G. particularly values.

76D1/041 "C." Corso, DeSole, Wagner, Singer, kid from village, Steve, Dave, interviewed by Phil Singer.

76S1/042 "C." June 8, 1976. Naropa, Boulder, Colorado. music w/Gregory, Thomas Campion sung by A.G. --When Thou Must Go Home, Oft Have I Sighed, 3rd Book of Ayres, If Thou Longst So Much to Learn Music, I Care Not for Thest Ladies, A Book of Ayres, O Dear with I Thee Might Live Twice, Where the Bee Sucks, Two Ravens.

76S1/043 "C." August 25, 1976. N.Y.C. w/S. Taylor, Allen Ginsberg--Father Death Blues (good version), Pussy Blues.

76S1/044 "C." March 1976 (K). Hammond final mix. Side 1--Lay Down Mountain, Gospel Noble Truths, Guru Blues, Sweet Oaha, Reef Mantra, Sickness Blues, NYC Outa Call (?). Side 2-- Blues, w/S. Taylor, Orlane Tune, James Alley.

76R1/045 "3." October 18, 1976 (K). Tape of letter of introduction from Kurt Schwarzkopf--Millbrook Road, Middletown, Conn. 06457.

76R1/046 "C." (K). Original songs by Dan Hutch--Guitar, harmonica, vocals.

76E2/047A November 29, 1976. Chicago--Studs Terkel with Allen Ginsberg re Karmapa visit; WFMT radio.
76E2/047B. Same as above.

76E2/048A "7." February 13, 1976. Allen Ginsberg Poetry Reading, Longhorn Radio Network, University of Texas at Austin.
76E2/048B "7." Same as above.

76F3/049 "7." 2/10/76. Univ. of Maryland--Chant Om Mani, w/ P.O.
76F3/050 "7." 2/10/76. Univ. of Md.--reel 2 of 3. Eyeball over Bay Area Poem.
76F3/051 "7." 2/10/76. Univ. of Md.--Mugging, Hadda Be, Sickness Blues, End Vietnam War, Gospel Nobel Truths, Gate, w/ P.O.

76A1/052 "7." 5/5/76. Reading, Chicago, Oakton Community College.

76A1/053 "7." 3/14/76. A.G. & P.O. (& John Sholle) at Bklyn Museum--Lay Down Mountain, Down in This World, Hadda Be.

1977

77A1/001 "7." February 27, 1977. Allen Ginsberg reading, Woodmere, New York--Steven Taylor, guitar and vocal--Kaddish, Louis Death Poems.

77A3/002A "C." June 22, 1977. Naropa Institute, Boulder, Colorado--Missing piece from Allen's poem.
77A3/002B "C." Same as above.
77A3/002C. Allen Ginsberg & Peter Orlovsky, poetry reading.

77S1/003 "C." October 6 or 7, 1977. Rehearsal--The Rune, w/S. Hall, A. Ginsberg, P. Orlovsky (Rasberry Song, All Around the Garden).

77A2/003A "C." October 13, 1977, River Falls, Wisc., Evening Seminar.
77A2/003B "C." October 12, 1977. Evening Seminar--reading Contest of Bards.

77A1/004 "7." April 7, 1977. Robert Duncan & Allen Ginsberg reading at Colorado State University. Side 1--first set. Side 2--second set.

77S1/005 "C" (K). Blake Songs of Innocence & Experience, Vol. II.

77A1/006 "C." July 31, 1977. Allen Ginsberg & P.O., reading, Fairplay Hospital--Fairplay, Colorado.

77E1/007 "C." December 7, 1977. WOR Radio--Allen Ginsberg on Arlene Francis Program.

77A1/008 "C." August 21, 1977. Gregory Corso, K Libre.

77A1/009 "C." Dec. 4, 1977. Allen Ginsberg reading Contest of Bards, Passion Coffeehouse.

77S1/010 "C." May 4 & 5, 1977. Rune Music--Allen Ginsberg-vocal, harmonium, organ; first composition tape; Evening at Kesey's--May 8th, 1977.

77A1/011 "C." May 7, 1977. Hoohaw 2--Hoohaw Field, Eugene, Oregon--Allen reading Contest of Bards; Peter Orlovsky--Rasberry Farm; Gregory Corso--Nagging God; plus various performers, and poets.

77F2/012A "C." April 1977. Allen Ginsberg, N.Y. Dharmadhatu Society, Poetry and Meditation.
77F2/012B. Same as above.

77A1/013. A.G. --University of Wisconsin.

77P1/014 3/25/77. A.G. & friends, Passim's, Cambridge, Mass. Sides 1 & 2--A.G. Lindisfarne 2/3/77.

77P1/015 "7." January 26, 1977. Troubador, Los Angeles--1st show.
77P2/016A "7." 2nd show.
77P3/016B "7." 2nd show.

77A1/016C "C." Recorded summer 1977 for Institute for Regional Ed., Santa Fe--A.G., voice, harmonium.

77F2/016 "7." March 5, 1977. Allen Ginsberg at Other End, N.Y.C., 1st Show--Broken Bone Blues, Guru Blues, Hardon Blues, Don't Smoke, Gospel Noble Truths, CIA Dope Calypso; Peter Orlovsky--Rasberry Song, Sweet You Are.
77F2/016A "7." 2nd Show.

77P1/017 "7." March 2, 1977. Other End, N.Y.C. 1st Show-- Allen Ginsberg--vocal, harmonium, song sticks; Denise Mercedes--guitar and slide guitar; Steven Taylor--guitar; Steven Hall--guitar; Arthur Russell--cello; CIA Dope Calypso, Father Death, Nurse's Song.

77P1/018 "7." March 2, 1977. Other End, N.Y.C. 2nd Show. Same personnel as above.

77P1/018A "7." March 4, 1977. 2nd Show--Other End, N.Y.C. Same personnel as above plus Peter Orlovsky and Artie Traum.
77P2/018A "7." March 4, 1977. 1st show--Nurse's Song, Guru Blues, Broken Bones, Gospel Noble Truths, Don't Smoke, AM Dirty Jersey Blues, Everybody Sing, CIA Dope Calypso.

77P2/019A "7." March 3, 1977. Other End, 1st Show.
77P2/019B "7." 2nd Show--The Lamb, Hardon Blues, Broken Bone Blues, Gaté Gaté, Gospel Noble Truths.

77P1/020 "C." March 26, 1977. Allen Ginsberg singing at Passim's, Woodstock, N.Y.
77P2/020 March 25, 1977. First and second shows.

77A1/021 "C." December 17, 1977. Philadelphia YMHA.
77A2/021. Same as above.
77A3/021. Same as above.

77A1/022 "C." June 6, 1977. Naropa Institute, Boulder, Colorado-- Allen Ginsberg and Peter Orlovsky reading.

77S2/023A "C." March 1, 1977. Rehearsal--Arthur Russel's studio.
77S2/023B. Same as above.

77D1/024 "C." September 27, 1977. Conversation w/Kenneth Koch for New York Times, 25 Claremont Ave., N.Y.C., 4-7 PM.

77S1/025 November 20, 21, 1977. Rehearsal--A.G., P. Orlovsky, S. Taylor, S. Hall. Side 1--Peter--All Around the Garden, Rasberry Song, Keep Clean in Between, Goin' Out in the Garden.

Side 2--Allen Ginsberg-- 3 AM Blues, NY Blues, Xmas Blues, MacDougal St. Blues, Troop St. Blues, Bus Ride Song, Prayer Blues, 2 AM Jersey Lites, Dope Fiend Blues.

77E1/026 "C." January 25, 1977. Lou Hunter interviews Allen Ginsberg; Nam Nammy Ho Reng He Ho; Peter singing.

77S1/027 February 4, 1977. Allen Ginsberg--When the Years Come, Father Death. Side 2--W. Biermann songs--September 24, 1976, East Berlin--Sufferings of Christ, 3 Encouragements.

77A1/028 "3 3/4" December 15, 1977. Allen Ginsberg reading at Bard College; Reading Contest of Bards in presence of Mr. Robbins from Hellen Kelly Lindenwood House, Kline Commons, Annandale-on-the Hudson.

1978

78E1/001A "C." Ginsberg on "Renaldo and Clara," WBAI interview by Lynn Samuels.

78D1/001 "C." March 1, 1978. Conversation at Branford College of Yale University, Connecticut 06520.

78R1/002 "3." Tape by Sheri Martinelle, California, 1978, reading Eternal Love by Ezra Pound and Emily Brontë's Cold in the Ear.

78D1/003 "C." March 1, 1978. Yale University--lunch talk.

78A3/004A "7." March 1, 1978. Yale University Art Gallery, Lecture Hall reading.
78A3/004B "7." Contd.
78A3/004C. Contd.

78D3/005A "C." February 16, 1978. M.D. Institute College, Maryland--Workshop Tapes.
78D3/005B. Contd.
78D3/005C. Contd.

78A2/006A "C." February 19, 1978. Allen Ginsberg reading--Port Washington Public Library, New York.
78A2/006B. Contd.

78A2/007 "7." 2/16/78. Reading--Maryland Institute--A.G.
78A2/007 "7." 2/16/78. Press Talk, post-reading at Maryland Institute.

78A1/008A "7." January 27, 1978. Steven's Point Wisconsin--Allen Ginsberg reading.
78A2/008B. Contd.
78A3/008C. Contd.

78A2/009 4/19/78. Boston, Church of Covenant--Allen Ginsberg
& friends, Mind Breaths, P. O.
78A2/010. Contd.

78F2/011 1/24/78. Workshop--Ann Arbor, Mich. Side 2: blank.
78F2/011A. Workshop, contd.

78A1/012 1/24/78. Public Reading?

78K1/013 "7. " 4/21/78. Allen Ginsberg, Evening Hartford--Real
Art Ways, PM--"voices in music, as recorded. "

78A2/014 "C. " 4/21/78. Univ. of Hartford--Poems, Songs, Discussions.
78A2/015 4/21/78. Includes reading FBI letters.

78F2/016 4/25/78. Meditation Poetry--A. R. Ammons class,
Cornell. Side 2: Parlato: Two O'Hara poems made into
songs.
78F2/017 4/25/78 A. R. Ammons Poetry Meditation, both sides.

78E1/018 3/25/78. Ginsberg, WPFW: Washington, D. C.

78A1/019 "7. " 4/25/78. A. G. --Poetry, Cornell, FBI documents.

78E1/020 5/7/78. A. G. on WBCU Boston, interviewer Bill Kates,
1 hour edited to 10 minutes.

78P1/021 "7. " 5/2/78 Rutgers University (N. J.)-- A. G. w/Stephen
Taylor--1. Gospel Nobel Truths, Spring, Cointel Pro Files
Speech, Dope Fiend Blues, Kaddish Poem (Russian-faced),
Aunt Rose. 2. Don't Grow Old, Junk Mail, Punk Rock, Grim
Skull Notebook, Grant Application, Nurse's Song.

78P1/022 "7. " 4/18/78. Student Union Lecture Society, Westfield
State College, Westfield, Mass. --A. G. & P. O.

Tapes Unclassified

Stewart Meyer. 934-4482.
Sons of the Tenth Guru. The Khalsa String Band.
Swami Muktanda Chants "Sri Guru Gita" & "Deva Storm. "
Peter's voice leading Chant ? unmarked.
Rabbi Schachter's Double Album dubs.
Amus Moore: Hip Men. Recorded in Performance at Apollo.
Manifesto Italian.
Charlie Morrow Personal Chants.
Barbara Reumensnyder--Bucknell. Songs of Innocence & Experience.
Anna Blume.
John Lief.
Happy & Artie's Woodstock Album.

APPENDIX C

1. UNDERGROUND NEWSPAPERS
From Bell & Howell Microfilm
Collection (1963-1975)

Key to Press Services*

AFS	Alternative Feature Service
APLQ	Agence de Presse Libre du Quebec
APM	Anarchist Press Movement
COSMEP	Committee of Small Magazine Editors and Publishers
CPS	College Press Service
ENS	Earth News Service
FRINS	Free Ranger International News Services
INS	Intertribal News Service
IWB	Intergalactic World Brain
LNS	Liberation News Service
LP	Last Post News Service
NYNS	New York News Service
PL	Presna Latina
PNS	Pacific News Service
UPS	Underground Press Syndicate (formerly Free Ranger Intertribal News Service)
ZNS	Zodiac News Service

To the best of my knowledge the UPS is still existent as the Alternative Press Service in New York City. No further information is available on the existence of the other underground sources. The predominant services over the last decade were APS, LNS and UPS.

Actuel [UPS]. 60 rue de Richelieu, Paris 2, France. O. P. E. 20-20. (In French.)

Alternative Features Service (AFS) [UPS]. P.O. Box 2250, Berkeley, California 94702. (415) 548-7000. Member of UPS, but only AFS members can use material with written permission.

Ann Arbor Argus [LNS]. 807 S. State Street, Ann Arbor, Michigan.

Ann Arbor Sun [Community News Service]. Published by Rainbow People's Party, (1975) 603 E. William St. , Ann Arbor, Michi-

*Appearing in brackets following newspaper titles.

gan 48104. Bus. and Ed.: (313) 761-7148; Home: (313) 994-4337.

Aquarian [LNS/APS, ZNS, PNS, Indelible Inkworks]. The Crescent, Montclair, N.J. 07042. (201) 746-0868. Published twice monthly.

Berkeley Barb [UPS, APS, LNS, ENS, ZNS, IWG, NYNS]. Ed. and Bus. Offices: 800 Heinz Street or Box 1247, Berkeley, California 94710. (415) 849-1040. Pub.: International News Keyus, Inc.

Berkeley Tribe. Published by: The Red Mountain Tribe, Inc. P. O. Box 9043, 1701½ Grove St., Berkeley, California 94709. (415) 549-3391.

Chinook [UPS, LNS, Intermind, FRINS]. 1452 Pennsylvania St., Suite 21, Denver, Colorado 80203. No association with defunct Mountain Free Press.

College Press Service. 1764 Gilpin St., Denver, Colorado 80218. (303) 388-7647.

Common Sense. Springfield, Mass. (Springfield College?)

Daily Planet [UPS, FRINS, LNS, CPS]. 3514 So. Dixie Highway, Coconut Grove, Florida. (Miami Free Press--copyright 1969 by Daily Planet). (305) 444-5882. "20th Century Schizo Paper."

Dallas Notes [UPS, LNS]. P. O. Box 7140, Dallas, Texas 75209. Formerly: Notes from the Underground.

Damascus Free Press [UPS, LNS]. Damascus, Maryland.

The Drummer. 4221 Germantown Ave., Philadelphia, Pa. 19140. (215) DA9-7270. Formerly: Thursday's Drummer; Distant Drummer.

East Village Other [UPS]. 20 East 12th St., New York, N.Y. 10003. (212) 255-2130, 31, 32. Copyright 1970.

Fifth Estate [UPS, LNS, ZNS, PNS]. 4403 Second Avenue, Detroit, Michigan 48201. Copyright 1975.

Floating Bear. The Poets Press, 1915 Oak Street, San Francisco, California 94117.

Free Ranger Tribe [UPS, INS]. Box 26, Village Station, New York, N.Y. 10014. (212) 242-3888. "All the Boogie That's Fit to Print!" Formerly: Free Ranger.

Fusion. Boston, Mass.

GAR [APS, COSMEP]. Box 4793, Austin, Texas 78765. (512) 453-2556.

Gay Sunshine, A Newspaper of Gay Liberation. P. O. Box 40397, San Francisco, California 94140. (415) 824-3184. Ed.: Winston Leyland.

Georgia Straight [UPS, LNS, LP, APM, PL, APLQ]. 2110 W. 4th Ave., Vancouver, B. C., Canada V 6 KIN 6. (604) 736-2994. Ed.: Roland Morgan. G. S. Publishing Ltd. Copyright 1975. Member: Adult Bureau of Circulations; Anarchist Press Movement.

Good Times. 2377 Bush Street, San Francisco, California 94115. (415) 922-9981. Copyright 1970, Good Times Commune: 1969-- formerly San Francisco Express Times.

The Grape (Western Organization). 324 Powell Street, Vancouver 4, B. C., Canada. (604) 688-3713. Owned and produced by The Grape Collective.

Great Speckled Bird. P. O. Box 7847, Atlanta, Georgia 30309. Published by Atlanta Cooperative News Project, 448 Forest Ave., N. E., Atlanta, Georgia 30312. (404) 875-8301. 1975.

The Green Revolution (Official Journal of the School of Living). School of Living-West, $442\frac{1}{2}$ Landfair Ave., Los Angeles, California 90024. 1974. Published bimonthly: Jan. 15, Mar. 15, May 15, Sept. 15, Nov. 15; except June, July, August. Publ. Material: F. Paul Salstrom, c/o Box 8074, Huntington, W. Virginia 25705. Subscriptions: Larry Lack, School of Living, Rt. 1, Box 129, Freeland, Md. 21053. (301) 357-5530.

Harbinger, P. O. Box 751, Station F, Toronto, 5, Canada.

Harry [UPS, LNS, CPS, FRINS, AFS, ENS]. 233 East 25th Street, Baltimore, Md. 21218.

Hartford's Other Voice [UPS, LNS]. P. O. Box 2424, Bishops Plaza, Station West, Hartford, Conn. 06117.

Helix. 3128 Howard Avenue E, Seattle, Washington 98102.

Hi (Subtitle: Young People's Newspaper). Bombay, India.

Inquisition [UPS, LNS]. Box 17543, Charlotte, N. C.

It. 27 Endell Street, London, England WC 2. Copyright 1969.

Kaleidoscope [UPS, LNS]. Kaleidoscope Publishing Co., P. O. Box 90526, Milwaukee, Wisconsin 53202.

Liberation. 339 Lafayette Street, New York, N. Y. 10012. Copyright 1974.

Liberation News Service. New York address: 160 Claremon-
nue, New York, N.Y. 10027. (212) 749-2200. Massacs:
LNS of the New Age, New Media Project, Inc. , Box 269).
#1, Chestnut Hill Road, Montague, Massachusetts 01351
Formerly: The New Media Project, Washington, D.C. al
office, 1968. Published twice a week. Political split in,
one office in New York, the other in Massachusetts. Re
later to one New York office/address. Now "published s
taneously in two locations under different editorial contro
each retaining the name of Liberation News Service. "

Logos (Montreal Free Press). Montreal, Canada.

Los Angeles Free Press [UPS, APS]. 5850 Hollywood Blvd.
Angeles, California 90028.

Madison Kaleidoscope. P.O. Box 881, Madison, Wisconsin .

Nickel Review. Box 65, University Station, Syracuse, N.Y.).
Published 50 times a year.

Nola Express [UPS]. Box 2342, New Orleans, La. 70116.
525-1632. 1971. Published every other week at 606 Co,
New Orleans, La. , by the Southern Louisiana Media Cor
a non-profit corporation.

North Carolina Anvil [UPS, LNS]. P. O. Box 1148, Durham.
27702. (919) 688-9544. 1971.

Northwest Passage. Offices: 100 Harris St. , Bellingham, W:-
ton 98225. Other: P.O. Box 105, S. Bellingham Static
Bellingham, Washington 98225. Published every other
day, 24 times a year. 1975.

Octopus [UPS]. Box 1259, Station B, Ottawa 4, Ontario, Ca
Published every 3 weeks.

Omphalos [UPS, LNS]. Pub. by: Territories Publishing Co. ,
Sherbrook St. , Winnepeg 2, Manitoba, Canada. (204) 77.

Open City [UPS, LNS]. 4369 Melrose, Los Angeles, Califor
90029. Renaissance--A Bimonthly magazine of the arts.
(special section).

Prospectus [LNS]. Charleston, Illinois. Slogan: The Freep
Serving Downstate Illinois. Published semi-monthly.

[Worchester] Punch [UPS, LNS]. P. O. Box 352, Worcheste
Mass. 01601. Published monthly.

Quicksilver Times, Inc. [UPS, LNS]. Washington Independen
Publishing Co. , 1736 R Street, N.W. , Washington, D.C.).
(202) 483-8000. Staff Collective.

New York, N.Y.

,ouis Outlaw [UPS, LNS, AFS]. P. O. Box 9501, Cabanne
Station, St. Louis, Missouri 63161. (314) 721-3170. 1972.
Published every 3 weeks.

Diego Door [APS, LNS, ZNS, PNS]. P. O. Box 2022 (Main
Office), San Diego, California 92112. (714) 233-9678. Los
Angeles Office: (213) 874-2200. Copyright 1973, APS. For-
merly: San Diego Free Door, San Diego Door to Liberation,
Good Morning Teaspoon, San Diego Free Door to Liberation,
Teaspoon and the Door, Door to Liberation.

San Francisco Phoenix [UPS]. P. O. Box 15081, San Francisco, California 94115. (415) 626-6431. Publisher: Waller
Press, 79 Beaver St. , San Francisco, California 94114.

. Barbara News and Review. Pub. by: Santa Barbara News
and Review, Inc. , 424 N. Nopal Street, Santa Barbara, California 93203. (805) 966-3928. An every other weekly.

. 2551 N. Halstead St. , Chicago, Ill. (312) 929-0133.

e City [UPS, LNS]. 1217 Wichita St. , Houston, Texas 77004.
Red Coyote Movement. Formerly: Space City News.

tator [UPS, LNS]. Southern Indiana Media Corporation, P. O.
Box 1216, Bloomington, Indiana. Founded: Feb. 5, 1966.

ane Natural [UPS, LNS]. P. O. Box 1276, 41 W. Main St. ,
Spokane, Washington 99210.

ise. Sunrise Folks, P. O. Box 271, Macomb, Illinois 61455.
Advs. : (309) 837-1307. Main: 837-3733. Home: 776-4569.
Published monthly.

rlove (In Danish). Redaktion and Ekspedition, Larsbjornstraede
13, 1454 Copenhagen K. , By 6897, Copenhagen, Denmark.

, from the Bottom. New Haven, Conn.

tport Trucker [UPS, LNS]. Divine Guidance, 4044 Broadway,
Kansas City, Missouri 64111. (816) 561-5429. Published
weekly by: Mother Love Tribe of Westport.

. Flowers. Red Acre Road, Stow, Mass. 01775. Alexandra
Brown, Editor.

iamette Bridge [UPS, LNS]. 522 West Burnside Street, Portland,
Oregon 97204. (503) 224-1727. ASH--a supplement edited by
Michael Marsh and Michael Burgess.

[UPS, LNS]. 503 Atlantic Ave. , 5th Fl. , Brooklyn, N.Y. 11217.
(212) 624-8337; 624-8595.

2. NEWSPAPERS AND PERIODICALS
From The Ginsberg Collection

Advocate. 1730 S. Amplett St., Suite 225, San Mateo, California 94402. (415) 573-7100: TWX (910) 374-2807. Liberation Publications, Inc.

After-Image. P. O. Box 10144, Towson, Maryland 21204. Eds: Joe Magri and Ray Sibol.

American Jewish Ledger. 1020 Broad St., Newark, NJ 07102. (201) MI2-0545.

Apocrypha Press. Box 12519, Tucson, Arizona 85711. A.G. association.

Appalachian. Boone, N.C.

Attaboy! 3874 N. Broadway, Boulder, Colo. 80302. Copyright 1976. Prose/poetry, little, alternative magazine. "This issue of Attaboy! has been partially supported by a grant from Poetry Project at St. Mark's Church In-the-Bowery, New York City."

Austin Sun. 404 B West 15th St., Austin, Texas 78701. (512) 472-1780.

Big Sky Books. Box 389, Bolinas, Calif. 94924. (Editor Bill Berkson) Dist. by Serendipity Books: 1790 Shattuck Avenue, Berkeley, Calif. 94709.

Black Sparrow Press. P. O. Box 3993, Santa Barbara, California 93105.

Bombay Gin. c/o Naropa Institute, 1111 Pearl Street, Boulder, Colo. 80302. Magazine.

Boxspring. Hampshire College, Amherst, Mass. 01002. "Boxspring is a literary magazine published semi-annually in fall and spring by students of Hampshire College and printed by Gazette Printing, Northampton, Mass."

Burlington Free Press. Burlington, VT.

Camels Coming Newletter. P. O. Box 703, San Francisco, Calif. 94101. Ed. by Richard Morris.

Caterpillar. 4434 Matilija Avenue, Sherman Oaks, Calif. 91403. Ed. by Clayton Eshleman.

Changes, A Metropolitan Monthly of Art & Trends. P. O. Box 631, Cooper Station, New York, N.Y. 10003. (212) 533-3246; 533-2604. Tabloid/journal of arts and trends.

Cherry Valley Editions. Box 303, Cherry Valley, New York 13320.
Charles Plymell, ed.

Chicago. The Chicago Press, 1973 (copyright), 29 Belle Vue Road,
Wivenhoe, Essex, England. Editor: Alice Notley. European
Edition.

Chicago Sun-Times. Chicago, Ill.

Christopher Street. Pub. by The New Magazine, 60 West 113th St.,
New York, N.Y. 10011. Gay magazine.

City Lights Journal, City Lights Books, San Francisco, California
94133.

City on a Hill (newspaper). University of California at Santa Cruz,
Stonehouse, UCSC, Santa Cruz, Calif. 95064. (408) 429-2430.

City Publishing Co. 531 Pacific Avenue, San Francisco, California
94133.

Cold Mountain Press Poetry Postcard. 4406 Duval St., Austin,
Texas 78751.

College English, National Council of Teachers of English. Ed.
Richard Ohmann, Dept. of English, Wesleyan University, Middletown, Conn. 06457.

College Reporter. Franklin and Marshall College, Lancaster, Pa.

Colorado-North Review. Edited by James Inskeep, Ronn David
Silverstein. Copyright 1977 by Associated Students of the Uni-
versity of Northern Colorado, University Center, University of
Northern Colorado, Greeley, Colorado 80639.

Columbia Flier (newspaper). Columbia, Maryland.

Columbia Today. Published by Columbia University and copyrighted
1976 by the Trustees of Columbia University in the City of New
York, William J. McGill, president, 202 Law Memorial Library,
New York, New York 10027.

Countdown, a subterranean magazine [UPS]. 450 W. 24th Street,
New York, N.Y. 10011.

Creative Arts Book Co. 833 Bancroft Way, Berkeley, California
94701. (415) 848-4777.

Creem Magazine Inc. 187 S. Woodward, Birmingham, Mich. 48011.

Daily Nexus. University of California, 1035 Storke Communication
Bldg., PO Box 13402, University Center, Santa Barbara, Calif.
(805) 961-2691 (Ed. office).

Daily World. 205 West 19th Street, New York, N.Y. 10011.

Deciduous. 3212 Lorain, Cleveland, Ohio, 44113.

Drummer. Ed. by Richard Flood. 4221 Germantown Avenue, Philadelphia, Pa. 19140.

Earth Read-Out. 439 Boynton, Berkeley, Calif. 94707. Orange and black mimeographed newsletter.

Eastwest Journal. 233 Harvard St., Brookline, Mass. 02146.

End of the Year (literary magazine). Ed. by Pat Nolan. Box 798, Monte Rio, Calif. 95462.

Era, the magazine of the New Age. P.O. Box 3269, Hollywood, Calif. 90028. (213) 666-0876. Monthly. Distribution: Parliament News, Inc., 21314 Lassen Street, Chatsworth, Calif. 91311.

Ethos. SUNY at Buffalo, 345 Norton Hall, 3455 Main Street, Buffalo, New York 14214.

Everyman (magazine). 2900 Cuyahoga Community College, Cleveland, Ohio 44115.

Extra (newspaper). 1775 Broadway, New York, N.Y. 10019.

Fervent Valley. Box 571, Placitas, New Mexico 87043. Eds.: Larry Goodell, Bill Pearlman, Steve Rodefer, Charlie Vermont.

Florida Flambeau. Florida State University, Tallahassee, Fla. 32306.

Focus Magazine (The Sunday Camera's Magazine). P.O. Box 591, Boulder, Colorado 80306.

Folio. Brandeis Literary and Visual Arts Magazine, Brandeis University, Waltham, Mass. 02154. Eds.: Andrea S. Aronson and David Rosenberg.

Folio/a publication of KPFA-FM 94 (Listener-Sponsored Pacifica Radio). KPFA-FM 94, 2207 Shattuck Avenue, Berkeley, Calif. 94704.

Fruit Cup. Edited by Mary Beach. Beach Books Texts and Documents, New York, N.Y. Fruit Cup was a magazine put out in only one edition in 1969.

Gainesville Sun. Division of New York Times Media Company, Inc., 101 SE 2nd Place, Gainesville, Fla. 32601. (904) 378-1411.

Gay Community News. 22 Bromfield St., Boston, Mass. 02108.

Gay News. Europe's Largest Circulation Newspaper for Gays of All Sexes. Gay News Ltd., Bsmt. 34 d Redcliffe Square, London SW 10. Tel: 01-373-0586. Fortnightly.

The Gazette. Montreal, Canada.

Globe and Mail. Toronto, Ontario, Canada.

Grape (now The Western Organizer). Owned and produced by The Grape Collective. 324 Powell Street, Vancouver 4 BC, Canada. (604) 688-3713.

Green Revolution. Official Journal of the School of Living (SOL). See this entry in section 1 of this appendix.

Happy Times (newspaper). Philadelphia, Pa.

Herald. By and for the Hobart and William Smith Colleges Community. Geneva, N.Y. 14456.

Holy Beggars Gazette, A Journal of Chassidic Judaism. Copyright 1975 by House of Love & Prayer Inc. Dist. by Judaic Book Service, PO Box 22043, San Francisco, Calif.

A Hundred Posters. Copyright, Alan Davies, 1977. Box 415, Kenmore Station, Boston, Mass. 02215. Newsletter: 7 pages, mimeographed, of poetry.

Independent and Gazette. Published daily except Sunday by Brown Newspaper Co., Inc.

International Education, A Bi-annual Journal. Editor: Anand Malik. College of Education, University of Tennessee, Knoxville, Tenn.

Intrepid (alternative small mag). Published by Allen De Loach; edited by Intrepid Press. Member of COSMEP, P.O. Box 1423, 297 Oakmont Ave., Buffalo, New York 14214.

Iowan. Iowa City, Iowa.

Iron (new quarterly mag). 92 Avenue Road, Gateshead 8, County Durham, England. G632-74430.

Juice (magazine). Phantom House, 4629 Keswick Road, Baltimore, Maryland.

Kaliflower (little magazine/alternative publication). Irving E. Kaliflower, 3145 23 St., San Francisco, California. (415) 285-7522.

Kliatt (paperback book guide). W. Newton, Mass.

Klipsun 1970 (yearbook). Copyright 1970 Klipsun, Western Washington State College, Bellingham, Washington.

Kuksu, A Journal of Backcountry Writing. Ed. by Dale Pendell. Kuksu Press, Box 980, Alleghany Star Route, Nevada City, Calif. 95959. Regional emphasis of this magazine is rural North California.

Kumanitu. Edited by Michael Gizzi, Wendy Lamb, Judith Grossman. Bonewhistle Press, Box 4 S. A. O., Brown University, Providence, R. I. 02912.

La Huerta Magazine. Editors: Gerald McCarthy and Jody Swilky. Box 27B, Lakeville, New York 14480.

Laomedon Review. Published by the University Journal in coopera- tion with the Students Administration Government of Erindale College. Printed in Canada.

Limberlost Review, A Magazine of Poetry. Ed. : Richard Ardinger. 73 Kingston Street, Lawrence, Massachusetts 01843. Alterna- tive Press Journal.

Litmus, Inc. , 574 3rd Avenue, Salt Lake City, Utah 84103. Valga Krusa

Loveland Publishing Co. P. O. Box 59, 1 Cleveland Avenue & East Fifth Street, Loveland, Colorado 80537, (303) 669-5050.

Magic Ink. Newsletter produced by Ian King of the "Underground/ Alternative Press Service/Europe" (shortened to UAPS/Europe and previously known as UPS/Europe). BCM Box 9620, London WCI 6XX.

Maine Edition (poetry magazine). Ed. : Stephen Charles Cook. 22 Bridge Street, Topsham, Maine 04086. (207) 729-8563.

Mass Media. University of Massachusetts at Boston, Boston, Mass.

Metropolis, The weekly newspaper of the Twin Cities. Flour Ex- change Building, Minneapolis, Minn. 55415. (612) 339-8321.

Militant. 14 Charles Lane, New York, N. Y. 10014. (212) 243- 6392.

Minnesota Daily. 10 Murray Hall, University of Minnesota, Minne- apolis, Minnesota 55455. (612) 373-3381.

Mt. Alerno Press. P. O. Box 5143, Santa Monica, California 90405.

Mouth of the Dragon/Poetry Journal of Male Love. Editor, Andrew Bifrost. Box 107, Cooper St. , New York, N. Y. 10003. Mem- ber of Committee of Small Magazine Editors and Publishers Coordinating Council of Literary Magazines.

Mystery Gate; AUM Foundation Newsletter. 515 7th Street Apt. "B,"
Huntington Beach, California 92648; or 512 36th Street, New-
port Beach, Calif. 92663. Mailer, 8½x11, mimeographed, 4
pages.

Nelly Heathen (newspaper). Neorap Book, Sensexual Pagan Media
freaks, P.O. Box 4000J Sather Gate Station, Berkeley, California 94704. Copyright 1973 Psychedelic Venus Church.
First ed. August 1973.

New (literary magazine). Ed. by Elaine Gill. The Crossing Press,
Trumansburg, N.Y. 14886.

New Departures (literary serial). Michael Horowitz, Piedmont,
Bisley, near Stroud, Gloucestershire, England GL6 7BU

New Sun. 807 Avenue N, Brooklyn, N.Y. 11230. (212) 627-0620.
Published by Bruce Silvey, copyright 1977.

News Record. 1201 W. Hwy. 14-16, Box 960, Gillette, Wyoming
82716.

NewsART, The New York SMITH. (Publ.) The Smith, 5 Beekman
St., New York, N.Y. 10038. Member COSMEP, Committee
of Small Magazine Editors and Publishers, Box 703, San Francisco, Calif. 94101. Copyright October 15, 1977 by the
Generalist Association.

Newsletter (on the state of the culture). Harry Smith, editor; Sidney Bernard, roving editor. 5 Beekman Street, New York,
N.Y. 10038. (212) 732-4821. Copyright February 4, 1977.
16 x 11 folded to form 4 pages, soft paper, stencil typed.

Nimrod (lit. mag.). University of Tulsa, Oklahoma 74104.

Noah's Ark, Inc., 2054 University Avenue, Berkeley, Calif. 94707.
(415) 849-4471. Ramparts published by the above.

Oklahoma Daily (newspaper). University of Oklahoma, Norman,
Oklahoma 73069.

Oregon Journal. Portland, Oregon.

Organ. (Publ.) Himalayan Watershed Properties, Inc., Box 4520,
Berkeley, California 94704. (415) 434-0470.

Out There. Editor: Rose Lesniak. 6944 W. George St., Chicago,
Ill. 60634. 1976 copyright--Out There Press. Alternative/
small press collection.

Pacific Sun Publishing Co., Inc., 1714 Stockton Street, San Francisco, Calif. 94133. 433-5055.

Paideuma; a journal devoted to Ezra Pound Scholarship. Hugh Kenner, Eve Hesse. University of Maine, Orono, Maine 04473.

The Painted Bride Quarterly. R. Daniel Evans, Louise Simons, editors. 527 South Street, Philadelphia, Pa. 19147.

Peace Press Inc. 3828 Willat Avenue, Culver City, Calif. 90230.

Phoenix. Queens College, Flushing, N. Y. 11367.

Poetry Project Newsletter. St. Mark's Church, 2nd Avenue and 10th St., New York, N. Y. 10003. 4 pp. stencil, 2 sides, $8\frac{1}{2}$ x 11, mailed.

Poughkeepsie Journal. Poughkeepsie, N. Y.

Press Herald (newspaper). Portland, Maine.

Publication of Chögyam Trungpa, Rinpoche at Lama Foundation. San Cristobal, New Mexico.

Pushcart Press. P. O. Box 845, Yonkers, New York 10701.

Quarterly West. Ed. by James Thomas. University of Utah, Salt Lake City, Utah 84112.

Real Paper ("Boston's Weekly Newspaper"). 116 Austin Street, Cambridge, Mass. 02139.

Response: A Contemporary Jewish Review. 523 W. 113th Street, New York, N. Y. 10025. Member Jewish Student Press Service.

Retriever. University of Maryland, Baltimore County, 5401 Wilkens Avenue, Baltimore, Md. 21228.

River Styx. Editor: Michael Castro. Big River Association, 7420 Cornell Avenue, St. Louis, Mo. 63130. Published twice a year/alternative press literary magazine.

Riverton Ranger (Riverton Review, Riverton Times). 531 East Main St., Riverton, Wyoming 82501.

Rocky Mountain Musical Express (newspaper). Gale Pub. Corp., 1977, Box B, Boulder, Colo. (303) 443-2061.

Rocky Mountain News (newspaper). Denver, Colorado.

Roof. Published by Segue, James Sherry, Ed. 300 Bowery, New York, N. Y. 10012. Collection of poetry and prose/magazine.

San Francisco Review of Books. 2140 Valleju St., San Francisco, Calif. 94123.

Santa Barbara News & Review (newspaper). 424 N. Nopal Street, Santa Barbara, Calif. 93103. (805) 966-3928.

Scottish International Review Ltd. 23 George Square, Edinburgh, Scotland EH 8 9LD. Tel: 031-667-7622.

Search and Destroy: New Wave Cultural Research. c/o City Lights Bookstore, 261 Columbus St., San Francisco, California 94133. Copyright 1977.

Sebastian Quill. Editor: James Mitchell. Hoddypoll Press, San Francisco, Calif. Primarily erotic homosexual poetry, drawings and prose magazine.

Second Aeon (literary magazine). Ed.: Peter Finch. 3 Maplewood Court, Maplewood Avenue, Cardiff, Wales CF4 2NB. Tel: 0222-562423. Welsh arts council support.

Sevendays. Published by the Institute for New Communications, 206 Fifth Avenue, New York, N.Y. 10010.

A Shout in the Street; a journal of literary and visual art. Edited by Joseph Cuomo. Queens College, Flushing, New York 11367. Published 3 times a year/$6.00.

Simpsonian ("Oldest continuously published newspaper in the United States"). Simpson College, Indianola, Iowa. Journalism Practicum.

Sitting Frog. Poetry of Naropa Institute, Ed. by Rachael Peters and Eero Ruuttila. Boulder, Colorado 80302. Unpaged--alphabetical listing "book" of poetry.

Six-Thirteen Magazine (Hasidic). 530 Avenue R, Brooklyn, New York 11223. Copyright 1976, Kol Hai.

Sixpack (alternative literary magazine/innovative and/or experimental fiction/poetry). Eds.: Pierre Joris and Victoria Smitter, 19 Deal Road, London, SW, 17; Ed.: W.R. Prescott, Box 158, Lake Toxaway, North Carolina 28747.

Skyway Peninsula. Brad Pearman, Editor. c/o Naropa Institute, 1111 Pearl St., Boulder, Colorado 80302. 17 x 8½, 1 sheet folded for 4 pp., printed words and illustrations (drawings).

Soft Need No. 9. Printed by Weender Buchdruckerei, Werner-Rosenthal, Go Hingen; distributed by Pociao's Bookshop, Herwarthstrasse 27, D-5300 Bonn. (Tel.: 02221/655887). Produced in Western Germany, Expanded Media Editions, Bonn, Göteborg.

Soho Confidential. (Publ.) Johnny-on-the-Spot, Inc., P.O. Box 4137, Grand Central Station, New York, N.Y. 10017. Stencil-typed leaflet, $8\frac{1}{2}$ x 11 (horizontal), folded to form 4 pp., pink with black letters.

Southwest Review. Southern Methodist University Press, Dallas, Texas 75275.

Star-Tribune. Casper, Wyo.

Statesman. Stony Brook, New York.

Straight Creek Journal. 1030 13th Street, Boulder, Colorado 80302.

Stupa, Naropa Institute Student Magazine. c/o Brad Pearman, Ed. 1111 Pearl St., Boulder, Colorado 80302. Poetry, graphics, broadsides.

Stylus. Student Press at Brockport, State University of New York, Brockport, N.Y.

Sub 70. Published by Sub 70 Press, 6 Cambridge Gardens, London W 10.

Sun Herald. Winter Park; Maitland, Florida.

Takeover Newspaper. Peter Newton, 509 Rolfsmeyer Dr., Madison, Wisconsin.

Toothpick, Lisbon & The Orcas Islands (The Wiater/Scott Issue). (Ed.: Michael Wiater.) 922 East Alder, Seattle, Washington 98122. Designed by Don Scott. 8 x 8 spiral in black and white.

Toy Sun. An occasional tabloid is published by the Somerville Chapter of the Poetry Conspiracy (SPC) 42 Grove St., Somerville, Mass. 02144.

Transatlantic Review. Editor: J.F. McCrindle. London: 33 Ennismore Gardens, SW, 7IAE; New York: Box 3348, Grand Central Station, New York 10017.

Tufts Observer. Tufts University, Medford, Mass. 02153. (617) 668-8281/628-5000, x 550.

UMBC Retriever (weekly newspaper). Free State University Press, University of Maryland, Baltimore County, 5401 Wilkins Avenue, Baltimore, Md. 21228. (301) 455-2224/2226. Member of Association of Collegiate Press.

University Magazine; A Journal of Writing and Visual Art. Published by Publications Council, The University of Utah, 141 A, Ray Olpin Union Bldg., University of Utah, Salt Lake City, Utah 84102.

University Review (newspaper). Copyright Entelechy Press Corp.,

Published 8 times/yr. 2929 Broadway, New York, N.Y. 10025. (212) 866-4604.

Unmuzzled Ox (literary magazine). Box 533 Planetarium Station, New York, N.Y. 10024. Ed. by Michael Andre, Box 374, New York, N.Y. 10024; The Print Center, Inc., 194 State Street, New York, N.Y. 11201.

Villager. 72 Fifth Avenue, New York, N.Y. 10011 (212) 929-7315.

Waves Magazine; A Tri-Annual York Magazine/Edited by Bernice Lever, Heid Bouraoui, Robert Clayton Casto, Pier Giorgio DiCicco, John Oughton. Copyrighted as Waves in New York; belongs to Canadian Periodical Publishers' Assc., 3 Church Street, Suite 407, Toronto, Canada.

Wellesley News. Wellesley, Mass. 02181.

West End; a magazine of poetry and politics. New York, N.Y.

Westport Trucker [UPS/LNS]. Divine Guidance, 4044 Broadway, Kansas City, Missouri 64111. (816) 561-5429. Weekly by Mother Love Tribe of Westport.

Wisconsin Patriot; Voice of the Wisconsin Alliance. 1014 Williamson St., Madison, Wisc. 53703. (608) 251-2821.

Woodstock Times. Woodstock, N.Y.

3. TRANSLATORS OF GINSBERG'S WORKS

Danish

Dan Turell
c/o Ulrich
301 E. 47th St., Apt. 6A
New York, N.Y. 10017
(212) 688-3029.
Istedgade 25
1650 Copenhagen U
Denmark.

French

Mary Beach Pélieu
85 Chestnut St., Apt. 4
Cooperstown, N.Y. 13326.

Yves Le Pellec
9 rue Darquié
31000 Toulouse
France

German

Carl Hanser Verlag
Kolbergerstrasse 22
8000 München 80.
Postanschrift: Postfach 86
04 20
8000 München 86
Telefon: 985861
Telex: 05-22837.

Spanish

Ugo Ulive
Apartado 50678
Caracus, Venezuela.

Russian

A.Y. Sezgeiev

Apt. 32
Zvezdnyboul 5, block 2
U.S.S.R., Moscow 12 9085.

Udo Breger, E.M.E.
Valands Konstskola
40070 Götesborg
Sweden.

City Lights List

City Lights Publishing
House (San Francisco,
California) supplied the
following list of trans-
lators of Ginsberg's work
into foreign languages.

Manuel de Seabra
Plaza de la Sagrada Familia,
10 ent.
1a Barcelona, Spain.

Heiner Bastian
Beenstrasse 48
1 Berlin 37, Germany.

Jean-François Bizot
5 rue des Feuillantines
Paris 75005, France.

Robert Cordier
33 bis, rue Docteur Roux
Paris 16.

Marcelo Covian
Avda. de Ballamar
12 Castelldefels
Barcelona, Spain.

Gosta Friberg
Sveavagen 68
Stockholm, Sweden.

Miguel Grinberg
El Correo Central 1933
Buenos Aires, Argentina.

Jean Jacques Lebel
16 Blvd, Raspail
Paris 7e, France.

François Legros
87 rue St-Antoine
Paris 5, France.

Gerard Georges Lemaire
56 rue du Turenne
Paris 3, France.

Spyros Meimaris
23 Limnou
Athens 823, Greece.

Philippe Mikriammos
56 rue du Turenne
Paris 3, France.

Fernanda Pivano
14 via Manzoni
20121 Milano, Italy.

Carl Weissner
77 Feldbergstr.
68 Mannheim, West Germany.

4. FOREIGN PUBLISHERS AND PERIODICALS

French

Pierre Belfond Editeur (publisher)
8 rue Garanciere
Paris 75006, France.

Christian Bourgois, Editeur
(publisher)
8 rue Garanciere
Paris 75006, France.

Bretagnes; Revue Litteraire et
Politique (magazine)

12 F. Directeur de la publication Paol Keineg
address impasse de la Fontaine-au-Lait
29210 Morlaix, France
trimestrielle

Cahier Noirs du Soleil (publisher)
7 rue Notre Dame des Lorettes
Paris 75009, France.

Cosmose (magazine)
Cuilleré
09420 Rimont, France.

Didier (publisher)
15 rue Cujas
55005 Paris, France.

Ellipse (journal)
C. P. 10, Faculté des Arts
Université de Sherbrooke
Sherbrooke, Quebec, Canada.

Entretiens, beat generation
(review/journal)
subervie éditeur: 21 rue de
l'Emberque
12000 Rodez, France.
Publié sous La Direction de
Yves Le Pellec
copyright 1975.

Le Journal des poetes (journal)
Edited by Pierre Bourgeois
and Arthur Haulot
Maison Internationale de la
Poesie
147 Chaussee de Haecht
1030 Brussels, Belgium.

Mandala
Belfond: Pierre Belfond Editeur
8 rue Garanciere
Paris 75006, France.

Mandala (Dossiers LSD)
Les Cahiers Noirs du Soleil
7 rue Notre Dame des Lorettes
Paris 75009, France.

Oeuf (alternative newspaper)
16,1Communes-Reunies

1212 GD-Lancy
Geneva, Switzerland.

Seghers (publisher)
31 rue Falguières
Paris 750015, France.

Starscrewer
Bernard Froidefont
Place de la Halle
24590 Salignac
Eyvignes, France.

Les Temps Modernes (monthly
review)
Directeur: Jean-Paul Sartre
Redaction, Administration: 26
rue de Conde
Paris 6e, France.
Tel: 362-47-81

German

Deutsch Heft, literatur Zeit-schrift (magazine)
Autorenverlag Pohl & Mayer
(publisher)
Kemptener Str. 98
D-8950

Exempla, Eine Tübinger Liter-aturzeitschrift Texte aus
Nordamerika (literary maga-zine)
c/o Seminar für Allgemeine
Rhetorik der Universität
Tübingen
Wilhelmstr. 50
7400 Tübingen, West Germany

Expanded Media Editions (pub-lisher)
Udo Breger
D-34 Göttingen
Reinhäuser 20a, West Germany
Telephone: T0551/59662

Gesprachsfetzen, ein rundbrief
für freunde erscheint, wenn
es sich ergibt
Karl O. Paetel
68-49 Burns Street

Forest Hills, Long Island
(in German)

RIAS-Quartral (magazine)
Kufsteiner Strasse 69
1000 Berlin 62, West Germany
Tel: (0 30) 85 03-1; Telex:
01-83 790
Publisher: Intendanz und Ge-
samtbetriebsrat

Italian

Fuori! fronte unitario omo-
sessuale rivoluzionario
italiano/mensile di liberazione sessule (newspaper)
Redazione: via San Francesco
d'Assisi, 21-10121
Torino, Italy.

Japanese

Goru (magazine)
Shogakukan Pub. Co., Hirose
Bldg.
S. Shinamoto, 3-17 Kanda-
Nishikicho
Choyoda-Ku, Tokyo, Japan.

Norwegian

Vinduet (literary magazine)
Oslo, Norway

Spanish

El Corno Emplumado (review/
literary magazine)
Mexico City, Mexico
Ed.: Margaret Zandall

APPENDIX D

SELECTIVE CHRONOLOGY, 1968-1978

(Ginsberg's published books, letters, essays/statements,
interviews, etc.)

Airplane Dreams: Composition from Journals. San Francisco:
    House of Anansi/City Lights Books, 1968.
Ankor Wat. London: Fulcrum Press, 1968.
Planet News, 1961-1967. San Francisco: City Lights Books, 1968.
T.V. Baby Poems. San Francisco: Beach Books, Texts & Docu-
    ments, Number 2. (Distributed by City Lights Books), 1968.
T.V. Baby Poems. New York: Grossman Publishers, Inc. (in
    association with Cape Goliard Press Ltd., London), 1968.
"Remarks on Leary's Politics of Ecstasy." Village Voice, 12 De-
    cember 1968, v. XIV, n. 9, p. 8.

"Consciousness and Practical Action." Counter Culture, The Crea-
    tion of an Alternative Society, 1969.
Kohn, Jaakov. Interview. East Village Other, 4:15, 12 March
    1969, pp. 6-7, 19.
"Ginsberg--Arts 1," Interview. Georgia Straight, 3:49, 14-20
    March 1969, pp. 10-11.
Carroll, Paul. Interview. Playboy, XVI:4, April 1969, pp. 81-92,
    236-244.
Webster, Jack. Interview. Georgia Straight, 3:52, 4-10 April
    1969, pp. 9-12.
"Inspired by An Attack of Bells' Palsy: For The National Institute
    of Arts and Letters." April 8, 1969. Available from the In-
    stitute.
Interview. Ann Arbor Argus, 1:5, 14-28 April 1969, pp. 12-13.
Gross, Amy. Interview. Mademoiselle, 69, August 1969, pp. 343-5.
"Kerouac." Rat, Subterranean News, 29 October-12 November
    1969. Reprinted in Georgia Straight (1969).
Fraser, David. Interview. Fifth Estate, 4:13 (91) 30 October-12
    November 1969, pp. 8-9. Reprinted in Extra (1969), Good
    Times (1969), Chinook (1970), Los Angeles Free Press (1970),
    San Diego Door (1970), Win, (1970).
Krown, Johnny. Interview. View from the Bottom, 1:3, [17] No-
    vember 1969, p. 10.
Prescott, Bill, Pierre Joris and Steve Kushner. Interview. Bard
    Observer(?) Annandale-on-Hudson, New York (Bard College), 3
    December 1969.
"Ecology and Progress/Ginsberg...." Interview. Octopus, 2:16,
    11 December 1969, p. 4.

Indian Journals, May 1962-May 1963. San Francisco: Dave Haselwood and City Lights Books, 1970.

The Moments Return. San Francisco: Grabhorn-Hoyem, 1970.

May Day Speech. (pamphlet), by Jean Genet. Description by Ginsberg. California: City Lights Books, 1970.

"Allen Ginsberg Comes Down on Speed." This is an article which
resurfaced in the 1970's in this form (from an interview by Art
Kunkin of the Los Angeles Free Press in the 1960's). The
first reprint appeared in the Nickel Review, 9 January 1970,
v. 4, n. 18, p. 5. It has since been reprinted in Chinook
(1970), Door to Liberation (1970), Harry (1970), Los Angeles
Free Press (1970), Nola Express (1970), Spectator (1970),
The Agitator: A Collection of Diverse Opinions from America's
Not-So-Popular Press, Chicago: American Library Association
(A Schism Anthology).

"My Free Bill of Rights." Daily Planet, 24 January 1970, 1:VIII, p. 4.

"No Money, No War." East Village Other, 5:7, 21 January 1970,
p. 2. Reprinted in Win (1970).

"Focus on Poetry/An Article by Allen Ginsberg." University Review, February 1970, n. p.

Interview. Logos, 3:1, March 1970, unpaged.

"Ransom." Good Times, 13 March 1970, v. III, n. 11, p. 3.

"Ginsberg Won't Pay for Vietnam." Chinook, 26 March 1970, v. 2,
n. 11, p. 6.

"Leary/Leary Defense Fund." Helix, 11-15, 9 April 1970, n. p.

"Ginsberg Interview." Good Times, 3:16, 17 April 1970, p. 11.

"Ginsberg and Swami A. C. B. P." Interview. Chinook, 2:16, 30
April 1970, pp. 6-7, part II. Continued in 2:17, 17 May 1970,
pp. 6-7.

"Ginsberg on Junk." Good Times, 17 April 1970, v. III, n. 16, p.
11. Reprinted in several versions in Georgia Straight (1970),
Harry (1970), Los Angeles Free Press (1970), Berkeley Tribe
(1971), Quicksilver (1971).

"Read Any Good Books Lately?" WIN, 15 June 1970, v. 6, n. 11, p. 25.

"A Conversation with Allen Ginsberg," Interview. Organ, 1:1, July
1970, pp. 4-9.

"Refusing to Look Through Galileo's Telescope," Interview. Crawdaddy, IV: 10, 6 July 1970, part 2, section 2, pp. 26-28.

"Symposium: The Writer's Situation II." New American Review,
10, August 1970, pp. 212-213.

"Continuation of Notes on Tim Leary's Public Career and Politics
of Ecstasy." August 7, 1970. Reprinted with some 1968 remarks as the preface to Tim Leary's Jail Notes (New York:
Douglas Books, 1970).

"Card to Ed (Sanders)." Quote on dust jacket of Shards of God
(New York: Grove Press, 1970).

"Fast Notes Reading Cats Language." Quote on dust jacket of
Spencer Holst's Language of Cats (New York: Avon, 1973).

"AG Pot Art Blurb." Quote on book cover of Stone Mountain's Pot
Art and Marijuana Reading Matter (Tucson, Ariz.: Apocrypha
Press, 1972).

Head, Robert, Interview. Nola Express, 67, 30 October-12 November 1970, pp. 4-5. Reprinted in Berkeley Barb (1970),
Chinook (1970).

"Adept McClure's Prose Maturity." Quote on dust jacket of Michael
   McClure's Adept (New York: Delacorte Press, 1971).

Howl and Other Poems. (1956) San Francisco: Grabhorn and Hoyem,
   special edition, 1971.
"En Marge de Howl et autres poems." ("Notes written on finally
   recording 'Howl'") (1959), ellipse, Quebec: Faculté des Arts,
   Université de Sherbrooke, 8/9, 1971, pp. 124-127. French.
"Ginsberg." Self Interview. Intrepid, 18/19, 1971, pp. 52-61.
"Two Interesting Dreams." IO, 8, 1971, p. 80.
Colbert, Alison, Interview. Partisan Review, 38:3, 1971, pp. 289-
   309.
Colbert, Alison and Anita Box. Interview. West End, 1:1, Winter
   1971, pp. 32-43. (Excerpt)
"To Young or Old Listeners: Setting Blake's Songs to Music, and
   a Commentary on the Songs." Blake Newsletter, 4:3, Winter
   1971, pp. 98-103.
"Blake Notes." Caterpillar, 14, January 1971, pp. 126-132.
Scharfman/Mandell. Interview. College Press, 46, 15 January
   1971, p. 1.
"Craft Interview with Allen Ginsberg." New York Quarterly, 6,
   Spring 1971, pp. 12-40.
"Allen Ginsberg and Richard Howard 1971 National Book Award
   Poetry Judges, Explain Themselves." New York Times, VII,
   4 April 1971, p. 4.
"Allen Ginsberg on the New Dylan." Outlaw, 7-28 May 1971, v. 2,
   n. 2, p. 12.
Tedesco, Frank. Interview. Berkeley Barb, 12:21:303, 4-10 June
   1971, pp. 2-3, 11. Reprinted in Georgia Straight (1971).
Aronowitz, Alfred G. Actuel, 9 Juin 1971, pp. 12-16. (French)
"Entretien avec le même Ginsberg." Interview. Actuel, 10-11,
   Juillet-Août, 1971, pp. 20-22. (French)
"DECLARATION OF INDEPENDENCE FOR DR. TIMOTHY LEARY,
   July 4, 1971/Model Statement in Defense of the Philosopher's
   Personal Freedom Proposed by San Francisco Bay Area Prose
   Poets' Phalanx." San Francisco: Hermes Free Press, July
   1971 (pamphlet). Reprinted in East Village Other (1971); Los
   Angeles Free Press (1971).
East Village Other. 10 August 1971, v. 6, n. 36.
Harris, James T. Interview. Alternative Feature Service, 1:13,
   10 September 1971, pp. 1-4. Reprinted in Chinook (1971);
   Good Times (1971); Great Speckled Bird (1971); Harry (1971);
   Space City (1971); Staff (1971).
"Raps with Allen Ginsberg." Interview. All Hands Abandon Ship.
   2:6, December 1971, n. p.

Bixby Canyon Ocean Path Word Breeze. New York: Gotham Book
   Mart, 1972.
The Fall of America; Poems of These States, 1965-1971. San
   Francisco: City Lights Books, 1972.

The Gates of Wrath: Rhymed Poems, 1948-1952. Berkeley, Calif. :
Grey Fox Press, (dist. by Book People), 1972.

Improvised Poetics. San Francisco: Anonym Press, 1972.

Iron Horse. Toronto, Canada: The Coach House Press, 1972.

New Year Blues. New York: Phoenix Book Shop. Oblong Octavo
Series, 1972. (pamphlet).

Open Head. (bound with Open Eye by Lawrence Ferlinghetti). Victoria, Australia: Sun Books Pty. Ltd. , 1972.

"Mysterious impersonality ... Patient genius ... old Indian Aboriginal storyteller...." Statement among others used on dust
jacket of the hardcover edition of Spencer Holst Stories (New
York: Horizon Press, 1972).

"On the New Cultural Radicalism." Partisan Review, 39:3 (1972),
pp. 423-4.

Giangreco, Dennis. Interview. Westport Trucker, 2:22 (46) ("Eighth-
ninth") (1972) (Undated issue), pp. 8-9.

"Television Address, 1972." Charlotte, North Carolina. "Response
to Charlotte television station's editorial denouncing violent behavior of some protestors at Republican convention proceedings
at Miami Beach late August (1972). "

Quote under 2-page illustration. Good Times. 28 January-10 February 1972, pp. 14-15.

"A Letter to Claude Pélieu and his translator Mary Beach...." Unmuzzled Ox, February 1972, v. 1, n. 2, pp. 19-20. (letter)

" 'No fuss on Blues'/Ginsberg Reply to the University." Westport
Trucker, 2 February-7 March 1972, v. 2, n. 21, (45?), p. 5.

Lester, Elenore. Interview. New York Times, II, 6 February
1972, p. 1, column 4.

Loewinsohn, Ron. Interview. Daily Californian, 10 March 1972,
n. p.

"mind consciousness be-in--San Diego." Win, 1 April 1972, v. 8,
n. 6, pp. 14-15. Reprinted in Los Angeles Free Press (1972).

Nolan, Frank. Interview. Polar Star, XXIX:24, 14 April 1972,
p. 8.

Production of Kaddish (Arthur Ginsberg). New York, Spring 1972.

Foehr, Stephen and Richard Lutz. Interview. Straight Creek Journal, 1:15, 18 May 1972, pp. 1, 10.

"Ah, WAKE UP!" Newsday, 27 August 1972, n. p.

"Lennon-Ono: Deporting the Great Swan." It, 2-16 November 1972,
n. p.

"P. E. N. Supports Lennon-Ono." La Star, 9 November 1972, n. p.

"A Manifesto for Nonviolent Revolution." Win, 15 November 1972,
v. 8, n. 18, p. 4.

Castro, M. Interview. Outlaw, III:11, 17 November-14 December
1972, pp. 13, 23 (see Allen Verbatim, "The Death of Ezra
Pound" pp. 179-187).

"Writers Protest Grant." Los Angeles Free Press, 15-25 December 1972, v. 9, n. 50, issue 439, p. 8.

Iron Horse. (American edition). California: City Lights Books,
1974.

Preface to Kerouac: A Biography, by Ann Charters. California:
Straight Arrow Books, 1973.

"Brother Poet." Introduction to Rites of Passage, by Eugene Brooks. New York: The Author, 1973.

"How Kaddish Happened." In Poetics of the New American Poetry. New York: Grove Press Inc., 1973, pp. 344-347.

"On Improvised Poetics." (Independence Day, 1973) in Poetics of the New American Poetry. New York: Grove Press Inc., 1973, p. 350.

"Introduction to Gasoline." (Amsterdam, Holland/October 1957) in Poetics of the New American Poetry. New York: Grove Press Inc., 1973, pp. 322-323.

"Notes for Howl and Other Poems." (1959) in Poetics of the New American Poetry. New York: Grove Press Inc., first edition, pp. 318-321. Reprinted in America A Prophecy, A New Reading of American Poetry from Pre-Columbian Times to the Present. New York: Random House 1973, p. 382.

"Poetry, Violence and The Trembling Lambs." (1959) in Poetics of the New American Poetry. New York: Grove Press Inc., 1973, pp. 331-333.

"Prose Contribution to Cuban Revolution." (Athens, Greece/October 16, 1961) in Poetics of the New American Poetry. New York: Grove Press Inc., 1973, pp. 223-244.

"Some Metamorphoses of Personal Poetry." (September 10, 1966) in Poetics of the New American Poetry. New York: Grove Press Inc., 1973, pp. 348-349.

"When the Mode of the Music Changes the Walls of the City Shake." (1961) in Poetics of the New American Poetry. New York: Grove Press Inc., 1973, pp. 324-330.

"Advertising Trade Publication...." Art Direction/The Magazine of Visual Communication. January 1973, p. 41 (prepared November 6, 1972).

Young, Allen. Interview. Gay Sunshine, 16 January-February 1973, pp. 4-10. Continued in 17, March-April 1973, p. 18. Reprinted in Berkeley Barb (1973), Georgia Straight (1973), Northwest Passage (1973), Real Papers (1973), College English (1974), Gay Sunshine Interviews. California: Gay Sunshine Press, 1978.

Robbins, Al. Interview. Drummer, 233, 6 March 1973, p. 9.

Clarke, Gerald. Interview. College Press Service, 40, 14 March 1973, p. 6.

Clarke, Gerald. Interview. Esquire, 79:4, April 1973, pp. 92-95, 169, 170.

"Ginsberg in Newcastle." Iron, 1, Spring 1973, pp. 2-3. An excerpt is reprinted in Madeira & Toasts for Basil Bunting's 75th Birthday. North Carolina: The Jargon Society, 1977, unpaged.

"Watergate Apocatastasis: G. Gordon Liddy from Millbrook to Vancouver Airport." Georgia Straight, 14-21 June 1973, v. 7., n. 297, pp. 12-13. Reprinted in Berkeley Barb (1973).

"Allen Ginsberg ... Rennie Davis and the Underground Press." Interview. Georgia Straight, 7:298, 21-28 June 1973, p. 11.

Aldrich, Michael R. Interview. Part 1. Grass Roots Gazette. n. 3, July 1973 (?), pp. 1, 4-6, 14.

Lemon, Denis and Stephen MacLean. Interview. Gay News (London), 27, 12-25 July 1973, pp. 10-12.

"Free Willie." nelly heathen, 15 August 1973, p. 13. (letter)
"Sisterbrother Allen Says to Say Ah!" nelly heathen, 15 August
   1973, p. 15. (letter)
"First Thought Is Best Thought." Interview. Scottish International.
   September 1973, pp. 18-23.
"Watergate Statement." Changes, 3 September 1973. (Dictated by
   telephone to Susan Grahm).
"Dear Readers of the Georgia Straight." Georgia Straight, 20-27
   September 1973, v. 7, n. 311, p. 1. (letter)
"Letters from Ginsberg/Abbie Hoffman-Political Poet...." Georgia
   Straight, 20-27 September 1973, v. 7, n. 311, pp. 4-5, 21.
   (letter)
"Allen Ginsberg Defends Abbie...." Liberation, September-October
   1973, v. 18, n. 2, pp. 7, 43. (letter)
"Defend Abbie Hoffman and Individual Rights...." Hi, 4 October
   1973, v. 5, n. 23, pp. 1, 7, 12. (letter)
"Abbie Hoffman...." Berkeley Barb, 5-11 October 1973, v. 18,
   n. 13, issue 425, pp. 4-5, 14. (letter)
"Ginsberg Makes Plea for Hoffman Defense." College Press Service,
   6 October 1973, n. 5, pp. 5-6. (letter)
"Requests for Help/Info Inc./Appeal on Behalf of Abbie Hoffman."
   Magic Ink, 14 October 1973, pp. 61-65. (letter)

Allen Verbatim. Lectures on Poetry, Politics, Consciousness.
   New York: McGraw-Hill, 1974.
Gay Sunshine Interview. California: Grey Fox Press, 1974.
Iron Horse. (1974) California: City Lights Books, 1973.
The Visions of the Great Rememberer. Amherst, Mass.: Mulch
   Press, 1974.
"Interju med Allen Ginsberg." Interview. Vinduet, 1974, 28 yr.,
   n. 3, pp. 16-20. (Norwegian translation).
"Encounter with Ezra Pound." City Lights Anthology, San Francisco:
   City Lights Books, 1974.
"The Fall of America Wins a Prize." New York: Gotham Book
   Mart & Gallery, 1974, folder, 4 leaves (Speech prepared by
   Ginsberg on April 18, 1974, Grand Valley/presented on his
   behalf by Peter Orlovsky).
Tytell, John. Interview. Partisan Review, 1974, pp. 253-262.
   Reprinted in Berkeley Barb (1974), Tel Quel (1974, in French).
Cargas, Harry. Interview. Nimrod, 19:1, Fall/Winter 1974, pp.
   24-29.
"Thoughts on Israeli Arguments." Liberation, 18:6, February 1974,
   p. 14.
Bockris-Wylie. Interview. Drummer, 12 February 1974, pp. 3-4.
   Reprinted in Berkeley Barb (1974), Georgia Straight (1974).
Freeman, Deborah. Interview. Green Revolution, 12:3, February-
   March 1974, pp. 11-14.
"OM AH HUM: 44 Temporary Questions on Dr. Leary." Original
   prepared March 1974. Reprinted in Berkeley Barb (1974),
   City (1974), Georgia Straight (1974) Soho Weekly News (1974),
   Win (1974) and San Francisco Phoenix (n.d.).
"Corso, Ginsberg, Orlovsky...." Interview. Gone Soft, v. 1, n.
   3, Spring 1974, n.p.

304 / Appendix D

Bradenburg, John. Interview. Oklahoma City Times, 25 April
1974, p. 10.
Lovell, John. Interview. Press Herald, 27 April 1974, p. 26.
"I Love Abbie Hoffman." Win, 10:6, 2 May 1974, p. 19.
Desauisseaux, Paul. Interview. Pacific Sun, 16-22 May 1974, pp.
12-14.
Jones, Lauren, Barbara Weinberg and David Fenton. Interview.
Ann Arbor Sun, 2:10, 17-31 May 1974, pp. 14-15, 22. Re-
printed in Georgia Straight (1974).
Interview. Maine Edition, August 1974, pp. 7-11.
"Interview with Allen Ginsberg." The Noiseless Spider, IV:1, Fall
1974, pp. 2-15.
Goodwin, Michael. Interview. City, 7:52, 13-26 November 1974,
pp. 30-34.

Chicago Trial Testimony. California: City Lights Books, 1975.
(pamphlet, Trashcan Series, No. 1).
Sad Dust Glories, Poems Written During Work Summer in Woods.
California: The Workingman's Press, 1975. (pamphlet)
"Allen Ginsberg: Interview." Unmuzzled Ox, 3:2, 1975, pp. 14-25.
"First Thought Best Thought" (from the Spiritual Poetics Class,
July 29, 1974), in Loka 1, A Journal from Naropa Institute.
New York: Doubleday, 1975, pp. 89-95.
Clark, Thomas. Interview. End of the Year, 1975, unpaged, pp.
22-23. (excerpt-original interview, Spring 1966).
Hochman, Sandra. Interview. entretiens, beat generation, 1975,
pp. 59-76. (French)
Pellec, Yves. Interview. entretiens, beat generation, 1975, pp.
41-58. (French)
"Ginsberg on Trantino." Liberation, February 1975, v. 19, n. 2,
p. 25. (letter)
"N. I. A. L. Grant in Arts & Letters" (for William Seward Burroughs).
Prepared on February 15, 1975. New York: The National
Institute of Arts & Letters.
Ziomek, Jon. Interview. Chicago Sun-Times, 17 March 1975, p.
36.
Geneson, Paul. Interview. Chicago Review, 27:1, Summer 1975,
pp. 27-35.
First Blues: Rags, Ballads and Harmonium Songs, 1971-1974. New
York: Full Court Press, 1975.

'"The Dream of Tibet' from New York Journals, August 1960."
Attaboy! 1976, pp. 68-74. Reprinted in The Retreat Diaries,
by William S. Burroughs (New York: The City Moon, 1976
Broadcast No. Three); and in Ginsberg's Journals. (New York:
Grove Press, 1977).
To Eberhart from Ginsberg. Lincoln, Mass.: Penmaen Press,
1976.
Afterword to Death College & Other Poems, by Tom Veitch. Cali-
fornia: Big Sky Books, 1976.
Foreword to Amphetamine Cowboys, by Claude Pélieu. German:
Expanded Media Editions, 1976.

Introduction to Stories and Illustrations by Harley, by Harley Flana-
gan.   n. p. :   Charlatan Press, 1976.
"An Exposition of William Carlos Williams' Poetics. " Loka 2, A Jour-
nal from Naropa Institute. New York: Doubleday, 1976, pp. 123-
140.
"Poets' Colloquium. " Loka 2, A Journal from Naropa Institute.
New York: Doubleday, 1976. p. 164.
Bockris-Wylie.   Interview.   Unmuzzled Ox, IV:1, 1976, p. 140.
(excerpt)
Levine, Sharon.   Interview.   American Jewish Ledger, 31 January
1976, pp. 7-8.
Lanser, Hinda. Interview. Six-Thirteen, February 1976, pp. 64-67.
"Citation for 1976 N. I. A. L. Award. "   Prepared on March 4, 1976
on behalf of Louis Zukofsky.   New York: National Institute of
Arts & Letters, 1976.
Billotte, Louise.   Interview.   Berkeley Barb, 8:577, 3-9 September
1976, p. 11.

As Ever: The Collected Correspondence of Allen Ginsberg and Neal
Cassady.   Berkeley, Calif. : Creative Arts Book Co. , 1977.
Journals: Early Fifties, Early Sixties. New York: Grove Press,
1977.
Mind Breaths, Poems 1972-1977. San Francisco, Calif. : City Lights
Books, 1977. Pocket Book Series No. 35.
Introduction to Junky, by William S. Burroughs. (Reprint ed. , New
York: Penguin Books, 1977).
"Allen Ginsberg on New Wave/Ginsberg SEZ. " Search & Destroy,
New Wave Cultural Research, 1977, n. 1, p. 13.
Clark, Thomas.   Interview.   Writers at Work, Paris Review Inter-
views. (Reprint ed. , New York: Penguin Books, 1977).
Portugés, Paul.   Interview.   Boston University Journal, XXV:1,
1977, pp. 47-59.
"What Six Nice People Found in the Government Drawers. "   Oui,
February 1977, v. 6, n. 2, pp. 116-117.
" 'Junky' Restored/Guest Word. " New York Times Book Review,
6 February 1977, p. 35.
"Allen Ginsberg. " Interview. Goru.   24 February 1977, n. 4, pp.
46-51. (Japanese)
Belov, Miriam and Elliot Sobel.   Interview.   New Sun, 1:4, March
1977, pp. 12-15, 35.
"General Purposes and Objectives. "   Excerpted from pamphlet
Naropa Institute Study Report for North Central Accreditation
Committee.   April 1977. (Prepared by Ginsberg, touched up
by Michael Brownstein and Anne Waldman).
"Some Different Considerations in Mindful Arrangement of Open
Verse Forms on the Page. "   Prepared on April 21, 1977 at
Jack Kerouac School of Disembodied Poetics, Naropa Institute,
printed in less than 100 copies for classroom distribution.   Re-
printed in City Lights Journal, 1978, n. 4, p. 137.
Westerman, Keith F. Interview.   Mass Media, XI:24, 12 April
1977, p. 16.
"On Mindfulness/Presentation to Conference on Life Cycle Planning. "

Part I, II, III, IV. One page statement signed and dated April
21, 1977. Available from Washington Dharmadattu, 3220 Idaho
Ave. , Washington, D. C.
Fox, Herb. Interview. Santa Barbara News & Review, VI:19,
(221), 20 May 1977, pp. 28-30.
Bockris, Victor. Interview. National Screw, June 1977, pp. 6-10.
First Blues "linear notes. " August 5, 1977 (First Blues/record/
pending release, 1978?).
"Interrogation of a Businessman by the Interior Police. " Interview.
Kaliflower, 3:17, 26 August 1977, unpaged.
Johnson, Bryan. Interview. Globe and Mail, 4 September 1976, p. 1.
Bageant, Joseph L. Interview. Rocky Mtn. Musical Express, Oc-
tober 1977, pp. 14-15.
Golden, Daniel. Interview. City on a Hill, 11:4, October 1977,
pp. 3-7.
"Ginsberg on Lowell. " Poetry Project Newsletter, 1 October 1977,
n. 48, p. 7.
Koch, Kenneth. Interview. New York Times Book Review, 23 Oc-
tober 1977, pp. 9, 44-46, section 7.
"Time; Squeezing the Most Out of it/We Asked 32 Busy, Successful
People How They Do It. " TWA Ambassador, 10:11, November
1977, p. 23.
Stuttaford, Genevieve. Interview. Publishers Weekly, 14 November
1977, pp. 6-7.
Gengle, Dean. Interview. Advocate, 16 November 1977, pp. 25-28.
Litterine, Lynn. Interview. Philadelphia Inquirer, 10 December
1977, pp. 7-8A.
Maroney, Tom. Interview. Acton Minute-Man, 15 December 1977,
p. 5. Appearing simultaneously in Bedford Minute-Man, Bil-
lerica Minute-Man, Burlington Times-Union, Concord Journal,
The Hansconian, Lexington Minute-Man.

Careless Love, Two Rhymes. Wisconsin: The Red Ozier Press
(Chapbook, limited edition, 1978).
Introduction to William S. Burroughs, A Bibliography, 1953-1973,
compiled by Joe Maynard and Barry Miles. Virginia: Univer-
sity Press of Virginia, 1978.
Faas, Ekbert. Interview and Essay. Towards A New American
Poetics: Essay & Interviews. Santa Barbara, Calif. : Black
Sparrow Press, 1978.
"T. S. Eliot Entered My Dreams, " in City Lights Journal. San
Francisco, Calif. : City Lights Books, 1978, n. 4, pp. 61-65.
"Blurb" for cover of Gay Sunshine Interviews. (San Francisco,
Gay Sunshine Press, 1978).
Chowka, Peter Barry. Interview. East West, February 1978, pp.
52-55.

AUTHOR INDEX

Aaron 668
Abhishaker, M. J. 1208
Abramson, Neal 1158
Adams, Leonard P. 1363
Albert, Stew 1159
Aldrich, Michael 319, 669
Alexander, Floyce 981
Alkabutazolidan 982
Allen, Bruce 1293
Allen, Donald 249, 250, 1322
Allen, Henry 670
Allen, Walter 619
Allison, Alexander W. 251
Altman, Dennis 1103
Alton, Lawrence 680
Alvarenga, Teresa 967
Amram, David 1093
Andre, Kenneth Michael 1336
André, Michael 1094
Andrews, Lyman 1161
Antin, David 1095
Arcaini, Dan 1324
Ardinger, Rick and Rosemary 1096
Arguelles, Jose A. 620
Aronowitz, Alfred G. 1279
Ashley, Richard 1352

Bacon, Leslie 682
Bageant, Joseph L. 323
Ball, Gordon 2, 16, 351, 985, 1367
Bangs, Lester 683
Barber, James 684
Barberis, Robert 969
Barg, Barbara 324
Barnes, Clive 685, 686
Barnet, Sylvan 252
Barry, Ann 687
Bartley, Bruce M. 688
Bartnatan, M. R. 316
Bastian, Heiner 37
Beach, Mary 29-33
Beck, David L. 690

Bell, Steve 352, 571
Belov, Miriam 325
Belt, Byron 691
Bender, Donald 1209
Bender, Todd 253
Berg, Stephen 254
Berkson, Bill 986, 1244
Berman, Morton 252
Bernard, Sidney 621, 693, 987
Bertlet, Chip 988
Bess, Donovan 1306
Betting, Richard A. 1337
Billotte, Louise 326
Blickstein, Steve 1329
Blake, Harry (translator) 404
Blum, Peter 695
Bockris, Victor 327, 696, 697
Bockris-Wylie 328, 329, 1097, 1326
Bowering, George 1073, 1098, 1354
Box, Anita 337
Bradley, John 989
Bradley, Soulley 255
Brady, Frank 256
Braitman, Stephen M. H. 548
Bramwell, Murray 1103
Brandenburg, John 330
Brinkmeyer, Robert 1132
Brinnin, John Malcolm 1133
Brodey, Jim 1194
Brooks, C. 257
Broughton, Panthea R. 262
BrownJohn, A. 1149, 1245
Brownstein, Michael 493, 990
Bruchac, Joé 698
Bruno, Salvatore 1355
Bryan, John 699, 700
Buccino, Anthony 701, 702
Bukowski, Charles 703
Burns, Glen 1079, 1080
Burroughs, William, Jr. 1327
Burto, William 252

TITLE INDEX

(including primary works, anthologies, and journals)

SUBJECT INDEX

(See also specific titles of Ginsberg's works
in Title Index for comments and criticism)

Baez, Joan 654, 781, 790;
   see also Rolling Thunder
   Revue
Baldwin, James 1041
Ball, Gordon 2, 16, 351, 583,
   597, 985, 1367
Baraheni, Reza 672, 782, 843
Baraka, Imamu Amiri [LeRoi
   Jones] 265, 622, 1361
Beach, Mary 29, 30, 31, 32,
   33, 884, 1053, 1097
The Beatles 402, 784
Beats 323, 332, 403, 624, 638,
   639, 746, 1053, 1114, 1345
   cultural movement 627, 631,
   637, 639, 642, 775, 849,
   976, 998, 1015, 1018, 1024,
   1026, 1036, 1050, 1077, 1084,
   1103, 1111, 1339
   cultural movement and poetry
   260, 626, 635, 646, 658,
   666, 667, 802, 845, 897,
   911, 1124
   poetry 249, 475, 645, 653,
   656, 657, 772, 967, 972,
   984, 987, 993, 1000, 1027,
   1068, 1076, 1100, 1101, 1117
Bell, Steve 352, 571
Bellow, Saul 1046
Bell's Palsy 677, 857
Berrigan, Daniel 465, 622, 1338
Berrigan, Ted 747
Bethlehem Asylum 671
Bhagavan Das 719, 723, 728,
   758, 770, 907
Bibliographies 509, 603, 604,
   605, 606, 607, 608
The Black Mountain Poets 249,
   769, 972
Black Panthers 494, 879
Blake, William 276, 354, 404,
   474, 602, 541, 1059, 1359
   recording of his poems by Gins-
   berg 401, 416, 467, 524, 536,
   652, 669, 683, 731
   Ginsberg singing his poems 337,
   394, 438, 600, 602, 698,
   735, 790, 1062
Blakely, Ronie 654
Blankfort, Jeffrey 383a
Bleeker, Nancy 12
Bly, Robert 344, 455, 544, 629a,
   636, 646, 699, 999, 1089,
   1125, 1341

Book Awards 341, 378, 411,
   422, 705, 727, 918, 938,
   959, 1002, 1009
Bookchin, Murray 566
Borges, Jorge Luis 388a
Bowie, David 371
Bowles, Paul 658
Boys, Barry 545
Bradstreet, Anne 265
Brautigan, Richard 267, 1103,
   1312
Brooks, Eugene 498, 552, 553
Brown, Jerry 326
Brown, Richard Rabbit 495
Brownstein, Michael 493,
   747, 990
Bruce, Lenny 998
Buffalo LEMAR Conference
   322, 523, 675
Bukowski, Charles 267, 703,
   895, 911, 1312
Bunting, Basil 426, 932
Burgess, Anthony 261
Burroughs, William S. 348,
   455, 641, 658, 697, 747,
   835, 969, 970, 982, 992,
   1022, 1328, 1329, 1342,
   1360
   appearances with Ginsberg
   324, 398, 567, 594, 711,
   742, 807, 872, 896, 906,
   958, 980, 1032, 1084
   Ginsberg's opinion of 322,
   327, 368, 370, 371, 379,
   396, 404, 460, 478, 509,
   629a, 696, 697, 776, 1044
   his effect on Ginsberg's
   writing and other writers
   344, 393, 403, 436, 443,
   458, 475, 499
   on Ginsberg 991
   Yage Letters 25, 46, 48, 53,
   61, 721

C. I. A. and F. B. I. 321, 322,
   358, 401, 404, 472, 588,
   1062
   drug involvement 352, 361,
   366, 388, 780, 862, 983,
   990
CKNW 394
Calais, Maris 439
Capote, Truman 261

Liddy, G. Gordon 469
Lindfors, Viveca 545
Lindner, Richard 975
Litman, Steve 352, 571
Living Theatre 643, 820
Lowell, Robert 428, 622, 693,
    809, 834, 875, 999, 1095
Lowenfels, Walter 1099
Lower East Side 306, 325, 373,
    623, 644

Macadams, Lewis 747
McCartney, Paul 327, 835
McClure, Michael 267, 405,
    516, 699, 891, 904, 1047,
    1350
McCoy, Alfred 366, 388, 469,
    723, 1363
Macdiarmid, Hugh 345, 932
McNamara, Robert 429
McReynolds, David 439
Mafia 427, 742
    and drugs 361, 385, 427, 486
Mailer, Norman 388a, 637, 1046
Malamud, Bernard 947
Malanga, Gerard 638, 1022,
    1109
Malina, Judith 643, 820
Mao Tse-Tung 429
Marcuse, Herbert 267, 1312
Marquez, Gabriel Garcia 388a
Marshall, Jim 383a
Max, Peter 432
May Day 795
Mayers, Patric 569
Media 347, 352, 365, 359, 385,
    629a
    Ginsberg's image in 347, 352,
        360, 365, 788, 807, 830, 831,
        1021
Meditation 325, 334, 344, 347,
    352, 355, 365, 366, 375,
    378, 383a, 395, 401, 406,
    407, 414, 451, 576, 655,
    681, 712, 719, 782, 841,
    930, 939, 943, 954, 1016;
    see also Writing and medi-
    tation
    and social change 325, 334, 337,
        342, 346, 347, 351, 362, 387,
        404, 410, 414, 418, 441, 429,
        732, 806, 978

Ginsberg as leader of public
    meditation 352, 358, 712,
        719, 728, 729, 788
Meeropol, Michael 963
Mekas, Jonas 596
Melo Nato, Joao Cabral 388a
Melton, Barry 904
Meltzer, David 736
Mercedes, Denise 413, 790
Meredith, William 1105
Merriam, Eve 1059
Merrill, James 544
Merwin, W. S. 636, 982
Metaphysics 332, 347, 354,
    361, 377, 392, 403
Miami Convention 321, 410,
    480, 1110
Michaelson, Peter 1049
Michaux, Henry 478
Micheline, Jack 838
Mikriammos, Phillippe 28
Miles 337, 698, 835, 840, 884,
    1097
Millan, Fernando 317
Miller, Rabbi A. W. 889
Miller, Henry 1099
Miller, Dr. Orville C. 298
Minzey, Rev. Wilbur 481
Mirabai 355
Mitchell, Pat 588, 670
Moore, Marianne 1113
Moraes, Dom 1028
Moraes, Vinicius de 388a
Morden Tower 426
Morse, Linda 765
The Movement (counter-cul-
    ture; New Left) 321, 348,
        362, 366, 368, 385, 396,
        458, 569, 620, 633, 649,
        655, 784, 789b, 901, 987,
        993, 1024, 1029, 1067,
        1103, 1112
Mugging 814, 862
Murao, Shig 706
Music 365, 368, 383, 394, 404,
    629a, 678, 834, 843,
        1078; see also New Wave;
        Blake; individual groups
        and people
    albums 351, 352, 379, 652,
        890, 945
    appearances by Ginsberg with
        musicians 352, 375, 380,

AFTERWORD

Public access to nontraditional information was the motivating force behind this compilation. As computer technology is adapted to library systems one hopes that this process of data retrieval will be simplified. However, in lieu of advances in application, this sourcebook has been provided with material that is not readily available. Furthermore, a model has been constructed for further inter-disciplinary, nontraditional and creative research.

In retrospect, the issue of public access is fundamental. Teaching, learning and scholarship cannot survive in a system that does not allow such. This work on Allen Ginsberg illustrates the potential of these endeavors.

Finally, this book was a labor of love, an historical inquiry, a frustrating experience, and a cooperative venture into the unknown: underground culture, literature and the Lower East Side. Allen was my tour guide; without him this book could not have been completed. Thanks are extended again to all those who shared in making this project possible.

M. P. K.

DATE			